GENUS AMERICANUS

Genus Americanus

Hitting the Road in Search of America's Identity

LOREN GHIGLIONE
with ALYSSA KARAS *and* DAN THAM

The University of Georgia Press   *Athens*

Ortiz, Simon J. The words "the bones of this nation will mend after the revolution." In *From Sand Creek: Rising in This Heart Which Is Our America*. Copyright © 1981 by Simon J. Ortiz. Reprinted by permission of University of Arizona Press.

"The Dry Salvages" by T. S. Eliot from *The Complete Poems and Plays, 1909–1950*. Copyright © 1930 by T. S. Eliot. Copyright © 1932 by Houghton Mifflin Harcourt. Used by permission of Houghton Mifflin Harcourt Publishing Company.

Viscusi, Robert. "An Oration upon the Most Recent Death of Christopher Columbus." Copyright © 1993 by Robert Viscusi. Reprinted by permission of Robert Viscusi.

The version of Tet Ming Yee's poem "On Re-visiting Angel Island" that appears in Felicia Lowe's documentary *Carved in Silence*. Reprinted by permission of Felicia Lowe.

Yamada, Mitsuye. "Evacuation." In *Camp Notes and Other Writings*. New Brunswick, N.J.: Rutgers University Press, 1998. Copyright © 1998 by Mitsuye Yamada. Reprinted by permission of Rutgers University Press.

Paperback edition, 2024
Published by the University of Georgia Press
Athens, Georgia 30602
www.ugapress.org
© 2020 by Loren Ghiglione, Alyssa Karas, and Dan Tham
All rights reserved
Designed by Erin Kirk
Set in Garamond Premier Pro

Most University of Georgia Press titles are
available from popular e-book vendors.

Printed digitally

Library of Congress Cataloging-in-Publication Data

Names: Ghiglione, Loren, author. | Karas, Alyssa, author. | Tham, Dan, author.
Title: Genus Americanus : hitting the road in search of America's identity / Loren
    Ghiglione with Alyssa Karas and Dan Tham.
Description: Athens : The University of Georgia Press, [2020] | Includes
    bibliographical references and index.
Identifiers: LCCN 2020022375 | ISBN 9780820358000 (hardback) | ISBN
    9780820358017 (ebook)
Subjects: LCSH: Ghiglione, Loren—Travel. | United States—Description
    and travel—21st century. | United States—Politics and government—21st
    century. | National characteristics, American—History—21st century.
    | Multiculturalism—United States—History—21st century. | Cultural
    pluralism—United States—History—21st century. | Group identity—United
    States—History—21st century. | Ethnicity—United States—History—21st
    century.
Classification: LCC E161.5 .G45 2020 | DDC 917.30493—dc23
LC record available at https://lccn.loc.gov/2020022375

Paperback ISBN 978-0-8203-6705-7

For the next generations:

Jessica and Laura;

Alyssa and Dan;

Emily, Matthew, Joy, Rose, and Theodore

Contents

GENUS AMERICANUS

Introduction

Is America's Identity at a Turning Point?

In search of America's identity, during the last three months of 2011 I traveled more than fourteen thousand miles by auto and airplane, ferry and foot, rail and riverboat, taxi and trolley to interview Americans in all their diversity.

On the road, I soon learned that the diversity of Americans' identities cannot be fully captured in the oversimplified either-or labels often applied to people—Black or white, male or female, gay or straight. Identity is complicated, even paradoxical.

Multiracial people challenge the Black-or-white boundaries associated with the illusory, imposed (and self-imposed) social construct of race. Some people choose identities inconsistent with their physical appearance. Walter F. White, head of the National Association for the Advancement of Colored People from 1931 to 1955, had white skin, blond hair, and blue eyes. But he wrote: "I am a Negro." His declaration distinguishes his authentic inner identity from the identity assigned by those viewing his outer self.[1]

Other either-or identity labels suggest additional complications. A person's gender and sexual orientation are not immutable. In 2019, the *New York Times* asked readers to say, in ten words or less, who they were. A number of respondents listed multiple identities not captured in the male-or-female, gay-or-straight binaries: "I am a Latino who identifies as genderfluid and pansexual"; "I am a nerdy nonbinary trans-femme film editor who loves reptiles!"; "I am a proud ginger, breakfast-lover, Eagle Scout, and transgender bisexual journalist."[2]

Identity labels also do not capture what scholars call intersectionality, the complex ways in which a person's multiple identities may interact. The comedian Chris Rock, who owns a New Jersey mansion and luxury cars, turned his multiple identities into a joke: "As a black man, I'm against the cops, but as a man with property, well, I need the cops. If someone steals something, I can't call the Crips!"[3]

Despite the limitations of identity labels, I use them here as a quick, socially recognized way to suggest the variety of the 150 Americans interviewed for this book—many of whose voices usually go unheard: an adopted refugee from Vietnam who called himself an Italian Vietnamese; a female Roman Catholic priest who had been excommunicated by the church; an African American death row inmate, freed after forty-four years in prison, who said whites run the entire criminal justice system; an intersex male who transitioned at age fifty to living as a woman and, because of past harassment, asked to be identified only by her first name; a gay Jewish expert on anti-Semitism who worried that a Hitler-style demagogue could foment the public targeting of African Americans, Muslim Americans, or gays; a young immigrant of Tanzanian-Indian descent who had been brought to the United States as a child and was facing the possibility of deportation; a Black female honorary mayor of a predominantly white male homeless camp on the Mississippi River; a Mexican American university student who said of America, "We're expanding beyond labels, but it's still slow going."

I hoped their stories would capture the ambiguities and ambivalences and the contradictions and commonalities that make up Americans' identities today. I also hoped their stories would help answer the question of whether those discriminated against on the basis of color, ethnicity, gender, sexual orientation, gender expression, religion, class, or immigration or refugee status contribute to the nation any less than those citizens usually identified as "real Americans."

The search for the nation's identity struck me as extraordinarily timely. Americans twice elected as president Barack Obama, the son of a Black man from Kenya and a white woman from Kansas; Obama symbolized globalism, multiculturalism, and a uniting inclusiveness.

In 2011, the year of my cross-country trip, Donald Trump, the real estate magnate and (un)reality TV star, toyed with a presidential run, briefly led in the polls for the Republican nomination, and began his birther campaign, which falsely claimed Obama had been born in Kenya, not the United States, and therefore was ineligible to be president.[4]

Trump's successful pseudopopulist 2016 presidential campaign, race-baiting and Obama-denigrating in its agenda, divided and excluded. He sought to shut U.S. doors in the faces of refugees, immigrants, and Muslims. He tried to exclude civil rights protections for transgender people and scale back legal protections for gay people. He declared war on cosmopolitan elites, people clustered in universities, the arts, and urban centers whom he branded disloyal to America and condescending toward ordinary Americans. He demeaned women, bragging about grabbing them "by the pussy" (the comedian Michelle Wolf responded by calling him "a racist fake gynecologist").[5]

I wanted my odyssey to deepen my understanding of America's identity. But in the age of identity politics, my own identity suggested to some a degree of cluelessness so profound it discredited my authority to undertake the trip. I am white, a default identity that Nell Irvin Painter, an expert on race, has called a "toggle between nothingness and awfulness." More specifically, I am a white, able-bodied, straight, Christian, cisgender male who lives in a largely white, upper-income suburb, the kind that one writer portrays as populated by self-righteous, overeducated, elitist snobs.[6]

However, I am not required to be a self-loathing, self-flagellating prisoner of my privilege. As the writer bell hooks said, "Privilege is not in and of itself bad; what matters is what we do with privilege."[7] What I wanted to do was give voice to Americans who lacked my privilege and often faced marginalization. The trip would provide opportunities for me to question white supremacy, male supremacy, and all the other supremacies said to go with being who I am.[8]

I sought a peripatetic white male of privilege as a role model. Mark Twain, who wrote about his travels in *Roughing It*, *Life on the Mississippi*, and other memorable books, served as an exemplar. He overcame boyhood biases to speak for the downtrodden and despised. Toni Morrison, the Nobel Prize–winning novelist, said, "Mark Twain talked about racial ideology in the most powerful, eloquent, instructive way I have ever read." The activist-comedian Dick Gregory proclaimed Twain "so ahead of his time that he shouldn't even be talked about on the same day with other people."[9]

Gregory overstated. Twain had his blind spots. While he could be "counted on to take the side of the oppressed over the oppressor," the author Richard Russo writes, Twain offered "some pretty cringe-worthy stuff" about Native Americans.[10] And, as the coauthor of *The Gilded Age: A Tale of Today* (1873), he critiqued his era's greed and graft, but he also lived the life of a Gilded Age plutocrat. He resided in an ornate, nineteen-room mansion and repeatedly pursued get-rich-quick ventures.

However, I hoped his insights into the late nineteenth-century soul of America would help me understand the America of today. After all, the America of the 1880s, Twain's peak years, was "uncannily like our own."[11]

This era's anti-immigration policies echo the Immigration Act of 1882 and the Chinese Exclusion Act of 1882. The post–Civil War Jim Crow laws banning intermarriage and requiring segregation virtually everywhere have been followed today by "the New Jim Crow"—a second-class status for African Americans that is marked by white police officers' killing of unarmed Black men and higher rates of Black unemployment and imprisonment.[12]

My road trip loosely followed the path of a young Mark Twain, beginning in his boyhood hometown of Hannibal, Missouri, and heading east to New York and other northern cities where a teenage Twain worked as a printer and writer.[13] I detoured to Hartford and other New England cities where he later wrote and lectured. Then I meandered south along the Mississippi, where Twain took up piloting steamboats. Finally, I went north and west from New Orleans, as did Twain when the Civil War forced him to retire from steamboating. Twain reported for newspapers in the Nevada Territory and San Francisco. Fittingly, my final stop on the West Coast was Seattle, the last major U.S. city from which an aging Twain began a yearlong worldwide lecture tour in 1894 to recover from bankruptcy.

After my 2011 trip, I came to believe that one who travels America to discover its identity must retravel the country. Even in the most ordinary of times, taking a snapshot of America's identity is difficult. But recent years, filled with political and cultural turmoil, required reinterviewing people in greater depth and conducting more interviews. So from 2012 to 2016, I crisscrossed the country—Boston to Seattle, Chicago to New Orleans—to reinterview Americans from the 2011 trip and undertake new interviews. I hoped the additional research would help me better understand the swiftly changing meaning of Americans' identity.

I sought to use three dramatically different ways of capturing Americans' complex identity.

First, I visited sites that allowed me to examine the enduring legacy of Twain. He exhibited the self-contradictions that were America. His friend William Dean Howells labeled him a theoretical socialist and a practical aristocrat.[14] Twain embraced the American dream of financial success and the exploitation of the nation's natural resources (American Indians' land rights be damned). But he regularly rooted for America's underdogs and attacked U.S. racism and imperialism. His life and writings offered opportunities to reflect on America's identity today.

Second, in a nation known for its citizens' coming from someplace else, I set out to explore the identity of immigrants and their descendants, especially Italian Americans. They were exploited as strikebreakers in U.S. coalfields, lynched by Louisiana mobs in the 1890s, and regularly vilified by nativist bigots as biologically inferior anarchists (a 1906 *Washington Post* editorial said 90 percent of arriving Italians were "the degenerate spawn" of "Asiatic hordes," traveling to America "to cut throats, throw dynamite, and conduct labor riots and assassination").[15] Congress passed the racist Immigration Act of 1924, with its ethnically based quota system slashing Italian immigration by 98 percent—from 222,260 in 1921 to 2,662 in 1925.[16] I focused on my own family, beginning with the arrival from Italy in 1872 of my great-grandfather Angelo Francesco Ghiglione, a barely literate indentured pasta maker. Angelo, his sons Charles and Frank (my grandfather), and his grandson William (my father) all made pasta or bottled wine. As a fourth-generation Ghiglione, removed like other third- and fourth-generation Italian Americans from occupations and neighborhoods associated with being Italian American, who am I? To complicate matters, only one of my grandparents was of Italian ancestry; another was born in France, and two others—a Fletcher and a Haskin—were of English heritage. And to stir the ancestral bouillabaisse even more, I married a Jew whose ancestors came from Austria, Germany, Hungary, Poland, and Russia. By interviewing immigrants and their descendants about their identities, I hoped to better understand my own.

Third, I interviewed ordinary Americans and experts about contemporary identity issues. The color line remained a scourge. In 2014, 75 percent of white Americans had no nonwhite friends. Many whites believed antiwhite bias—"reverse racism"—was more prevalent than anti-Black bias.[17] And America in the time of Trump embraced fault lines beyond race. Altrighters, neo-Nazis, and white supremacists dehumanized Americans based on religion, immigration status, and other factors.

Americans also seemed to be dividing themselves into two political tribes. A 2017 poll found about 65 percent of Democrats, versus 35 percent of Republicans, said the mixing of global cultures and values was important to American identity. Fifty-seven percent of Republicans, versus 29 percent of Democrats, said a culture grounded in Christian religious belief was important. Another study, in 2018, reported 90 percent of devoted conservatives thought immigration was bad, and 99 percent of progressive activists thought it good.[18]

On my journey, I set out to describe the America of today and perhaps tomorrow. Those who have recently emigrated from Asia, Africa, and the

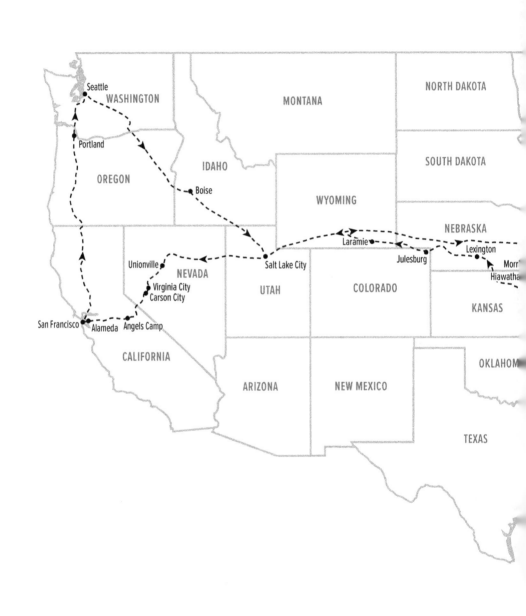

The Route

Americas add greater diversity to a nation that once was largely European. Many Americans, who in an earlier generation felt ashamed of being racially or ethnically mixed, take pride in their multiracial, multiethnic, and multicultural status. Transgender, intersex, and other gender ambiguous or androgynous individuals are more outspoken, challenging the notion of a gender binary of only males and females. Many Indigenous people envision a future revolution in which restored and enlarged sovereign Native nations within the United States will help heal the country; the Acoma poet Simon Ortiz writes that "the bones of this nation will mend after the revolution."[19]

And yet the Donald Trump revolution—his polarizing presidency—foretells a quite different future for America. Identity issues today are linked to a wide range of stubborn societal challenges. Income inequality grows. An antidemocratic, authoritarian agenda surfaces in democracies. Politicians' posttruth "alternative facts" (that is, lies) contribute to a worldview in which truth-seeking journalists are "the enemy of the people." Global warming—with humanity's survival at stake—goes unchecked. The nuclear threat looms.

I shared the drive with Alyssa Karas, a 2011 graduate of Medill, Northwestern University's journalism school, and Dan Tham, then a junior at Medill who received course credit for the trip. They had experienced their own identity issues. Dan grew up gay, Asian, and Buddhist in Salt Lake City, a largely straight, white, and Mormon community that had only begun to overcome its history of homophobia. Alyssa, a white, Catholic heterosexual from a suburb of Pittsburgh, said her identity issues involved money and men. To a scholarship student, well-heeled classmates made Northwestern sometimes feel like "a rich kids' playground." And during her journalism internships married men hustled and harassed her.

Traveling with Alyssa and Dan made me appreciate the bond between young and old. Neither young nor old need give in completely to the serious, sober world of adults between their ages. Whatever a graybeard has to offer twentysomethings, they allow a seventy-year-old to more fully experience the beat of contemporary life.

"Old elephants limp off to the hills to die," Hunter S. Thompson writes in *Fear and Loathing in Las Vegas*. "Old Americans go out to the highway and drive themselves to death."[20] But I drove to live—to take the pulse of America, to experience the education of the open road.

Dan and Alyssa, joyous June bugs, increased my chance of success. While I had visited virtually every town and city on our route, Alyssa and Dan were experiencing most of them for the first time. Also, Alyssa and Dan, as targets of homophobia, misogyny, and other forms of discrimination, experienced the people we met differently than I experienced them. I encouraged Dan and Alyssa to write about the people who most interested them. Their fourteen contributions are italicized and appear in the body of the chapters.

I also encouraged them to be humble and not rush to judgment. As journalists, we were to write about what we heard and observed. We were not psychiatrists, political scientists, or sociologists, trained to psychoanalyze, theorize, or philosophize. At trip's end, after taking time to review our three months of reporting, we would summarize what we had learned about America's identity.

At the beginning of our trip, I wondered what America Alyssa, Dan, and I would find. John Steinbeck, the Nobel Prize–winning author of *Travels with Charley: In Search of America*, sought what was uniquely American about Americans, what he called Genus Americanus.

We, too, were searching for Genus Americanus.

The Constitution's preamble begins, "We the people of the United States." An early national motto, "E pluribus unum," also suggests a unified United States: "Out of many, one." Was such unity anything more than a myth about American pluralistic exceptionalism? Was the United States becoming increasingly hostile to the many that made the one?

I hoped our trip would help us answer such questions.

CHAPTER I

Hannibal, Missouri

Which Way Is "America's Hometown" Going?

On September 18, 2011, Alyssa Karas and I, to paraphrase Twain, lit out for the territory. From the Northwestern University campus in Evanston, Illinois, we drove south in a nondescript black Dodge Grand Caravan that would acquire a crater-sized dent in Salt Lake City, a smashed window in San Francisco, and other eye-catching reminders of three months on the road (Dan Tham was completing a research project in India and would not catch up with us for two days). In anticipation of the trip, Alyssa and I ignored sensible advice about packing toilet paper, wet wipes, first-aid kit, and mosquito spray. Instead, we crammed the van with cameras, laptops, Twain tomes, and eight large bins of clippings, photos, and research files. At least I left my bust of Twain behind.

I got to know Alyssa better during the early hours of our drive on Interstate 57 toward Twain's hometown of Hannibal, Missouri. She described herself as "a product of the European Pittsburgh melting pot." Her guess as to that melting pot's contents: "Irish, German, Polish, Slovak, probably English, among other things, with rumors of some Native American roots that are absolutely unverified." That motley mix, she said, "made me feel very thoroughly American."

Like many Northwestern journalism students, Alyssa had reported on serious stuff—a governor's election, a president's visit, and a car-bomb plot. But she also had edited *NU Intel*, a buzzy news and culture website that student media competitors hailed as rambunctious, risqué, and rebellious.[1]

I began to think those adjectives applied to Alyssa. When we talked religion, she said, "My father likes to joke that he was *born* and *raised* Catholic, while I was merely *born* Catholic." And after graduating from Northwestern in June 2011, she had rejected immediately pursuing a prestigious journalism job—the goal of many graduates—to serve as our trip's $1,000-a-month everything: navigator, travel agent, copy editor, tech specialist, and photographer.

I soon experienced the merry, mischievous side of Alyssa, whose motto is "Everything is a good time or a good story." Halfway to Hannibal, Alyssa and I stopped at the Cahokia Mounds State Historic Site in Collinsville, Illinois, which had been inhabited by Indigenous people as early as 700 CE. The museum's information center attendants prohibited pens and other writing implements because "writing has been done on our gallery exhibits."[2] They insisted Alyssa and I wear laminated "Writing Permit" badges on strings around our necks. I thought of Nathaniel Hawthorne's Hester Prynne, the bearer of an illegitimate child, who was required to wear a scarlet *A* for "adulteress" on her dress. At the end of our Cahokia visit, I grumbled to a staff person about the writing permit requirement as I returned my laminated badge. Alyssa did me one better. She stole hers.

Twain wrote, "There ain't no surer way to find out whether you like people or hate them than to travel with them." I was finding out that I liked Alyssa—her sense of humor, her intelligence, her generosity, and her humility. She described herself as "quite frankly ordinary: white, straight, lower-middle class, healthy, with a vague notion of religion and an intact nuclear family. I grew up in a very, very homogeneous place, where everyone else had more or less the same amount of money, and the population was overwhelmingly white. I think I knew *maybe* 1.5 Jewish kids until I went to college. And anything beyond that? Forget about it."

Perhaps living in a homogeneous place helped explain Alyssa's interest in making our trip. She said, "For me, the question that begets all other questions is, 'Are people different or are they the same?'" Our trip would be an opportunity to answer that question, she said.

Late that first day, Hannibal presented Alyssa and me with a sobering no-star motel and roadside restaurant and reminders of the town's racial history. The Twain scholar Shelley Fisher Fishkin says Hannibal whitewashed its history of slavery auctions and Ku Klux Klan rallies, avoiding "chapters of the past that were still painful and difficult."[3]

Alyssa and I chose not to ignore those painful and difficult chapters. Our first morning in Hannibal, with summer green giving way to golden fields of dead cornstalks, we drove about thirty miles west to the Mark Twain Birthplace State Historic Site in Stoutsville, Missouri. A modern museum shelters a two-room clapboard cabin that had been moved from Florida,

Loren Ghiglione interviews Connie Ridder.

Missouri, where Twain was born in 1835. Eight people—Twain, his four siblings, his parents, and the family's young slave—were said to have occupied the tiny rented cabin.

Our museum guide, sixty-one-year-old Connie Ritter, turned stern when she recalled the playground beside the birthplace museum. She and other African American children played there, but they never entered the museum. "No one ever told us we couldn't go inside," she said. "But we knew we couldn't go inside. And now I work here."

Ritter said the museum attracted few Black visitors: "We're always happy to see one." She made clear, however, that times had changed during her sixteen years at the museum, which is part of the 2,750-acre Mark Twain State Park. More African Americans were working at Missouri's state parks. She had been promoted from tour guide through several positions to interpretative research specialist II. For a year she had served as the museum's acting administrator.

She said that, at the beginning, "Mark Twain wasn't my cup of tea. I hated Mark Twain. Because of Nigger Jim." She questioned Twain's use of the African American character in *Adventures of Huckleberry Finn*. "It took me a while to understand what I understand about *Huck Finn* now." Ritter considers the novel an assault on racism.

In a memorable scene Huck agonizes about his friendship with Jim and his belief that helping the runaway slave is a sin. Huck writes a letter revealing where Jim is, then tears up the letter, saying, "All right, then, I'll go to hell!"

Ritter used her position at the museum to highlight the role of slavery in the area, which was nicknamed Little Dixie. The area had a disproportionately large number of plantations, slaves, and lynchings. In 2010 she added a slavery display to the museum's exhibit. The display showed a reproduction ball and chain—a foot-wide, 7¾-pound ball attached by a short chain to a slave's ankle—that demonstrated how hard it would have been for a slave to escape.

Some descendants of slaves resisted telling the truth about their family histories. In the 1990s Ritter interviewed African Americans who had been members of the Civilian Conservation Corps, a New Deal public works program (1933–42) for unemployed, unmarried men aged eighteen to thirty-five. They refused to talk candidly on tape about their ancestors, she said: "They told people what they wanted to hear." The danger, said Ritter, is that by "talking good," the lie, not the reality, "becomes your memory." Ritter was determined not to let that happen at the museum.

When I returned to the museum in 2015, I learned Ritter had retired in December 2014. The museum no longer employed any African Americans. Her slavery display had been taken down, supposedly only for as long as it would take to get proper permission to use the photos in the display. But in late 2017, three years after Ritter's retirement, the slavery display remained in the museum's basement. Marianne Bodine, an interpretive research specialist, talked about renovating the museum's exhibits as a ten-year project. If the museum displayed the slavery exhibit, she said, it would be "down the line a bit," not any time soon.

I telephoned Ritter at her Monroe City home. She hoped the slavery display would return. "I received so much positive feedback," she said. The exhibit's removal seemed to foreshadow, in the time of Trump, regression on race.

After our interview with Ritter, Alyssa and I drove ten miles west on back roads to Paris, Missouri, to see a recently restored post office mural. Completed by Fred Green Carpenter in 1940, the mural shows Twain's parents and their slave entering Florida, Missouri, in a horse-drawn buggy. Twain joked about his 1835 birth in Florida: "I increased the population by one percent. It is more than many of the best men in history could have done for a town."

Paris, population 1,220 (down from 2,500 in the 1880s), portrayed itself as an idyllic, real-life version of the humorist Garrison Keillor's fictional Lake Wobegon, "the little town that time forgot, and the decades cannot improve."[4] Lake Wobegon had the Chatterbox Cafe ("The place to go that's just like home"), Paris had Jonesy's Cafe. A row of American flags lined the Main Street sidewalk in front of Jonesy's, as if the town celebrated the Fourth of July year-round.

Following a double bacon cheeseburger lunch at Jonesy's, Alyssa and I headed east on Highway 24 to get back to Hannibal, which bills itself as America's hometown. Of course, the typical American's hometown was no longer a Paris or a Hannibal. Two-thirds of Americans were living in metro areas of a half-million or more. The rural and small-town America of white Protestant farmers was turning into an urban nation of Native Americans and the descendants of refugees, immigrants, slaves, and free Blacks, a pluralistic nation decreasingly white and Protestant.

Alyssa and I drove to the St. Louis airport to pick up Dan Tham, the third member of our team. He was returning from a summer in Germany and India that reflected his interest in reporting on the world's outliers. Credit his upbringing. He recalled his time in white-bread, heavily Mormon Salt Lake City as a quadruple minority: Asian, gay, Buddhist, and vegetarian (sextuple, if you count left-handedness and colorblindness): "My dad practiced tai chi shirtless in our driveway every morning, no doubt scaring the neighbors, while my mom observed a militant veganism as a disciple of Supreme Master Ching Hai, the flamboyant, blonde Vietnamese overlord of the Loving Hut restaurant chain, whose ostentatious lifestyle was financed by sales of fake meat and vegan cosmetics and generous donations from her supporters."

While Dan achieved in the way most journalism students wanted to achieve (as a senior, he won Medill's top broadcast journalism award), he also explored what it means to be a minority in America. He was the first man to live with a woman in Northwestern's inaugural gender-neutral housing. He coproduced *Diva*, a documentary about Rae Lewis-Thornton, a Black woman activist living with AIDS. For a course on Chicago's immigrant and multiethnic communities, he reported on Koreans and Tibetans, at one point finding himself in the middle of a protest for Tibetan freedom outside the Chinese embassy. And for the *Daily Northwestern*, the student newspaper,

Dan interviewed Maher Ahmad, a gay Palestinian who helped found a gay liberation student organization on campus in the early 1970s.

Hannibal had a history of creating outliers. Dan Vogel, author of *Mark Twain's Jews*, portrays the Hannibal of Twain's time as a "hotbed of bigotry." Whether based on religion, race, or immigration status, discrimination thrived. During a 1909 labor dispute at a local cement factory, the *Hannibal Courier-Post* attacked striking immigrant workers as "beer-demented foreigners."[5] Old-fashioned racism led Hannibal's whites to dismiss both African Americans and Native Americans as savage subhumans.

Twain's childhood loathing of American Indians helps explain his later characterization in *The Adventures of Tom Sawyer* of Injun Joe as a thieving, essence-of-evil murderer. Injun Joe deserved to die a horrible death and did. Joe Douglass of Hannibal, who had African American and Osage ancestry, denied on his tombstone "that he was the 'Injun Joe' in Mark Twain's writings as he had always lived an honorable life."[6]

From the airport, Dan, Alyssa, and I went straight to an early evening event at the Mark Twain Boyhood Home & Museum, Hannibal's centerpiece. We found it far more forthcoming about Hannibal's history than the museum once was: its exhibits discussed the Clemens family's slave ownership, and the museum held summer training sessions for teachers to help them address Twain's writings about race and racism. But the museum's Tom & Becky Program, a look-alike contest for schoolchildren, made Tom Sawyer and Becky Thatcher, white children from Twain's *Adventures of Tom Sawyer*, the symbols of the museum.

During our visit the museum was holding a preview party for its two-disc CD, *Mark Twain: Words & Music*. Despite Twain's fondness for Black vocalists and musicians, all the preview party performers and the dozens of artists on the CD were white.

I wondered whether "America's hometown" felt like home to its gay residents. Gayle Rubin, the theorist of sex and gender politics, writes that such residents are "more closely monitored in small town and rural areas"; they flee to cities to avoid "being isolated and invisible."[7] In August 2004, three months after Massachusetts began allowing same-sex marriages, 71 percent of Missouri voters ratified a state constitutional amendment that restricted a valid marriage in Hannibal and the rest of the state to the union of one man and one woman.

Michael Gaines

Mary Lou Montgomery, editor of the five-day *Hannibal Courier-Post*, said sexual orientation in Hannibal was "pretty quiet—not secretly hidden, not talked about in polite society." She spoke of the community's tolerance, but three years later the Baptist-affiliated Hannibal-LaGrange University refused to readmit an honors-caliber student after he came out as gay on Facebook.[8] "Most gay folks will move to Quincy," a nearby Illinois city, Terrell Dempsey, a Hannibal attorney, had told us. "It's still outwardly hostile here."

Montgomery and Dempsey recommended that we talk with Michael Gaines, the forty-three-year-old executive director of the Hannibal Arts Council and the Missouri Association of Community Arts Agencies, about what he faced as a gay man in Hannibal. Alyssa and I interviewed Gaines the next morning (after his transatlantic flight, Dan was sleeping in). Gaines reassured us about his life as a gay man: "It's not like they're dumping people in the river. I certainly haven't experienced outward hostility or anything like that at all." He said it took him time to figure out who he was. "That has nothing to do with any societal pressure, community pressure, or family pressure," he said. "My sexual orientation was just there, unspoken." He had grown up on a farm near Bethel, Missouri, a town of 108 people that was established as a religious communal colony by German immigrants in 1844.

Gaines said he had to come to terms with the "institutional religious baggage I carried my whole life."

At one point, addressing his sexual orientation meant "wanting to die every day," he said. But his parents proved they loved him unconditionally. He added, "When I came to love and accept myself, I was okay. I didn't care what the rest of the world thought."

Eventually he shared a home with his partner in nearby Bowling Green, Missouri (city motto: "Where the Grass Is Always Greener"). He attended community events with his partner. While they did not broadcast their sexual orientation—"I haven't put an ad in the paper," Gaines joked—they were neither isolated nor invisible. "It's not like we can't be ourselves," Gaines said. "We choose to live without labels. Is that cowardly? Who knows, but it's the best way I can answer."

Three or four times a year Gaines would return to Bethel to play the piano at the Bethel Christian Church, his church since junior high. "It was as much my family as my family was," he said. When church elders learned he and his partner had been living together, they took Gaines aside and told him he never again would be allowed to be part of the "worship team" and play the piano during services.

The church's rejection bothered Gaines. But he still played the piano almost every day. He was certain that God, who gave him the gift, heard him playing. He joined a Bowling Green Disciples of Christ church that welcomed his piano playing during services. "The church I grew up in might change their attitude, or they may not, but it is really not of my concern now," Gaines said. "Moving on."

Gaines talked optimistically about cultural changes. "Sometimes they take a while to trickle down to small-town America," he said. But he remained committed to Hannibal. "I feel loved and appreciated for who I am and for the work I do. That's pretty good for anyone." He mentioned a young man who came up to him at a party and told him how much he valued Gaines's being himself in the community. "My doing that made a real difference to some of his gay friends in high school," Gaines said. "Made my day. The trade-off for me to move to a bigger city would be that I would actually lose a part of myself, something that most people might say I lose by staying here."

I felt an obligation to contact Gaines after Donald Trump won the presidency. Trump had described same-sex marriage as settled law that he was "fine with." His supporters portrayed him as the most gay-friendly Republican president in U.S. history. But his Justice Department rolled back LGBT protections. I asked Gaines's opinion of the state of Trump-administration LGBT rights. Gaines answered, "I don't talk politics."

———

I managed to resist much of Hannibal's hucksterism—the souvenir Twain T-shirts and the ride on the Too-Too Twain—but for a lunch with Montgomery, the editor of the *Hannibal Courier-Post*, I was seduced by the Mark Twain Dinette's twelve-foot rotating mug of root beer atop a twenty-five-foot pole.

I admired Montgomery's grit. In 1975, long before the #MeToo movement began to make it more acceptable for women to address workplace harassment and discrimination, she started at the *Courier-Post* as a part-time proofreader. A quarter-century later, after a series of promotions, she became the first female editor in the *Courier-Post*'s 173-year history.

At first, as an editor, she "tried being a man," carrying a day planner instead of a purse. But she eventually learned an important life lesson: "I can only be myself, and that's good enough." Suburban Newspapers of America named her editor of the year for daily newspapers in 2011. The judges credited her with being "an advocate for her community."

While I admired Montgomery's determination to overcome the discrimination she and other women faced in the news industry, I questioned her hiring record. She volunteered that the *Courier-Post*'s staff of 5¼ was 100 percent white. "We don't get many minority applicants in Hannibal," she said. "Like none." She mentioned a young new hire, Dominic Genetti: "He's the closest thing. He's Italian."

I also questioned Montgomery's vision for the paper, however sensible it sounded. Montgomery said she strived for thorough coverage of everything Hannibal. "Now we're virtually all local," she said.

As the former editor of a dinky daily in Southbridge, a Massachusetts town the size of Hannibal, I also valued local coverage. But Montgomery's local coverage emphasized bulletin board news and soft features and photos. For Groundhog Day she had invited children to submit photos of their pets. "My motto is 'Look what we can accomplish together,'" she said. "It is not 'my' paper but rather 'our' paper. We belong to our readers." She recalled her first job at the paper in 1975: "When I was a pup, we would run people's dead deer photos. We're back doing them."

She spoke in the past tense about the Watergate generation of journalism school graduates, "who were going to change the world." She thought

Mary Lou
Montgomery

the current generation of journalism school graduates should focus, instead, on the details of local life. "If traffic accidents are boring to you, you are in the wrong business," she said. I felt, however, that even the smallest newspaper should act as its community's feisty watchdog. The 5,700-circulation *Southbridge Evening News* investigated industrial pollution of the local river, reported on funeral homes that covered up suicides, campaigned against schools' censorship of student journalists, and sued when an agency sought to conduct the public's business behind closed doors.

Montgomery worried about the survival of the *Courier-Post*, which was slashing expenses. In 2013 the paper laid off Genetti in what Montgomery called "a cost-cutting sweep." Asked to put out a daily paper with a news staff of two, Montgomery retired at the end of 2014. "I couldn't work up to my own standards," she emailed me. "I equate what I did at the newspaper to that of a horseshoer when the Model T came along and virtually eliminated the need for the farrier," she added. "But I'm a really good horseshoer."

When Montgomery described Genetti, an Italian American, as "the closest thing" on her Hannibal staff to an applicant of color, I recalled Malcolm X's description of Hannibal, the great Carthaginian military commander of the Second Punic War and occupier of Italy after whom the town of Hannibal was named. Malcolm X had declared that Hannibal was a Black man from Africa and therefore the pappy, as Malcolm put it, of the Italian; the Italian "knows how he got that [dark] color."[9] In saying that, Malcolm was drawing on a long history of discrimination against Italians, especially southern Italians, in the United States. They endured such racist epithets as "white nigger" and "nigger wop."[10]

Curious about local Italians, whatever their color, I checked the Hannibal telephone directory for Ghigliones during a 2015 return trip. Wherever I travel, I look for Ghigliones, almost as scarce as feathers on a fish. I saw a family name as a powerful symbolic marker, an identifier that encodes a person's ancestry.[11] Alas, Hannibal's directory had no Ghigliones. But elsewhere, on what would have been the directory's Ghiglione page, were entries for Genovese, also the name for people from Genoa, the northern Italian city close to my great-grandfather Ghiglione's village. I telephoned Cheryl and Sammy Genovese.

The Genoveses' story struck me as a stereotypically triumphant American dream story of an immigrant family that had been in America for three or four generations, except the latest chapter was not ending happily.

The story of the Genovese family began not in Genoa but in Papanice, a town in southern Italy. A representative of the U.S. Immigration Commission who was touring the region in 1907 noted the residents' illiteracy and marginal existence; day laborers were earning an average of less than fifty cents a day.[12]

Sammy Genovese's grandfather Pantaleone Genovese was part of what has been called "the greatest movement of a single nationality in recorded world history."[13] Between 1820 and 2004, 5.5 million Italian immigrants flooded the United States. Eighty-four percent came from southern Italy and Sicily, primarily as poorly educated manual laborers and agricultural workers. Many Americans treated them as doubly alien, different physically, psychically, and morally from both earlier European immigrant groups and lighter-skinned, better-educated, and often less-destitute groups of northern Italian immigrants.[14]

Sammy said Pantaleone Genovese left Papanice at age twenty-one, a year after his marriage in 1907 to sixteen-year-old Rosa Raimondi, a laborer on the olive farm of Pantaleone's parents. Lured by Atlas Portland Cement Company labor agents, Pantaleone and other Papanice residents moved to Ilasco, an Atlas company town four miles from Hannibal. Soon Pantaleone and Rosa had thirteen children, U.S. citizenship, membership in Holy Cross Catholic Church, and eighty acres. Pantaleone farmed the land with a horse-drawn plow on evenings and weekends while continuing to work a shift at Atlas.

Cheryl Andrews and Sammy Genovese graduated from Hannibal High School in 1965, married in 1971, and, in the same year, purchased at foreclosure for $7,000 a three-bedroom southside house. It remains their home to this day. A painted sign at the front door lets visitors know angels guard the premises.

Sammy and Cheryl Genovese were not part of a visible Italian American community in Hannibal. Sammy, whose wife is of Irish descent, said, "Most of them [Italian Americans] didn't marry Italians." They melted into Hannibal's predominantly white population, achieving a kind of invisibility.

But certain values associated with Italians survived in the Genoveses, starting with an emphasis on family togetherness. The historian Mark Stolarik says many immigrant families, in the name of family togetherness, accepted lower-paying jobs nearby instead of pursuing a distant career opportunity or a college education: "It was all right to be a blue-collar worker, to drop out of school at an early age, and to live in the same neighborhood all your life."[15]

Talking with the Genoveses made me understand the different values of the Genovese and Ghiglione families. Both families prized togetherness. But my great-grandfather and great-grandmother decided Angelo would not remain an indentured blue-collar worker. And they expected their descendants, if they did not enter the family pasta business, to get an education—the best they could afford—and go out on their own.

The Genoveses, however, emphasized togetherness more than my family did. In the late 1940s, Armenia, the eleventh child of Pantaleone and Rosa Genovese, graduated as valedictorian of her high school class and won a teaching scholarship. Instead of attending college, she sewed linings on the tongues of shoes at a Hannibal factory. She delighted in being able to buy her mother "a real slip and dresses," because her mother, as well as her sisters, usually wore dresses her mother created from feed sacks.[16]

Cheryl and Sammy Genovese made clear their family was not living the American dream. They described the decline of their southside neighborhood. "Most of our past neighbors have either moved or passed away," Cheryl said. "The property has become mostly rental. We now have fifty-three abandoned homes. I am involved in a Neighborhood Watch because of the level of crime in this area. What was once the middle class in Hannibal is now poverty level."

In 2017, Hannibal's newly elected mayor, James Hark, began promoting the city's Community P.R.I.D.E. (Planned Renovation, Investment, Development Endeavor) Project in the neighborhood of the Genoveses, demolishing structures beyond repair and selling decaying houses to developers for one dollar apiece, so long as the developers committed to quickly restoring and flipping them. The first P.R.I.D.E. home went under contract 10 days (versus typically 90 to 120 days) after being offered for sale.[17]

But the Genoveses, like other members of Hannibal's middle class, remained victims of the changing local economy. Dura Automotive, Alpharma, and other companies were closing their factories. The cement plant workforce shrank from more than a thousand to a couple of hundred. Montgomery, the local editor, said, "The plant has sold a couple of times, reducing the 'good' jobs and benefits down to 'average.' Unless you want to make soup at General Mills, or farm chemicals at BASF, there's not much going here. We have a large population of kids who get free lunches at school and senior citizens who live in subsidized housing. There is a saying that anyone with any get up and go has already got up and gone."

Hannibal occupied the losing side of a divide that the economist Enrico Moretti calls "the Great Divergence." The Great Divergence, which began in the 1960s, was economic. College-educated, skilled workers with good jobs lived in certain growing, usually larger, communities. The less-educated workers with fewer skills lived in the smaller Hannibals of America. The Great Divergence also was about the social fabric of communities: their crime and divorce rates, and the quality of their health services and housing.[18]

Perhaps these economic realities affected the attitudes of whites on the losing side of the Great Divergence, with the result that they blamed their plight in part on African Americans. A 2017 psychological study suggests that, when white Americans fear a threatening future, "then anybody who is seen as not part of that group [of white Americans] is seen as more of a threat," said Jennifer Richeson, a Yale psychology professor who was one of the study's researchers.[19] Whether Richeson was correct, commentators took the 2016 Trump landslide in Missouri and racial incidents in the state as evidence that it had become "the new Mississippi" and, to quote one headline, "the Heart of Racial Tension in America."[20]

In their view and experience of that racial tension, G. Faye Dant and other Black Hannibal residents differed dramatically from the Genoveses and other white Hannibal residents. The sixty-two-year-old Dant recalled the segregated Frederick Douglass School for Black students. In 1955, the school, abiding by a federal desegregation order, held its last graduation. But the order went only so far. The school system hired none of Douglass's former instructors, all of whom were Black, to teach at the newly integrated high school.[21]

As a high school student, Dant protested a 1968 presidential campaign rally in Hannibal's Central Park for former Alabama governor George Wallace. Flanked by Ku Kluxers, Wallace ("Segregation now! Segregation tomorrow! Segregation forever!") represented white supremacy as well as segregation.

Echoing Connie Ritter, Dant said local African Americans were required to possess an unspoken knowledge of the places in town where they could and could not go. "We were not the kind of community that had signs," Dant said. "But we knew." Hannibal restaurants insisted Black customers use the back door for takeout. Movie theaters relegated them to balcony seating only. The local skating rink made Black children bring their own skates.

Dant left Hannibal for college and bigger cities in Michigan, Minnesota, and Illinois. She and her husband, Joel, moved back to his family's Hannibal farm in 2009. Although Hannibal had changed, Dant felt the need to acknowledge the past of the city's African Americans, who made up less than 10 percent of the population. She called them "the invisibles," evoking the novelist Ralph Ellison.

On September 10, 2011, not long before we met her, Dant invited Hannibal to view the project she had cooked up in less than six months. In the back of the Hannibal History Museum, Dant unveiled the Hannibal African American Life and History Project. The exhibit showcased the sprinter George Poage, who became the first African American medalist in Olympic history by winning two bronze medals at the 1904 Games; Hiawatha Crow, a schoolteacher who, in 1983, was the first African American elected to the Hannibal City Council; and Blanche Kelso Bruce, a freed Virginia slave who headed a Hannibal school for African Americans, later served as a U.S. senator from Mississippi, and won eight votes for the nomination for vice president at the 1880 Republican National Convention.

When the Hannibal History Museum relocated in 2013, Dant moved her exhibit to the Welchman's House, a one-room, city-owned stone structure (annual rent: one dollar) built by slaves around 1839 and mentioned by Mark Twain in *Tom Sawyer*.[22]

Dant renamed her project Jim's Journey: The Huck Finn Freedom Center. She celebrated Twain as an antiracist humanitarian and the first white writer to treat an African American slave as a human being, not as an object or

G. Faye Dant

caricature. She also honored Daniel Quarles, a slave who was the inspiration for Jim in *Adventures of Huckleberry Finn*. As a boy, Twain heard Quarles describe the terror of slave families separated at auction. "I listened as one who receives a revelation," Twain said.

When I last spoke to Dant in 2017, she worried aloud about the 70 to 80 percent of northeastern Missourians who voted to elect Donald Trump president ("Those were scary numbers"). (The vote was not entirely surprising, of course: Missouri had been a slave state, admitted to the Union as such after Maine was admitted as a free state under the Missouri Compromise of 1820.) Dant participated in marches organized by the local Indivisible, a citizens' organization with six thousand chapters nationwide designed "to show Congress there is broad resistance to Trump's agenda."

In Missouri, resistance to racism predated Trump's election. In 2015, a year after the Ferguson demonstrations, protesters took over the University of Missouri's flagship Columbia campus in response to racist incidents. The football team said it would refuse to play until the university system's president resigned. The president and the university chancellor both resigned. In 2017, the Missouri NAACP issued a travel advisory for Missouri, the first the civil rights organization ever issued for any state. The advisory cited a 2016 state attorney general's report that Black drivers in Missouri were 75 percent more likely than whites to be stopped by the police (a 2018 update said Black drivers were 91 percent more likely than whites to be stopped).

Were white Missourians blind to the systemic racism that infected many Missouri institutions, from its legal system to its schools? The historian Carol Anderson, who once lived in Missouri, concluded that the press and public missed the point by focusing on the rage of protesters in Ferguson and other Missouri communities. She said white rage had fueled Black protesters' rage: "White rage is not about visible violence, but rather it works its way through the courts, the legislatures, and a range of government bureaucracies. It wreaks havoc subtly. . . . It's not the Klan."

Black advancement triggers white rage, Anderson concluded. When Black parents sought to desegregate Missouri's schools, whites fought to maintain separate and unequal schools. "Thus in the twenty-first century," Anderson writes, the school district of Michael Brown, the young unarmed Black man fatally shot by a white Ferguson police officer in 2014, "had been on probation for fifteen years, annually accruing only 10 out of 140 points on the state's accreditation scale. It was the same with policing, housing, voting and employment, all of which carried the undercurrents of racial inequality—even after the end of slavery, the triumphs of the Civil Rights Movement, and the election of Barack Obama to the presidency."[23]

Dant's museum played an important role in Hannibal. A sign by the entrance read: "In order to live in the present and prepare for the future, we must first understand and appreciate the past. Welcome!!" The museum reminded Dan, Alyssa, and me that the artificial tourist town that celebrated Twain masked the reality of an earlier Jim Crow industrial Hannibal, a town now in decline.

That earlier Hannibal once featured factories that turned out seventy thousand cigars a month and twenty-four thousand pairs of shoes a day, and it had a bustling Broadway that served as the area's commercial center. But the factories died. Retail outlets on Broadway gave way to empty storefronts, a Salvation Army Family Store, and, next door, Hard Times Tattoo.

The sorry state of Broadway prompted questions Hannibal seemed to raise about America that might dog the rest of our trip. Would the idyllic image of America's small towns that I carried in my head, for example, be replaced by real small towns that were, at best, standing still, if not slowly withering?

The sorry state of Hannibal's Broadway also brought to mind Twain's flight from Hannibal as a teenager one evening in June 1853. He boarded

Dan Tham (left), Alyssa Karas, and Loren Ghiglione about to board the Mississippi riverboat *Mark Twain* in Hannibal, Missouri, at the beginning of their three-month trip around the United States.

a Mississippi River packet and "fled to St. Louis." His brothers also left Hannibal that year. Twain idealized his Hannibal boyhood in his fiction. But Hannibal, like many small towns, could, as Greil Marcus writes, "grow in on itself and shut out the rest of the world."[24] As an adult Twain chose to live in New York and other cities.

Toward the end of our time in Hannibal, however, Dan, Alyssa, and I took a two-hour dinner cruise up the Mississippi on the *Mark Twain Riverboat*. The presence of the Mississippi—what the poet T. S. Eliot, a St. Louis native, called "a strong brown god—sullen, untamed and intractable"—made Hannibal special to us.[25]

Dan's first time on the Mississippi mesmerized him. "This was the same river that Jim and Huck were on," he said. Later he identified the Mississippi as our odyssey's "connecting thread": hearing a Mississippi riverboat's steam calliope in New Orleans, riding a stretch on a Louisiana State Penitentiary patrol boat, and, toward our trip's end in Seattle, meeting an overweight Mississippi River–traveling cat that went by the name of Coyote George the River Pig.

CHAPTER 2

St. Louis

Decoding Race in a Largely Biracial Metropolis

To pay for the trip the eighteen-year-old Twain would take to New York in August 1853, he set type for two months in St. Louis for the *Evening News* and other local newspapers. During the 1850s, racism and nativism thrived in St. Louis. In 1854, anti-immigrant, anti-Catholic Know-Nothings—advocates of "pure Americanism"—attacked Catholic schools and Irish and German pubs, churches, and businesses.[1]

In 1857, the U.S. Supreme Court ruled that Dred Scott and his family, who were enslaved in St. Louis, could not gain their freedom based on having traveled and lived with their owner in states where slavery was illegal. Chief Justice Roger B. Taney wrote that Blacks were "so far inferior that they had no rights which the white man was bound to respect."[2]

In recalling 1850s St. Louis, Twain sounded confused, as if he did not know whether he loved or loathed the city. In 1867, he called it a "happy, cheerful contented old town." But later Twain said he hated the city. Visiting it, he said, was a "ghastly infliction." St. Louis was home to his mother and sister, and their presence, the biographer Fred Kaplan claims, "was part of the problem."[3]

More than a century later, I, too, found the city confusing. St. Louis seemed to be the stereotypical U.S. manufacturing metropolis in decline—its population of 856,796 in 1950 had shrunk to 318,172. The 62.9 percent loss was the largest percentage loss of any U.S. city with more than 100,000 residents in 1950. The relative absence of Latinxs and Asians, however, made it anything but stereotypical. Its diversity was defined almost entirely in Black (49.2 percent) and white (43.9 percent).

Gerald Early, the fifty-nine-year-old Merle Kling Professor of Modern Letters and director of the Center for the Humanities at Washington

University in St. Louis, struck me as the perfect person to explain race relations in this confusing city. He was an African American insider. He had spent almost three decades in St. Louis and soon would be awarded a star on the St. Louis Walk of Fame. But Early was also an outsider. He had graduated from Ivy League universities, Penn and Cornell, after growing up in a poor working-class Italian section of South Philadelphia.

In his book-lined university office, Early quietly decoded for us the difficult history of race in St. Louis, the nation's fifth-most segregated city. "St. Louis is southern but not quite," Early said. "St. Louis is midwestern but not quite." The city wanted to think of itself as cosmopolitan, a Midwest capital rivaling Chicago. St. Louis showcased its 632-foot, silvery Gateway Arch that, Early has written, "defines what the Middle West is."[4]

Early said St. Louis is southern because of its history of slavery and rigid segregation. In the twenty-first century, the southern end of St. Louis continued to be predominantly white, whereas northern St. Louis and nearby suburbs were predominantly Black. In 2014, in Ferguson, one of those northern suburbs, a white police officer named Darren Wilson fatally shot Michael Brown Jr., an eighteen-year-old unarmed African American man. His death led to more than a week of protests and criticism of the police's militarized response to the protests. An FBI investigation cleared Wilson of civil rights violations in the shooting, but the conduct of the St. Louis–area police continued to provoke protests.

In 2017, a white St. Louis police officer, Jason Stockley, fatally shot a young Black man, Anthony Lamar Smith. When a judge acquitted Stockley, another St. Louis police officer, Dustin Boone, anticipating protests that night, texted: "It's gonna be a lot of fun beating the hell out of these s——heads once the sun goes down and nobody can tell us apart!!!!" That's what Boone and two other officers did two days later to one Black protester, even though he was obeying their orders. What they did not know was that the Black protester, Luther Hall, was a police officer working undercover. They beat him so badly, according to news reports, "that he couldn't eat and lost 20 pounds." In November 2018 a grand jury indicted Boone and the other two officers in the attack; they faced other felony charges as well. As this book went to press, Boone and another officer were awaiting trial; two other officers had pleaded guilty, and the U.S. Attorney's Office was planning to seek indictments of still others.[5]

Many white St. Louisans continued to look at Black people as inferiors, deserving of only subjugation and segregation, Early said. "Even now, with all the talk of diversity, it's been very hard in St. Louis. Black people are still at the bottom" in terms of income, educational opportunities, and health care. "Things have changed," he said. "But on another level, nothing has changed in so far as their overall relationship with whites in this city."

Many well-meaning whites wanted race relations to improve, Early said. But their approach was often paternalistic. And the absence of a strong political machine and mayor—the kind evident in Chicago and some East Coast cities—prevented "really innovative policies or social change," he said.

Early recounted what he termed his own superhumiliating experience twenty years earlier at Le Chateau Mall, home to Neiman Marcus and Saks Fifth Avenue, in Frontenac, an affluent suburb that was 98.5 percent white. Early, his wife, Ida, who was a vice president of the Junior League of St. Louis, and their two daughters had gone to the mall to attend the Junior League's Christmas bazaar.

A bored Early paced the mall briefly, returned to the family van to read for about half an hour, and then walked back through the mall—past a jewelry store at closing time—to retrieve his wife and daughters from the Christmas bazaar. The jewelry store owner called the police, saying, "There is this Black guy walking around the mall here, and we think he is going to rob us,'" Early recalled.

Early started to rub his hand across his forehead nervously as he told Alyssa, Dan, and me what happened next: "The police came and they wanted to see my identification, and they wanted to know why I was there." His children and a growing crowd witnessed the police grill him spread-eagled.

Although Early was not arrested, his irate wife went to the Frontenac police chief to ask for an explanation. The chief, Early recalled, said, "'Well, he's a Black man and he was in this mostly white mall. He should expect something like this.'" The chief used the analogy of needing to check out the driver of a jalopy on a street full of luxury cars.

Ida Early demanded an apology from Frontenac. Frontenac's mayor refused. Letter-writing campaigns and threats to boycott Frontenac businesses followed. "It probably was the worst three weeks of my life," Early said, looking down and rubbing a forefinger around the inside of his shirt collar. "We got threatening phone calls. We got called racial epithets. 'Who do you think you are?'

"But, on the other hand, we found out we had lots of friends. There were lots of white people who came out to support us who didn't know us," Early said. "Just talking to you about it, the pain of it just returned to me. It was a very painful experience."

We ran out of time before I had a chance to ask the question that haunted me. What was the impact of this humiliating experience on Early's two daughters? I tried to compare it with a humiliating moment of mine, when after a quarter-century of owning and operating community newspapers in New England, I faced losing the papers and going through bankruptcy. I had to explain to my two daughters how our lives would be disrupted, beginning with the loss of our home.

Although I did give up the newspapers and left the area for an academic job in Atlanta, I escaped personal bankruptcy. But I was sure the experience for my family, even if I had gone through bankruptcy, could never have matched what Early and his family had endured. In a 1994 book, *Daughters: On Family and Fatherhood*, Early writes that his experience with the Frontenac police reminded him "that I was a nigger."[6]

The experience also "nearly wrecked" his relationship with his children. His daughters, both upset, avoided Early's efforts to discuss the incident and the issue of race with them. Talking with daughter Linnett, who was sick in bed, Early, "growing hysterically angry," grabbed her arm and shouted: "Do you see this? This skin color? This is what determines what goes on in this world. This, and only this. Nothing but this. Has never been anything but this."

Daughter Rosalind rushed into the room. "Stop it!" she insisted. "Leave her alone!" Early told Rosalind to shut up and lectured Linnett about how white people had always treated him as if he were nothing but an animal. When Ida entered the room, Early, who had never before told his children to shut up, "was struck dumb by the horror of what I had been doing."[7] Under stress and scrutiny by the public, his own insecurities about race, and perhaps about parenting, had taken control of him, he said.

Later, Linnett told her father that she was sorry she had not been with him that night as he walked through the Frontenac mall. If she had, she said perceptively, "The guy wouldn't have called the police." Early put his arm on Linnett's shoulder and told her. "Thank you, thank you. It's nice to know I've got a daughter who can protect me."

That, for me, was perhaps the saddest part of Early's story. "If a Black man is alone or with other Black men, he is a threat to whites," Early said. "But if he is with children, then he is harmless, adorable, the dutiful father."[8]

Racial prejudice, of course, was not the only form of bigotry evident in St. Louis. Missouri law allowed discrimination against gays and lesbians. They could be fired from a job or evicted from an apartment. That reality, and our interview of Michael Gaines in small-town Hannibal, had left us curious about the experience of gays and lesbians in St. Louis, Missouri's second-largest city, and their coverage in the *St. Louis Post-Dispatch*, famous for the platform of its previous owner, Joseph Pulitzer: "Always fight for progress and reform . . . never be afraid to attack wrong."[9]

The city served as an oasis for the region's white gays and lesbians, despite municipal laws against cross-dressing (from 1864 to 1985) and consensual sodomy (from 1812 to 2006). Only months after Stonewall—the gay riots in New York sparked by a police raid on a Greenwich Village gay bar on June 28, 1969—members of St. Louis's gay community protested at police headquarters the arrest of nine men for being in drag at a Halloween party. The charges against them eventually were dropped, and a gay rights organization began hosting an annual drag ball on Halloween.[10]

A monthlong study in 1999 of the *St. Louis Post-Dispatch*'s lesbian and gay coverage—compared with that in the *New York Times*, *Los Angeles Times*, and *Atlanta Journal-Constitution*—showed the *Post-Dispatch* provided the least coverage. One hundred percent of straight readers surveyed viewed *Post-Dispatch* coverage as "about right," but 89 percent of gay and lesbian readers surveyed thought coverage was largely limited to national events. "I wish they'd look in their own backyard and see how many great stories there are," said a gay man who lived in St. Louis.[11]

Dan Tham interviewed a journalist who could speak to whether the *Post-Dispatch*'s coverage had improved in the dozen years since the survey:

We drove to the Post-Dispatch *to talk with Doug Moore, the forty-eight-year-old openly gay diversity and demographics reporter for the* Post-Dispatch. *"In a city like New York, they have happy hour every week," joked Moore, president of the local chapter of the National Lesbian & Gay Journalists Association. With only ten members in the St. Louis chapter, which included journalists from as far away as Nebraska and Iowa, weekly NLGJA gatherings for cocktails were virtually impossible in St. Louis, Moore said.*

Moore was raised Southern Baptist in Neosho, Missouri, a town of ten thousand in southwest Missouri. "Every Sunday we were told these [gay and lesbian] people are sinners and are going to hell," Moore said. "You always romanticize your childhood. But my life was threatened and I was called 'fag.'"

Moore didn't come out until his midthirties when, to combat newsrooms' "bungling [of] gay coverage," he helped found the NLGJA chapter in 2004. After serving as chapter president for seven years, Moore believed that every newsroom needed an advocate for covering issues of sexual orientation and gender expression.

He gave the example of a reporter who was working on a story about a horse trainer at Rainbow Ranch in Morse Mill, Missouri. The reporter didn't know, and perhaps felt uncomfortable asking, about the woman's romantic partner, even with the "rainbow flag flying above the sign for Rainbow Ranch" and photos in the living room of the women together, Moore recalled with a chuckle. For instances like those, Moore felt a responsibility to educate other journalists.

"There is a hesitancy," he said. "They don't want to make that person [being interviewed] uncomfortable," and they don't want to be uncomfortable themselves. But when it came to matters of identity, for example, whether someone refers to herself as African American or Black, for instance, Moore said reporters shouldn't be afraid to ask. "Ninety-nine percent of the time, people are actually happy that you did [ask]."

Moore was thankful that his paper supported him. He strongly encouraged other gay journalists to come out. "If you just have straight white guys running the newsrooms, you would have very narrow coverage. I think I've added a lot more stories that wouldn't have been in the paper."

He recalled Missouri's first same-sex marriage case. A lesbian couple of thirty-four years had wed in Iowa in 2009, although Missouri did not recognize their marriage license. The couple, along with nine others, brought a lawsuit challenging the state's ban, and the case headed into court in September 2014. "If I weren't here [at the paper], we probably would not have spent the resources or manpower to cover it. We would have just run the wire [service account]."

Moore said achieving diversity in newsrooms remained an important goal, but achieving it was far from inevitable. "Ideally, it would be great to say there's an expiration to my beat," he said. But he realized "there's still a lot messed up in this country. There's always a class of people being treated differently."

One of Moore's recent stories featured Mazy Gilleylen, a transgender girl from the city of Overland in St. Louis County. Moore profiled the *eleven-year-old and her family as they grappled with Gilleylen's being bullied at school and the onset of puberty. "The story is the real struggle of a parent between protecting your kid and allowing your kid to be who they think they are." The multimedia feature about Gilleylen on the* Post-Dispatch's *website included photos, a short documentary, and a podcast, in which Moore talked about his reporting process.*[12]

Moore said he hopes his reporting causes readers to relate to his subjects, regardless of their sexual orientation or gender identity. "They're really no different than anyone else. They're leading your typical, boring life, except they're dealing with this very abstract and complex issue."[13]

In St. Louis, Alyssa, Dan, and I located a homeless camp called Hopeville. Alyssa reported on our visit:

Finding the homeless camp was difficult. No address. No directions. Hopeville, one of the three largest homeless camps in St. Louis, came with nothing more than "north of the Arch, next to the river."

Sure enough, it was there at the end of Mullanphy Street, between the railroad tracks and the Mississippi River floodwall. Tarps, tents, rusty vans, fires in trash cans, dozens of cats, and a highway-style sign that said "Welcome to Hopeville" announced the civilization on the fringe of society. That, and the smell, which was a combination of unwashed people and campfire smoke.

The three of us approached the camp, and a man poked his head out of a van and waved. We all shook hands. Loren explained our project and asked if there was someone the three of us could speak to.

The man didn't hesitate. "Big Mama," he said.

"Sorry, who?"

"Big Mama." He pointed.

Big Mama lumbered over to us. Within seconds it was clear that she was not only Big Mama, as in size 24 big, but big in position. Tedra "Big Mama" Franks was the mayor of Hopeville.

She had just woken up. She said she needed to sit down, but, yes, of course, she was the one we could talk to. She plopped down on a wooden swing and pulled me down next to her. Loren lugged over a green wingback armchair, fitting for a professor, and Dan settled down on a tree stump.

Big Mama began to talk, a skill at which she was particularly adept. She didn't hem and haw about anything, even the unsavory pieces of her past. Yes,

Tedra "Big Mama" Franks

she had anger management issues. Yes, she used to carry guns. Yes, she had stabbed a man. Yes, she saw a friend shot and killed.

"That just gave me the mentality to trust no fuckin' body," she said. "Nobody."

She also had flown first class next to a woman in fur and diamonds, she told us, had held a steady job, and had a six-foot, ten-inch son playing basketball in college.

Her ability to communicate and her frankness in mediating disputes had turned Big Mama into the mayor of Hopeville. "I'm the glue that sticks it all together," she said.

Many, though not all, of Hopeville's residents were drunks or addicts or mentally ill. But a new community was forming, somehow. At the very least they had a mayor, and Big Mama's role seemed more than honorary.

According to an unofficial census, Hopeville had thirty-four permanent residents, meaning they owned their tents, Big Mama said. Seven Black people (Big Mama among them), and the rest were white folks, she told us when we asked.

Big Mama had arrived in Hopeville a little more than a year earlier. She remembered the event with an unnerving precision. On May 12, 2010, she was laid off. Then her last paycheck arrived. On May 15 she came to Hopeville.

She'd been mayor for about two months. In her leadership role she was no-nonsense. "You ain't gonna win in a conversation [with me]," Big Mama said. She doled out advice, and it wasn't always pleasant. And you didn't come to her if you weren't sober. You'd have to deal with her anger management problem.

"I could be aggressive, especially when it comes to things I can't tolerate, like sloppy drunks," she said.

Cooking was one way that Big Mama unwound. Even the people she didn't get along with wondered when she was going to make her next big meal.

"You ever had fried pizza on the grill?" she asked Dan, who was sitting across from her on his tree stump. He smiled and shook his head. She shot him a look and paused. Dan was diligently taking notes and appearing particularly clean-cut that morning. He looked like he'd never had fried pizza. "You ain't ready," she told him, and he nodded in agreement.

She and the person she called "my man" received a generous food subsidy, she said. Hopeville coolers were filled with baloney, hot dogs, and cheese. Big Mama's cooler was full of rib tips and roasts.

Despite her community meals, Hopeville was not a sentimental, fuzzy, welcoming place—one resident had been stabbed to death four months earlier. Its residents primarily operated autonomously.

"You look at us as a community. Each individual household has its own issue. You pull together when it's true or right," she said. "As long as you a Christian, ain't you supposed to share?"

She said she'd been approved for a shelter and care program. After she provided proof of income through unemployment checks, she'd move into an apartment, she hoped in about two months. Then she'd work with a temp agency that would place her in light industrial work.

"Now is the time to make up your mind. What are the areas I need to change?" Big Mama said to herself.

Hopeville was headed for change as well. Not only did St. Louis want to clear out the settlement, but winter was coming. In a homeless camp Mother Nature's caprice was more than just annoying. When the Mississippi rose over the levee, the camp flooded. "I started rolling like a river raft," Big Mama said. Her tent (she called it her "estates") started to rise up and float away.

"I don't believe everybody will be able to be placed in a home, but I believe those that are able [will be]. Go out and handle your business," she said, as if speaking to those candidates for placement.

A train rolled by, so close to the camp it looked like it would barrel over a couple of tents. One ran through Hopeville eight times a day.

"We so used to it, it's nothing," she said, raising her voice to be heard over the metallic clamor. "It don't even exist no more."

Hopeville's name began as a mockery of what the tent city stood for—people without jobs, without stability, without any kind of permanence in society. But Big Mama had grown accustomed, maybe even numb, to the harsh conditions of Hopeville and had found a kind of peace.

"It might have started out as a joke," Big Mama said, "but I really found hope when I got back down here."

Hopeville was razed in 2012. Big Mama continued to keep in touch with everyone from Hopeville, although she estimated 30 percent of its residents have since died. With the help of a housing voucher Big Mama moved into a one-bedroom apartment near Tower Grove Park in what she described as a quiet, close-knit neighborhood. She marveled at the proximity to boutiques, restaurants, the botanical garden, grocery stores, and more. When reached again in 2018, she was engaged to be married to a hardworking man, pursuing her education, and focused on improving her health, which included receiving psychiatric help, she said. "Lately I been doing pretty good."

The distance between Hopeville and the Hill can be measured in more than miles. Dan, Alyssa, and I visited the fifty-two square blocks that make up the Hill, St. Louis's Little Italy, in search of Ghigliones, both dead and alive. If you can trust the quotations attributed to Twain about genealogy, he treated the topic with doubt bordering on disbelief. He reportedly joked he had spent twenty-five dollars to research his family tree and then had to shell out fifty dollars to cover it up.[14]

But I took genealogy more seriously. With no parent or grandparent alive to tell me about the family's history, I read books like *Mastering Genealogical Proof* and took a course, Genetic Genealogy. Part of looking forward to America's future, I felt, was looking backward to the history of one's family members to find the meaning of their lives. I wanted to believe that the life of each Ghiglione family member, not just those who first came to America, had meaning that helped shape the meaning of my life.

Alyssa, Dan, and I knew we had reached the Hill when the fire hydrants suddenly started to look like Italian flags, striped green, red, and white. When a wave of Italians arrived in St. Louis in the 1880s, they found the neighborhood sparsely settled by African Americans and German immigrants. By 1914 the editor of *La Lega Italiana*, a local newspaper, described the Hill as an isolated island of five thousand Italians, devoid of streetcars, settlement houses, and other services provided to the rest of St. Louis.

Perhaps the physical isolation had at least one benefit: the Hill was the only St. Louis ethnic-immigrant settlement (German, Irish, Czech, and Polish included) of the late nineteenth and early twentieth centuries that had survived. It remained a tight-knit community of modest but well-maintained homes.

The Hill boasted two branches of the local Ghigliones, the pasta makers and the saloon keepers. The saloon keepers of the 1880s and 1890s—who "held exalted positions in the community," according to the historian Gary Mormino—included Joseph Ghiglione.[15] He was labeled "the King of Dago Hill" by the *St. Louis Post-Dispatch* (later the media removed *Dago*, a slur, from the neighborhood's name).

Dance halls adjoined the saloons. The saloon keepers hired drink-and-dance women from the city and paid them one dollar a night. Joe DeGregorio, the Hill historian, told us the dance hall women—"prostitutes or women looking for husbands or both"—served the predominantly male Italian community. The 1900 census, he said, listed three hundred Italian men and only three Italian women.

Joseph Ghiglione's was the first of a half-dozen Dago Hill saloon–dance halls raided by the police on Sunday, August 22, 1897. The police arrested Ghiglione and his dance hall women. But Ghiglione had connections. The police released him. Of the raided saloon–dance halls, only his remained open: "There dancing went on as if nothing had happened. A dozen girls had escaped the clutches of the police," the *Post-Dispatch* reported.

Years before police were hassling Joseph Ghiglione and his dancing women, another Ghiglione, Antonio F., became half of Ghiglione & Rossi, a manufacturer of macaroni and vermicelli—reportedly the first pasta maker west of the Mississippi. By 1882, Ghiglione had moved to Colorado and declared his intention to become a U.S. citizen, renouncing allegiance to his homeland of Switzerland. But the firm of Ghiglione & Rossi continued in St. Louis, with another generation of Ghigliones helping to run the company.

John C., in that next generation of pasta-making Ghigliones, had two sons, Lawrence P. and John L. Seventy-nine-year-old Audrey Ghiglione

Bender, daughter-in-law of Lawrence, remembered him and his wife for a set of values similar to those of my Ghiglione family, also pasta makers.

When Dan, Alyssa, and I interviewed Audrey, she lived alone in a South St. Louis brick bungalow on a predominantly African American block of Alaska Avenue. That weekend she had celebrated her eightieth birthday, four months ahead of schedule, by inviting forty family members to join her at a Cardinals–Chicago Cubs game. Audrey had downed three beers, and the Cardinals had won, on their way to victory in the World Series.

Calling me Sweetie, Audrey directed me to sit on the living room couch, with its two Budweiser beer pillows, seventeen stuffed animals, and a St. Louis Cardinals banner for the team's 2009 Gold Glove Award winners. She talked about living alone after the deaths of her husbands. Her first husband, Kenneth J. Ghiglione, died in 1981, her second husband, Robert S. Bender, in 2011.

Seated in front of a pillow that read "Don't Mistake Me for That Nice Little Old Lady," Audrey spoke candidly ("Holy crap, uh, crumb") about life with her Ghiglione in-laws. They stressed cleanliness. "You had to clean from the top to the bottom," she said, demonstrating her housecleaning technique.

Sunday family dinners were sacred family events. Lawrence Ghiglione served ravioli and other family favorites beginning at exactly 4:30. "If you weren't there by 4:30, there was war in the camp," Audrey said.

Her description of Lawrence's rule echoed stories I had heard about my great-grandmother Maria Strada Ghiglione, a four-foot, ten-inch, ninety-five-pound tyrant. Her Sunday dinner, which began at 2:00 p.m., earlier than weekday dinners, meant not only fine food but also family rite. Everyone had to attend. Even when dinners were held at her sons' homes in Seattle, she dictated what was to be served.

Maria hung on to the Old World. Her Ligurian dialect was incomprehensible to a grandchild who had learned classical Italian (those who disobeyed Maria were called *teta de rapa*—turnip head, or idiot). Maria's superstitions ruled. "We couldn't have thirteen at the dinner table, and we always had thirteen in the family," Maybelle Lucas, a granddaughter, said. "She didn't want a handkerchief as a gift—a handkerchief meant crying—or sharp things because they would cut a friendship."

Maria sought perfection in everything. Later in life, "she rinsed her hair in kerosene, which whitened it," Hazel Rispoli, another granddaughter, recalled. "Even her hair had to be perfect." Sometimes the search for perfection resulted in rudeness. When she visited her children's families, "upon

Maria Strada
Ghiglione

sitting down to eat, she would pick up the plate and rub her finger across it to make sure there was no grease on it," her granddaughter Marie Wilham said. "Everything had to be sparkly clean."

When cooking dinner at home every day except Sunday, Maria began at 3:00 p.m. She insisted on the freshest of vegetables and fruits from her garden (everything planted by the moon) or from Seattle's Pike Street Market, founded by Joe Desimone, also an Italian immigrant. Maria ordered the Pike Street Market vendors to give her their best or else. She required each ravioli—of finely chopped brains (for moisture), veal, pork, chicken, eggs, parmesan cheese, and spinach—to be made thin and tiny, no larger than a postage stamp.

Dinner ended with a theatrical flourish. Maria placed two sugar cubes in a teaspoon, poured Five Star Hennessey over the cubes, lit the brandy, allowed it to burn until the sugar melted and the flame died, and then poured the remainder of the teaspoon's contents into her demitasse.

Traditional values—honor, cleanliness, thrift—constituted a holy trinity in Maria Ghiglione's home. To ensure a fingerprint-free dining room table, the children were not permitted to touch the table. Their chairs sat on oil cloths. Each day, one room was cleaned thoroughly, the furniture hauled outside, the paintings and mirrors taken off the walls, the curtains removed and washed.

Maria's thrift bordered on miserliness. Her husband, who was expected to bring her every cent of his pay each week, once returned home with only five dollars. "I bought a few rounds for the boys at work," he said. Maria exploded. "Okay, if you're going to drink it up, I'm going to burn it up," she screamed, tossing the five-dollar bill in a parlor stove.

The values of my Ghigliones and those of the St. Louis Ghigliones differed in one way. The St. Louis Ghigliones were more devoted to their religion, Catholicism. My great-grandmother, the committed Christian, endured my great-grandfather, the committed nonbeliever who echoed the French writer Émile Zola: "Civilization will not attain to its perfection, until the last stone from the last church falls on the last priest!"[16] Audrey Ghiglione Bender insisted Alyssa, Dan, and I visit her son, Jim Ghiglione, forty-eight, a deacon and the unofficial family historian.

We took an early morning, 122-mile drive to Our Lady of the Holy Spirit in Mt. Zion, Illinois, which is just southeast of Decatur. Deacon Jim had been serving as the church's parish life coordinator for eight years. He said the entrepreneurial spirit ran deep in the Ghiglione family. His father, Kenneth, owned a *St. Louis Post-Dispatch* paper route for five years and also sold cars.

But clearly a spirit other than the entrepreneurial one moved Deacon Jim. Educated at Catholic schools in St. Louis, he remembered "having a spirituality different than the rest of my family," he said. "At best we would say grace and pray before a meal during Christmas. I really gave all the praise and glory to God."

Jim took a job as a mechanical design engineer partway through college and worked in that field for seventeen years. Attracted by the idea of becoming a deacon, he also attended seminary three nights a week for five years. Following ordination, he served as deacon at churches in Carthage, Missouri; Collinsville, Illinois; and then Mt. Zion.

Deacon Jim did not envision that women would ever become priests in the Catholic Church. He praised women's role in the church. But the role had limits, he emphasized. "I could never be a mother, biologically speaking," he said. "A woman can never be a father, biologically speaking. Those differences transfer from a spiritual standpoint as well."

Deacon Jim also espoused the church's position on sexual orientation. He tried to approach sexual orientation, he said, "in a kind, caring, and compassionate way. But to shy away from the truth—the teachings of Jesus Christ, the truth of God's law, if you will—to shy away from that is a lack of compassion. Christ loves the sinner but hates the sin."

Deacon Jim's faith gave him certainty and sincerity in his answers about women priests and sexual orientation. But what if his faith was mistaken? "Faith is the one thing," the biologist and naturalist Edward O. Wilson writes, "that makes otherwise good people do bad things."[17]

I could not accept Deacon Jim's opinion about sexual orientation or women priests. I was struck by a contradiction: although the church labeled homosexuals "deeply disordered," an estimated 30 to 40 percent of U.S. priests were gay (the French author Frédéric Martel called the Vatican "one of the biggest gay communities in the world"). I felt the biblical arguments precluding women from being priests qualified as what the scholar Garry Wills labels "pseudo-biblical justifications" for women's subordination: "It was always against the Gospel for men to treat women as inferior. . . . If we are all Christ, then how can one 'pull rank' on a woman? She is Christ." The author Karen Armstrong, a former Catholic nun, interprets Genesis 1:27—that male and female human beings were created in God's image—to mean that "both sexes, therefore, are capable of expressing the mysterious divine essence."[18]

Deacon Jim's interpretation of scripture also bothered Dan. "I see religious traditions as often beautiful, but I see dogma as disastrous," Dan said. "I was ready to leave that interview about half an hour in." Dan purposely tried to "downplay my gayness, especially after Deacon Jim's comments about his duty to help guide gays led astray—that if he doesn't act on his part, he is abetting the sin. I also found his views on female leadership in the church old-fashioned and hewing to the party line."

Alyssa heard Deacon Jim's message to be that God was a man, men were made in his likeness, women could never attain that, and their role was to support their husbands. "Of course, I found it offensive, being a woman, and sitting next to my very dear friend Dan, who also happened to be gay," she told me. "I suppose it was especially irksome because Deacon Jim wasn't a hateful person. He was merely a dutiful follower of his religion, espousing a sanctioned doctrine to those he has been tasked with taking care of. It just happened to be one that insulted everything I personally believed in."

Alyssa, Dan, and I again picked up the path of Twain's 1853 trip from St. Louis to New York by driving west from Mt. Zion to Springfield to visit the Abraham Lincoln Presidential Library and Museum (I would subject Dan and Alyssa to thirty-six museums during the trip). We then took Interstates 72 and 55 to Chicago. Whereas Twain rode slowly by stage coach (5 mph) and train (25 mph) from Springfield to Chicago for two days, we streaked northeast at 70 mph in only three and a half hours. But Twain was in no rush to experience Chicagoans. In *Following the Equator*, Twain's Satan tells a newcomer to hell: "The trouble with you Chicago people is that you think you are the best people down here; whereas you are merely the most numerous."

CHAPTER 3

Chicago

Confronting a Bevy of Biases

If only Twain were still around to challenge Chicago's self-image as a world-class city. Twain might remind Chicagoans of their city's reputation for high taxes, long commutes, lousy weather, ceaseless corruption, drive-by killings, and segregation. When the Reverend Martin Luther King Jr. mounted a northern civil rights movement in 1966, he chose to live in segregated Chicago, which he saw as the ultimate racial war zone.

A famous battleground site was Cabrini-Green, twenty-three towers of public housing for twenty thousand people, predominantly Black, built in the 1940s atop Little Hell, a largely Italian slum. Italian property owners lobbied the Chicago Housing Authority to segregate Black residents within one portion of Cabrini-Green "in order to preserve the character and values of the neighborhoods on the north side."[1] King led a 1966 march in a white enclave to protest such housing segregation. He was met by white counter-protesters carrying placards that bore such sentiments as "King would look good with a knife in his back." A hurled stone struck King in the head. He said he had never experienced white opposition "so hostile and so hateful." King's marches led to "little tangible change."[2]

Given the city's reputation for segregation and Twain's focus on racism, Dan, Alyssa, and I decided we should begin our time in Chicago by seeing Bruce Norris's Pulitzer-winning play, *Clybourne Park* (2010). In 1974, Supreme Court Justice Thurgood Marshall said America's metropolises were becoming "divided up each into two cities—one white, the other black."[3] Thirty-seven years later, the Steppenwolf Theatre production portrayed the neighborhood face-offs that accompanied the shifts in boundaries between the white and Black Chicagos.

After the performance, we interviewed Karen Aldridge, the thirty-nine-year-old who offered the play's most powerful performance. *Clybourne Park* focuses on neighborhood turf in 1959, borrowing its plotline and year from Lorraine Hansberry's *A Raisin in the Sun*. In act 1, Aldridge plays Francine, a uniformed African American maid for a clueless white middle-class couple (the husband: "For some reason, there is just something about the pastime of skiing that doesn't appeal to the Negro community"). The couple is fleeing to a white neighborhood, selling their modest bungalow to what becomes the neighborhood's first Black family.

Francine tries to limit her conversation with Bev, the white wife, to "Yes, ma'am" and "No, ma'am." "The less you speak," Aldridge explained, "the faster you can get out. But if you try to engage, you're in a whole whirlpool of trouble. Just to keep quiet—not meek quiet but to hold your tongue and know when to fight your battles—takes a lot of power."

In act 2, fifty years later, a young white couple from the suburbs is buying the same house, now rundown. The couple plans to raze it to build a McMansion, a symbol of urban gentrification. Aldridge now plays Lena, one half of the Black couple selling the house. Lena spews anger over the sale, unhappy that white people are planning to move into her Black neighborhood, "a part of my history and my parents' history."

Aldridge drew on her own experience living on Chicago's South Side for thirteen years with an aunt from Auburn, Alabama, who stayed in a largely Black world south of the downtown Loop. "I don't think she has white friends, she has white acquaintances. The way she looks at the community changing . . . she's resistant," Aldridge said.

Toward the end of act 2, Steve, the male half of the white couple, tells an unfunny racial joke—"What is long and hard on a Black man?" Lena retaliates: "Why is a white woman like a tampon?" Kevin, her husband, interrupts, "Baby, don't." When Steve cannot answer Lena's question, she says, "Because they're both stuck-up cunts."

Although the actors do not laugh or smile, Aldridge said that joke got a laugh from the audience every night. "I have to admit I got some pleasure from telling the joke," she said. "Of course, I don't think white women are c-u-n-t-s, but it's weird how, when you tell these racial jokes, is it more that you truly feel that way or is it the payoff and the pleasure you get from telling the joke? How do you keep Black kids from jumping on the bed? Well, tape Velcro to the ceiling. It's more the payoff than something personal."

Karen Aldridge

Aldridge said the Dominick's grocery store in the Steppenwolf Theatre's neighborhood provided evidence of a real-world transition: "Poor Blacks, mixed with these upper-class white people, newly rich, interact." But still, she said, "the city's so split. Latinos live here, Blacks live here, and then, when you get into the different white categories, they live in their worlds—it's neat if you want to go shopping and go to the real Polish whatever. But when you step back, it's kind of sad."

Norris began writing *Clybourne Park* in 2006, before the election of President Obama, a Chicagoan with a message of hope and change. Although he was an Obama supporter, Norris recalled for the drama critic Frank Rich, "I thought to myself, 'Good luck.'" Norris's pessimism about what Obama faced led him to add a line to the play, Rich noted. Norris has a well-meaning white character say naively at play's end, "I really believe things are about to change for the better. I firmly believe that."[4]

But no theatergoer could believe that after experiencing the play's verbal warfare between Blacks and whites. In the *Playbill*, Martha Lavey, artistic director of the Steppenwolf at the time, writes, "It's tantalizing to imagine a third act for *Clybourne Park*. An act set in 2059. Will we still be negotiating territory through the prism of race? Will we have learned a language that accommodates our increasingly diverse America?"

Aldridge said, "I don't think this is going to be resolved in the next fifty years, if ever."

She wondered whether human territoriality goes beyond matters of race and ethnicity. In a shopping center parking lot, she said, "someone's getting into their car and they see you waiting [for their spot]. There was a study done that they'll be less inclined to hurry up and leave the spot knowing someone's there [waiting for it]."[5]

"Right now, it's theirs," she continued. "And that's insane, is that not? And it's just human nature. My spot in the line. I can't even explain it better than that. We are as humans very territorial, and once we have our space, it's ours. Magnify that and it's the United States. Weird."

At a discussion about race relations after the performance of *Clybourne Park*, we met the leader of the discussion, Michael Fosberg, who offered an unusual perspective on race, as Alyssa Karas reported:

Michael Fosberg played the race card, literally. He joked about it as he handed us his business card. RACE is emblazoned on the back in big black letters.

The other side lists Fosberg's contact info and accomplishments: actor, writer, director, teacher, and—perhaps the culmination of all those things— diversity trainer.

Fosberg grew up as a white kid in Waukegan, Illinois. In his early thirties, his mother and stepfather—the man who had raised him—divorced.

"I realized at this time that I didn't really know who my biological father was," Fosberg said. "And here I was, losing my stepfather, and I decided perhaps I needed to know some information about [my biological father]."

Fosberg sought to find him. "I knew his name and that twenty-five years prior to this he lived in the Detroit area—and this was before we used the internet for everything—I went to the library and they had phone book sections."

He copied down the six names and numbers listed in the Detroit telephone directory. He went home. He called the first number on the list. It was his father.

"During that phone call, my father proceeded to tell me, as he said, 'a couple of things you should know I'm sure your mother's never told you,' one of which is that you're African American."

Fosberg had spent his entire life thinking he was white.

"Well, I was living in an apartment that was about the size of this chair at the time, but I remember being stunned, not so much from the idea of 'Oh

my God, I'm Black' but the idea that 'Let's see, this is a big story.' I've always felt, my whole life, I've always felt a deep connection to African American people, to African American culture, and I never could explain why." He felt reassured to learn he was half Black.

"I remember looking across the room I lived in, it was a little apartment, and there was a mirror there, and my dad was sort of filling me in on family history, and I kind of glanced over and caught a reflection of myself, and I thought, 'Oh, my God, did I just change? Have I gone Black and then back to white?' It was sort of a surreal experience."

A lot of Fosberg's friends weren't surprised. An old friend said, "'Damn, I always knew you were Black.' And I was like, why did you know that?" Fosberg said. "A lot of my friends had said this. They always had an inkling, and, I don't know, I suppose it's pretty easy after the fact to say that, but people said, 'You know, you were so cool, your hair, you had an Afro.'"

Although Fosberg was furious with his mother for withholding his identity, he later made peace with her.

His newfound family and its history enriched his life. He could trace his roots back to slavery. His great-grandfather was a member of the Fifty-Fourth Regiment Massachusetts Volunteer Infantry, free African Americans who fought in the Civil War. His grandmother's father was an all-star pitcher in the Negro Leagues. His grandfather was a genius who started the science and engineering departments at Norfolk State University.

For ten years Fosberg had used his story as a springboard for talking to Americans about diversity. He published a book and performed his one-man show, Incognito, sixty to seventy times a year for schools, colleges, corporations, and the government.

In the play, Fosberg discovers his identity at the same time the audience does.

"Some people are kind of disappointed," he said. "To be frank, white audiences are sometimes more disappointed that I'm not more outraged, perhaps, by the discovery. And I am perplexed by that, because what would I be outraged about? Would being part Black be outrageous or bad? I'm confused by that kind of response to it. I was overjoyed. I was like, 'Damn, I figured out who I am.'"

Fosberg saw dialogue as the key to improving race relations. He saw it in politics, in audiences, and in the media. Fosberg said it seemed like people wanted to have a conversation about race, but they didn't know how to start it.

"There also seems to be a faction of people who feel like, 'Oh, man, do we have to talk about race?'" he said. "When in fact they haven't really talked about race. They think they have. And that's mostly from white people, almost exclusively. And then, yes, the dialogue about race is so difficult to have.

"When you're in mixed company and you want to have a dialogue about race, white people approach the dialogue from a place of caution, because you want to be careful that you don't say anything that sounds racist. On the other side of the issue, people of color are ready to pounce on anyone, anything, that sounds remotely racist, and so we're polarized, and we don't have the dialogue."

Fosberg suggested creating a space "to allow people to say whatever they're gonna say and not jump on them like they're a racist. There are definitely, definitely racist things being said all over the place. You see them, you hear them, but rather than jump to calling it racist, why don't we have some dialogue about it?"

The same constraints were evident in mainstream media. "I've been interviewed by all kinds of media," Fosberg said. "I've been on CNN, All Things Considered, Tavis Smiley Show, blah, blah, blah," Fosberg said. "Who has interviewed me to talk about race and identity? People of color. Those are the only people in the media who are talking about it. Why is that?"

A few days later I struggled to write about our conversation. One question remained, one that I hadn't brought up because I thought it might be unprofessional or stupid.

So I pulled out Michael Fosberg's RACE card and called him.

He answered, although it was well past normal working hours.

"Michael, I have one more question," I began. "So I'm a white girl. I don't know how to start a dialogue about race. What questions should I even be asking?"

The difficult part, he said, is the expectation to be an expert, but we don't know all there is to know about race. No one does.

"Come up front and say, 'Hey, I want to be honest, this is where I'm coming from,'" he told me. Everyone has a different experience. "It's up to you to discover and uncover what you know about race."

Twain's anti-Catholic prejudice—his belief that the church practiced deception of the gullible ("Jesuit humbuggery")—had crossed my mind in Mt. Zion, Illinois, while listening to Deacon Jim Ghiglione talk about gay Catholics and

Barbara Zeman

the ordination of women. In Chicago, Alyssa, Dan, and I found Catholics with perspectives quite different from Deacon Jim's. Barbara Zeman served as a priest for Chicago's LGBT Catholics. Zeman's lay assistant—who asked to be identified by only her first name, Joanna, for fear of harassment—described herself as intersex, born with ambiguous genitalia.

We watched Zeman preside over the fortieth anniversary Mass of Dignity Chicago, which ministers to the city's LGBT Catholics at the congregation's home, Broadway United Methodist. Zeman and Joanna led fifty-five Dignity Chicago congregants in singing, "For everyone born, a place at the table, / to live without fear, and simply to be."

Later we interviewed the sixty-four-year-old Zeman as she sat by herself in the empty sanctuary of Broadway United Methodist. She said her path to becoming a priest began with a traditional Catholic upbringing. She attended Catholic schools in Cleveland and then earned a bachelor's degree from the University of Detroit Mercy.

She felt a call to the priesthood. The Second Vatican Council (1962–65) suggested anything might be possible. Pope John XXIII insisted the church "look to the present." Zeman thought the church soon might "open the doors to women leaders and allow laypeople to take ownership of our church," she said.

But that failed to happen. "I felt betrayed almost," Zeman recalled. Her life in the 1970s took a different course. She married and later divorced her husband. She took TV production jobs usually held by men.

In 1998, still seeking answers about the place of women in the church, Zeman earned a master's in theology from Loyola University of Chicago. She began participating in the interfaith United Power for Action and Justice and an organization of Catholics named Call to Action. She committed, she said, "to bringing justice to our church and to speaking to the lack of leadership in the church for women."

In 2002, she learned that male bishops in Europe were ordaining women as priests. But they were doing so in secret, she said, "because if their identities became known, they would be removed from their duties and put under house arrest by the Vatican."

In 2008, the Vatican decreed excommunication for any woman who sought ordination. The decree saddened Zeman. If she chose to become a priest, she knew she could no longer be a sacristan, sing in a church choir, or do anything else in a Catholic setting. She also worried that Catholic zealots might try to attack her physically or prevent her from working as a hospital chaplain.

Nevertheless, in 2008 a female bishop from Roman Catholic Womenpriests, an organization not sanctioned by the Catholic Church, ordained Zeman in Chicago. Hundreds of Catholic women have been similarly ordained worldwide since then. In response, subsequent Vatican pronouncements have gone beyond an excommunication decree. In 2010, the Vatican categorized ordinations of women as *delicta graviora*, crimes against the church so serious that they ranked with priests' sexual abuse of children.

In 2012, Pope Benedict XVI insisted an exclusively male priesthood had been "set forth infallibly." It could never be changed. A year later, Pope Francis urged a greater role for women in the church but reaffirmed the ban on women priests.

"I'm going to be who I am," Zeman said. She served as a nondenominational chaplain at a large Chicago hospital (her agreement with the hospital required her not to name it) and led services for Dignity Chicago. At the start, some Dignity Chicago members were uncomfortable with a woman priest. "I think 20 percent left," Zeman said. But "more than 20 percent of new people have come in—younger people, women, straight guys. It's becoming much more of a mix of everybody now, which is nice."

Contacted in 2019, Zeman said she had taken on additional duties as a meditation group facilitator and a transplant hospital's advocate for living organ donors. She makes sure their decisions to donate are informed and free from coercion. She continues to "minister to all who feel marginalized" and remains committed to the role of women priests: "I do see our movement causing a sea change in people's thinking." In 2018, 60 percent of U.S. Catholics felt women should be permitted to be priests.[6] But Zeman doubted the Catholic Church would change its position on the role of women priests. "These guys are playing hardball," she said. "It's about power, not about Jesus."

———

Joanna, Barbara Zeman's lay assistant during services for Chicago's LGBT Catholics, puffed on a Pall Mall as she talked nervously in her apartment about her winding, wearying journey to a new gender identity. She sat in an armchair in a corner of her tiny apartment's living room–dining room–kitchen, which was filled with signs of her different lives.

Beneath a large window overlooking Lake Michigan, two Yamaha keyboards stood ready for Joanna to play her favorites, everything from opera to jazz. A small table held a microscope, from her days as a biology student at Columbia University and her career as a physician's assistant until she retired in 2010.

The only child of Polish immigrants who arrived in the United States in the 1930s, Joanna was born Joseph in 1946 in Dover, New Jersey. "Shortly after I was born, a decision was made for my parents and me, of course, as far as what gender I was to be assigned," Joanna said. "The good doctor at the time said, 'You know, the plumbing is kind of not here nor there, let's just make it a him.'" Joanna's parents, who treated the family doctor as God, assumed he knew best. They agreed to have Joseph take male hormones and undergo surgical procedures.

"My parents didn't do anything maliciously; they did the best they could," Joanna said. "Nowadays, it's far from a unilateral decision. The hospital gets medical ethicists involved, and there's a whole chain of decision makers involved. It's rare that, if any surgery is to be done, it is . . . done . . . [before] the person has achieved some degree of maturity to participate in that decision."

While Joanna grew up classified as a male, she said, "I never really felt like I belonged." She also came to feel, because of the 1962–65 reforms of

Vatican II, that she no longer belonged in the Catholic Church. While many Catholics saw reforms, such as the use of vernacular languages in place of Latin, as long overdue, she viewed Vatican II as impermissible permissiveness.

"I left the church," Joanna said, "and became interested in the Eastern Orthodox Church," an even more traditional church. As Joseph, she studied three years for the Eastern Orthodox priesthood. "I got to the point of being a deacon and then, as they say, the substance hit the ventilating system. I developed an acute illness and had to be taken to the hospital.

"It was then that they discovered, shall we say, my unique physiological status," she continued. As an intersex individual, she possessed genitalia with both testicular and ovarian tissues. "Well, that spelled the end of that," Joanna said. "I was summarily cashiered out of the court, so to speak."

Uncertain as to both her religious identity and gender identity, Joanna struggled with depression and substance abuse. Alcohol led to such prescription pain relievers as Oxycontin and Vicodin. The pills left no odor on her breath, so she could hide the abuse.

"But my head was going crazy," she said. She felt she had to transition, at age fifty, to living as a female. At the same time, she said, "I had this feeling I needed to have a spiritual home."

Joanna tried Roman Catholic churches again. "And that's when things started getting dicey," she said. "Depending on how I'm dressed, I can be taken for either male or female." She stood five feet, ten inches tall, with shoulder-length, light-brown hair, and a strong jaw.

"I was feeling very much not accepted and not welcome in the Roman Catholic churches," she said. As a last resort, she attended four masses of the Archdiocesan Gay and Lesbian Outreach at Our Lady of Mt. Carmel Church in Chicago. "It was very cold, very sterile, I felt, very nonwelcoming to all those who were not male or those who did not identify as such," she said.

Then she read an advertisement for Dignity Chicago in the Chicago Gender Society's newsletter. She decided, "One more time. One more time, and then I don't know what I'm going to do."

Dignity Chicago was "like one of those storybook situations where I walked in and they had the welcome table set up. Within five minutes, my thought was, 'I'm home.' The biggest part of it was the acceptance. No questions asked. 'You are what you are, and we love you for that.' Everything, fortunately, came together. I stopped using [drugs], and, coincidentally or not, my sobriety anniversary was the day I walked into Dignity."

Joanna, an eight-year veteran of Dignity, has not found it easy to adjust to all the changes in the Roman Catholic Church that Dignity represents. "You might think I'd be jumping for joy at the inclusion of women priests," Joanna said. "But there's an old saying, 'Once a Catholic, always a Catholic.'" Women priests were totally foreign to the Roman Catholic Church and Eastern Orthodox Church of Joanna's earlier life.

But she loved Dignity's inclusivity—"both sexes in any aspect of the services, the liturgy, and in the wording of the prayers that are used," she said. In the Lord's Prayer, for example, "Our Father who art in heaven" became "Our Maker who art in heaven."

She saw the Roman Catholic hierarchy as a patriarchy resisting reality: "Things can't go as they are. The situation with priests—they're dwindling [in number]. So what are some possibilities if you're only going to limit it to male clergy? Either start accepting married males or, God forbid, homosexual males. And what about females? 'No, no, no, no, no, we can't have that.' I don't see the hierarchy changing significantly."

As for her transition from Joseph to Joanna, "I feel like I've been extremely blessed and fortunate," she said. "I've had two lives in one." Her childhood doctor gave her notes to get her out of the hell of gym. "Having to jump in and out of showers, taking showers with towels around me," she said. "Essentially it was fear of the unknown. But finally I got to the point where, once the substance abuse kicked in, I started dealing with therapists. They started learning my story and said, 'Of course, you're half screwed up.'" The counseling, she said, "gave me the push that I needed." She stopped abusing drugs and transitioned to Joanna.

Although Joanna experienced harassment, she questioned whether her gender transition was an act of bravery. She had reached a crossroad, she said, "where I'm either going to do it or I'm going to end up in a box. Substance abuse is a more subtle way of committing suicide. And I was doing a pretty damn good job of it, in ways not too terribly subtle."

Joanna said she was far from radical, definitely not an intersex activist. "That's just not me," she added. But she criticized the way the LGBT community addressed intersex issues: "They say they support transgender people in terms of equality, but they're just paying lip service. And in terms of intersex, that's nonexistent. 'Intersex, what's that?'"

Joanna did not expect any significant change in public attitudes toward intersex people in her lifetime. Intersex "is too esoteric for most people to get an accurate take on," she said. Coverage of intersex issues focused on the sordid and sensational, she said. "Until or unless that starts to change, nothing will happen.

"I would say that most people need to enlarge their concept of sexuality," she added. "Human sexuality is a continuum. A vast continuum. I'm sure that there are parts of that continuum that haven't even been identified yet."

She emphasized how difficult it is to understand the continuum. On one end, she said, are people who "get their jollies from dressing in the clothing of opposites." On the other end are people who "honestly feel like they are in the wrong body."

She advised people not to come to intersex individuals with preconceived notions. She has met people who clearly wondered whether, as she said, "I'm fish or fowl. As we get to know each other, over the course of time, we have real conversations and they'll say, 'Oh, my gosh, Joanna, I feel so bad how negatively I thought of you when I first met you. Freak city here. And you've turned out to be so totally opposite that.'"

Joanna said, "Take me for what I am, who I am, how you find me right now."

A mile southwest of Joanna's apartment, the banh mi sandwich shops of Argyle, the busy hub of the Vietnamese community in uptown Chicago, featured steaming bowls of pho and French-style baguettes. Dan Tham reported on our visit:

We skipped the gastronomic goodies to visit the Vietnamese Association of Illinois (VAI), situated in a nondescript brick building on Broadway, shyly distanced from the heart of Argyle. Founded in 1976, the VAI serves Vietnamese refugees who fled their homeland after the Vietnam War. Some called it the American War.

According to the 2010 U.S. census, nearly seventeen thousand Vietnamese live in Illinois; a large portion have helped create a thriving neighborhood enclave in Argyle.

At the VAI, Dung Nguyen, bespectacled and attired in a safari vest, looked like a sort of bookish explorer. The seventy-year-old Nguyen directed the association's community care program, which assisted seniors. Even in his second-floor office, we could hear the screaming and laughing of the children playing on the floor below. "The after-school program," Nguyen explained, shaking his head and smiling at the same time.

Born in Phan Thiet, a coastal town in central Vietnam, Nguyen moved at seventeen to Saigon to pursue an education in English and American literature. He recalled being particularly fond of Hemingway, Steinbeck, and Twain.

A photograph of Nguyen's younger incarnation as a handsome jet fighter pilot in the South Vietnamese Air Force looked over his shoulder from the table behind him. The table served as an altar to his proud military past.

Nguyen fought alongside American soldiers on Vietnam War combat missions. For that he was imprisoned for almost ten years in a "reeducation camp" after the Communists took Saigon and renamed it Ho Chi Minh City.

A journalist interviewed him shortly before he immigrated to the United States in 1992. The reporter asked where he would most like to live in America. "Anywhere in the United States," Nguyen said, "because this is a free country and everywhere it's the same."

When the Vietnamese arrived in Chicago after the war, their main problem with adjustment to life in America was the language barrier, Nguyen said. Few could speak English as well as he could. Still, he lamented the irony that second-generation Vietnamese Americans were forgetting Vietnamese and communicating with one another almost exclusively in English.

To counter that trend, the VAI offered free weekend courses in Vietnamese for children in the community. Nguyen said the nonprofit also tried to attract young people with its yearly festivals; the biggest was the Lunar New Year celebration, or Tet. VAI encouraged children to participate by giving them small red envelopes (li xi) containing five dollars.

Despite his support for preserving Vietnamese culture, Nguyen was not interested in going back to Vietnam. He hadn't returned in twenty-two years. Nguyen was skeptical of the government that had imprisoned him. He was also reluctant to visit because he no longer had friends living in Vietnam. "I won't have anyone to talk to," he said.

Nguyen proudly described a book filled with the biographies of successful Vietnamese Americans, from politicians like Anh "Joseph" Quang Cao, who represented Louisiana's second congressional district from 2009 to 2011, to prosperous entrepreneurs. Nguyen laughed and said, "Some have big businesses, they are millionaires."

America stands for education and opportunity, Nguyen said. Children of South Vietnamese officials would have faced discrimination and received a poor education if they had stayed in Communist-controlled Vietnam. "Here they receive a very good education," he said. "And they grow up in a modern society. They become good citizens."

Outwardly cheerful, Nguyen refused to play up his harrowing experiences in the war or in prison. He was still enamored of literature. In his free time he translated French poems into Vietnamese and published them in the VAI's monthly magazine.

He also looked forward to seeing more of the United States. "When I was in school in Vietnam, I studied American literature and we talked about Atlanta in [reading] Gone with the Wind. So when I came here, I traveled to Atlanta to have a look."

Twain, too, traveled around the United States, Nguyen said as he zig-zagged his finger across an imaginary America. He shared a knowing laugh with us. Travel symbolized the freedom so precious to Nguyen. In the United States, if he wanted, he knew he could join us any time, anywhere on the road.

———

We visited suburban Evanston, where our trip had started, to interview Leezia Dhalla, a student at Northwestern's journalism school and an undocumented immigrant subject to deportation. Dhalla grew up in San Antonio, she said, "very all-American": Girl Scout, National Honor Society member, student newspaper coeditor, summa cum laude graduate of Ronald Reagan High School, and organizer of a $10,000 fund-raiser for a leukemia patient in desperate need of a bone marrow transplant.

Dhalla returned home to San Antonio in November 2010, during her junior year at Northwestern, to find a notice from the U.S. Department of Homeland Security that said she was "not a citizen or national of the United States" and faced the possibility of deportation for overstaying a Canadian visa.

"I was in shock," Dhalla said. "I grew up completely unaware of my legal status." She felt the notice classified her as "not American enough"—not sufficiently devoted to U.S. ideals—to remain in the country. She grew emotional as she described to us how she had spent her twenty-first birthday, "so monumental for young Americans," in the office of her immigration lawyer. "What am I supposed to do with my life?" she asked her attorney.

Of Indian and Tanzanian descent, Dhalla was born in Canada. But in October 1996, when she was six years old, "financial struggles led my parents to move the family to San Antonio," she said. Dhalla memorized the Pledge of Allegiance, rooted for the San Antonio Spurs, spoke Spanish as well as English, and regularly said "y'all."

She felt she was "a normal American kid." Her room at Northwestern featured pictures of such American icons as Marilyn Monroe and Bob Dylan

Leezia Dhalla

and the jersey of Clay Matthews, then a Green Bay Packers linebacker (traded to the Los Angeles Rams in 2019). Although she was from Texas, Dhalla reminded us that the Packers, not the Dallas Cowboys, had received the most votes in a recent poll asking which was America's team.

"There's a lot of dissonance," Dhalla said. "Even now I don't know what to think. At first, at least for me, it's like, 'Oh, my gosh, what did I do wrong?'" She realized, however, she had not done anything wrong. "All I did was listen to my parents and they said, 'We're moving to Texas.'"

Dhalla had dreamed since high school of working for CNN or another major U.S. news organization. But the notice from Homeland Security left her feeling that her career in journalism was over before it started. She wanted to spend a required semester-long internship reporting for a South African newspaper. But without a valid passport, she would be unable to reenter the United States.

Four months after her graduation from Northwestern, she spoke of good and bad news. She had been one of the first young undocumented immigrants in the country to receive a conditional work permit and deferred action status under the Deferred Action for Childhood Arrivals (DACA) program. That Obama administration initiative lifted her fear of being deported for at least two years.

Her plan to become a journalist had morphed into a desire "to pursue a career in immigration law and human rights advocacy in some capacity."

She added, "Most Americans would not pass a citizenship test. Did you know that sixty-five thousand undocumented kids graduate from an American high school every year? Of those, only 5 to 10 percent go to college. And most of those are community colleges."[7] A degree from a university like Northwestern creates a sense of duty, Dhalla said. "It's almost as if you have a responsibility to do something on behalf of everybody else. You can be vocal about it, and you're educated enough to do it."

I contacted Dhalla in August 2019. A provision of the 2000 Legal Immigration Family Equity (LIFE) Act allowed her, unlike most DACA recipients, to apply—and be approved—for a green card. But the cap on the number of green cards available to Canadians was so low that she could not be certain that she would ever be allowed to permanently live and work in the United States. "It could be another ten years [until a green card becomes available to me]," she said. "I have no idea."

She was working in Washington, D.C., as press director for FWD.us, an organization founded by Facebook CEO Mark Zuckerberg and fourteen other tech innovators and entrepreneurs to keep the United States competitive in a global economy by, in part, achieving immigration reform.

FWD.us—and Dhalla—sought passage of a law to protect from deportation the estimated 690,000 young immigrants known as "Dreamers" (after the never-enacted Development, Relief and Education for Alien Minors [DREAM] Act). In three TED Talks, newspaper articles, a presentation before U.S. senators and representatives, and a *Washington Post* op-ed, she argued her case. Dhalla had made the most of her years since her 2012 graduation from Northwestern: she had bought a home and car, paid off more than $114,000 in student loans, started a small business that helped job-seeking Americans and immigrants write résumés and cover letters, and paid her share of federal and state taxes. The DACA program allowed her, she said, "to give back to the country I consider home."

She was doing her best to be an American and live a version of the American dream. Each year she celebrated not only her December birthday but the October day she arrived in the United States.

What would she do if the United States deported her to Canada? "I just don't have plans to go anywhere," she said. "I really don't have a plan." Except to remain in America, her home country.

As for those politicians who continued to insist on deporting Dreamers like Dhalla, I know how Twain would have regarded them. Twain demonized Americans who sought to rid the nation of California's Chinese immigrants:

"Only the scum of the population do it . . . they, and, naturally and consistently, the policemen and politicians . . . for these are the dust-licking pimps and slaves of the scum, there as well as elsewhere in America."

———

I invited the transgender baseball expert Christina Kahrl to Evanston to talk with us about her life. As she spoke, I imagined a conversation between Kahrl and Mark Twain. A lover of base ball (as it was spelled then), Twain called the game "the very symbol, the outward and visible expression of the drive, and push, and rush and struggle of the raging, tearing, booming nineteenth century!"

Twain might have been interested in talking with Kahrl about gender too. His "1002nd Arabian Night," a tale of switched babies, suggests the challenges faced by transgender individuals. The sultan's male baby is raised as a girl, Fatima, with his hair parted in the middle; the female baby is raised as a boy, Selim, with her hair parted on the side. Their behavior disturbs people. Selim is dubbed a milksop and Fatima a defective.

Kahrl recounted for us the moment at age thirty-five when she told her mother, father, and youngest brother that she planned to transition from being Chris to Christina. Kahrl's mother suggested Christina, like Fatima, would be in one sense defective. She said that her daughter would have to quit "sports and military history and all that stuff."

Kahrl responded, "Mom, I know the woman who teaches military history at West Point. She's good at it and she's not a guy. There are great sports reporters who are women." Kahrl resisted the notion that a gender change required her to redefine her personality and interests: "I just needed to change this one feature of me, and if that makes me one of the girls who likes sports, that makes me one of the girls who likes sports."

Kahrl disagreed with the idea that all transgender individuals—who sometimes grappled with their gender identity as early as age three or four—had tormented childhoods. "I had a wonderful childhood," she said. Kahrl, forty-four, called her parents hip; they were only twenty years older than she. Her father, her intellectual role model, "had me reading Goethe or Schiller at an early age," she said. Her Italian American mother taught her to ride horses and make marinara from scratch.

But, she said, "about third, fourth, and fifth grade, I started realizing I was different. I wasn't like the boys. Although I was playing with the girls on the playground, I didn't really know where I fit until fifth-grade health, when

I learned about gender dimorphism, reproductive health, and all of that. I thought, 'Hell, I'm in the wrong bin.'"

As a fifth-grader she did not yet know the "terminology to explain that I'm transgender," she said. But she was also self-assured enough to believe that she would figure it out. She decided not to worry about it.

Kahrl's gender identity evolved over decades. At her Sacramento-area high school she chose not to date. "I didn't know necessarily how to act on my attractions to both men and women because I wasn't sure about myself," she said.

While an undergraduate at the University of Chicago, Kahrl made a conscious choice to be a man. As Chris, she joined the Phi Kappa Psi honor society, grew a mustache, and "tried to be as butch as I could be, which wasn't necessarily all that butch."

Although her family never pressured her, Kahrl felt "the expectation to be the alpha-male, firstborn son, [and] fulfill all the pride they had in me. Fulfill what I would say is a feedback loop. That you expect to be the person your friends [and family] expect." As Chris, she married a college friend, a "very Catholic and very heterosexual" woman. Kahrl soon regretted the marriage, which she later termed selfish. The couple parted in an amicable divorce.

In 1995, also as Chris, Kahrl helped found Baseball Prospectus, a pioneering baseball think tank that performed contract work for *Sports Illustrated* and ESPN. "I felt very comfortable with where I was professionally," she said. "But I also felt fundamentally unhappy with myself. And unhappy with my sense of self."

Kahrl said to herself, "Whose life am I living? You don't get do-overs in life. You get one shot at life." She committed to not "playacting through my own life anymore." She stopped stressing "the Chicago guy thing"—the buzz cut, the mustache, "the butching it up."

Earlier she had researched transsexuality. She was relieved to learn, she said, "that there are other people like me [an estimated 1.4 million transgender Americans] and that I'm not crazy."[8]

In 2001, she embarked on the transition from Chris to Christina. "When I decided to transition, I was forty pounds heavier, much bigger in the shoulders," she said. When I interviewed her a decade later, she weighed 165 pounds.

In 2002, she started hormone replacement therapy, laser hair removal—"all that kind of incremental agony," she said. "This was an opportunity to remake my life pretty much from top to bottom and be very thorough

Christina Kahrl

about it." The remake, as was true for most transgender Americans, did not initially entail bottom surgery.

When she informed people at work of the transition, "all of them were exceptionally supportive," Christina said. "I got a lot of notes from people telling me I was incredibly brave."

It could have gone differently. In a majority of states, companies could legally fire transgender people from their jobs because of their identity. Transgender people faced unemployment at twice the national rate. Ninety percent experienced harassment, mistreatment, or discrimination or sought to avoid such behavior by hiding their identity.[9] Transgender Day of Remembrance commemorates the many people murdered each year as a result of transphobia.

But Christina downplayed her bravery: "No! It's not courage. It's exhaustion from a lifetime of fear. It's about finally moving on from that and just trying to live.

"I liked my past. I'm not ashamed of my past. I was assigned male at birth, but fundamentally I was also trans. My need to transition was just an eventual fact of my life. On that level I was in a healthier head space about my own transition than some. I didn't feel the need to adopt a persona or personality. If anything, I think the butching-up of my life from college onwards—that fifteen-year stint in my life—is the one thing that I'm uncomfortable with.

"I know a lot of trans people commit suicide," she said, mentioning three trans people who had killed themselves. "Do I ever feel suicidal? No. I like being alive. I wouldn't want to cheat myself of the possibilities that this life holds."

Her life and career had turned out, she said, "better than anybody could have possibly predicted." She was voted into the Baseball Writers' Association of America, not as a man but as a woman. She was hired by ESPN "because they cared about my quality as a professional, trans or not," she said. "It didn't matter."

Whether in a press box or locker room, people did not seem to care about Kahrl's trans status. But she also thought her acceptance might have been based on "a superficial element." As a statuesque redhead, she said, "I'm not appallingly ugly or something like that, and I have to be frank that we live in a superficial society, so being slightly easy on the eye makes life easier than if you're grossly overweight or not remotely passable as a trans person."

She predicted public acceptance of trans people would take longer than acceptance of gays and lesbians. "Part of that is because there are so few of us, so it's easier to caricature or stigmatize us," she said. "We have so few spokespeople. We have so few role models."

Transgender people historically had felt the need, Kahrl said, "to achieve stealth, to bury their past and hide who they were. Unfortunately, the mistake there is that you feed into the idea that trans people are misleading you. Or lying to you about who they are."

She believes people should be candid about being transgender, if they can deal with the stigma. "I think by living out loud, my hope is that I get people used to the idea that trans people can just be public about being trans without making a big deal about it," she said.

A recently acquired tattoo on her left ankle suggested her confidence in her new identity. The tattoo carries the name of Sjöfn, the Norse goddess, who, Kahrl said, "grants love to those for whom it's forbidden. If LGBT people are supposed to have a patron saint in Norse cosmology, that would be Sjöfn."

Kahrl became an activist on transgender issues. She helped organize a protest against Hunters Nightclub Chicago, a gay-owned business in Elk Grove Village that was illegally screening people at the door. "If your ID did not conform to your gender presentation," Kahrl said, "they would turn you back." Seventy people protested by cross-dressing. The nightclub stopped its screening, she said.

Kahrl also worked to develop a new Chicago Police Department policy on the treatment of transgender people. She said homeless transgender youths were frequently abused, "the police asserting their right to grope genitalia to determine gender. No other class of citizens has to put up with that as part of the shakedown the policeman feels he gets to do."

After a two-year negotiation, then-police superintendent Garry F. McCarthy signed an order in 2012 directing police to treat transgender, intersex, and gender nonconforming individuals respectfully and without bias. The order also prohibited strip searches to determine gender characteristics and required police officers to be trained in the respectful treatment of detainees.

The next stage, Kahrl said, would be to extend oversight of police performance across Illinois. Her message to police departments statewide that target transgender individuals: "You're going to be sued out of existence if you let guys with guns get away with this." She hoped the appeal to police departments' instinct for self-preservation and their respect for justice would stop police discrimination and abuse statewide.

Kahrl also participated in a sports coalition that sought to end anti-LGBT bias in athletics. To achieve equal rights at the K–12 level, the coalition pushed for a national law that, like a California law, would give a transgender student the right to use bathrooms and participate in sports consistent with his or her gender identity. "It is a never-ending fight," Kahrl said. "We just have to keep battling."

With this thought in mind, we left Chicago to visit Rust Belt cities to learn of other identity battles being fought, about immigration, poverty, and race.

CHAPTER 4

The Rust Belt

Where Immigrants and Refugees Aid Recovery

We departed Chicago at 7:00 a.m., anticipating a thirteen-hour trip to Cleveland that day, given the stops we planned. Alyssa drove, Dan napped, and I read the Sunday *New York Times* and *Chicago Tribune* hamster-style, shredding the papers as I ripped out articles to save. We spoke little. Were we trying to avoid thinking about what lay ahead in Marion, Indiana? We planned to visit the county courthouse where a mob had lynched two Black teenagers—Thomas Shipp and Abram Smith—on August 7, 1930, supposedly the last lynchings in the North.

The two teenagers, along with a third, sixteen-year-old James Cameron, had been accused of the murder of Claude Deeter, a white factory worker, and the rape of Mary Ball, his white companion. An 1869 *Buffalo Express* column attributed to Twain came to mind: "An avenging mob" in Memphis had hanged a Black man for the rape of a white woman, only to have another man confess his guilt. Twain wrote: "Ah, well! Too bad to be sure! A little blunder in the administration of justice by Southern mob-law, but nothing to speak of. Only 'a nigger' killed by mistake—that's all."

Aware of lynchings in the North as well as the South, Twain later called the nation the "United States of Lyncherdom." He proposed writing a multivolume history of U.S. lynching but soon retreated for fear that "I shouldn't have even half a friend left" in the South (a redacted version of "The United States of Lyncherdom," his 1901 essay, was published only posthumously by his literary executor).

Dan, Alyssa, and I met at a Japanese restaurant with William F. Munn, a Taylor University professor who had taught history at Marion High School until 2010, and two of his former high school students. The students, his son

Evan Munn and Meredith Kuczora, had written papers for his U.S. history course that touched on the local lynchings.

Without asking our preferences, the restaurant server plopped chopsticks in front of Dan, the Vietnamese American member of our team, and forks, knives, and spoons in front of the rest of us. Dan joked about the experience later: "I guess you could say I was racially profiled! I know Meredith said she was half-Asian, half-white, and she wasn't chopsticked, but I guess I have a harder time blending in as 'all-American' in places like Marion."

Dan described what he called a "perpetual foreigner syndrome that some-times compels me to maybe overplay my American-ness." Growing up, he was aware of Vietnamese aunts and uncles who still had heavy accents, "even after having lived in the States for many, many years." In middle school, he always carried a pocket dictionary to look up the unfamiliar words he encountered. In high school, he tried especially hard to be well read in American literature. He was a finalist in a state English competition started by two Mormon me-dia companies. "Talk about trying to fit in with the white, heteronormative Mormon hegemony," Dan said.

Over lunch, the six of us discussed the lynchings in Marion, a town of about thirty thousand that is between Indianapolis and Fort Wayne. Kuczora said she came to understand the town's silence. "A lot of the families that were involved still live in Marion," she said. "It's a sensitive subject." In trying to grasp the reasoning of the people who participated in the lynchings, she wrote her course paper about human ritual sacrifice.

Evan Munn wrote about the absence of a lynching marker or monument in Marion. The city exhibited what the historian Michael Kammen calls highly selective memory: "Recall the good but repress the unpleasant."[1] Evan Munn contrasted Marion's resistance to acknowledging its lynchings to the response of Duluth, Minnesota, to three lynchings there in 1920. In 2003 the City of Duluth created a memorial as an expression of shame and regret.

Evan Munn said a 2003 Reconciliation Day in Marion, organized by Black and white ministers, provided helpful healing for hundreds of citizens. A white minister apologized and asked for forgiveness on behalf of white Christians. A Black minister responded: "We forgive those who failed to stand up. From this day forward, we will rise up out of the ashes of disgrace."

After lunch, William Munn took us to a small church at Eighteenth and Meridian. At that church, Munn said, white workers from the nearby factory of Superior Body (what irony in that name), some of whom were reportedly Ku Klux Klan members, had plotted the 1930 lynchings. But perhaps the

The lynching of Thomas Shipp and Abram Smith in Marion, Indiana, on August 7, 1930, as photographed by Lawrence Beitler.

story about Superior Body workers was too good to be true. The historian Kevin Boyle, an expert on the Marion lynchings, later told me the lynch mob leaders did not work together at Superior. Boyle thought the story about KKK workers at Superior could have been a way, unconscious perhaps, to obscure the roles of the father and uncle of the alleged rape victim, Mary Ball, in leading the lynch mob.

The leaders planned to snatch the three accused Black teenagers from the Grant County jail and lynch them from trees in front of the county courthouse. Cameron recalled that the noose was removed from his neck after a sharp but sweet female voice, unlike any he had ever heard, shouted, "Take this boy back! He had nothing to do with any raping or killing!"[2]

All the trees in front of the courthouse were later cut down, locals said, to remove the lynching apparatus from view. But an iconic photo by Lawrence Beitler, a studio photographer, survived. His photo of the two hanging bodies, with a crowd of white men and women gawking and pointing at them from below, shook Abel Meeropol, a schoolteacher from New York.

Meeropol, a Jew who wrote poems and songs under the gentile-sounding name of Lewis Allan, composed "Strange Fruit." The song was published in 1937 and memorably recorded two years later by Billie Holiday (when her Columbia label refused to record the song, fearing retaliation by southern distributors, she arranged to record it with Commodore).[3]

The song's simple, stark images of lynching's brutality—Black body swinging, eyes bulging, mouth twisted, flesh burning—caused the record producer Ahmet Ertegun to call the song's cry against racism "a declaration of war . . . the beginning of the civil rights movement."[4]

Forced to take the freight elevator to stages where she performed, Holiday knew firsthand the racism she attacked in "Strange Fruit." Meeropol said, "She gave a startling, most dramatic, and effective interpretation which could jolt an audience out of its complacency anywhere. This is exactly what I wanted the song to do and why I wrote it."[5]

As we left Marion, we played Holiday's "Strange Fruit." Then we played it again. The haunting last line about the lynchings' bizarre and bitter crop evoked memories of James Cameron, the teen who was not lynched and produced a bountiful and beautiful crop.

After serving four years as an accessory to murder, he started three NAACP chapters, directed Indiana's Office of Civil Liberties, and founded America's Black Holocaust Museum in Milwaukee in 1988. The bricks-and-mortar museum closed in 2008, following Cameron's death at ninety-two. It continued online as a virtual museum, providing visitors, according to its website in 2012, "opportunities to rethink their assumptions about race and racism."

Cameron's message—"Forgive but never forget"—required seeing the lynchings for what they were, spectacle murders intended to terrorize Black people. Local whites, including Klan members, planned the lynchings in the morning "with the precision of a military coup," Cameron wrote.[6]

The victims of such spectacle murders died several times, Cameron wrote. They were severely beaten, often tortured and mutilated, then hanged or burned alive or dead. The crowd took as souvenirs body parts, hair clippings, clothing, lynch-tree bark, and pieces of the lynch rope. Finally, souvenir photos were shot of the spectators posing with their dead victims. In the ten days following the Marion lynchings, Beitler sold at a good profit fifty-cent prints of his photo of the white mob celebrating the hanging of the two beaten Black bodies.[7] Yes, forgive, but never forget.

After we left Marion, we drove across small-town Indiana and Ohio for four hours to reach Medina, Ohio, the hometown of John Anthony "Tony" Ghiglione. He was not a relative of mine, but he was a rarity in America, a Ghiglione. And he was a man Twain could have appreciated for his occupation. Travel eventually became for Twain a matter of business—stop after stop on the lecture circuit. Ghiglione trucked across America for almost four decades.

Ghiglione did not fit the trucker stereotype of country-western songs—a gear-jammin', citizens-band-chatter lover of the open road who barreled along in a chrome-plated eighteen-wheeler with mud flaps depicting a bosomy naked woman. He said he strived "to be different from what the norm is supposed to be in life."

That comment reminded me of Jack Kerouac's line about the road's being life.[8] My road trip was turning out to be a life revisited. Alyssa and Dan did not seem to mind. Alyssa, ever kind, said to me, "Dan and I often discuss how we feel like we are reliving your life with you, and that it is a privilege."

Sitting across from Tony Ghiglione, I relived my time as a senior at Haverford, a historically Quaker college in Pennsylvania. The dean, William E. Cadbury Jr., asked me what I planned to do about military service after my graduation in 1963. U.S. involvement in the Vietnam War was building. I told the dean I planned neither to enlist nor to become a draft resister. I hoped to attend Yale Law School, where Professor Fred Rodell, a Haverford alum, taught a highly regarded course on writing about the law. I wanted to put out my own newspaper or become the next Anthony Lewis, a Pulitzer Prize–winning *New York Times* columnist who was credited with creating the field of legal journalism.

I felt a twinge of guilt about following what Tony called the norm. Attending graduate or professional school was the norm for most Haverford graduates. Many could afford to attend professional or graduate school until age twenty-six, thereby avoiding the draft (my three years at Yale and my Congressional Fellowship qualified me). Tony, however, had no such option available to him and served in Vietnam.

He came from what he called a working-class family. His father, John Norbert Ghiglione, provided a role model for Tony that did not involve higher education; John graduated from the eighth grade at St. Francis School of St. Louis. Tony's sister, Kathy Hupe, said their father became a runner of bootleg booze for the mafia. He served almost four years during World War II as a medic with the U.S. Seventh Army in Normandy and other bloody battles. He won a unit citation, six bronze battle stars, and other commendations. After the war, "my old man was a baker for Tasty Bakery, a union man," Tony said. "That's probably all he wanted from life."

During the summer after Tony's graduation from St. Ann's Ritenour High School, he said, "me and the old man weren't seeing eye to eye." He told his father, "You know what, I'm outta here." Tony enlisted in the Marines. He called his 1970–71 Marine service in Vietnam "the greatest thing I experienced in my life—it made me the person I am." But he spoke modestly about his role in Vietnam. Although he took dangerous jobs as squad point man and later radioman, he said, "I was a grunt. I didn't do anything special. I was a nobody."

He remained proud, however, of military victories in Vietnam. "We beat them in every stage. But we lost the war." He attributed the defeat in part to the lack of political will of the Johnson and Nixon administrations. Upon Tony's return from Vietnam, he served temporarily as a military police officer at Camp Pendleton in California. He met Richard Nixon, who regularly visited the base in his black limo to "play golf with the generals," Tony said. Nixon gave Tony a golf ball that displayed the presidential seal and *Richard M. Nixon* in gold leaf. "I want you to have this," Nixon said. As the president drove away, Tony said, "I threw that fucking golf ball as far as I could heave it."

After his service, Tony returned to Missouri and became a trucker. He moved with his work for Yellow Roadway Corporation from Kansas City, Missouri, to Lincoln, Nebraska, and then Medina. He would drive 3.6 million miles before retiring at sixty-four in July 2014.

He spoke to us with the same pride about being a Ghiglione as about being a trucker and a Marine. He and his wife, Carolyn, had no children. "Of my family, I am the last Ghiglione," he said. "When I die the name Ghiglione from St. Louis, I believe, comes to an end." (We suspected he was incorrect.)

Tony said his parents and grandparents had lived on St. Louis's Dago Hill. Tony's grandparents and parents nonetheless discouraged him from learning Italian. "They wanted to be Americans," he said. "You have to remember, the war's only five years over with [when] I was born in 1950. The Italians were not looked upon as friendly during the war, until they got rid of Mussolini and pushed the Germans out [of Italy]."

Tony said his family had emigrated from Sicily. He recounted the time his father, a member of General George S. Patton Jr.'s Seventh Army, entered Palermo, Sicily, with other victorious Allied troops. Sicilian residents, Tony said, "recognized my father [as Sicilian]. They yelled at him, 'Heh, buddy, heh, buddy.'"

But later Tony showed me a family tree that led me to believe his family was from northern Italy or Switzerland, not Sicily. When we were in Mt. Zion, Illinois, Deacon Jim Ghiglione had told me that, because of a falling out between his grandfather and his grandfather's brother, "there's a whole Ghiglione clan in St. Louis that my family doesn't really know." Deacon Jim's Ghigliones and Tony's Ghigliones were part of the same St. Louis family.

Tony said his immigrant great-grandparents had entered the United States through Ellis Island in New York. "That's how I got my name," he insisted. "You know what Tony stands for? *To NY.*"

When Tony visited New York, locals encouraged him to change the way he pronounced his last name. "When they ask you your name and you say Ghiglione (Gill-e-yo-nee), they say, 'No, no, no, no, no, it's Gill-e-yon.'" Whatever the proper pronunciation (I was taught Gill-yo-nay), Tony remained proud of being a Ghiglione. I shared Tony's pride of family. But I hoped later in my trip with Alyssa and Dan to dig deeper, to learn more about the Ghigliones and what their experiences in the United States said about America.

Dan, Alyssa, and I drove the twenty-odd miles north from Medina toward Cleveland on Interstates 71 and 480 to spend the night at Americas [*sic*] Best Value Inn, which catered to customers who were willing to endure the worst accommodations to get the best price. A TripAdvisor reviewer rated the inn "Filthiest hotel in America" and advised, "Do not stay here!"

The depressing Americas Best Value Inn prepared us for the next day. We interviewed representatives of agencies serving the impoverished and homeless of Cleveland, a city ridiculed by critics as "the mistake by the lake," with a river so polluted that it more than once caught fire. Even Twain, who loved Cleveland and tried to become an owner of the *Cleveland Herald* in 1869, was quoted, though he never said it, as denigrating Cleveland: "America is New York, New Orleans, and San Francisco. Everywhere else is Cleveland."

We took a break from interviewing to have lunch in the city's Little Italy. The east side neighborhood had a reputation for festivities and food. The neighborhood's Columbus Day parade featured Little Miss Columbus, high school bands, and one hundred other units. Jay Westbrook, a member of the Cleveland City Council, once proposed Columbus Day be abolished in favor of Indigenous People's Day, first recognized by the Berkeley, California, City Council in 1992 to protest the conquest of North America by Europeans and to honor the contributions of Native Americans. Cleveland's Italian Americans rallied in opposition. Six hundred squeezed into the city council chambers. Westbrook withdrew his resolution.[9]

At Presti's Bakery, opened by Rose and Charles Presti Sr. in 1903, Alyssa ordered a meatball sandwich, Dan ordered a veggie stromboli and tortellini, and I a mountainous Italian sandwich, with ham, capocollo, salami, lettuce, tomato, provolone, pepper rings, pickle, and coleslaw.

We agonized about dessert. Presti's gelato case offered a wide variety of flavors on both sides of the Italian American divide, from American (peanut butter and apple pie) to Italian (spumoni and stracciatella). But the woman serving us insisted you could judge a good deli in part by its carrot cake. So Dan and Alyssa ordered carrot cake and three forks. While we devoured the cake, Alyssa asked us tough food questions. What were our favorite cuisines? Our favorite foods? Our favorite desserts?

As I rattled off tasty Ghiglione family dishes, I thought of what immigrants passed on to each succeeding generation.

My grandfather, from the first generation of Ghigliones born in the United States, spoke Italian, loved Italian opera (he collected 78-rpm Enrico Caruso phonograph records), and delighted in all of the family foods. My father spoke little Italian but kept alive my grandfather's passion for Italian opera and Ghiglione family dishes. I spoke no Italian, cooked no Italian dishes, and knew embarrassingly little about Italian opera.

Shouldn't I be doing more to foster in the next generations a love of Italian culture and heritage? Were my children just plain Americans? Should I care? After all, what's wrong with shedding insularity by assimilating and adapting to life in a pluralistic society?

Fortunately, I escaped having to address those questions. At the end of the meal, Alyssa, Dan, and I met with Michael Presti, the restaurant's thirty-nine-year-old pastry chef and a fourth-generation owner. Michael said he had a two-year-old son, Charlie. There might be a fifth generation of Presti's Bakery ownership. If my children and grandchildren became just apple-pie Americans and chose not to keep alive the Ghiglione family recipes, at least they might be able to visit Presti's to enjoy tasty Italian fare.

———

Priscilla Cooper

After Presti's, we returned to interviewing people about the intersection of race and poverty in Cleveland, a job that demanded humor as an antidote. Fact: Cleveland competed with Detroit for the title of Poorest Large City in America. Joke: Why do ducks fly over Cleveland upside down? There's nothing worth crapping on. Fact: Cleveland's culture of guns and gangs helped the city make *Forbes* magazine's list of the ten most dangerous U.S. cities. Joke: What's the only thing that grows in Cleveland? The crime rate.

We interviewed antipoverty activists in Cleveland about the region's increase in poverty. Priscilla Cooper, a former welfare recipient who started the Family Connection Center to empower Cleveland's poor, provided the most memorable interview. An African American, Cooper described the experience of Cleveland's Black women, 50 percent of whom were impoverished. The women were often forced to take low-paying housekeeping jobs. "The very poor are doing the same thing they were doing in slavery," Cooper said.

Cooper recalled her visits to poor people's homes as a truancy officer for the Cleveland school board: "They would say, 'I really would have had my daughter at school today but she doesn't have a coat.' Or, 'My son had to stay home [to watch the kids] because I'm required to go to work; if I miss a day they'll stop my checks.'"

Cooper saw poverty as more than an economic challenge. Now many people see poverty, Cooper said, "as a moral issue, something must be wrong with you—[and] you are illiterately poor. It destroys the person that is poor."

Cooper thought poverty also hurts the prosperous people who are satisfied with the economic divide that separates them from the poor and who believe the well-off are morally and intellectually—not just financially—superior to the poor. Poverty also destroys the character of the prosperous.

Cleveland's increase in poverty correlated with a decrease in population. The 2010 census put Cleveland's population at 396,815, its lowest in one hundred years. The plummeting population translated into personal tragedies—underemployed and unemployed workers and homeless people.

Walter P. Ginn, executive director of Family Promise of Greater Cleveland, said the media focused on the visible homeless, individuals on the street and under bridges. But the media missed a large category of homeless, he said. The stagnant economy had caused a drastic increase in homeless families, who stayed with relatives and friends and therefore remained invisible. Whenever one of Family Promise's apartments for homeless families became available, the agency received thirty calls within an hour.

Ginn said the average pay, increasingly for fast-food and housekeeping jobs, had gone from twelve dollars an hour three years earlier to ten dollars an hour. Karen Brauer, the Salvation Army's director of social services for Cleveland, also bemoaned the job crisis: "We've lost our industry. It's very, very scary."

Her comment reminded me of a 2008 book by Richard Longworth, *Caught in the Middle: America's Heartland in the Age of Globalism.* Longworth recalled the days a century earlier when Cleveland was 50 percent immigrant. With the shrinking industrial base, that 50 percent dropped to barely 4 percent. "We even have a hard time attracting illegal immigrants," Ronn Richard, president of the Cleveland Foundation, told Longworth.[10] (Recent reports have described Cleveland as a city on the rebound.)

Some Americans vilify immigrants and refugees as the nation's enemies, but they actually may be saviors of Rust Belt cities. After Cleveland, we drove almost two hundred miles to Buffalo, New York, which was the nation's eighth-largest city in 1900. Buffalo's population had shrunk from 580,000 in 1950 to 261,310 in 2010. It shared with Cleveland not only a contracting population but also a shriveling business district with many empty buildings.

In Buffalo, however, the presence of refugees and immigrants had created a more positive atmosphere. Refugees from Bhutan, Eritrea, Sudan, Iraq, and Somalia continued to arrive daily. Hodan Isse, a Somali who was a professor

Hodan Isse

at the University of Buffalo's School of Management, took us on a tour of the West Side Somali community.

"This area is up and coming," Isse said, "and that's because of the refugee population." She introduced us to Abdinoor Jama and Aden Aden, who fled Somalia and started a clothes-mending business in a Kenyan refugee camp. In Buffalo, they operated Jubba Food Store and Tailor at 215 Forest Avenue. Isse also introduced us to Ali Mohamed, who had opened Hatimy Market at 278 Grant Street seven years earlier. He had expanded into serving the Nepali community. A nursing student at the University of Buffalo, Mohamed hoped to continue running his market while working three twelve-hour shifts each week as a nurse. Grant Street looked poor but alive. The entrepreneurs building their businesses created a sense of hope. Newcomers to America were more than twice as likely to start businesses than were native-born citizens. Edward Roberts, founder of the MIT Entrepreneurship Center, said that to immigrate is itself an entrepreneurial act.[11]

Isse, a founder of Help Everyone Achieve Livelihood (HEAL), showed us a large building on West Ferry Street that HEAL had purchased for about $20,000. After a $240,000 renovation, it would house HEAL offices and community meeting space on the second floor. Vendors from Africa, Asia, and Latin America would sell their wares on the first floor.

In what seemed to be a most unlikely place to meet a former prime minister, we interviewed Mohamed A. Mohamed, a New York State compliance specialist for civil rights, in the two-car garage of his suburban home. Mohamed had served as Somalia's prime minister for nine months during 2010–11. In addition, he had aided in the establishment of the Buffalo Immigrants and Refugees Empowerment Coalition. The organization assisted about twenty thousand Buffalo residents from twenty countries. It started after-school programs, mobilized people to vote, and endorsed candidates.

It also helped immigrants buy houses. The rundown houses immigrants had bought five years earlier for $1,000 to $20,000 and then renovated had increased the value of substandard houses still on the market. "You won't see them at $20,000 [today]," Mohamed said. The immigrants' purchases also helped eliminate neighborhood blight and restored houses to Buffalo's tax rolls that might otherwise have faced demolition.

The vitality that Buffalo's immigrants and refugees gave the city, however, did not overcome stark realities: an urban high school graduation rate of about 50 percent, immigrants' heavy use of social services, and the existence of food deserts—neighborhoods with little nearby access to healthy fresh foods.[12] But whatever challenges the newcomers represented, the city could have had a worse problem: the immigrants and refugees could have stopped coming.

In 2017, when President Trump was portraying refugees as potentially "dangerous people" intent on bringing "death and destruction" to America, Buffalo mayor Byron W. Brown told a meeting of recent arrivals, "One of the reasons that Buffalo is growing, that Buffalo is getting stronger, that Buffalo is getting better, is because of the presence of our immigrant and our refugee community."[13]

Buffalo was a mandatory stop on a trip of Twainiacs. As a seventeen-year-old headed to New York from St. Louis, Twain stopped off in Buffalo on August 22, 1853. He returned sixteen years later as one-third owner and managing editor of the *Buffalo Express*. Twain introduced himself to readers on August 21, 1869, with a promise to stick "strictly to the truth, except when it is attended with inconvenience." He wrote lengthy front-page pieces and editorials, produced funny "People and Things" compilations, excerpted *The Innocents*

Abroad, and inaugurated a series of Saturday features. The historian Thomas J. Reigstad said the *Express* "could have been renamed the *Buffalo Morning Twainian*."[14]

Fortunately for Dan, Alyssa, and me, the current editor of Buffalo's daily newspaper welcomed us into her home. Alyssa wrote:

Awaiting us in Buffalo, after our disastrous night at Cleveland's Americas Best Value Inn, were comfortable beds; a bottle of wine; a tray of cheese, crackers, and berries; and a statue of Mark Twain on the living room mantel. We were at the home of Margaret Sullivan, an alumna of Northwestern's journalism school who was vice president and editor of the Buffalo News.

"From summer intern to editor." It had a nice ring to it. In her years at the Buffalo News, *Sullivan had achieved just that. She had been the top editor at the* News *for twelve years, and one of her goals had been to enrich her newsroom through greater staff diversity.*

The diversity—and racial sensitivity—of her staff became an issue for Sullivan in August 2010, when the News *published a front-page story about the criminal records of seven of the eight victims of a shooting at the downtown restaurant City Grill. Four people died, and four others were injured in what the* News *labeled "one of the bloodiest shooting attacks in the region in recent decades."[15]*

Sullivan wrote a column in which she acknowledged reader resentment about the story. Readers demonstrated twice at the News *building and torched copies of the newspaper. "They are especially upset at the timing of the story's publication," Sullivan wrote, "coming only one day after the last of the public funerals. And, on a deeper level they believe that this treatment is tinged with racism. All of the victims were African-American, and some of the protestors have said they believe the* News *would not have reported on white crime victims the same way."[16]*

Sullivan quoted the protest leader Darnell Jackson, whom she described as a "community activist and former gang member." Jackson reacted to the description of him and coverage of the murder victims: "What does me being convicted of a crime, or me arrested for a crime, have to do with me getting murdered?"

Sullivan also wrote, "Jackson, and others, want the paper to apologize." Instead of apologizing, Sullivan defended the paper: "The News *had a clear obligation to pursue and publish this." She insisted white victims were not treated differently in the paper. She did agree that the story was displayed too prominently on page 1 and that the timing was unfortunate. The* News "could have waited a day or two," she wrote, but "to hold back the news is to distort the news."

Sullivan concluded by saying she was "truly sorry for offending people." She called on the community to address underlying problems—poverty, gang violence, public school failures, racism, and the drug and gun culture. "Sometimes the truth hurts," Sullivan wrote. "And only the truth can get us, as a society, where we need to go."[17]

At a community meeting attended by seven hundred people, Sullivan heard from readers still disappointed by the paper's coverage of the shooting victims. "I feel that we were victimized twice," said Cheryl Stevens, mother-in-law of Danyelle Mackin, one of the four killed in the shooting.[18] Sullivan wrote another column in which she said she left the meeting "both shaken and changed." She described several steps she intended to take, from the creation of a community diversity advisory council to a public opinion poll to gauge perceptions of the News among African Americans to diversity training in the newsroom.[19]

Newsroom diversity had been a goal of Sullivan's for years before the shooting. But the News, like most newspapers, had been hit by a decline in revenue from advertising and subscriptions that made hiring almost impossible. During our visit to the News, members of the Buffalo Newspaper Guild displayed desk cards that said, "The News has lost nearly 100 full-time Guild employees in the past two years through layoffs and buyouts." The News's management insisted it needed to cut an additional $1.8 million from the paper's annual budget.

Sullivan, the first female editor in the paper's 138-year history, estimated that diversity in the newsroom had increased from 3 percent to 12 percent, which reflected the racial makeup of western New York. Recently, she had observed just as many women as men and several people of color at the paper's news conference table, she said.

Lisa Wilson, forty-one, was a prominent example. In April 2011, Wilson became the only Black female sports editor in the country at a metropolitan daily newspaper, "which is just shocking to me," Wilson said. "I can't be the only one qualified."

Sullivan was frequently still the only woman in the room at news meetings. "You can feel alone," she said. "It's not an entirely pleasant feeling."

Sullivan preferred to speak as an individual, not for womankind, she said. She had laughed when an opinion editor asked her for the women's point of *view for an article. "I thought that was hilarious because I could never try to represent 51 percent of the population," she said.*

In fact, Sullivan represented a tiny percentage of the population. She was one of only about thirty executive editors in Buffalo's history. "One of them was Mark Twain, and one of them was me!" she said. "It's a great legacy."

On our way out of Buffalo, Dan, Alyssa, and I stopped at Niagara Falls, only twenty miles to the northwest. The presence at the falls of American Indians selling handicrafts reminded us of how eighteenth- and nineteenth-century white Americans—including Mark Twain—had demeaned Native Americans.

"A Day at Niagara" (1871), the first sketch in the *Buffalo Express* under Twain's byline, claims the Indian vendors, members of the local Tuscarora tribe, are actually Irish immigrants. The joke reflects, the historian Kerry Driscoll writes, "the widespread anti-Irish sentiment arising from the action of a radical nationalist organization called the Fenian Brotherhood" that hoped to force Britain to relinquish control of Ireland.[20] Twain's joke also erased the Indians.

Driscoll, who spent ten years working on a book about Mark Twain's relationship with Native Americans, told us Twain had grown up with African Americans. "Twain never had a corresponding experience with Indians," Driscoll said. "They're kind of an empty space into which imaginary things can seep." Twain had conflicted attitudes about Native Americans. They were the "hunted and harried" victims of the European settlers of the New World and of the U.S. government. They were also savages to be loathed. He mocked their appearance and squalid living conditions in the West, Driscoll writes, "as proof of intrinsic inferiority rather than a dire economic consequence of settler colonialism."[21]

From Niagara Falls, Dan, Alyssa, and I headed 163 miles southeast to Elmira, a railroad and manufacturing town of twenty-nine thousand that had lost 40 percent of its population since 1950. It promoted itself as Mark Twain Country—home to the gravesite of Twain and of the people he loved most, his wife, son, and three daughters. The octagonal, carved-wood gazebo, where he wrote *Huck Finn*, *Tom Sawyer*, and other important works during twenty summers, had been moved from its mountain perch to a place of honor at the center of the Elmira College campus.

What perhaps best honored Twain was not the gravesite or gazebo but the view from the front porch of Quarry Farm, Twain's summer residence. Alyssa wrote about its panoramic hilltop view of the Chemung River valley: "People have preserved everything Mark Twain might have ever touched—plates, sticks, paper—the most ridiculous trifles. But I certainly felt closest to him when there was nary an object he came into direct contact with. Just an open space. Some trees."

———

Twain was not the only nineteenth-century resident Elmira chose to honor. The hardworking, blue-collar town also memorialized a grave digger, John W. Jones.

Jones was a runaway slave who had escaped from Virginia to Elmira by Underground Railroad. He arrived in Elmira, after a three-hundred-mile trek, as a virtually penniless twenty-seven-year-old illiterate.[22] Jones became an Underground Railroad agent in 1851. He arranged for Northern Central Railway workers to hide slaves in baggage cars that eventually took them across the Canadian border to St. Catherine, Ontario. None of the eight hundred slaves he helped was captured for return to the South.[23]

As First Baptist's sexton, Jones also took charge of all city burials. He felt responsible for the 12,123 Confederate soldiers locked behind the twelve-foot stockade fence of Elmira Prison toward the end of the Civil War. In 1864–65, about a quarter of the prison's inmates died. Poor health, a severe winter, overcrowding, scurvy, and unsanitary conditions, including contaminated drinking water, caused the death of 2,963 inmates. Jones buried every one and kept careful records. Only seven were listed as unknown.[24]

In 1998, Jones's farmhouse at 1259 College Avenue was threatened with demolition. A local group decided to restore the house as the John W. Jones Museum. Carole Knowlton, sixty-nine, a member of the museum's board of trustees, recalled that when a mail carrier knocked on the front door of Jones's abandoned house, it fell open to reveal homeless people living there. "Even though Jones was no longer alive," Knowlton said, "he was still helping people."

The house's restoration stretched into a second decade. Lucy Brown, eighty-six, president of the museum board and a descendant of a former slave who married Mark Twain's cook, hoped the museum would open by 2014, the 150th anniversary of the founding of Elmira Prison. But when that did not happen, she remained upbeat: "I'm still hanging in there until we open."

A difference of opinion had split the museum's board of trustees. Knowlton said Black members of the board wanted to honor Jones's role with the Underground Railroad but not his role in burying the remains of imprisoned Confederate soldiers. Sheri Jackson, northeast coordinator for the National Park Service's National Underground Railroad Network to Freedom project, suggested to Knowlton that the Jones Museum seek funding from the United Daughters of the Confederacy, an organization of female descendants of Confederate soldiers. "I took the suggestion to our board meeting, and I was ripped apart," Knowlton said. "That is why I resigned [from the board in 2010], because I do not tolerate prejudice."

Board president Brown said, "I don't mind Confederates coming there [to the museum]." She sounded unhappy, however, about the Jones Museum's solicitation of an organization with a Confederate connection. To Brown, anything Confederate represented slavery. "Just don't come with that Confederate flag," she said. "Don't come with that flag."

But museum board members, past and present, white and Black, agreed that Jones deserved a museum. The board member Irene Langdon, who was ninety-one and whose family had helped hide Jones when he arrived in Elmira as a fugitive slave, said, "How he buried the Confederate soldiers with such dignity, he was a wonderful saint, a first-class gentleman." The John W. Jones Museum finally opened in June 2017.

Before embarking on our 230-mile drive to New York City, Alyssa, Dan, and I watched *7th Street*, a documentary by Josh Pais about changes over ten years in the Lower East Side, a neighborhood we planned to visit.[25] We discussed one line in the film: "There are two ways to learn about the world. One way is to travel all over the planet and see all the different lands. And the other way is to stay in one place." We were certain our time in New York, where people from all over the planet live, would confirm our commitment to travel.

CHAPTER 5

New York City

The Wondrous Capital of the World

My return to New York with Alyssa and Dan represented an opportunity to reconnect with the city in all its diversity and dazzle. I had grown up a bicoastal boy, born in New York in 1941 but raised in California from the age of one and a half. My parents divorced when I was five. My father moved back to New York and remarried. Except for a few weeks each summer with my father and stepmother, I lived with my mother. The two of us bounced around Southern California for a while—I attended four schools in five years—until we settled in Claremont, population nine thousand, where my mother had attended college. We lived (with a cat and eight kittens) in a small stucco house, two bedrooms and one bathroom, two blocks from the Memorial Park ball field and three blocks from Sycamore Elementary School. Soon I was comfortably at home in the neighborhood.

But my mother died when I was twelve, forcing me to move across the country to New York, population eight million, to live with my father and stepmother, William and Rae Ghiglione. I felt a bit like George Willard, the dream-filled young man in Sherwood Anderson's *Winesburg, Ohio*, a favorite boyhood book of mine. In Winesburg, Willard boards a train bound for the big city. I left Claremont the way Willard left Winesburg: "His life there had become but a background on which to paint the dreams of his manhood."[1]

New York, host to people from everywhere, encouraged cosmopolitan dreams. On the bicycle that I had brought from Claremont, I explored on light-traffic Sundays at least a dozen museums, the main New York City Public Library, the Strand Book Store ("18 Miles of Books"), Washington Square art shows, and Central Park, with its zoo and bicycle paths. Dad took me to Ebbets Field in Brooklyn for a Brooklyn Dodgers game. After Claremont, which had virtually no African American residents, I experienced the heroics of Jackie Robinson and other Black Dodgers. About that time, with the wisdom of a thirteen-year-old, I decided I would become a professional athlete.

Dad and Rae enrolled me in McBurney, a small, nonprofit, nonsectarian YMCA boys school that took advantage of the swimming pools and basketball courts next door at the West Sixty-Third Street Y and the playing fields of nearby Central Park. Whether I was trying to bury my grief at my mother's death or become the person I wanted to become (or thought my parents wanted me to become), I immediately began overdosing on McBurney activities. I started a four-page mimeographed newsletter grandly titled *Science Reporter* and competed at everything. It seemed important to win, whether it was my class section's presidency, the *Times*'s current events contest, the lower school's outstanding athlete award, or its leadership cup. Looking back, I wonder whether all the activities and the approval they generated were my way of responding to my mother's death. To lose a parent in the 1950s brought no grief support, an expert noted, just "stoicism, silence and suppression."[2]

I had been plopped down in the middle of my parents' great love affair and busy lives. My father commuted to his New Jersey wine-bottling company each morning and worked long hours. Rae, a TV backup singer, taught me what it meant to be a working mom. Barbara Mach, also a singer and Rae's close friend, described their demanding work schedule: rehearsals Monday, Tuesday, and Wednesday for the *Arthur Godfrey and Friends* variety show, which aired on Wednesday night. Then rehearsals Thursday, Friday, and Saturday for *Your Hit Parade*, which presented on Saturday evening the week's seven top-rated Tin Pan Alley songs. After rehearsing all day Saturday, the Hit Paraders completed a dress rehearsal, took a dinner break, and then performed live from 10:30 to 11:00 p.m. On Sundays and free nights "we did all kinds of things," Mach said, from recording with Frank Sinatra and other crooners to producing singing commercials to appearing on the *Ed Sullivan Show*.

Understandably perhaps, my parents did not offer the attention or affection that my birth mother, a sickly, stay-at-home parent, had provided. I had felt like the man in my mother's home (a study of the impact of the early death of a parent labels that prematurely adult child a "pseudoadult personality").[3] Though I worked adult jobs at my father's company during high school summers, unloading freight cars and inserting fifty-seven wine-filled bottles a minute into cardboard boxes, my father informed me that children were not really adults until the age of thirty. With a smile, he regularly called me a meathead or pinhead. I don't remember him praising me or telling me he loved me. Yet when he died, Rabbi Julius G. Neumann, who supervised the bottling of kosher wine at the company, wrote to me about my father, "He had great love for you and could speak of you for hours with a glow in his eye."

I admired my father. He was his own boss. He cooked with the skill of a professional chef. He could identify the violinist Jascha Heifetz and other classical musicians by name just from listening to recordings. He relished words. He sat on the toilet each Sunday morning until he completed that day's *New York Times* crossword puzzle. And, while he did not participate often in my school activities, he came through in a pinch. He and other fathers packed the swimming team into their cars to return to New York in a snowstorm after we won the Colgate University Prep School Swimming Tournament. Only Dad's car made it home that night; the other fathers and their charges were forced to stop overnight before completing the two-hundred-mile trek.

I also admired how he dealt with death. I don't know when, after decades of smoking four packs a day, he first learned he had terminal cancer. But during the last two years of his life, he got out of bottling wine and used his thirty-four-foot sportfishing boat, *Allegro II*, to follow a dream. He had taught Power Squadron courses on celestial navigation and sportfishing (a posthumous award read: "He found and spread happiness through teaching"). At the end, he started a sportfishing business that never made a cent. He fished out of Montauk, New York, customers or not (when Alyssa, Dan, and I discussed what we should name our trip's van, they kindly accepted my suggestion of *Allegro III*, in tribute to my father's end-of-life odyssey).

I was alone and lonely as a boy in New York (Twain described the city as "a domed and steepled solitude, where the stranger is lonely in the midst of a million of his race"). I lived far from most of my classmates, in an apartment on East Twenty-Eighth Street. I knew no girls in the neighborhood. Occasionally, I would insert ten dollars in quarters in the pay phone of a neighborhood Rexall Pharmacy to talk with Beth Booth, my sixth-grade girlfriend in Claremont. My senior-year yearbook listed me as a member of the "girl-out-of-town club" and used "But Beth . . ." as the caption for a photo of me talking on a pay phone. I was determined, however, to attend McBurney's senior prom. I took ballroom dancing lessons. Rae arranged for Gisele MacKenzie, a featured *Hit Parade* singer, to perform at the prom. But I failed to get a date and, embarrassed, stayed home.

I liked my East Twenty-Eighth Street neighborhood, which felt like a birth-to-death community: Bellevue Hospital to the east; Gannon Funeral Home across the street; Church of St. Stephen and its school next door; at the end of the block the Third Avenue El station to uptown jobs. The neighborhood tasted of Italy: Marchi's Restaurant ("No sign outside and no menu inside!") offered a northern Italian prix fixe five-course feast; Trinacria's Italian food store sold fragrant imported cheeses; Frank Spadola, an Italian immigrant, played opera (loudly) on his barber shop radio and handed out free copies of his book of love poems dedicated to God, America, and Italy.[4]

As much as I liked the neighborhood, New York had its unfriendly side. My bike and my father's Oldsmobile 88 were stolen off the street. A gang of schoolage boys mugged me on the Forty-Second Street crosstown subway but threw my book bag back at me once I cried. During a class trip to a movie, a teacher inappropriately touched me and a classmate who was sitting on the teacher's other side (when the classmate and I reported the teacher to the headmaster, the teacher was immediately fired).

After graduating from McBurney, I spent little time in New York. For the summer after my first year of college, I returned to Claremont to take a college philosophy course, deliver by truck for a local furniture store, and reconnect with my past. During my second college summer, I reported for the *Claremont Courier*. Seeing journalism as my calling, I took the Radcliffe Publishing Procedures Course, read unsolicited manuscripts for the *Atlantic* magazine, and freelanced for the *Boston Globe* during the summer following my junior year. After editing the Haverford College student weekly, I interned at the *Washington Post* following my senior year.

Returning to New York with Alyssa and Dan did not feel like returning home. "After wrestling with financial problems and declining enrollments," McBurney School had died in 1988.[5] All the relatives I associated with New York had either left the city or died. The El, Trinacria's, and Spadola's barber shop had disappeared. The apartments on East Twenty-Eighth Street and, later, West 100th Street, where I once lived, were now occupied by people I did not know.

But New York remained for me a dazzling, diverse city of dreams. I wanted to introduce Alyssa and Dan to that city.

———

I felt our first stop in New York, in my seventieth year, should provide a meal as memorable as the 1905 feast at Delmonico's for Mark Twain's seventieth birthday. Delmonico's nine-course, oysters-and-champagne extravaganza featured green turtle, timbales Perigourdine (not even Google can tell us what this was), filets of kingfish meunière, saddle of lamb Colbert, Baltimore terrapin, quail, and redhead duck.

I also wanted our meal to reflect New York's diversity, defined more broadly, I hoped, than the way the *New York Times* defined diversity in 1905. The *Times* reported on the 170 guests at Twain's dinner: "As many women there as men." The writers Willa Cather and Dorothy Canfield, and the other talented "young and pretty" women, were not "mere appendages of their husbands."

We were unable to reproduce that nine-course meal (the green turtle is on the endangered species list) or visit Delmonico's at 2 South Williams Street, which the immigrant Delmonicos from Switzerland had opened in 1827 (the current Delmonico's has no connection to the original). But Red Rooster Harlem, 310 Malcolm X Boulevard, opened by an Ethiopian Swede in 2010, provided an ambitious menu and a message about New York that went far beyond gender diversity.

Red Rooster reflects the vision of the owner and celebrity chef Marcus Samuelsson. He was born in an Ethiopian village without roads, running water, gas, or electricity. Orphaned at three, he was raised by an adoptive Swedish couple and trained as a chef in Sweden, Switzerland, Austria, France, and the United States. When he was twenty-four, a *New York Times* review ballyhooed him as a three-star chef. The White House chose him to prepare President Obama's first state dinner.

Along the way, Samuelsson kept a food journal to "play with the what-ifs of dishes that were taking shape" in his mind. He thought about cooking, he writes, in the same way an innovative jazz musician thinks about creating "a new kind of perfect."[6]

Our Red Rooster Gospel Sunday Brunch merged the flavors of southern comfort food with international flavors. The signature cornbread was served in inch-thick slices accompanied by homemade honey butter and a tomato jam spiced with curry leaves from South Asia. The cornbread also contained aleppo, a delayed-kick pepper from Syria. Greens, another soul food staple, were mixed with not only cheddar cheese but also rich Gouda and Comté cheeses from Europe.

Samuelsson sought to showcase all of Harlem. He celebrated Harlem as the old capital of Black America and as the old and new home of a multicultural mix of people who identify as American southerners, Latinx, Caribbean, Jewish, or Italian. My scrambled eggs with fresh tomatoes and mozzarella stirred pleasant memories of both my three years in Atlanta and visits to my great-grandparents' villages in northern Italy.

Next to the bar, a tall bookshelf displayed items that told the story of Samuelsson and Harlem: *Amharic for Beginners*, jars of lentils and pickled turnips, *African American Heritage Hymnal*, books of photos by Gordon Parks and poems by Maya Angelou, a Miles Davis *Bitches Brew* record album, and a special-issue Captain Marvel comic book that featured on its cover a Black masked figure flying above the city—*The Supersonic Sensation Reborn!*

Peter Crippen, Red Rooster's service manager, described the restaurant's clientele and staff as "a cross section of everything." Red Rooster welcomed straight and gay, Asian and Latinx, hometown and international, young and old, white and Black. The staff's diversity responded to a concern of Samuelsson's: "Blacks, and especially American blacks, are still shamefully underrepresented at the high end of the business."[7] I counted six chefs in the kitchen—five were African American—under the direction of Executive Chef Michael Garrett.

Garrett, a bearded thirty-eight-year-old African American with dreadlocks encased in a Rastafarian-style, black-and-white knit tam, had only line chef experience at Houlihan's and Olive Garden on his résumé when Samuelsson met him in 2000. Samuelsson said Garrett "had fried chicken in his bones" but needed more experience as a chef to learn how food from around the world should taste.[8] Red Rooster Harlem was giving Garrett that opportunity.

Wall hangings carried out what Samuelsson saw as his purpose as a Black chef: "To document, to preserve, to present, to capture, to inspire and to aspire."[9] He documented Harlem's history with the supper menu of Royal Roost, a jazz club from the late 1940s: southern fried chicken, $1.25; shrimp cocktail, 85 cents; coffee, 25 cents. A nineteenth-century poster from London advertised "the favorite Negro melody, 'Lucy Neal,' sung with rapturous applause at the St. James's Theatre by the Ethiopian Serenaders."

The songstress Roz Beauty glided around the bar and dining room singing "Soon and Very Soon" and other gospel songs. She talked modestly about the music, just piano and voice, but said that for diners "it's enough to feed their souls as they're feeding their bodies." The eyes of a transfixed child, seated with his Black mother and white father, followed Beauty's movement.

Red Rooster was succeeding at feeding the body too. Hung on a bathroom wall, a framed letter from "your friend" Ataliyah, a spelling-challenged Harlem third-grader, thanked Samuelsson: "I really injoyed the potatos and carrots. They were the best thing I ever had in my life."

A mile south of Red Rooster Harlem, in a block-long, high-rent, high-rise apartment building on Central Park West and 97th Street, we interviewed Ellis Cose. He had been addressing race and other identity issues throughout his career—as a weekly columnist for the *Chicago Sun-Times* at age nineteen, chair of the *New York Daily News*'s editorial board, and author of ten books.

The building's doorman waved us in without calling up to Cose to make sure we were expected. Cose greeted us at his apartment door with a broad smile. He said the doorman was much more likely to challenge his Latinx and African American friends. Cose did not blame the doorman. Stereotypes persist, Cose said. A cab driver worried about being robbed might ignore a casually dressed Black man trying to flag a taxi late at night. A postracial society does not exist, Cose said, except as an aspiration.

I thought of the 1989 rape and beating of a white female jogger in Central Park only six blocks from Cose's building. The attack "revived fears of black men preying on white women and engaging in random acts of violence," said Natalie Byfield, who wrote a book about the attack after reporting on it for the *New York Daily News*.[10]

Intent on instant justice, the police coerced five African American and Latinx boys aged fourteen to sixteen to plead guilty. They were sentenced to long prison terms in 1990. In 2002, a serial rapist and murderer serving a life sentence confessed to acting alone in the rape and beating. DNA evidence confirmed his role. The convictions of the five innocent men were vacated, and a New York City settlement paid them a total of $41 million.[11]

At the time of the attack, Donald Trump spent $85,000 for full-page ads in four major New York newspapers to argue for the death penalty's return. The five "crazed misfits," Trump said, "should be forced to suffer." As a presidential candidate in 2016, Trump refused to apologize, insisted the five were guilty, and called the $41 million settlement outrageous.[12]

Despite such cases, Cose saw progress before Trump was elected president—America had become postracist, if not postracial, unwilling for the most part to accept 1950s-style racism, racial epithets, and blatant discrimination. "I think we're getting there," he said during Obama's second term, pointing to less stereotyping, fewer glass ceilings, and more openness to interracial relationships.

Cose, who has written about race globally in such books as *Color-Blind: Seeing Beyond Race in a Race-Obsessed World*, noted the unusual way the United States categorized people racially. America's so-called one-drop rule meant that the offspring of Black and white parents were labeled—and labeled themselves—Black, which risked reinforcing racial hierarchies.

He recalled having dinner in Chicago with two light-skinned African American women who insisted they were Black. He bet them that two Portuguese-speaking women sitting at the next table, perhaps from Brazil, would not identify them as Black. One identified both American women as white, the other identified them as white and mulatto. "In neither case did they think the person was black," Cose said.

Twain told an equally thought-provoking story about skin color in a July 1865 issue of the Virginia City *Territorial Enterprise*. Whites were followed in a local parade by African Americans in order of Blackness, light to dark. "It was a fine stroke of strategy," Twain wrote. The day was dusty, and onlookers could not tell where the white marchers left off and the Black ones began. Mocking whites' belief in their racial superiority, Twain questioned the wisdom of whites' being on bad terms with Blacks "in the face of the fact that they have got to sing with them in heaven or scorch with them in hell some day in the most familiar and sociable ways, and on a footing of most perfect equality."

Cose believed the Black-white divide would eventually cease to be a crucial fault line in the United States: "The dividing line, I suspect, is going to be increasingly less about race and more about income, economic status, education, and things like that. The real battle of the future is getting us to be a society where there is a workable kind of equality. Where people, wherever they start out in life, can end up someplace decent. Where people, just because they come from certain neighborhoods, don't have to expect that their lives will be lives of poverty and, perhaps, prison."

Americans, whatever their race or ethnicity, have linked fates, Cose said. "How are we going to be an American family?" he asked. "What does it mean to be this America that is evolving?" In *The End of Anger: A New Generation's Take on Race and Rage* (2011), he describes the change in attitudes and opportunities across four generations: Americans born before 1945, those born between 1945 and 1969, those born between 1970 and 1995, and, as he told us in conversation, "the young kids who are coming up now."

The most striking contrast was between the first and fourth generations. The first generation, the civil rights generation born before 1945, Cose said, consisted of African Americans who demanded equality ("the fighters") and whites who, though their views may have changed over time, initially believed Black people were lesser beings and therefore resisted African Americans' push for equal citizenship.

Cose, sixty, said the fourth generation, that of his nine-year-old daughter, Elisa, was one of almost limitless possibilities. His daughter grew up with a woman as secretary of state and a Black president. "She assumes," Cose said, "with all the confidence of the very young, that she can be whatever it pops into her mind to be."

Still, Elisa had questions about skin color. As a preschooler, she asked her father why some nannies called one of her friends *fea*—or ugly—because she was dark skinned. When she was about four years old, Elisa asked her father to explain race to her. Cose, an African American, is married to Lillian "Lee" Llambelis. He described his wife as the color of wheat and said her "Puerto Rican features show conspicuous evidence of her African and Taíno ancestors." Elisa asked her father, "Okay, Daddy, I'm brown like you, and Mommy—is she white?" Cose laughed at his attempt to answer her: "Well, not quite."

Cose was clear, however, on how Elisa, at age nine, viewed race. She identified herself as African American and Puerto Rican, but "in terms of the way she sees people, and the way she includes people and does not include people, race really doesn't enter into the equation with her."

He recalled a conversation with Elisa when she was extremely young. She was painting people with purple faces. "I said to her, 'Why are you drawing people with purple faces?' She said, 'Oh, Daddy, don't you know people come in all colors?'" Cose laughed, recalling his response: "Oh, okay, sure, why not."

At the end of 2017, after almost a year of the Trump presidency, I called Cose to learn his reaction and the reaction of Elisa, who was then fifteen, to

Trump's reign. Cose had made his reaction to Trump clear immediately after his election, calling Trump a man "who comfortably trafficked in racism, xenophobia and misogyny; who appears to have contempt for non-white immigrants and disdain for an entire religion."[13]

Cose described Elisa's "intense dislike of President Trump, which is not surprising," and her "growing discomfort with the idea of spending all her life in the United States." When Elisa thinks of the almost 63 million Americans who voted for Trump in 2016, Cose said, "she thinks Americans are a little bit crazy." And racist too. "It's never been a secret that many Americans are racist," Elisa told her father. Whites don't want to be called racist, she added, but most "don't really try to fix anything" about their racism.

Ellis Cose suggested putting in perspective the period in which America's president pushed a racist agenda. Cose recalled generation after generation of U.S. laws, such as the Chinese Exclusion Act of 1882, and lynchings and imprisonings and other actions that targeted those deemed alien—whether they were Native Americans, Asians, Jews, Irish, Italians, Slavs, Greeks, or African Americans.

Even Trump's politics of fear, Cose said, had a precedent. Senator Joe McCarthy, the Wisconsin Republican, was a lying, bullying, media-manipulating demagogue who charged in 1950 that the State Department was loaded with hundreds of "card-carrying Communists." McCarthy accused President Harry Truman of refusing to purge "the enemy within." A Senate report eventually denounced McCarthy and his smears of patriotic U.S. citizens as a "fraud and a hoax on the American people." In 1954, the Senate censured McCarthy, 67–22. President Dwight Eisenhower quipped that McCarthyism was now McCarthywasm.

Cose ended our telephone call on an optimistic note. At a time when Black Lives Matter, #MeToo, and #OscarsSoWhite had gained traction, he said, "a growing array of Americans, particularly younger people," were finding racism, misogyny, homophobia, and other forms of discrimination intolerable.

———

We took a subway train south and stopped at what had become a tourist attraction, the Occupy Wall Street protest site. Alyssa ruminated on the experience:

One thing about the Occupy Wall Street protest in Lower Manhattan's Zuccotti Park: You couldn't visit too early. Like, before 2:00 p.m.

We made that mistake and arrived around 11:00 a.m. Many protesters seemed to be snoozing, curled up in their sleeping bags and, in one case, beneath a tarp.

Occupy Wall Street began when protesters descended on Zuccotti Park on September 17, 2011. Fueled by the rallying cry of "We are the 99 percent," the movement spread. People participated in hundreds of cities around the country and even the world.[14] We saw occupations from Boston to Boise. Zuccotti Park was the epicenter, and protesters claimed the entire park, which was privately owned but open to the public twenty-four hours a day. The encampment in New York lasted nearly two months, until police evicted the occupiers on November 15, 2011, a little more than a month after our visit.

The logistics of the protest were well organized. The manifesto of the movement was not. "The biggest challenge is figuring out whether we want student loan forgiveness or revolution," one occupier told us.

Cecily McMillan, who became involved with Occupy Wall Street before the Zuccotti Park occupation began, experienced the same frustration. McMillan, then twenty-three, had recently moved to New York to begin her graduate studies at the New School and served as the northeast regional organizer of the Young Democratic Socialists. She attended a weekly gathering, which eventually called itself the New York General Assembly, to establish the Occupy Wall Street movement's direction. She said she lobbied to pass a statement of nonviolence and a statement of purpose, but both were voted down.

"This thing that we had somehow miraculously managed to get off the ground was in a constant state of danger and crumble with our infighting about . . . demands, not demands, about violence, about nonviolence, about gluten-free alternatives in the kitchen," she said.

Many activists who joined the movement in its infancy were young, white, and held a bachelor's degree or higher. They railed against the same things I railed against: aging parents forced to get by without pensions, and friends who couldn't afford health insurance. My peers and I had followed what we thought was the right script—go to college, study hard, get involved—assuming that we would be rewarded.

Instead, I watched as some of my most talented college classmates accepted unpaid internships after graduation or settled for jobs in retail. I was fortunate to have received a Northwestern education. But at my exit interview, required of anyone with an outstanding student loan, I received the bill for my education, added neatly into one sum: $43,500.00.

The panic was immediate. I ended up on a bench in a manicured campus garden, called my mom, and cried. How was I going to pay for this? I wondered.

We hope that higher education will be the great equalizer. But throughout my four years on campus, I couldn't shake the feeling that I had been mistakenly dropped into a rich kids' playground. My friends at state schools threw on sweatpants to go to class; at Northwestern women wore Chanel ballet flats. Instead of cheap beer at parties, students drank Grey Goose. Friends had luxury apartments with rooftop pools, and they scarfed expensive sushi dinners with the same voracity as they ate late-night pizza. Sometimes I felt rejected by the same place that had sent me an acceptance letter.

After spending a morning with the protesters in Zuccotti Park, I didn't see how they were going to eliminate the wealth gap in our country. Dan and I observed the organization's General Assembly meetings and a small group addressing the press, but we also encountered plenty of people who appeared to be stoned.

Finding the perfect solution to the country's woes, however, wasn't exactly the point, said Todd Gitlin, who had been a founder and president of Students for a Democratic Society in the 1960s and now is a professor of journalism and sociology at Columbia University and the author of Occupy Nation: The Roots, the Spirit, and the Promise of Occupy Wall Street *(2012).*

"You can't look at them as if they're a failure at something, as if they're failed [political] parties or failed organizations," he told us. "They're not [political] parties, and they don't aspire to be parties. They aspire to be what they are, which is a form of encounter."

When we visited, colorful clothing, flamboyant signs, the sounds of drums and music, and the people's microphone filled the park. An older protester carried a sign with a Mark Twain quote, which he repeated to us: "Virtue has never been as respectable in society as money."

"Virtue has been replaced by money and greed," the protester added. Grayhaired women carried signs that said, "Wall Street stole our retirement."

The activists wanted what many underrepresented Americans wanted: to be recognized for who they are and what they stand for. "They were into an identity," Gitlin said during our interview. "And it was their own. They were the occupation. So their demand was not really a demand. They were right in a way to abstain [from making demands] because what they wanted to be was what they were doing. They wanted to be the encampment of Wall Street. So in that sense they succeeded. I think they helped make it legitimate

Dan Tham interviews an Occupy Wall Street protester carrying
a sign with a Mark Twain quote in Zuccotti Park, New York.

in conventional politics to talk about inequality. So the phrase people use for this is changing the conversation. And that was effective."

McMillan, an early organizer, changed her view of Occupy Wall Street as a result of what happened to her on the six-month anniversary of the protest. She was arrested and later convicted of assaulting a police officer—ironic, given her insistence on nonviolence. While she was being escorted out of Zuccotti Park, she said her breast was grabbed from behind. She instinctively struck out, not knowing a police officer was behind her, she said, and shortly after she suffered a seizure. But McMillan was found guilty of intentionally elbowing the officer in the eye. She served fifty-eight days of a three-month sentence at Rikers Island.

While she was in jail, McMillan learned the protests didn't reach every-one, especially those who might have needed its message the most. "It made me realize how limited [it was] in its scope of reaching everyday people of the 99 percent," she said. "Sure, in intellectual circles and powerful circles and the privileged circles, like, yes, we can say, 'It changed the dialogue.' [But not for] those people who don't watch CNN professionally or discuss the New Yorker over brunch or read the New York Times, which is most of the 99 percent."

During the protest, many Occupiers assumed McMillan came from wealth because of her penchant for secondhand designer clothes, she said, which earned her the nickname "Paris Hilton of Occupy." But in fact, she experi-enced periods of poverty and homelessness as a child growing up in Texas, calling it a "very volatile class position." After her parents divorced, she stayed with her mother, an immigrant from Mexico. McMillan, who identifies as white and Latina, said she feels "culturally Mexican, also very culturally working-class Irish."

"When I was in [Rikers], it was really difficult to explain what Occupy Wall Street was to people who had never heard of it. They're like, 'So this sounds like a party in a park.' And I'm like, 'Well, yes. Sort of.' And so then you try to do things like reference, to Black folks, the civil rights movement. And they're like, 'So you're like Martin Luther King,' and I was like, 'No! No, definitely not.' But then you try to explain things like Malcolm X, like the [Black] Panthers and how they were actually trying to effect [a] parallel soci-ety. And so they're like, 'So you ran around with guns?' And I'm like, 'Nope, nope. Did not do that.'"

One study of the movement suggested the participants were 63.5 percent white, 10.1 percent Hispanic/Latinx, 9.6 percent African American, and 5.4 percent Asian. A significant number held college or graduate degrees.[15]

McMillan said she'd realized what kind of privilege being an activist holds, and how important it is to put down the books and get out there. And if you want to get arrested, fine, but realize that even choosing to get arrested is a privilege. She added: "Like, nobody would ever, who I met in Rikers, go out and intentionally get arrested for anything. That's crazy!" Most people, she said, don't have access to lawyers who will be passionate about what you stand for.

"The thing is, at the end of the day, we may have not really have had a sense of exactly what we were doing or where we were going, we may not always have gotten along—that's an understatement—but we really respected one another. And that we all set out to say definitively and clearly for the whole world to hear, 'We dissent.'"

A fifteen-minute subway ride north from Zuccotti Park took us to the West 17th Street apartment of Dr. Lawrence "Larry" D. Mass. In 1981, before coverage by the mainstream media, Mass reported on what later became known as the AIDS epidemic.[16]

David Alexander's large painting of Mass and Arnold "Arnie" Kantrowitz, Mass's life partner since 1982, dominated their crowded living room. The painting captured telling shards of their lives: cats, fish, orchids, a small Buddha, videotapes, pieces of coral, opera recordings, monkeys, skulls, shells, and wall-to-wall books.[17]

In the background of the portrait, a book titled *Richard Wagner* arises from the head of a ceramic cat (in 1994 Mass published a memoir titled *Confessions of a Jewish Wagnerite: Being Gay and Jewish in America*). A yellow Star of David, an Alcoholics Anonymous triangle, a GMHC (Gay Men's Health Crisis) logo, the ACT UP slogan Silence = Death, and other symbols important to Mass appear in the painting.

Mass, a founder of GMHC, the world's first and largest AIDS service organization, had not been silent about death from AIDS in the gay community. He wrote a pioneering 1981 article about AIDS—"Cancer in the Gay Community." The article had appeared on the front page of, ironically, the biweekly gay newspaper *New York Native*, which, a historian of AIDS coverage wrote, "glorified the sexually promiscuous life-style and the most dangerous forms of risky sex."[18]

Mass grew up gay and Jewish in Macon, Georgia. He joked about being "twice blessed," but the experience deeply affected him. "There was social and historic anti-Semitism and a lot of internalized anti-Semitism among Jews," he said. "I didn't want to be Jewish." Secretly, he celebrated Christmas.

Growing up gay was even scarier for him, although he did not realize it then. "Being gay wasn't even thinkable," he told us. "If it was there, in me or others, it was inchoate and invisible. If you're Jewish, you know you're Jewish, even if you don't want to be. But there was no public acknowledgment of homosexuality or gayness, no context for understanding and accepting it. Nobody talked about it, except in derogatory terms like 'sissy,' 'queer,' 'pervert,' 'psychopath,' and 'homo,' and even those terms were rarely heard because what they were describing was so forbidden."

Even after moving to New York, which has among the largest gay and Jewish communities in America, he could not escape anti-Semitism. One of his first lovers, a former Christian seminarian, seemed "jocularly anti-Semitic" with him. A later lover sent Mass a postcard on which he wrote only "Merry Christmas." Mass took the words to mean, "Merry Christmas, Mr. Jew." Mass worried he was becoming paranoid about anti-Semitism. He fixated on an increase in anti-Semitic graffiti and wrote passionately in his memoir about a graffito painted in the bright yellow color the Nazis used to deface Jewish businesses.[19]

He saw the World War II genocide of six million Jews not merely as history but as a warning about scapegoating today. The post–World War II assurances that such atrocities could never happen again gave way to the genocides of millions in Cambodia, Bosnia, Rwanda, and elsewhere. "There's that famous saying by Santayana, 'Those who don't learn the lessons of history are condemned to repeat them,'" Mass said. "I've created an addendum to that: 'They will repeat them even if they've learned history, so long as they think they can get away with it.'"

"History can turn on a dime," Mass mused. He insisted a Hitler-style demagogue could foment public targeting of African Americans, Muslim Americans, or gays. "It doesn't have to be Jews," Mass said. "When the public starts going crazy, when the public starts getting that fever of bondedness about something, rationality drops away and the mass psychology of fascism takes over." Mass's description of inhuman human behavior recalled Twain's maxim that man is the only animal that blushes—or needs to.

For a long time, Mass had a sense as a gay man of impending disaster—radical-right Republicans or the whole country "going after gays again in a major way as a scapegoat, but even more so, the kind of things that they did to Jews." More recently, he had rejoiced in the impressive progress in public

Dr. Larry Mass

opinion—for example, in the public's acceptance of same-sex marriage—which he called "wonderful and hopeful."

Despite the public's progress, Mass felt the continuing need to be vigilant about gay bashing and other forms of bigotry. I telephoned him after Trump's election to the presidency. Mass said, "I'm a lot more skeptical than too many other minority persons of the strength of minority gains. I still think it could turn on a dime, as it seems to have done with the Trump presidency. Around the world, tyrants run police-state dictatorships. I've no doubt that what has happened throughout history—globally and here in America—can and will happen again. Complacency is always troubling. As Twain put it, 'Whenever you find yourself on the side of the majority, it is time to . . . pause and reflect.'"

Mass pointed to gay and Jewish communities that have practiced their own intolerance. Hasidim and Orthodox Jews have ostracized Jewish gays. Gays, in turn, have abandoned transgender and intersex individuals in the hope of getting a federal employment nondiscrimination act passed. Everyone has to address the most difficult forms of discrimination, the ones they themselves practice, Mass said.

"All I'm saying, and Twain might have been somewhat pleased with this, is tell the damn truth, especially if you're not going to do the right thing,"

Mass said. "Both the Left and Right compromise themselves to the extent that they are no longer speaking truth. In order to speak the truth, you have to speak the whole truth, not leave out the parts that are inconvenient."

In search of a different kind of truth—about the neighborhood that for generations has served as the first home for many immigrants to America—Dan, Alyssa, and I headed a mile south to the Lower East Side.

CHAPTER 6

Five Points

The "Loathsome" Home to Immigrants

The Lower East Side's infamous Five Points neighborhood has witnessed dramatic changes in its dominant immigrant groups. Most recently, new arrivals from China and other Asian countries have moved into spaces vacated by Italians and other Europeans.

In the 1840s, Five Points was home to poor Jews, African Americans, and immigrants from Ireland and Germany. When Charles Dickens visited America in 1842, he decried Five Points as crime infested and disease ridden: "All that is loathsome, drooping and decaying is here."[1]

By 1853, when Mark Twain arrived, New York's seven hundred thousand inhabitants made it America's largest and most diverse city. Twain walked through Five Points's multiethnic, multiracial slums from his Duane Street lodging to the Cliff Street printing house of his employer, John Gray. He observed homeless children surviving as pickpockets, panhandlers, and prostitutes.

After one walk, the racist teenage Twain of the white South, not the antiracist he would become, deplored in a letter to his Presbyterian Calvinist mother the racial and ethnic mélange of "trundle-bed trash. . . . I think I could count two hundred brats. . . . And to wade through this mass of human vermin, would raise the ire of the most patient person that ever lived." The literary historian Ann M. Ryan says the "human vermin" symbolized to Twain a moral stain, "an emblem of degrading poverty, savagery, and corruption."[2] Twain also wrote to his mother about "niggers, mulattoes, quadroons, Chinese, and some the Lord no doubt originally intended to be white, but the dirt on whose face leaves one uncertain as to that fact." Spending a lifetime learning about humanity changed Twain's attitude.[3]

In the 1880s, three decades after Twain's arrival in New York, Italian immigrants flooded Five Points. The *New York Times* turned up its nose at the "awful odors" of the Italians.[4]

The neighborhood's park appropriately took the name of Christopher Columbus in 1911. A century later, that 2.76-acre park symbolized a shriveling Italian neighborhood and an expanding Chinatown. The Italian neighborhood had been reduced to a few touristy blocks, "Historic Little Italy." The 2010 census reported not a single resident who had been born in Italy. A Mulberry Street block housed sixteen Italian restaurants and three Italian souvenir shops. Staffed mainly by Chinese, the shops sold refrigerator magnets and T-shirts with Italian themes ("I'm Not Yelling, I'm Italian").

Columbus Park had become, in effect, Sun Yat-sen Park. A statue of Sun Yat-sen, the founding father of the Republic of China, was erected in 2011 at the park's center. We watched Chinese perform tai chi in the park's pavilion, sing and play in choruses and bands on Chinese stringed instruments and drums, chat on benches in a Chinese-style garden, and compete at Chinese checkers and card games under billowing clouds of cigarette smoke.

At the nearby Museum of Chinese in America, Herb Hoi Chun Tam, the thirty-eight-year-old curator and director of exhibitions, chose to call himself Chinese, not Chinese American. "That's a very calculated, almost politically influenced, decision to identify that way," he explained. In 1974, he and his parents had settled in San Francisco's Chinatown, where his mother worked in a garment sweatshop and his father delivered groceries. They later owned and operated a laundry and moved to Millbrae, a suburb that Tam recalled as "pretty white."

He and his sister were called "chink" and other derogatory names. Other children "would make fun of our language," he said. As a student at San Jose State University, with its program in Asian American studies, he became aware of identity politics. But he "felt very uncomfortable lumping myself into this group [of Asian Americans] that formed because of a political movement . . . even though their issues were also my issues."

Tam moved to New York in 1998 to earn a master of fine arts degree from the School of Visual Arts. We interviewed Tam, the artist-turned-curator, at his museum, a twelve-thousand-square-foot converted machine repair shop on Centre Street. Maya Lin, who had designed the Vietnam Veterans Memorial in Washington, D.C., in 1981, designed the museum in 2009. The lobby features Lin's *The Journey Wall*, an art installation of bronze tiles that connect Chinese Americans' family names and emigration sites in China to the communities where they settled in the United States.

Tam used to think about returning to Hong Kong to work and "get back in touch with my roots." But after ruminating on his American-ness and Chinese-ness, he concluded, "the older I get, the more I understand how particularly American I am and how I don't think I would really feel comfortable in Hong Kong or China." America, especially New York—with its half-million Chinese residents, the largest Chinese population outside Asia—represented to him an energizing cultural diversity and freedom of intellectual pursuit.

"I don't belong to groups," he said. "Even though a lot of my political beliefs are aligned with Democrats, I would never say that I'm a Democrat. I would never say that I'm part of the Asian American community."

Similarly, he resided in Flushing, New York, rather than remain in Brooklyn, where he lived and worked as an artist for seven years, because he wanted to be "a little bit outside" the art community. Flushing was home to one of the city's three big Chinese neighborhoods and, like Millbrae, California, offered a suburban rhythm that suited him.

Tam said many residents of his neighborhood had fled Chinese communism and poverty in the 1960s, after a relaxation in U.S. immigration quotas. The Chinese became part of a wave of Asians that in 2010 surpassed Hispanics—430,000 Asians versus 370,000 Hispanics—as the largest stream of new immigrants to the United States.

Tam described the rapid evolution of his once virtually all-white hometown of Millbrae—by the 2010 census it was 47.3 percent white and 42.8 percent Asian. The local high school became, Tam said, "50 percent Chinese, and you're talking less than twenty years. I think that's pretty remarkable."

Growing up in Millbrae, he loved rap music and basketball. "I didn't have many Asian role models," he said. "It was mostly Black people, Black kids, Black music and athletes" because their cultural influences most appealed to him. The emergence of Jeremy Lin, the first American-born National Basketball Association player of Chinese or Taiwanese descent, provoked the 2012 "Linsanity" craze. Tam screened live at the museum six New York Knicks games in which Lin starred.

Tam saw Lin's performance as a way for the museum to stimulate a discussion about the identity of Asian American men. Lin was not only a "model minority"—the religious, Harvard-educated son of Taiwanese immigrants— he was also athletic and assertive. Aspects of his character, Tam said, went against stereotypes about Asian American males. "It's important that people like Lin 'make it,'" Tam added. "Hopefully that opens doors for others."

By 2011, the political arena had also opened to Asian Americans, he said. "The mayor of San Francisco [Edwin M. Lee] is Chinese, and the mayor of Oakland [Jean Quan] is Chinese and she's not very good. It's kind of okay that she's not very good because there's another [Chinese] mayor right across the bay."[5] In 2018, three new legislators—T. J. Cox of California, Andy Kim of New Jersey, and Michael San Nicolas, a nonvoting representative for Guam—brought the total number of Asian Americans and Pacific Islanders in Congress to twenty, a new high. In 2020, Andrew Yang, an entrepreneur and philanthropist whose parents emigrated from Taiwan, was a candidate for the Democratic Party's nomination for president (and he often ended his stump speeches with "I am the ideal candidate for this job, because the opposite of Donald Trump is an Asian man who likes math.")

Tam noted the changes in Millbrae (and elsewhere) since his childhood. "It's much different to be a young Asian American now," he said. "The way we think about race is different. The kinds of opportunities are different." But Nadia Y. Kim, a professor of sociology, writes that some analysts see Asian Americans as "forever foreigners, i.e., inauthentic Americans"; U.S. relations with China and other Asian nations, these critics argue, are likely to reignite talk of the Yellow Peril and Asian Menace and perpetuate the subordination of Asian Americans in the United States.[6]

I chose, however, to celebrate the changes that Tam observed—Asian Americans' socioeconomic success, assimilation into the nation's political structure, and greater opportunity to marry those they wish to marry, Asian American or not. Increasingly their offspring, multiracial Asian Americans, are creating their own identities. And, I like to think, they will play a key role in the political and cultural evolution of a diversifying, pluralistic America.[7]

Two and a half blocks east of Tam's Museum of Chinese in America, Joseph V. Scelsa presided over the Italian American Museum in a nineteenth-century brick storefront on the corner of Grand and Mulberry Streets. (By 2019, the building had been demolished; the opening of a new museum building on the site—with quadruple the space and an auditorium for lectures and film screenings—was scheduled for spring 2021.) As a member of the third generation of Ghigliones born in the United States, I wanted to

Joseph Scelsa

know from Scelsa, the museum's founder, when descendants of Italian immigrants stopped being Italian Americans and became Americans.

Bearded, balding, and wearing tortoiseshell glasses at sixty-six, Scelsa looked the part of a professor emeritus, which he was. In Little Italy, which had shrunk to fewer than a thousand people of Italian ancestry, he devoted his thousand-square-foot museum to the struggles and successes of Italians in America.

Successes did not mean the triumphs of mafia mobsters that Hollywood movies loved to celebrate. Scelsa had asked the owner of Groovies and Movies of Little Italy, the Grand Street shop next door to his museum (Scelsa held the shop's lease), not to display in front of the store the stereotypical Italian mobster movie photos that sold so well.

But Scelsa did not apologize for quality crime movies set in Little Italy such as *Mean Streets*. Directed by Martin Scorsese, who grew up on nearby Elizabeth Street, it stars Robert De Niro, who once lived on Bleecker Street, a half-dozen blocks north of Elizabeth. The critic Roger Ebert called the 1973 film "one of the source points of modern movies."[8] Scelsa said, "I think we would be foolish as a community who is so successful—I mean, I went to Columbia, my son went to Harvard—to be ashamed of some small aspect of our community that has a reputation for doing nefarious things." Organized crime, he added, has become disorganized crime, "if there's any remnant of it left."

Scelsa hoped to educate Americans—especially Italian Americans of the third and fourth generations who are researching their roots—about Italian American history. Scelsa put $800,000 of his own money toward the $3 million down payment for the purchase of the nonprofit museum's $9 million building.[9] He also provided guided tours of the eclectic one-room museum, discussing the significance of a huge Banca Stabile safe; an organ grinder's cart; hand-carved puppets; and a police revolver used by Frank Serpico, a New York officer who exposed widespread police corruption.

Scelsa pointed me to three neighborhood sites that captured the history of Little Italy—a park, a church, and a food store.

At Lafayette and Kenmare Streets sat a tiny (0.03 acre) triangular park named after Lieutenant Joseph Petrosino, a five-foot, three-inch immigrant who joined New York's police department in 1883 and became its first Italian American detective. Fluent in Italian dialects, he worked undercover and headed an Italian American squad that sent five hundred mob members to prison. In retaliation, he was assassinated in Sicily in 1909, reportedly the only New York police officer ever killed in the line of duty outside the United States.

Scelsa also sent me to the Church of the Most Precious Blood at 109 Mulberry Street. The predominantly Irish American Catholic hierarchy forced Italian immigrants entering Lower Manhattan to worship in the basements, never the sanctuaries, of existing New York churches (my Ghiglione grandfather had his first communion at nearby St. Rose of Lima, a church with Irish priests and strong ties to Irish politics). The Vatican responded in 1888 by establishing a temporary storefront and, three years later, the Mulberry Street church. It offered services in Italian (when I visited, the church's only foreign-language service was in Vietnamese) and, since most neighborhood Italians came from Naples, started a Feast of San Gennaro, the patron saint of the port city.

Scelsa's third site, DiPalo's Latteria at 200 Grand Street, symbolized the entrepreneurial Italian immigrant. Savino DiPalo left Italy in 1903 and opened a *latteria* (dairy store) in Little Italy. When I visited more than a century later, cheeses and meats hung from the tin ceiling. I was served by Marie, a fourth-generation DiPalo, who sliced me a sample of aged Genoa salami and took ten minutes, despite a line of customers, to tell me about the salami and the store. "This is more like a family home," she said. "That's how we were raised."

Her twenty-four-year-old daughter, Jessica, was studying the food business for her MBA at the University of Bologna. Salvatore, a fourth-generation DiPalo, joked that when he asked his father if he could study there, his father looked at the meat case and said, "There's the bologna. Study it." Salvatore said he started serving customers when he was eight years old. He hoped to keep serving them, although he worried about the parking problems faced by old customers—called suburban "Saturday Italians"— returning to a neighborhood virtually devoid of parking.[10] "If they park on the street and run in for a minute," Salvatore said, "they'll get a $115 ticket, so that hurts us."

Back at the Italian American Museum, Scelsa said his own family was typical of New York's Lower East Side immigrant families. His grandfather and grandmother came from Caccamo, a small Sicilian town, around 1900. Their marriage on the Lower East Side would not have been possible in class-conscious Sicily. Her family owned land, his did not.

Scelsa applauded Italian Americans' entry into the educational, cultural, economic, and political fabric of America. But he also said they had sacrificed in the process. "Closeness to family was probably the hardest to give up because over time you choose success over the closeness you had with your family," he said.

He suggested that Italian-ness may not be exclusively Italian anymore. "There are a lot of people today who feel Italian who don't even have Italian blood at all," he said. "I don't know necessarily that that's a bad thing." Scelsa accepted the wannabes—the Italophiles who love Leonardo da Vinci or Frank Sinatra. "There's a big tent, and there's enough room for everyone underneath it," he said.

Studies by historians and sociologists have shown that ethnic homogeneity—Italian-ness—among Italian Americans was virtually nonexistent by the third or fourth generation. A 2000 study of intermarriage in four generations of Italian Americans found that by the third generation "a solid majority had mixed origins." Children of mixed origins represented more than 90 percent of Italian Americans by the fourth generation.[11] Answering my question, Scelsa said, "After three and a half, four generations in America, we're American."

———

Scelsa's comments about his family prompted me on Columbus Day to resume, on the Lower East Side, my almost half-century search for the story of my great-grandfather. I had begun the search in 1966, when my father died of cancer, leaving three relatives—my stepmother, her mother, and my grandfather, Frank Achille Ghiglione—to share our tiny apartment on 100th Street in Manhattan. Sheets that hung ceiling to floor from a clothesline converted what had been my bedroom before I went off to college into two closet-sized bedrooms for my stepmother's mother and my grandfather.

Later in 1966, following my graduation from law school, I invited my grandfather to join me in Washington, D.C. (where I had lived between college and law school and tried to woo Nancy Geiger, who would eventually become my wife). Grandpa, who was then eighty-eight, and I were among the oddest of odd couples. At twenty-six, I was focused on the present and future—on learning as a Congressional Fellow how the House and Senate worked and on figuring out how to achieve my dream of someday putting out my own newspaper.

Grandpa concentrated on the past. He remembered key dates. On February 4, 1911, in Seattle, he married Theresa Fetta, a registered nurse. She was born in the French town of Rive-de-Gier on March 24, 1884. He became president of A. F. Ghiglione & Sons, a pasta manufacturer in New York and then Seattle, following his father's death on March 31, 1927. If angered when we argued, Grandpa would threaten to return to Seattle or San Francisco, where he lived after A. F. Ghiglione & Sons went out of business.

Grandpa and I argued about almost everything, even how to wash dishes. We lived in a small house on Tenth Street, SE, in a predominantly Black neighborhood that was giving way to whites, many of whom were gay. Grandpa dismissed our neighbors, white and Black, with an enthusiasm previously reserved for southern Italians, whom he saw as (I abbreviate his list) lazy and lower class, stupid and stiletto wielding.

His enlarged heart had given him the reputation since childhood of being sickly. My cousin Marie Wilham recalled: "We were always told, 'Uncle Frank is coming over and you must be very quiet.' We all thought Uncle was going to fall over at any moment." When he took his morning walk with Dante Alighieri Ghiglione, his brown-and-black dachshund puppy, Grandpa walked with a tilt. His rightward lean, physical as well as political, was so extreme that it appeared he might fall over at any minute. But he was a feisty featherweight—five feet, six inches, 126 pounds—who seemed to thrive on our verbal jousting and a daily routine that rarely varied.

One day in 1967, I returned from Senator Robert Kennedy's office to find Grandpa lying diagonally across the living room sofa, his left foot still

W. Fricke,   50 Bowery, N. Y.

Angelo Francesco Ghiglione

touching the floor. When a fly landed on his upper lip, he did not brush it away. I knew Grandpa was dead.

Later, when I went through his belongings, I came across two century-old documents written in Italian. A note of recommendation was signed by Angelo Cavero, an Italian employer, in elementary-school-style penmanship, as if he were writing his name for the first time. The note attested to my great-grandfather's good work for him from September 14, 1865, to July 11, 1868, interrupted only by my great-grandfather's service during the Third Italian War of Independence.

I translated the brief note with the help of an English-Italian dictionary. The second document, however, three-and-a-half pages in the most baroque of hands, proved inscrutable. The document detailed my great- grandfather's indenture to Uffreduzzi and Dart of New York. Claudio Capasso, the family friend who succeeded in translating the contract where I had failed, attached a note: "Please find herein the translation of the contract signed in 1872 by an honest and skilled Italian victim and his Yankee butcher."

My great-grandfather and others making the voyage from Genoa to New York were swindled at both ends. In Genoa, dishonest hotel owners, restaurateurs, and emigration agents duped those leaving Italy. Agents for U.S. companies circulated handbills promising work and wealth, multiplying a hundredfold the wages immigrants would actually earn.

My great-grandfather's indenture contract promised payment of his passage from Genoa to New York. In return, he would make Italian-style noodles for three years, putting in at least seventy-two hours a week at seventeen cents an hour ($12.24 a week) plus "appropriate quarters without linen." To guarantee that my great-grandfather remained at his job for three years, Uffreduzzi and Dart would deduct one dollar from his pay each week. If he left the firm early, he would lose the money.

The indenture contract led me to a microfilmed ship's passenger list at the National Archives in Washington, D.C. It revealed that my twenty-eight-year-old great-grandfather had arrived in New York from Liverpool on March 28, 1872, aboard the Inman Line steamer RMS *City of London*. That ship symbolized the development and danger of immigrants' travel. By 1870 the *City of London* and other Inman ships were landing forty-four thousand passengers a year in New York, more than any other company. On a trip from London to New York in November 1881, the *City of London* sank. All of its crew and passengers died.

Even passengers aboard ships that survived the Atlantic crossing risked death. On my great-grandfather's 1872 voyage of 816 immigrants, a one-year-old French girl died of "debility." The rate of shipboard deaths from unsanitary, overcrowded conditions, cholera, and other diseases sometimes reached as high as 9 percent and caused newspapers to call the vessels "plague ships."[12]

I was overcome by curiosity about the answers to questions I had never thought to ask my parents before they died. Where did my family come from? Why did my great-grandfather, Angelo Francesco Ghiglione, choose to leave Italy, which Twain called a land of quietude and comfort that allowed people "to comprehend what life is for"?

Beginning in the 1970s, I tried to find every Ghiglione relative in the United States. I peppered them with letters filled with my questions about our family's history. Angelo F. Ghiglione, my great-grandfather's grandson (my first cousin twice removed), wrote to me in 1978 about my headstrong great-grandfather's departure for America. Angelo made my great-grandfather sound like a proud, petulant teenager: "He served in the Italian army under the famous general Garibaldi [and] was decorated but refused to send for his medal because there was a charge for it. After his mother died young he couldn't get along with his dad so he sailed."

In 1979, I sailed, by airplane, to Genoa, a Mediterranean seaport city of 600,000 in northwestern Italy, to stalk the story of my ancestors—not necessarily back to Adam and Eve but at least to Angelo Francesco Ghiglione. To understand his immigrant life in America, I felt I needed to understand the life he left behind. As I would with my trip around the United States, I followed in the footsteps of Twain, who visited Genoa in 1867.

Twain joined about seventy pious, prosperous Americans for a five-month pleasure cruise so he could write *Innocents Abroad*. He loved Genoa, as would I. Stately Genoa, Twain said, "rose up out of the sea and flung back the sunlight from her hundred palaces." Of course, I also was influenced by Genoa's standing as the world capital of Ghigliones. Its telephone directory listed 232 Ghigliones, undoubtedly more than the number listed in all U.S. directories combined.

I drove nine miles by autostrada from Genoa to Pontedecimo, a farming village that developed into an industrial town by the end of the nineteenth century. With a population of about ten thousand, Pontedecimo was home to a foundry, underwear and sweater manufacturers, and producers of edibles—olive oil, mineral water, wines, sweets, and pasta made by Montaldo

Bernardino, Fratelli Barbarino, and perhaps, I fantasized, distant relatives of Angelo Francesco Ghiglione.

Pontedecimo's streets radiated from a town square dominated by an immense Catholic church, Parrocchia San Giacomo Maggiore. Nearby, as if to announce Pontedecimo was part of my family's past, sat, side by side, Ghiglione S.M., a furniture store, and the shoe store of Giuseppe Ghiglione.

A visit to the town hall led me to nearby St. Cipriano Serra Ricco. St. Cipriano, a church dating from 1000 CE, sat on a cliff overlooking Pontedecimo, which lay five hundred feet below. The opulent interior featured a huge sixteenth-century oil painting by Luca Cambiaso, two rows of pink marble columns down the length of the nave, and an ornately carved marble baptistery, added in 1899. Immigrants in the New World had paid for the renovations.

Giuseppe Risso, the parish's priest, sat at a backroom desk covered with papers. He was a native of Genoa who had served St. Cipriano for twenty-four years. Reverend Risso found the birth-and-baptism record of my great-grandfather, Angelo Maria Francesco Ghiglione, son of Benedetto, a weaver, and Maria Cambiaso Ghiglione, listed as *atta ai lavori di casa*, someone who did housework. The cleric said he was willing, despite a busy schedule, to make a copy of the birth-and-baptism record for me. ("Of course," he said, "you have to make an offering to the church.")

Also listed as godparents were Angelo Ghiglione, Benedetto's brother, a weaver, and Teresa Cambiaso, Maria's sister, a housewife. They picked my great-grandfather's two middle names, including Maria, after the Virgin Mary, a name my great-grandfather dropped before he arrived in the United States. The birth-and-baptism paper was signed by a priest, Carrozzo Giambattista, because my great-great-grandfather could not write his own name.

During that brief visit, I was struck by my early relatives' illiteracy and poverty. They were peasants to be pitied. Similar to the Central American migrants who today face starvation and gang warfare at home, my great-grandparents were "survival migrants."[13] During nineteenth-century famines, peasants occasionally "ate grass and seeds which sometimes killed them more quickly than starvation would have done." An 1872 *New York Times* article, headlined "The Poor Italians," described them as "helpless and destitute."[14] Twain took a harsher view of Italy's peasants. He saw them as idle victims of what he called "priestcraft." They suffered from "a happy, cheerful, contented ignorance, superstition, degradation, poverty, indolence, and everlasting un-aspiring worthlessness."

But I suspected my great-grandfather and other Italian immigrants were not examples of helplessness, indolence, or unaspiring worthlessness. An investigation by the Commissioners of Emigration of the State of New York reported the exemplary work of newly arrived Italian immigrants. In a letter to the editor of the *New York Times*, a Newark, New Jersey, executive who had employed hundreds of Italian immigrants during the previous three years declared that the Italians were "most industrious . . . and entirely free from the many vices which our laboring classes fall into."[15]

The executive's comment about Italian industriousness was on my mind when, on Columbus Day, Alyssa, Dan, and I walked east from Washington Square at the base of Fifth Avenue to 807 East Sixth Street, where my entrepreneurial great-grandfather and his ten to thirteen employees once made pasta. My great-grandparents lived nearby at 195 Lewis Street. After World War II, Lewis Street and many other streets made way for three massive public housing projects. I adopted East Sixth Street, which welcomed newly arrived Italians, Irish, and Eastern European Jews in the late nineteenth and early twentieth centuries, as my ancestral Lower East Side home.

By the 1970s, when I visited the street for the first time, what had been red-light residences and slum tenements with no running water a century earlier had become Curry Row. Indian restaurants (twenty-seven of them by the 1990s), most actually owned by Bangladeshis, dominated the street between First and Second Avenues (the joke was that the restaurants shared a kitchen).[16] To the east, in the alphabet city of Avenues A, B, C, and D, a few Puerto Rican storefront churches and social clubs survived amid deserted tenements and litter-strewn lots.

When I first saw the neighborhood, much of it looked like a war zone of bombed-out buildings, except for a row of Italian-language shops, including Farmacia Italiana, on East Seventh Street. The shops turned out to be part of a movie set for *The Godfather: Part II*, created to represent Vito Corleone's Italian neighborhood of 1917.

At the Ninth Precinct police station hung a row of seven framed photos of officers killed in the line of duty between 1964 and 1975. The real neighborhood, infested by gangs and drug dealers who turned dozens of abandoned buildings into shooting galleries, challenged the make-believe mafia-controlled neighborhood of *Godfather II* for violence. By the time of our 2011 visit, the neighborhood had been reborn. Myrna Megron, the Ninth Precinct's receptionist for twenty-five years and a neighborhood resident for fifty-six years, said police officers now died of "accidents and stuff," rather than shootings. Creative Little Garden and other pocket parks with waterfalls and fountains had replaced litter-filled lots.

The gentrified East Sixth Street boasted a new diversity. Peruvian, Mexican, Thai, Ethiopian, Argentinian, Vietnamese, Chinese, Japanese, and Moroccan restaurants shared the street with ten Indian restaurants. To the east Chinese-language business signs competed with Spanish-language signs.

But in my great-grandparents' era, East Sixth Street was a neighborhood that residents sought to escape. By 1900, in one generation, my great-grandparents achieved a key part of the American dream: they moved from a Lower East Side tenement to a Staten Island single-family house. I had conflicting clues to the location of that house. Dan, Alyssa, and I took a free, twenty-five-minute ferry ride from Lower Manhattan to Staten Island and grabbed a United Cars taxi driven by fifty-one-year-old Roger's Effehi (as he gives his name), who had arrived in the United States from Nigeria thirteen years earlier. Staten Islanders, 80 percent white and heavily Italian American, were more conservative and more Republican than typical New Yorkers (in 2016, 57 percent of Staten Island voters chose Donald Trump for president, while Hillary Clinton won 79 percent of the vote of the entire city).[17]

Effehi, our driver, represented the Staten Island of tomorrow—increasingly populated by Africans, Asians, and Latin Americans. Effehi drove us past the stadium where the Staten Island Yankees, a New York Yankees farm team, played and past Port Richmond (home to "very, very hardworking" Mexicans, he said).

In search of the Ghiglione home, we visited Arrochar and Rosebank, two heavily Italian American communities, and Richmond Avenue. Longtime Richmond Avenue residents told of old homes, vacant lots, and forests that were replaced by new housing after construction of the bridges to Staten Island from New Jersey and Brooklyn. We never found the Ghigliones' home, if it still existed.

I returned disappointed to my New York home-away-from-home, the Park Avenue apartment of Ann Ghiglione O'Keefe, my second cousin, and her husband, Jim O'Keefe. Ann and Jim spoiled Dan and me during our four nights in New York. (Alyssa stayed with a friend, Sylvi Sareva, in a sixth-floor walk-up on Bank Street, and wrote in her diary: "This trip does make me realize what wonderful friends I have. . . . I can call them and ask for their couch, and they give me their bed." Dan and I felt the same way about Ann and Jim.) As if to make up for my disappointment at failing to find the Ghiglione home on Staten Island, Ann gave me an old painting of the house and told me two stories, one about her own pursuit of the Ghigliones.

Ann's search story dated from the mid-1960s. She installed five-thousand-pound UNIVAC 1050 computers at major U.S. Air Force bases abroad. An amateur rally car driver, she zoomed around Europe and North Africa in a red Porsche. During a 1966 stop in Italy, she asked Pontedecimo residents for Ghigliones. "Somebody found a couple of Ghigliones for me," Ann recalled. The elderly Ghiglione couple invited her to their home. On a wall hung a painting from the 1700s—"a picture of me—it looked like me: my nose, my eyes, my face," Ann said. "It was like seeing a double. It almost scared me."

Ann's second story was also a disquieting one. Ann's father, Angelo F. Ghiglione, a cum laude graduate of the University of Washington and possessor of a photographic memory, "earned his master's degree in [civil] engineering at MIT in just one year with the highest grades ever earned to that date [1932] in the program," his son John had told me with pride.[18] Ann was accepted by MIT in 1958 and consulted her father about whether to attend.

Worried that she would find the derogatory comments and discrimination against women to be debilitating, he discouraged her from attending MIT. Typically, one-third of the women students quit MIT before graduation. A 1956 MIT committee, comprised almost entirely of men, had proposed the institute shut its doors to female undergrads, given the hostile environment for women. Ann chose to attend Penn State, which she steamrolled.[19]

The 1958 class of about one thousand MIT graduates included only fourteen women. Professor Emily Wick wrote later: "If they succeeded, fine! If they failed—well, no one had expected them to succeed."[20] Audrey Buyrn '58 and PhD '66, who had a distinguished career in the Office of Technology Assessment in Washington, D.C., said, "The boys—one can hardly call them men—could be pretty crude."[21]

Not until the women's and civil rights movements of the 1960s did more than a handful of women graduate from MIT annually. Like most U.S. research universities, MIT had almost no women faculty until the Civil Rights Act of 1964 required an end to gender discrimination. Even thirty years later, in 1994, when tenured women faculty and the administration at MIT collaboratively addressed the issue, women comprised just 8 percent of the science faculty. Lab spaces for women were smaller than men's by about half.

Women's salaries on average were 20 percent lower than men's. "Societal beliefs can overpower merit," said the molecular biologist Nancy H. Hopkins, Amgen, Inc. Professor of Biology at MIT, who joined MIT's faculty in 1973 as an assistant professor.[22]

Hopkins, the keynote speaker at a 2011 MIT celebration of women in the sciences and engineering, said the women who were admitted to previously all-male universities, even after the Civil Rights Act of 1964, faced four barriers that still have to be dismantled. The impact of those barriers is cumulative, and overcoming each of them takes about thirty years.

Hopkins experienced the first barrier, sexual harassment, although she said it had not affected her own career. She recalled writing up her lab notes as a Harvard undergraduate when Francis Crick, a codiscoverer of DNA's structure, entered the room, stood behind her, placed his hands on her breasts, and said, "What are you working on?"[23] While at the time Hopkins did not identify Crick's behavior as sexual harassment, she came to realize how such behavior reflected the attitudes that were a barrier to women's achieving workplace equality.

The second barrier, she said, was the dearth of mentors who encouraged women to become scientists. She had had a powerful mentor, Jim Watson, another codiscoverer of DNA's structure (Watson, however, has a history of racist, homophobic, anti-Semitic, and sexist comments, remarking about gene editing in a 2003 documentary: "People say it would be terrible if we made all girls pretty. I think it would be great.").[24] But other women lacked strong, supportive mentors.

Her response to the third barrier—the expectation that women scientists, whatever their family obligations, would work seventy or more hours a week—was to become "a nun of science." After obtaining her PhD and doing a postdoc, she divorced and "decided not to marry and not to have children," she said. "So much for that problem."[25] The residue of the system of gendered roles—the men working night and day, the women raising families at home—persisted. But the system failed to serve women's lives, and many men's as well, Hopkins added.

The final barrier resulted from the psychology of unconscious bias. Women and men alike undervalued work done at MIT by a woman. Hopkins said, "Sometimes the woman got no credit at all."[26]

In the 1990s, MIT worked with women faculty to address the issues of family-work balance and inequality resulting from unconscious bias and made significant progress. In fall 2018, women constituted 46 percent of the undergraduate and 35 percent of the graduate student body and about 22.5 percent of the science faculty.[27] MIT recruits women into administrative posts, provides family leave and day care centers, and monitors admissions and hiring progress annually.

Despite women's achievements at MIT, critics contend MIT women advance only because of affirmative action or some unfair advantage. Hopkins said that such beliefs are often examples of unfounded, unconscious bias. The challenge of overcoming women's undervaluation—even by women—persists.

Ann's story and MIT's history motivated Dan, Alyssa, and me to interview women at our next stop, Yale University in New Haven, Connecticut. There, the focuses of our trip, which had been primarily issues of race, religion, and ethnicity, shifted to questions of gender discrimination.

CHAPTER 7

New Haven

Interviewing the Overlooked Half of Humanity

With discrimination against women much on our minds, Dan, Alyssa, and I headed for Yale University, where Twain visited in the 1880s and my mother studied drama in the 1930s.

Perhaps it is inevitable that a son—an only child—looks to earlier generations of men in his family for role models and a sense of identity. But I regretted overlooking my mother, Rita Belle Haskin Ghiglione, who had proved the myths about single parents wrong. Our home never felt broken or deficient. Mom nurtured but tolerated no nonsense. She dragged me most weeks to Sunday school and made me say prayers nightly. She insisted I practice violin (I played in an elementary school orchestra), led my Cub Scout den, and watched over my softball team. She drove players to games and practices and cut out and sewed pale blue Y's on the front of ten white T-shirts so that my Yankees would have uniforms.

Mom educated me about everything, from academics to subjects that none of my teachers dared address. "She taught you a lot of English," recalled Robert E. Jones, a retired high school teacher of English. "You probably got more at home than at [elementary] school." When, at age ten or eleven, I expressed curiosity about smoking and drinking, she sat me in our living room, brought me a lit Chesterfield and a jigger of whiskey, and encouraged me to try both. I gagged and gasped uncontrollably. I never smoked or drank hard liquor again.

My mother qualified as an outlier in her generation of women. She was the daughter of Loren Hix Haskin and Hettie Fletcher Haskin, white Methodist farm-family Kansans who moved west to Pomona, California, at the beginning of the twentieth century. Neither had gone to college. But their daughter graduated in 1932 from Scripps, a new women's college in Claremont, California, where she gained the nickname "Birdie" because she was pint sized.

Marion Jones, my mother's first cousin, said childhood polio had stunted Rita's growth and required regular surgery "to lengthen and keep her spine as even as possible. I thought she was very brave." Virginia Willis, a Scripps classmate and childhood friend, said, "In all the years I never heard her complain."[1]

Many of my mother's college classmates regarded Scripps as a finishing school to prepare them for marriage ("a ring by spring or double your money back"). But my mother wanted a career in drama. Her high school and college classmate Frances Sumner recalled playing opposite her in a high school production of Shakespeare's *A Midsummer Night's Dream*: "At one point in rehearsal, she roundly scolded me for being so wooden, so uninvolved, that she could not portray her character properly."[2] My mother pursued theater at Scripps and then applied to Yale's graduate drama department.

Isabel F. Smith, dean of Scripps, recommended Rita as not "among our brilliant students" but "quick and humorous; diligent, conscientious and ambitious," with "an alert and original mind."[3] Henry Eames, a Scripps art professor, listed Rita's strengths as "keen mind, bright plus—I rather think she will make Honors rank—and unending desires and plans to achieve something." Eames applauded her performance in *Little Women* as the shy sister, Beth March, who develops scarlet fever and dies young.

Eames mentioned only one difficulty for my mother: "She has had to fight polio's effects and has *won* largely." Smith, too, wrote of my mother's polio—"slightly noticeable spinal curvature. It may be that her decision to go into [theater] production has been influenced by a realization of this handicap."[4]

Yale accepted my mother. Her parents scraped together Yale's annual tuition of $350, and in 1932 my mother started the three-year course. Mostly, she focused on play production. With the help of a third-year scholarship, she earned a master's in theater production in 1935.[5]

Not much came easily after that. She struggled to find work in theater production or teaching. She took a summer job with the Garrick Players in Kennebunkport, Maine. She produced a three-act play for the New Haven Women's Club while she held a part-time librarian's job at Yale's drama department. But her efforts led nowhere. By 1938, she was working at the Pinker-Morrison Literary Agency in New York; the firm closed within the year after an owner, Eric Pinker, was convicted of grand larceny.

Also in 1938, she married my father, William Ghiglione, in a chapel at St. Patrick's Cathedral in New York. The wedding shocked her friends back in California. A Methodist marrying a Catholic "was talked about," recalled Harold Pomeroy, a California friend of my mother's. "In the early days, really the only Catholics [in Pomona] were Mexicans."

Five years after my 1941 birth by Caesarean section, which threatened my mother's life (she was bedridden throughout her pregnancy), she and my father divorced.

Dorothy Martone, her cousin, recalled finding Rita in tears: "She told me that she had opened a bill for a jeweler for an expensive ring which she knew nothing about. Bill admitted it was for someone else." Affected by her polio and other health issues, my mother died young, at forty-four, in 1953.

Three-quarters of a century after my outlier mother graduated from Yale's drama department, Alyssa, Dan, and I decided to interview female graduate students there who felt they, too, were outliers. Our conversation with Prema Cruz and Carmen Zilles reminded us of the progress achieved at Yale Drama School and of new challenges there. In my mother's era, admissions rules declared "only one third [of a class] may be women."[6] By the time of our trip, women comprised a majority of each class. But other identity issues intruded on students' lives.

Cruz, a first-year acting student, was conscious of her ethnic and racial heritages. Born in the Bronx, Cruz, twenty-six, grew up in Sacramento with her African American mother. Only recently had she begun spending time with her Dominican-born, Spanish-speaking father in New York.

Cruz and her father had visited the Dominican Republic together. Cruz, who considered herself Black and was much darker than her father, found herself faced with a wrenching moment of decision in a culture with blatant colorism. She needed to board a flatbed truck that served as a bus. Dark-skinned women sat in the back, and light-skinned locals sat in the truck's cab.

Her father sat in the cab, Cruz recalled, her eyes tearing. "I didn't know what to do. Do I sit in the back or the front with my father? I'll never forget that moment." She sat in the back.

Color also may have been a factor in the men Cruz dated. She said she was "never raised to think about color." But she had not dated African American or Dominican men. Whomever she married, she said, her children would know the family histories of their parents and grandparents. "They must

Carmen Zilles

know who they are and where they came from," she said. "It's important to know what those roots dig into, what they are soaking up."

Carmen Zilles, a twenty-four-year-old Mexican American, said she was the only Hispanic member of her second-year class. The drama school accepted just one acting student for every eighty who applied. Zilles wondered sometimes whether her ethnicity had something to do with her admission.

As a scholarship student at Sarah Lawrence College, where "most people had a lot of money, I felt like a huge Other," she said. Zilles, who was born in Boston, had spent more time with her mother's family from Mexico than with her father's family from Ohio. "I feel connected to my Mexican heritage and family," Zilles said, but at times she saw herself as an outsider to her relatives in Mexico. "Sometimes I feel very American," she said.

Yale's drama school, with its generous financial aid, created a sense of equality, she said. People at the school did not talk about ethnicity, she said, "but it's definitely there." She had already been cast in a Yale play as a Cuban. "I'm not Cuban," Zilles said. "I don't necessarily walk around feeling like a Hispanic person. I just kind of walk around feeling like a person."

I corresponded by email with Zilles two years after her graduation from Yale. Using capital letters to emphasize her points, she wrote about her experience as an actor in New York: "Basically, fundamentally, I feel very much now like my identity as a Latina is one of the primary things that potential employers latch onto about me."

She felt pigeonholed "in ways that don't always feel representative of the multifaceted person I am." She wrote of having had "a multitude of influences that have NOTHING to do with having Mexican heritage." She did see progress: "We are getting more comfortable with people having MULTIPLE ways of defining their identities, and we're expanding beyond labels, but it's still slow going."

When Mark Twain visited Yale in 1885 to lecture, Warner T. McGuinn, one of the first African American law students there, served as Twain's campus guide and introduced him at a public meeting. Impressed by McGuinn, Twain quietly arranged with Francis Wayland III, the law school's dean, to cover McGuinn's expenses. That permitted McGuinn to stop waiting tables, checking hats, and collecting students' bills.

Twain wrote to Wayland: "I do not believe I would very cheerfully help a white student who would ask a benevolence of a stranger, but I do not feel so about the other color. We have ground the manhood out of them & the shame is ours, not theirs, & we should pay for it."

Alice Rufie Jordan, who graduated from Yale Law the year before McGuinn, well could have been a white student Twain would not "very cheerfully help." But, as a woman, she, too, faced systemic discrimination. Twenty years old when she graduated from the University of Michigan, Jordan entered its law school, and, at the end of the first year, passed the exam to practice law in the state. She wanted more of a legal education, though. The law schools at Harvard and Columbia rejected her. Yale seemed likely to do the same.

Jordan, by many accounts, applied to Yale using her initials instead of her first name. The law school admitted her. But the university's registrar explained to her that Yale did not admit women. "You'll have to admit me," Jordan responded. "There isn't a thing in your catalogue that bars women."[7] She was right.

The next June, Yale's board approved a law degree for Jordan but directed that future Yale catalogues state the university was open to "persons of the male sex only, except where [as in the art school] both sexes are specifically included."[8]

Jordan's experience led me to contact the nine surviving women in my Yale Law graduating class, who entered the school exactly seventy years after

Jordan's death and graduated in 1966. They represented the tough transition between the nineteenth-century Yale Law that rejected women and the twenty-first-century Yale Law that welcomed them. In 2000, women for the first time represented a majority of the first-year class. The twenty-first-century school honored such notable alumnae as former secretary of state Hillary Rodham Clinton, LLB '73, and Supreme Court Justice Sonia Sotomayor, LLB '79, with its Award of Merit in 2013 and 2014, respectively. Heather Gerken became the school's first female dean in 2017.

But my female classmates entered a different school in 1963. While Yale Law had been officially opened to women beginning in 1919, few women were admitted each year after that, even into the 1960s. "Somehow in each class," Betsy Levin asked sarcastically, "Yale could only find a small number of qualified women?"

Carolyn Jones, an African American who had attended Stanford as an undergraduate, said, "It wasn't until I got to the law school that I realized I had two strikes. Before that it was only race." Jones's Stanford class had been 40 percent female. Our Yale Law class was 6 percent female—ten of 167 graduates.

Male law students lived in the elegant, fireplace-adorned singles of the Sterling Law Building. The women had to live in off-campus boardinghouses or on the campus's edge in Helen Hadley Hall. Vincent J. Scully Jr., Yale's renowned architecture professor, called it "late modernist design at its most banal."[9] Linda Sato Dalby Kennedy, who lived in Helen Hadley, was more succinct. She dubbed the dorm a dump.

The women frequented a Yale Law basement bathroom-lounge, known as the kiss-and-cry booth, or dungeon, "which was a sign we were second class," Jones said. But she and other women recalled that bathroom-lounge somewhat fondly, as a cozy cubbyhole with sofas and chairs where women could nap, chat, and commiserate.

The perhaps apocryphal story holds that Yale Law added bathrooms for women only after a female student jumped on the desk of Associate Dean Jack Tate and threatened to urinate on it unless the school added them.

The Yale Law faculty consisted entirely of men, except for Associate Professor Ellen Ash Peters. Nina Zagat found "a lot of the male professors encouraging." But other women experienced a "kind of invisibility," said Betsy Michel. "Women were simply not as important as men. Law school and the legal profession were defined in the context of a man's world." Robert H. Bork's antitrust exam "was one long football question" that focused on the pro football quarterback Y. A. Tittle, Levin said. "I had never heard the name." She told Ronald Dworkin, the legal philosopher, that she was having some problems writing her paper for his jurisprudence course. He replied, "That's all right. Women don't think abstractly anyway."

Some professors never called on female students in class. Professor Leon Lipson, who called on women once a week in alphabetical order, could be quick with the hurtful quip. He replied to Kennedy's analysis of a case in front of eighty or so of her classmates: "Your response reminds me of the clock that strikes thirteen. Not only does one reject the value of the thirteenth chime but it casts doubt on the twelve chimes that preceded it."

Some women in the class of 1966 were offended, if not outraged, by Professor Friedrich "Fritz" Kessler's teaching of contracts to first-year students.

"I was picked on," my classmate Cynthia Jacob said. "There was just no other way to describe it." She recalled that once, after lobbing a hypothetical at her and listening to her response, Kessler said, " 'Pardon me, Miss Jacob, that's the dumbest thing I've ever heard.' He just didn't think women should be there." Given today's law, Jacob said, "I would have had a good 'hostile environment' case, based on sex."

Sheila Avrin McLean said she had to remain on her feet through three or four classes straight in Kessler's first-year contracts course as he embarrassed her with an endless hypothetical that, she said, "contained more sexual overtones or undertones as he changed it." The ending of the hypothetical was mortifying for McLean, "filled with sexual innuendo. I had to climb a flagpole and at the top was a golden eagle."

But Jones, a student in Kessler's third-year contracts seminar, and Judith McGuire Pickering, who took his first-year course, found his behavior acceptable. Pickering labeled him "tough, tough, tough, but with the students' best interests at heart. He called on me on a day when I was unprepared. I struggled through it as best I could until finally, exasperated, Professor Kessler said, 'Miss McGuire, if you put half as much effort into answering the question as you do into avoiding it, you would be a very fine student indeed.' The greatest humiliation was that he was right. His advice on that occasion has stood me in good stead for my entire life."

Yale Law's deans appeared more encouraging of women students than did deans at other law schools. At Harvard, Dean Erwin Griswold and his wife, Harriet, would invite the first-year women to their home for dinner. The dinner ended with interrogation for dessert, said Judith Richards Hope,

Harvard Law, '64. The dean, famous for his interest in civil rights, gruffly asked the women: "Why are you at Harvard Law School, taking the place of a man?"[10]

To some female students' answers, he barked, "Ha! Ha! That's not a very good reason." By the time Griswold got to Ann Dudley Cronkhite, '64, she was riled and rebellious. She told Griswold that she was at Harvard because she had been rejected by Yale. Pat Scott, '64, recalled that Griswold became "flaming crazy, saying, 'That's not true, Yale always lets more women in than we do,' and so forth, the implication being that Yale had much lower standards than Harvard."[11]

Eugene V. Rostow, Yale Law's dean from 1955 to 1965, supported the women students. One law firm said it wanted to interview only white Christian gentlemen. Another firm held a lobster-and-cocktail reception for students at Mory's, a private club that refused women; an interviewing partner for that firm told Harriet Bograd and Levin he would interview them later, over a cup of coffee at the corner drugstore. Rostow disinvited the white-Christian-gentlemen firm and banned law firm receptions at Mory's, Levin said.

Many male students at Yale Law also supported their female classmates. But other male students treated the school as if it belonged only to them. Jones said, "The guys would grab a [male] prof after class and go out for coffee," an opportunity that seemed less available to women. Although a few women students were on the *Yale Law Journal*, it appeared to be "Exclusive Club No. 1" for men, said my classmate Hope Babcock, a tenured professor and codirector of the Institute for Public Representation at Georgetown Law School. "You didn't have a sense of belonging to the law school," McLean said.

Organizers of moot court, a simulated court proceeding in which students argue a case, pitted McLean against her female classmate Pickering. A magna cum laude graduate of Vassar, Pickering had won several beauty contests and been a finalist in the 1962 Miss Rheingold contest. "The guys always referred to her as Miss Rheingold," Jones said. "I rarely heard them call her by name."

Pickering and McLean faced off in the largest available moot courtroom before a mob of male students. "My 'adviser,' a second- or third-year student, recognized that they were doing this to poke fun at Judy and me and advised me to ignore the very crowded room and do the best I could," McLean said. "I followed his advice and lived to see another day but never to litigate!"

Whatever challenges Yale Law represented for female students, most of them agreed with Levin: "The real problem for women was getting summer or permanent jobs." Milbank, Tweed, Hadley & McCloy, a century-old Wall Street firm, offered to hire Levin but only if she accepted a position in trusts and estates. That department's clients were dead.

McLean had numerous interviews with firms during which the hiring partner would say: " 'It's not that we have anything against women, it's that our clients don't like women lawyers,' or, 'We're afraid that you'll get pregnant over the summer.'"

Jacob was hired as a litigation associate by a prominent Newark firm. But, she said, "every research project got tossed my way. All the court assignments went to the guys." She switched to New Jersey's Office of the Public Defender.

Following Jacob's first victory in a Superior Court jury case, Baruch Spinoza Seidman, the judge in the case, asked to see her boss. Later her boss reported to Jacob that the judge had said, "Did you know that Miss Jacob doesn't wear a girdle?" The judge suggested Jacob's boss should monitor her attire for propriety. Jacob, who would later be elected president of the New Jersey State Bar Association, laughed, "He's looking at whether my fanny wiggles."

Whatever career paths they chose, the women of the class of 1966 remained sensitive to the challenges women still faced. Kennedy mentored younger women lawyers to not, for example, make statements that sounded like they were asking a question—"like they were asking for approval." Jacob, part of an informal group of women lawyers who called themselves "the old broads," advised women lawyers how to make partner, obtain maternity leave and child care, and gain judgeships and equal pay. According to a 2009–11 survey, women lawyers and judges earned 82 percent of what comparable male lawyers and judges did.[12]

The earnings gap between young male and female lawyers was often nonexistent at the start of their careers. But fifteen years out, when women lawyers, as mothers, experienced job interruptions and worked fewer hours, the law firms often encouraged a gender pay gap, concluded the Harvard economics professor Claudia Goldin. Law firms undervalued the part-time work that fit many women's schedules and overvalued the eighty-hour workweek. "The more hours worked," Goldin writes, "the higher the hourly fee reported."[13]

I took Michel's advice, to read a 1988 paper by Peggy McIntosh of Wellesley's Center for Research on Women titled *White Privilege and Male Privilege*. McIntosh's paper and Kennedy's comments highlighted the interlocking advantages that went with being what I was, a white male. The advantages for white males existed when McGuinn and Jordan studied at Yale Law

Linda Sato Dalby Kennedy

in the 1880s, they remained during my time there in the 1960s, and I suspect they continue.

Kennedy was especially sensitive to white male privilege. Her great-grandparents had immigrated to Hawaii from Japan in the 1890s. She grew up in multiracial Honolulu, where ethnic Japanese were in the majority. "I had no sense of being a minority," she said.

Her first off-island trip, to attend virtually all-white Smith College in Northampton, Massachusetts, shocked her. A mainland student arriving at Smith to move into a college suite "probably would be expected to choose the best bed and desk, the next student the next-best spot," Kennedy said. "According to the culture in which I was raised, the student who arrived first probably would choose the worst bed and desk, as a sign of humility and deference to others."

After four years at a women's college, Yale Law represented, she said, "a double whammy," a white male world. She recalled only one Asian American in her second or third year.

After graduation, she practiced law in Boston as what she called "an accidental pioneer"—a woman who made partner at three major law firms. She survived, she said, "by working harder and better than the men." At

Gaston & Snow, which had no partner-track women attorneys before hiring Kennedy, maternity leave did not exist in 1978. So Kennedy gave birth to her son during her Christmas vacation.

"I did not skip a beat. Most of my clients never knew. Women had to fit into the model," Kennedy said. "And they still do."

According to a 2017 report, women made up 50.3 percent of U.S. law school graduates but fewer than 35 percent of attorneys employed by law firms and only 20 percent of the firms' equity partners.[14]

So, when it comes to the legal community, Twain missed the mark a bit. The shame is ours, not only about African American men but about women too.

CHAPTER 8

North toward Boston

Gays, Muslims, and Small-Town "Whitesville"

Dan, Alyssa, and I drove six miles north from New Haven to hear a different perspective about a different kind of discrimination—that against gays and lesbians. Alyssa wrote:

> *The Saturday morning we went to see Edward Alwood, a journalism professor at Quinnipiac University, it happened to be parents' weekend. The campus was abuzz.*
>
> *We pulled up to the entrance gate and rolled the window down to speak to the security guard. Loren managed a few words before the security guard held up a piece of white paper with, bizarrely, Loren's headshot on it. She compared the image to the real thing and then waved us through. A hundred feet later, another security guard stopped us. She held up the same photo, grinned, and pointed to the face on the piece of paper. We were VIPs.*
>
> *Alwood had interviewed Loren in 1993 for a history of gays and lesbians in American journalism,* Straight News: Gays, Lesbians, and the News Media. *As president of the American Society of Newspaper Editors in 1989–90, Loren had initiated a study of gay and lesbian journalists at the nation's daily newspapers.*
>
> *In* Straight News, *Alwood wrote: "Not one to shy away from controversy, Ghiglione had served on the National News Council and was on the panel that reviewed the CBS documentary* Gay Power, Gay Politics *in 1980 and found it biased against gays."[1]*
>
> *Alwood quoted Loren: "I'm a leftover from the sixties. I knew gays had a second-class citizenship in our newsrooms. The atmosphere made about as much sense as having a bilingual reporter who could not acknowledge that*

he or she was bilingual. That leaves editors unable to take advantage of that strength. In addition, I saw it as a civil rights issue. It was my feeling that newspapers would be better able to report their full community if gays were freer to acknowledge themselves."[2]

Before entering academia and writing Straight News, Alwood had a long career in journalism and public relations, including working as a CNN correspondent in Washington, D.C., and reporting for television stations in Virginia, Florida, and Washington, D.C.

Alwood, who is gay, had had a frontline view of the gay rights movement from the pre-1974 era, when homosexuality was classified as a mental illness, to the first gay march in Washington, D.C., in 1979 to the current movement.

As late as 1964, the New York Times was reporting on a newly released study by the respected New York Academy of Medicine that declared homosexuality "an 'illness' that can be treated successfully in 'some cases' but is more easily dealt with by early preventive measures."[3] Alwood finished college in 1972, when "gays were still 'mental cases,'" he said. "I wasn't out at work, whatever 'out' is. How are you out at work? Bring in a banner? Oh, I didn't have any boyfriends' pictures at my desk."

Being gay sometimes left Alwood feeling vulnerable on the job, but it also occasionally helped him find and air a story. Riding in a van with his television crew sometime in the early eighties he heard chatter on the police scanner about a three-alarm fire in Washington, D.C. "I'd never been to the gay porno movie theater, but I knew where it was," Alwood said. "In that day the gay movie theater would advertise the movie it was showing in the Washington Post.

"I heard the address and I looked at the Washington Post, and I thought, 'That's the gay movie theater!'" he said. "Then I thought, 'Well, how do I handle this?'" Alwood laughed at the memory, but his story also was proving Loren's point about the presence of out gays on a reporting staff making a newsroom "better able to report their full community."

Alwood picked up the tale: "So, I made up this convenient story, and I got on the walkie-talkie, two-way radio, and I said, 'Listen, we were riding along here and I heard this police thing, and I just happened to be reading the Washington Post and just happened to notice that the address of the fire is this gay movie theater.' And they went, 'Oh, really?' and I said, 'Yeah, I think we need to go there.'"

It turned out to be a big story: several people died in the fire.

From Quinnipiac, we headed north on Interstate 91 for about thirty miles to Hartford, Connecticut's capital, America's insurance center, and Mark Twain's home for longer than any other place, from 1871 to 1891.

For us, Hartford provided a tale of two cities. Twain's mansion on Farmington Avenue represented the elegant, affluent Hartford of old. The Twain biographer Justin Kaplan dubbed Twain's burnt-orange gothic behemoth "part steamboat, part medieval stronghold, and part cuckoo clock."[4]

But Hartford now ranked as the nation's second-poorest city. Its modest population growth relied on immigrants who were arriving from Asia, the Balkans, Central America, and the Caribbean. Its population of about 125,000 in the 2010 census was 43.4 percent Hispanic or Latinx, 38.7 percent African American, and 15.8 percent white not of Hispanic or Latinx background.

Andrew Walsh, associate director of Trinity College's Greenberg Center, which studies the role of religion in public life, took Alyssa, Dan, and me on an afternoon-long tour of Hartford's neighborhoods that ended at the El Mercado Marketplace on Park Avenue. There, Walsh told us Hartford's future depended on the contribution and economic impact of immigrants and the education of their children. "If we succeed in raising educational levels, Hartford will continue to do very well," he said. "If we don't, Hartford will have real troubles."

———

Muslim immigrants were generally better educated and more affluent than other local immigrant populations. But many Americans viewed Muslims' religion, Islam, as an anti-Christian faith—fraudulent, destructive, and evil. In *Innocents Abroad*, Mark Twain portrayed Muslim leaders as child-eating, bloodthirsty savages, on a par with American Indians, whom Twain also denounced as subhuman: "The Koran does not permit Mohammedans to drink. Their natural instincts do not permit them to be moral."

That perception of Muslims and of Islam was reinforced by the coordinated terrorist attacks on New York's World Trade Center, the Pentagon, and the planned attack on Washington, D.C., of September 11, 2001. Many Americans chose to dismiss Islam, a fast-growing major religion with 1.6 billion followers, as a fringe faith inspiring mass-murdering terrorists.[5] Dan, Alyssa, and I talked about this with Ingrid Mattson, whom the *New York Times* labeled "perhaps the most noticed figure among American Muslim women."[6]

Ingrid Mattson

Mattson directed Hartford Seminary's Macdonald Center for the Study of Islam and Christian-Muslim Relations (in July 2012 she would become the London and Windsor Community Chair in Islamic Studies, Huron University College, at the University of Western Ontario, London, Canada). She also was the first woman, the first nonimmigrant, and the first Muslim convert to head the Islamic Society of North America.

Mattson grew up as the sixth of seven children of Roman Catholic parents in Kitchener, Canada. Her father had a Norwegian-Irish background, her mother a German-English background. Mattson attended a Catholic girls high school but stopped going to Mass at sixteen—"a precocious unbeliever I was"—and identified as an agnostic. She enrolled at the nearby University of Waterloo, focusing on philosophy and fine arts.

In the summer of 1986, after her junior year, she studied in Paris and met Muslims for the first time. The Muslim students from Senegal and other West African nations had, she said, "a dignity and a generosity of spirit that really impressed me and opened my heart." She started reading the Qur'an. "It was through the Qur'an that I regained my faith in God," she said. She converted to Islam a year later.

After college, she volunteered to teach Afghan women in a Peshawar, Pakistan, refugee camp that exposed her to the broader Muslim world. There, she met and married Amer Aaetek, an Egyptian engineer who was installing a water system at the camp.

She enrolled at the University of Chicago in 1989 and earned her doctoral degree in Islamic studies a decade later. She began to think about what it meant to be a Muslim in America.

She offered an answer that drew on the Qur'an and the philosophy of the Indigenous peoples of Canada. The Qur'an emphasizes avoiding excess or extravagance. Natural resources should be used sparingly, to serve the larger community of people, plants, and animals. The community of faithful North American Muslims should be ethical, productive, and healthy.

Mattson stressed the importance of educating North Americans to treat Muslims as individuals and to recognize that Islam is not anti-Western or antimodernity. The few immigrant Islamists who saw U.S. culture and commercialism as the height of secular hedonism might resist integration into American society. To them, Mattson writes, "America can be defined only in absolute negative terms."[7]

But the vast majority of America's five to eight million Muslims—a quarter of whom are African Americans—integrated themselves into U.S. culture. Some adopted Anglicized names, married non-Muslims, and thoroughly assimilated. Others proudly held on to distinctive Muslim names, dress, and traditions, still pursuing the American dream. They saw the United States by and large as a multicultural democracy that, while often flawed, valued law and liberty, including religious freedom.

Mattson struck me as a fan of those values—as a modern Muslim woman who was as progressive as a Muslim woman can be and still show respect for traditional aspects of Islam's culture. She sided with the majority of Muslims who felt that the imam, the officiating priest of a mosque, should be a male if called on to lead prayer for a congregation of men and women. But she kept her surname when she married. She mowed the family's lawn while her husband served as primary family cook. She shared equally with her husband in raising their daughter, Soumayya, and son, Ubayda.

American Muslims, Mattson said, have had an unfair burden placed on them since 9/11: they are expected to eradicate radical Muslim terrorists and their sympathizers. "We would love to, but we are not in control of those people," Mattson said. She explained that Islam does not have a hierarchical structure. Muslims lack the equivalent of a pope. Neither the Islamic Society of North America nor the local mosque has the power to dictate the beliefs and behavior of its members.

American Muslims feel as threatened as other Americans by cultlike terrorists who pursue "a revolutionary fantasy in religious guise," Mattson said. At the same time, she said, American Muslims object to the U.S. government's "surveillance state" tactics in the name of protecting Americans from terrorists. In a 2010 meeting with John O. Brennan, then deputy national security adviser for homeland security and counterterrorism, Mattson called on the U.S. government to live by the rule of law it claims to be defending.

She criticized government raids on Muslim immigrant neighborhoods, the naming of American citizens as enemy combatants, and other post-9/11 government tactics. In 2010, the United States ended a policy of subjecting passengers from fourteen countries, most of them Muslim, to special scrutiny at airports. Donald Trump, however, called for a "total and complete shutdown" of Muslims entering the United States. As president, he tried to block visitors from select Muslim countries. Mattson could empathize with those visitors. She had endured "countless hours," she said, stuck in Toronto immigration offices on her way to the United States.

Mattson strived to demonstrate that the clash of civilizations—the West versus all the rest—was not inevitable, as some analysts insisted.[8] She encouraged interfaith dialogues by pairing synagogues and mosques and reaching out to evangelical Christians. She opposed violence and discrimination against Muslim women, including criticism of them for wearing full veils.

She wore a hijab, a headscarf, and covered all but her hands and face. She viewed wearing it not as an act of subjugation or repression but as a form of equality and empowerment that helped free her from being judged on her appearance and exposed to unwelcome male advances. Dan Tham later talked to me about his post-9/11 "prejudicial notion that veiled women were veiling secrets and weren't forthcoming." It was a revelation, he said, to meet Mattson, "so mirthful and blunt and the total opposite of my stereotype: open and candid."

Being a Canadian in the United States may have helped her as vice president (2001–6) and president (2006–10) of the Islamic Society of North America, an umbrella organization of three hundred affiliates and an estimated twenty thousand Muslims, three-fourths of whom had immigrated to America. She laughed as she described a Red Rover–style game she played as a child growing up in Canada. She and her elementary school classmates locked arms, raced in giant strides across the playground toward the opposing team, and shouted: "Heh, heh, get out of my way, I just got back from the

USA." She thought the words helped convey the Canadian perspective on the United States as a "big, pushy, imposing presence on our border."

But many Americans, however big and imposing, see Muslims as threatening. A Gallup poll the year before our trip reported 43 percent of Americans "admit to feeling at least 'a little' prejudice toward Muslims."[9] Stereotyping, employment discrimination, and hate crimes targeted Muslims, especially younger Muslims. Counselors told Mattson of a dramatic rise among younger Muslims of depression, anxiety, and other indicators of stress. "They have to prove themselves, that they are not violent," Mattson said.

By 2014 the task appeared to be getting more difficult. The Sunni militant group known as the Islamic State of Iraq and Syria (ISIS) and other terrorist groups abroad were attracting foreign fighters on an "unprecedented scale," a United Nations report concluded. The report said domestic terrorism could rise as the fighters from more than eighty nations returned to their home countries.[10] Mattson stressed that "these horrible people are terrorizing everyone. I think it is most important for Americans to understand that more Muslims—including Sunni Muslims—have been killed by ISIS than non-Muslims. Muslims are like other people in that we have our good guys and our bad guys. Don't judge Muslim people by the worst of them."

As his fortieth birthday approached, Mark Twain joined his walking buddy, Rev. Joe Twichell, on a hundred-mile hike from Hartford to Boston. They walked thirty-five miles to North Ashford, Connecticut, before Twain's aching knees and the subzero weather led them to jump on the next train for Boston.

I wished they had managed to walk seventeen miles beyond North Ashford to stop in Southbridge, Massachusetts, where I put out the *Evening News* from 1969 to 1995. Twain, who worked for several small-town newspapers, understood the satisfaction derived from reporting in a town the size of Southbridge: "There you can know your man inside and out—in a city you but know his crust and his crust is usually a lie."

Inspired by William Allen White, the Pulitzer Prize–winning owner of the four-thousand-circulation *Emporia (Kansas) Gazette*, I had bought the struggling fifty-seven-hundred-circulation *Evening News* when I was twenty-eight. I dreamed of becoming a progressive, politically independent version of White, writing fire-breathing editorials and putting out the best small-town paper in America.[11]

I was no William Allen White. But I, like White, served as president of the American Society of Newspaper Editors (1989–90). In that role, I sought to overcome the underrepresentation in newsrooms of women, people of color (more than one-third of dailies' newsrooms were all white), and those whose sexual orientation or gender expression made them outliers.

Gwyneth Mellinger, the historian of ASNE's diversity efforts, writes that other hiring advocates may have matched my "passion for social justice, but none was as evangelical or uncompromising in commitment to the cause." In the "Ghiglione era," Mellinger continues, "support for racial diversity had become a social and professional expectation. The hiring initiative had finally gained legitimacy, if not universal support, within ASNE." But did the initiative make a difference?

Mellinger concluded that newspaper and corporate hiring efforts "were more intense because of the pressure that ASNE brought to bear." ASNE failed, however, to overcome "the institutionalized and exclusionary professional norms that constructed segregated newsrooms to begin with," Mellinger added.[12]

She was right. In 2015, ASNE reported a stagnant decade in which the percentage of journalists of color declined to 12.76 percent; "our industry isn't making progress," said Karen Magnuson, editor of the *Rochester (N.Y.) Democrat and Chronicle* and cochair of the ASNE Diversifying the News Committee.[13]

It was easier for me to have an impact in Southbridge, a town that a Black newsroom intern labeled Whitesville. By recruiting aggressively, I was able to achieve a newsroom staff by the mid-1980s that was 40 percent reporters and editors of color. When Alyssa, Dan, and I returned to Southbridge in 2011, however, the staff was again all white.

The town was quite different too. Once home to American Optical, the world's largest eyewear manufacturer, Southbridge showed the effects of American Optical's decision in the mid-1980s to move its manufacturing operation to Mexico.

Two videos I found on YouTube portrayed Southbridge as a poor town of loonies and losers. Rod Murphy's documentary, *Greater Southbridge* (2003), made Jerry Sciesniewski, a stuttering collector of empty soda and beer cans, into a symbol of the community. Jordan Forget titled his video *10 Reasons That Southbridge Sucks*. Forget complained that Friendly's was one of the few restaurants in town and criticized the town's schools.

But the fates had a worse future in store for Southbridge than the 2011 state of affairs that roused Forget's ire. Friendly's soon closed. Its building was razed. The state placed the town's schools in receivership in 2016, after they were declared "chronically underperforming." And environmental groups sued the town and the local landfill and its owner for groundwater contamination. Four days later, Casella Waste Systems announced it would close its fifty-one-acre regional landfill by December 31, 2018.

The Southbridge during my time at the *Evening News* was a hardworking, blue-collar town, independent (51 percent of voters were unaffiliated), religious, patriotic, and patriarchal. Women were largely invisible in the leadership of local organizations and businesses. When the League of Women Voters changed its by-laws in 1974 to admit men, I became its lone male member and, as an experiment to increase the visibility of women, invited them to put out a special issue of the *Evening News*.[14] The women offered their perspectives in editorials, sports columns, and news analyses.

But the employment of women journalists in leadership positions did not change dramatically at the *Evening News*, I confess, until the mid-1970s. I promoted Linda Megathlin, a 1973 graduate of Smith College, from women's editor to news editor to managing editor. She was twenty-five when she became the paper's executive editor. She was more than qualified to be a member of the American Society of Newspaper Editors. But many ASNE members wanted to keep the society "a male country club," said Jean S. Taylor, associate editor of the *Los Angeles Times* and reportedly the first woman ever (in 1974) on the *Times*'s masthead.[15]

In 1964, Robert Atwood of the *Anchorage Daily Times*, who was an ASNE member, had dismissed women employees as unpredictably charming or snarling: "They are always in one of four stages: premenstrual, menstrual, post-menstrual, or pregnant. We call it 'moon phases.'" As late as 1973, ASNE had only seven female members in a membership of 749.[16]

Most women editors worked for papers the size of the *Evening News*, but an ASNE constitutional amendment in 1974, designed to increase the number of women members, applied only to papers with circulations greater than twenty thousand. With Megathlin in mind, I lobbied ASNE's membership committee to extend the amendment to smaller papers as well. Eventually, ASNE relented and elected Megathlin a member in 1976.

Forty-two years after I first arrived in Southbridge, I fondly recalled the vitality of the town's diverse ethnic communities in 1969. Half a block from Friendly's had stood Edwards, a Main Street department store that dated from 1844. On the evening of American Optical's payday, the store would be flooded with French-speaking Canadian immigrants. I loved to hear the conversations in French and the many other languages spoken on the street.

Each ethnic group, it seemed, had its own church and club. The Poles prayed at St. Hedwig's and drank at the Pilsudski Polish-American Club. The Italians worshiped at St. Mary's and raised a glass at the Italian American Club.

In 1969, shortly before I bought the *Evening News*, Frank McNitt, the owner, allowed me to learn about the paper and community by working as his assistant. Before retiring to my $18-a-week boardinghouse room, I often ate dinner at Mario's, a tiny Main Street restaurant.

Because he was feeling sorry for an *Evening News* novice who clearly knew nothing about Southbridge, Mario Piccione, the restaurant's owner, insisted on buying me dinner during my first week in town. When he later read I had become the paper's owner, he sent me a small celebratory orange tree, an act of kindness I will never forget.

So I wanted to see Piccione during my return to Southbridge. Ron Tremblay, Jean Ashton, and Mark Ashton, managers crucial to the success of the *Evening News* during my time there, joined Dan, Alyssa, and me for lunch at Mario's, which had moved to Central Street.

We swapped stories. Some stories I was willing to forget: about the time I challenged the sports editor to a mile race and wound up losing, my knees full of cinders; about my self-indulgent 106-part editorial series on nuclear arms issues; about my equally self-indulgent photo-filled editorial on the Lamaze-style birth of our first daughter, in which I used the royal *we*, as if Jessica were coming out of my womb as well as Nancy's.

Each local ethnic group, I learned soon after joining the *Evening News*, contributed to the community in its own way. Piccione showed us a 1991 plaque that celebrated the hundredth anniversary of the arrival in Southbridge of the first Italian immigrants. The plaque applauded the "thrifty, hardworking people who quickly learned the English language and contributed to this community as masons, contractors, craftsmen, and industrialists."

Piccione told us how Italian pick-and-shovel workers, paid fifty cents a day, rid themselves of an Irish crew boss who urinated on them. The Italian-speaking crew insisted the Irish boss had to go: "Italian crew, Italian boss." Piccione also recalled his father's burial in St. Mary's Cemetery, which in its early days served a heavily Irish congregation: "The Irish were buried in the front, the Italians in the back. Even the crosses [in the back] were really small."

Only one other customer entered Mario's during our lunch there, a reflection of how difficult it was for businesses to survive in Southbridge. Across the street from Mario's, the Ink-Toxicating Tattoos parlor occupied space once held by a high-end retailer, as did Clockwork Tattoo on Main Street. On one prime Main Street block that had been occupied by top-quality clothing stores—Tot to Teen, Tiger's Den, and Goodwin's—many storefronts stood vacant. One storefront was an evangelical church, Iglesia Evangelica Sanando al Herido, a reminder that the town was now 26 percent Hispanic.

Soon the *Evening News*, the daily I had spent more than a quarter-century trying to strengthen, would be forced to retreat to weekly publication. Mark Ashton, who was at that lunch, would die. The downtown of Southbridge—the town I loved, the town where my children were born, the town where I once planned to live my entire life—would look more and more like a ghost town.

CHAPTER 9

Boston

Pot, Harvard, and Women's Experience on the Road

After an exhausting month on the road, Alyssa, Dan, and I drove the sixty miles east from Southbridge for a day of recovery in Boston. Mark Twain said a visitor "feels more tranquility and satisfactorily at home in it in three hours than he could in New York in as many years."

But generations of people of color have felt less tranquility and less at home in Boston than in other U.S. cities. Dan, Alyssa, and I vowed to interview Boston-area experts who could address racial discrimination nationally as well as locally. Supposedly liberal, Boston best represented all the racist northern cities that resisted desegregation as fiercely as the most redneck of southern cities. Even Boston's founding reeked of racism. The Massachusetts Bay Colony "made room for what is now Boston by setting the palisaded village of the Pequot Indians on fire in 1637 and killing the men, women and children when they tried to flee."[1]

A 2017 *Boston Globe* Spotlight Team report on the city's racism began: "Google the phrase 'Most racist city,' and Boston pops up more than any other place."[2] The Spotlight Team focused on the structural inequalities that have existed in Boston for generations. Surveys in 1983 and in 2017 found the unemployment rate about twice as high for Blacks as whites; in 1983, 4.5 percent of Black workers were officials or managers; in 2017, 4.6 percent were.[3]

Boston's white households had a median wealth of $247,000, its Black households a median wealth of "close to zero," according to a 2015 report by the Federal Reserve of Boston.[4] The city's wealth inequality was part of a national problem. The Federal Reserve study reported that even Blacks who had moved into the upper half of American incomes would see 60 percent of their children fall into the lower half as adults. If those trends continued, the Fed's study concluded, "black Americans would make no further relative progress."[5]

But before Dan, Alyssa, and I embarked on our interviews, our highest priority was rest. Dan and Alyssa (who described Boston as "my rock bottom of the trip") met friends in the Boston Common and Public Gardens. They "sat on a bench and got high, which, apparently is no longer a criminal offense in Massachusetts," Alyssa wrote in her diary.

Alyssa, who rarely smoked marijuana, "got too high, and not in an enjoyable way." At that moment Alyssa could have been a character in Kerouac's *On the Road* or other road-trip narratives where misogynistic males abandon themselves to drugs, booze, and sex. I wondered what was different about how Alyssa and other women experience the road than how men experience it.

Scholars suggest women road-trippers focus more on relationships and roots than on individualism, power, and other goals of male travelers. The way Alyssa thought about our trip paralleled how Simone de Beauvoir, the adventurous philosopher-rebel, reveled in a four-month trip across America in 1947. Beauvoir devoted much of her subsequent book to waxing philosophical. Just as Alyssa would end our trip with a "deep, deep love for America," so Beauvoir would "feel such a dizzying attraction for America, where the memory of the pioneers is still recent and palpable, because it seems to be the realm of transcendence; compressed in time, magnificently expanded through space, its history is the creation of a world."[6]

The interview Alyssa, Dan, and I had with Henry Louis "Skip" Gates Jr., director of Harvard's W. E. B. Du Bois Institute for African and African American Research, provided another example of how Alyssa was experiencing our road trip differently than I was. My email request to Gates for an interview had gone unanswered. The reporter in me refused to assume no answer was a no. Dan, Alyssa, and I visited Gates's Harvard office on a Monday morning.

A Du Bois Institute receptionist seemed intrigued by our trip. She said we were in luck. Professor Gates had his weekly student visiting hour from 1:00 to 2:00 p.m. that day. The three of us departed for a quick lunch, returning before 1:00 p.m. We were second in line. When our time came, Gates invited us into his office and, before learning the purpose of our visit, greeted us warmly and then said, Alyssa recalled, "And one of you is pretty."

Later, when Alyssa and I discussed Gates, I did not remember that comment. Perhaps my ears, plugged with hearing aids, missed it. Perhaps I chose at the time to ignore the comment as meaningless flattery, similar to the greeting by restaurant servers and other women I don't know who call me Honey or Sweetie. Perhaps women or millennials are more attuned to sexist comments than I or men of my generation.

At any rate, Gates told us he wanted to speak first with all his waiting students. He encouraged us to leave our video equipment in his office (we were posting videos on our Traveling with Twain website) until our turn came. When we returned to his office to interview him, he explained his desire to control who video-interviewed him—he had many requests—and questioned the ethics of how we wound up in his office (his visiting hour, he said, was intended only for his students). He said he planned to reprimand the receptionist who informed us of his student visiting hour.

Gates agreed to answer three questions on camera. His answer to one question stayed with me. Since the Reverend Martin Luther King's assassination in 1968, two distinct socioeconomic classes of African Americans had developed, Gates said: "On the one hand, it's the best of times for a segment of the African American community; on the other hand, it's the worst of times."

Gates said the African American poor have an infant mortality rate higher than that during King's time (today Black mothers and babies die at more than twice the rate of white mothers and babies in the United States).[7] But the Black middle class has grown: "Two distinct classes, one with what my mother used to call white money, as opposed to colored money, and the other, mired in poverty, and both self-perpetuating. It will take drastic intervention from the federal government and private enterprise, on the one hand, and within the African American community through individual will, on the other hand, to transform this."

Gates was not optimistic. "We need, within the community, a second civil rights movement, about moral and individual responsibility," he said. "I don't see that on the horizon. So I'm very pessimistic about massive social change affecting poor people and/or African Americans in our lifetime. I wish that I were wrong, and I hope that I am wrong."

As we left, Alyssa recalled, Gates commented on my having "such an attractive team." Alyssa said Gates's comments about physical appearance certainly were not "terribly offensive. I suppose I was just disappointed that he wasn't more professional. Comments about our appearance didn't seem necessary in that setting."

Alyssa said women in journalism still struggle to be taken seriously. "In two out of three newsrooms I've interned in, I've had to deal with married male editors' becoming *too* friendly, whether they were hanging around my desk frequently or inviting me out for one-on-one drinks," she said. Sometimes male colleagues would grumble that she had gotten plum assignments from male editors or better access to a male source only "because you're a girl." She wondered if that was true. A married editor once pressured her to attend a group outing. When she arrived, he was sitting at the bar waiting for her. Alone.

"I remember one of the first stories I ever reported for the *Pittsburgh Tribune-Review*," Alyssa continued. "As I was talking to the county commissioner, another reporter approached and politely asked if he could also get a few quotes. The commissioner replied to the male reporter, 'Of course—I was just hitting on her!' and let out a big laugh."

In the crowded, closet-sized office of the Massachusetts Transgender Political Coalition, Alyssa, Dan, and I met with Gunner Scott, who tutored us on the treatment of transgender women, especially those of color. Alyssa wrote:

> *Thirty-four-year-old Rita Hester was brutally murdered in Allston, Massachusetts, on November 28, 1998.*
>
> *Her death rippled through her family, social circle, and community. In a video commemorating Hester, a woman's voice chokes out, ringing with the pain of losing a loved one, "It's such a great loss to me, I can't even hardly explain it."*
>
> *But Hester, a transgender woman, was just one of many people murdered worldwide that year—and every year—because of her gender identity.*
>
> *Hester's murder still resonated with Gunner Scott, a transgender political activist, more than a decade later. Scott, a stocky man with short hair and a trace of a beard, directed the Massachusetts Transgender Political Coalition, which aimed to use political channels to end discrimination against the transgender population. In 2013, he became director of programs at the Pride Foundation in Seattle.*
>
> *Scott met Hester briefly once, outside a twenty-four-hour convenience store. His roommate introduced them. He remembered her smile and long braids. Hester, who was involved in the music community, was talking about her band. A few weeks later, someone stabbed her to death.*
>
> *Hester's murder, which remains unsolved, deeply affected Scott, not only because he had known her but also because the coverage of her murder was*

Gunner Scott

so unjust. Although she was the victim of the crime, Hester became the target of unfavorable media coverage because she was a transgender woman. Scott began to understand the magnitude of violence against the transgender community.

"When I'm at a conference or I'm in a space with a lot of trans people, particularly trans women of color, I cherish that time with them even more so, because there have been instances where I've been in that space, and I will hear six months later that one of those folks has been murdered. And it's something I keep in the back of my mind," Scott said.

Scott's reaction helped to fuel his activist work. Hester's murder also energized the transgender community in Boston and beyond.

"The mood in the community was one of great frustration, I think," said Nancy Nangeroni, activist and chair emeritus of the Massachusetts Transgender Political Coalition. Three years before Hester was killed, another woman of color from Boston's transgender community, Chanelle Pickett, twenty-three, was viciously beaten and found dead in William Palmer's apartment in Watertown, after he had picked her up at the Playland Café.

"Palmer's defense was that he thought Pickett was a woman and that when he discovered otherwise, Pickett went into a rage and attacked him," the Boston Globe *reported. Pickett's friends, however, noted that Palmer had*

frequented the Playland Café, known to be a popular transgender hangout. They doubted Palmer's defense.

Palmer was convicted of assault and battery. He received two years of prison time.

At the sentencing, Pickett's twin sister, Gabrielle, also transgender, said, "I don't think it is fair that someone should lose their life and assault and battery is the verdict. I don't think it is fair that the state of Massachusetts wants to push [the victim] aside and not treat her like a human being."

Nangeroni, a transgender woman, said, "The transgender community was very unhappy because that was a gross injustice. So, when the Rita Hester murder happened, and when the transgender community was joined by the local rock 'n' roll community from Allston, there was just a lot of upset and frustration, and sort of a very strong call for change."

Hester's death spawned a candlelight vigil and a web project titled Remembering Our Dead. A San Francisco candlelight vigil followed in November of the next year. Transgender Day of Remembrance, memorializing Hester and all other victims of gender violence, is now recognized internationally each year on November 20.

Activists like Scott and Nangeroni were struck by what they consider repeated disrespect toward trans people from the media.[8] Hester was murdered a little more than a month after Matthew Shepard, the victim of an antigay hate crime. Two men tied Shepard to a split-rail fence, assaulted him, and left him for dead in Wyoming. Scott contrasted the respectful national media coverage of Shepard and that given to Hester. Outlets like the Boston Globe referred to Hester as "he" and questioned her "apparent double life."[9] They used her male name, even though she had identified as female for a decade.

"She was a person," Scott said. "And she had a community that loved her. She had been very integral in the music community and the drag community and the trans community and the gay community. To reduce her to calling her a 'she male' or other really horrible things, and treating her death like it was her own fault," is unfair.

Nangeroni said, "It's like being insulted to your face in your own home, I guess, to read that kind of slander and gross mischaracterization in the media." In 2008, Nangeroni wrote a letter to the Boston Herald after it published an article about a police operation and an undercover detective who had been "trapped inside houses of ill repute by giant naked trannies."[10]

"Of course, I'm older now and nearing retirement, and my life is pretty good and pretty stable, and so I personally don't have to fear anymore,"

Nangeroni said. "But people who are not just gender different but also are nonwhite, nonmale in this culture suffer multiple oppressions, and the oppressions don't just add, they multiply. A person who is of color and poor and trans is much more at risk. And these are the people I fear for."

When we first approached Scott about an interview, he was hesitant. Part of Scott's job was to be an advocate, but even he had reservations about having his image appear on our website. One reason was the frequent bungling of transgender issues, he said, but also he believed having his name and image easily accessible opened him up to threats and even violence from Internet trolls.

Media relations have definitely improved, he said, but there's still a long way to go. "I think the media has tokenized a few of us that are presentable and passable and are celebrities," Scott said, citing the actress Laverne Cox and the writer Janet Mock, among others.

"But for poor trans women of color, particularly [those] who don't pass well and who aren't English speaking, the media is still really terrible," Scott said. "The assumptions that they, particularly young Black women, young Black trans women, and young Latina trans [women] are sex workers, that's the first assumption about them. I think that, still, the issue around racism and how folks of color are talked about in the media becomes glaringly apparent when it comes to trans people."

Nangeroni wanted people to understand that gender is a language, a way to communicate, and people should be able to freely express their gender without recrimination. Until then, Transgender Day of Remembrance will continue as a reminder of injustice, not as a celebration, she said.

"The world gets changed when we remember the injustices that have been committed," Nangeroni said, "and when we renew our commitment to do something about it."

We could not leave Boston without somehow addressing its status as an educational capital of the world. Metropolitan Boston contains more than fifty institutions of higher education. Mark Twain, who quit school at twelve, regarded such institutions with distrust. "I never let my schooling interfere with my education," he is attributed to have said. Yet I could imagine the seventy-two-year-old Twain, upon the opening in 1908 of Harvard Business School, the first school to offer a master's degree in business administration, saying that finally a school had been invented for him. He saw himself as an entrepreneur.

But his many get-rich inventions did not make him rich. His book publishing company failed. He invested disastrously. The Paige Compositor, intended to automate the tedious typesetting job he had performed as a teenager, cost him $6 million in today's dollars.[11] During a 1901 banquet of business leaders, the sixty-five-year-old Twain admitted he had not "turned out the great businessman that I thought I was when I began life. But I am comparatively young yet, and may learn."

To William J. Ghiglione, my Depression-era dad, however, Harvard Business School represented an opportunity for what one writer called "a golden passport to the good life."[12] His first-generation parents had not attended college. Both worked, she as a nurse, he as manager of A. F. Ghiglione & Sons, the small Seattle family pasta company that soon would go out of business.

Dad knew he needed to create his own opportunity. He studied economics and business at the University of Washington, graduating in 1935. Then he borrowed $1,210 from his father and worked eighty-four-hour weeks that summer unloading boxcars and barges for American Can Company so that he could attend Harvard Business.

Three-quarters of a century after Dad's graduation from Harvard Business, I was curious about the current student body at one of the world's most elite—some say elitist—business schools. My father's all-male class of '37 included only three international students of color—two from China and one from the Dominican Republic—and no African Americans. Lillian Lincoln Lambert, '69, the first African American woman to attend Harvard Business (although she was not allowed to live there), recalls being "one of thirty-five women, and one of nine blacks in a student body of approximately sixteen hundred. I can't say I faced overt racism or sexism—it was more a feeling of being invisible." She adds, "There were no black or female faculty."[13]

I requested an interview with Deidre Leopold, fifty-nine, who directed Harvard Business's admissions and financial aid office. Months later, I obtained a twenty-minute appointment (that number was "hard," I was warned) to interview Leopold in her cramped office, which featured a "Keep Calm and Carry On" wall poster. Admissions numbers covered portable whiteboards.

The base of one whiteboard displayed a postcard to Leopold from a member of the admissions staff. It reproduced Alex Katz's painting of Anna Wintour, the demanding editor-in-chief of *Vogue* whose assistants had dubbed her "Nuclear Wintour." University admissions consultants similarly portrayed Leopold, a 1980 graduate of Harvard Business, as hard-nosed and haughty ("Her Royal Highness"). I remembered the reaction of the journalist David Carr to coverage of Wintour: "Powerful women . . . always get inspected more thoroughly than their male counterparts."[14]

The year of my father's graduation, five women had arrived at Radcliffe College to begin a one-year, certificate-granting personnel program.[15] More than a generation later, in fall 1963, eight women were allowed to enroll in Harvard Business's MBA program as fully matriculated students. Women accounted for 42 percent of the Harvard Business class of 2019.

Other kinds of diversity—socioeconomic status, class, ethnicity, and religion—were harder to compare. In the 1930s, when Harvard and other universities discriminated against students and faculty on the basis of religion and ethnicity, Harvard Business asked applicants to provide their "extraction" and religion (a request that ended in 1947). My father listed Italian and Episcopalian (family lore said he converted to Catholicism while at Harvard).

The school already knew his economic status because he had to apply for a $150 loan—at a time when tuition cost $600—to cover his second-year expenses of $1,720. For the class of 2019, tuition stood at $72,000 and annual expenses totaled $106,800; 50 percent of the 928 enrolled students were eligible for need-based fellowships. But many students were from the moneyed class—graduates of elite private institutions who had worked for prestigious businesses around the world. The *New York Times* reported in 2013 on Section X at Harvard Business, an "on-again-off-again secret society of ultrawealthy, mostly male, mostly international students known for decadent parties and travel."[16]

Harvard Business, however, appeared far more welcoming to a wider range of students in the twenty-first century than in 1937. Leopold pointed to student organizations for African Americans, women, and gay, lesbian, bisexual, and transgender students.

But Duff McDonald, who wrote a 2018 history of Harvard Business, thought that diversity has failed to overcome troubling realities at the school—for example, its faculty's "ingrained sexism" and the corrosion of the school's educational mission. The corrosion, McDonald charged, led to a focus on maximizing corporate profits, not on the needs of society. With the election of Donald Trump, the move toward emphasizing corporate interests was, McDonald concluded, complete.[17]

Students at Harvard and other business schools, however, were encouraging the introduction of courses that deal with sexual harassment, gay rights, and other issues of ethics and values. Prominent schools, including Harvard, were starting groups called Manbassadors, "for men committed to gender equity in business."[18]

Leopold emphasized that Harvard Business stressed not only inclusion but also internationalization. Thirty-five percent of students were international, up from 13 percent in 1985. Leopold said she would like each class of nine hundred to include "all that sort of difference in the room"—engaged citizens of the world, technology-savvy thought leaders, and risk-taking entrepreneurs. "I'm a big fan of quirky," she said. Maybe even Mark Twain would be admitted today.

CHAPTER 10

Philadelphia

Then and Now, In and Out of the College Closet

After Boston, we began a three-week, two-thousand-mile drive through Philadelphia, Washington, D.C., Pittsburgh, and Cincinnati into the South. Our path roughly followed that of Mark Twain in his twenties. In April 1857, after knocking about New York, Philadelphia, and other cities as an itinerant typesetter-journalist, he met Horace Bixby, a steamboat pilot. Bixby took Twain on as an apprentice pilot. Until the outbreak of the Civil War in 1861, Twain was a steamboat pilot on the Mississippi River, between New Orleans and St. Louis.

The South was bound together by ultraconservative politics, fundamentalist Christianity, a distrust of government regulation, and what the writer D. H. Lawrence called "the myth of the essential white America."[1] Before we headed south, I hoped we could interview Isabel Wilkerson, a Boston University professor who had written *The Warmth of Other Suns: The Epic Story of America's Great Migration*. The book describes the flight of six million African Americans from the caste system of the South to the cities of the North and West. The book also connects two of our trip's key topics, race and immigration; it compares African Americans' flight northward and westward to the crossing of the Atlantic by Italians, Swedes, and other European immigrants to reach a new world, America. African Americans moved from their old country—a South of salt pork, superstition, and segregation—to their new world, cities such as Chicago, New York, and Los Angeles.

But I was unable to catch up with the fifty-one-year-old Wilkerson until a year after our trip, when I met her at the 2012 convention in New Orleans of the National Association of Black Journalists. She told a standing-room-only audience that the subject of the Great Migration had "called to me." Raised in Washington, D.C., by her Georgia-born mother and Virginia-born father, Wilkerson felt connected to the South of her parents and grandparents.

But she sought to tell more than the story of her family. "This is everyone's story," she said. Many there agreed. Betty Baye, sixty-six, a journalist and adjunct lecturer at Bellarmine University in Louisville, Kentucky, told me how her parents moved to New York in the early 1940s, her mother from Union Bridge, Maryland, and her father from the Richmond, Virginia, area. "They never moved back," she said. "My father said, 'Don't even take my body back.'"

Baye appreciated Wilkerson's accounts of Miles Davis, John Coltrane, and other talented African Americans who moved north and west at a young age to become the advance guard of American culture and, in some cases, of the civil rights movement. "Otherwise they might have been cotton pickers," Baye said. "It's amazing."

Ava Thompson Greenwell, fifty, told me about her parents from Yazoo City, Mississippi, and Henderson, Kentucky, who came to Chicago in their teens and twenties. She especially enjoyed Wilkerson's description of the life of Ida Mae Gladney, a Mississippi sharecropper who headed north, eventually to Chicago, in the late 1930s. Gladney's descendants in the North included bus drivers, secretaries, government workers, teachers, administrators, a bank teller, and a lawyer.

Greenwell, a colleague on the journalism faculty at Northwestern University, admired the thoroughness of Wilkerson's research—the hundreds of hours of interviews of more than a thousand people and Wilkerson's recountings of subjects' trips north and west.

Accompanied by her parents, Wilkerson drove the route from Monroe, Louisiana, to Los Angeles taken by Dr. Robert Foster in 1953. He had driven his Buick Roadmaster through Texas towns and eventually into the desert darkness of Arizona. There, he was unable to find a motel that would rent him a room. After Wilkerson almost fell asleep at the wheel near Yuma, her parents insisted she stop at a hotel for the night, something Foster could not do in 1953.

When Wilkerson met with high school students, they expressed surprise at her description of Jim Crow—the law in Birmingham, Alabama, that made it illegal for whites and Blacks to play checkers together, the requirement of a North Carolina court for separate Bibles for Blacks and whites to swear upon, and the rule throughout the South that a Black motorist must not pass a white motorist, however slowly the white motorist drove.

One high school student told Wilkerson, "Well, I would have honked." Another said, "I would have tailgated." Wilkerson explained: "Acting like a white person" might result in lynching. Every four days on average, Wilkerson said, an African American was lynched.

The young, impoverished participants in the Great Migration did what Lincoln and the Emancipation Proclamation could not do for them. "They freed themselves," Wilkerson said.

She shared the response to her book of a grandmotherly woman from Greece who said she could not discuss the book without crying. "This book is my story," the woman said. Wilkerson made clear, however, that African American migrants from the South not only started on the lowest economic rung but also faced greater discrimination in the labor market than did immigrants. A Black worker in the North and West made a median annual income in 1950 of $1,628, an Italian immigrant made $2,295, and a Polish immigrant $2,419.[2]

Yet Wilkerson emphasized the similarities in the mind-sets of immigrants from abroad and African Americans who moved out of the South. Individuals in both groups experienced the power of making their own decisions about where they would reside and what they would do for a living. And, in acting on their decisions, they not only achieved a personal freedom, they transformed America.

Wilkerson suggested future social change will require the effort of whites and Blacks alike. She quoted a ninety-year-old study by the white-led Chicago Commission on Race Relations that emphasized the responsibility of whites: "Both races need to understand that their rights and duties are mutual and equal and their interests in the common good are identical. . . . An understanding of the facts of the problem—a magnanimous understanding by both races—is the first step toward its solution."[3] "We've come a long way," Wilkerson told her audience, "but we still have a long way to go."

Philadelphia offered Alyssa, Dan, and me a variety of striking symbols, from the well-known Liberty Bell to the little-known plaster casts of historic Siamese twins. The Mütter Museum houses not only collections of abnormal skeletons, tumors, and other human body parts but also extraordinary white plaster casts of Chang and Eng Bunker, the original "Siamese twins," made after their autopsy in 1874. Twain featured them in a fanciful 1869 *Buffalo Express* column and drew on them in part for *The Tragedy of Pudd'nhead Wilson* and *Those Extraordinary Twins*, written in 1893–94.

The satirical *Express* column, "Personal Habits of the Siamese Twins," explored the connection between union and division. During the Civil War, members of the same family sometimes fought on opposing sides. The twins' physical linkage did not prevent conflict. The sedentary Chang endured Eng's fondness for running errands. Chang, the Roman Catholic temperance reformer, became just as drunk as Eng, the whiskey-guzzling Baptist.

While subjected to anti-Asian racism, the Bunkers wiggled through loopholes in U.S. laws, becoming citizens in 1839, even though the 1790 Naturalization Act supposedly applied only to the "free white person." The brothers claimed whiteness, married white women, championed the Confederacy, owned as many as thirty-two slaves, and sent two of the twenty-one children they fathered to fight for the South in the Civil War.[4]

Philadelphia, with the second-largest Italian American population in the United States after New York, was an especially appropriate location to read Twain's farcical *Those Extraordinary Twins*, about "a youthful Italian 'freak'—or 'freaks,'" Luigi and Angelo Cappello, with two heads, four arms, one body, and a single pair of legs.

Angelo—described by Twain as blond, with "a noble face" and "kind blue eyes, and curly copper hair and fresh complexion"—suggests the stereotype of the northern Italians who began settling Philadelphia in colonial times. They came largely from Liguria, a region known for its receptiveness to the progressive thinking of the Italian Enlightenment. They were primarily merchants, entrepreneurs, scientists, scholars, philosophers, artists, and musicians.

Twain's Luigi—a hardy, dark-skinned whiskey drinker and heavy smoker—recalls the stereotype of working-class southern Italians who participated in the mass migrations to Philadelphia that began in the 1870s and 1880s. A historian describes the new arrivals as "less educated and less skilled" and more menacing to other Philadelphians than the earlier northern Italian immigrants.[5]

Twain's story, set in Dawson's Landing, Missouri, plays with the issue of identity. Luigi tells his local hosts: "The truth is, we are no more twins than you are." The story ends with an aldermanic election in Dawson's Landing. Luigi wins the election but "could not sit in the board of aldermen without his brother, and his brother could not sit there because he was not a member." Twain quickly resolves the dilemma by having the citizens of Dawson's Landing hang Luigi.

Twain's story caused me to think about the highly polarized, highly ideological political system—liberal/conservative; Democrat/Republican; blue state/red state; alt-right/left-wing antifa—that encourages the United States to gridlock. Scholars suggest a long list of culprits, including gerrymandering in the redistricting process, one-sided media programming (people consuming only personalized web content with which they agree), and greater participation in the political process by "the most ideologically oriented and politically rancorous Americans."[6]

While the center shrank, Democrats lurched left and Republicans rolled right, with both parties exhibiting increased contempt for each other. Writing in 2012, the Harvard professor David A. Moss called it "politics as war."[7]

Perhaps Twain's Angelo and Luigi offer a life lesson for today's polarized Left and Right. A two-party system, for survival's sake, requires both sides to commit to more than party, ideology, and difference. A democracy may need political parties, however polarized, to cooperate, coordinate, and compromise, like conjoined twins, or die.

While in Philadelphia, I could not resist visiting Bryn Mawr College, my wife's alma mater, and Haverford College, my alma mater, to interview people about identity issues there.

The sight of the late nineteenth-century gothic dormitories of Bryn Mawr, founded as a college for women in 1885, recalled a bit of history about sexuality and gender and stories about Twain's daughter, Susy, who entered Bryn Mawr in the fall of 1890.

The history: despite the temptation to believe that society's attitudes toward sexuality and gender "follow an even and upward march of progress toward freedom," writes Jason Baumann, editor of *The Stonewall Reader*, cycles of freedom and repression alternate. Susy's time at Bryn Mawr was during an era when same-sex relationships were "discreetly tolerated . . . in the form of romantic friendships," Baumann concludes. The twentieth century brought increased medical and legal regulation.[8]

Early in her first year, Susy developed a relationship, whether sexual or not, with Louise Brownell, a sophomore who would become editor of the college literary magazine and president of the self-government association. In thirty letters addressed to "Dear Sweetheart," and "My beloved," Susy wrote of her "violent and demanding" love of Louise and wanting to "kiss you *hard* on that little place that tastes so good just on the right side of your nose." Susy desired to "throw my arms around you and kiss you over and over again."[9]

By April 1891, Twain and his wife had removed Susy from Bryn Mawr. Some biographers blame Susy's departure on her poor health and homesickness, others on the family's need to economize. But still other scholars argue that Twain and his wife wanted, in Linda A. Morris's words, "to put distance between" Susy and Brownell.[10]

Students at Bryn Mawr exploring same-gender relationships, whether sexual or not, had faculty role models. M. Carey Thomas, who would become president of Bryn Mawr, lived with her companion, Mamie Gwinn, during Susy's year at the college. In 1894, Gwinn and Thomas separated; Mary Garrett joined Thomas on campus in a life together until Garrett's death in 1915.

How was it today for lesbian and gay students at Bryn Mawr and Haverford, I wondered, and how was it during my student days in the early 1960s? I had arrived at Haverford in September 1959 with the dating experience of an oak tree and extraordinary cluelessness about sexual orientation.

I sought dates with dozens of Bryn Mawrters, including Karen Burstein, a coquettish, curly-haired, five-foot-four-inch first-year student with a Woody Allen wit and twelve-cylinder energy. Misreading her active brain for an active body, I thought a perfect date with her would be bouncing on a trampoline together at a nearby YMCA. Somehow that date never happened.

I followed Karen's career after Bryn Mawr—as a New York state senator, president of the state civil service commission, Brooklyn Family Court judge, and candidate for New York state attorney general. She lost a tight 1994 race to a Republican whose campaign tarred her as a left-of-Lenin liberal and "admitted lesbian." What, I asked Karen, was it like for her at Bryn Mawr?

Karen, seventy, started at the beginning. "I was a girl until I was about seven years," she said. "I remember being deeply in love with a boy in the second grade." But soon there was a moment, she said, when she wanted to be a boy. "From that minute on, I thought of girls as attractive," she said. At age eleven, she read Richard von Krafft-Ebing, who in *Psychopathia Sexualis* describes a lesbian relationship as "a congenitally abnormal inversion of the sexual instinct."[11]

Karen said, "I found myself described as psychopathic and aberrant. There cannot be a worse introduction to the question of sexuality for an impressionable preteen." Krafft-Ebing failed, however, to explain the complexity of Karen's feelings. "While I preferred girls to boys, I was interested in the latter as well." But, she said, "I'm not in the middle—I'm not bisexual."

Karen Burstein

She talked candidly about the depression that had accompanied her in life. She wrote to a mentally ill friend: "I know about closets not only from the noonday demon of depression who lurks in one of mine," but, she explained, because of her childhood realization that she was a lesbian. The lesson she learned from living was, she said with a laugh, "lesbianism is insanity."

Lesbianism at Bryn Mawr under Katharine E. McBride, president from 1942 to 1970, went largely unacknowledged. Bryn Mawrter Brenna Levitin, '16, who studied the history of sexual orientation and gender expression at the college, said administrators tried to "minimize or suppress the perception of Bryn Mawr as a lesbian-friendly institution."[12]

Karen had found it difficult to declare her sexual orientation. Her father, a prominent international lawyer, had told her, "Bursteins are not homosexuals." Early at Bryn Mawr she had fallen in love with a classmate. Later the classmate "decided she didn't like women anymore," Karen said. "I was devastated."

Karen slept with other women at Bryn Mawr and, in her junior year, for the first time, with a man. After later visiting Europe, she tallied her relationships to that point in her life: "Slept with four women and loved three of them very much, slept with fifteen men, loved one very much."

On November 19, 1972, as a New York state senator-elect, she married Eric Lane, a lawyer who had been her campaign manager. Their divorce decree was granted in September 1998.

"Eventually, I met someone I could seriously love, and she and I lived together for ten years," Karen said. Karen had come out to her husband before they married, and she came out to some close friends, her siblings, and mother in the early 1980s (her father died in 1983). But not until the ceremony to swear Karen in as a family court judge in 1990 did she go public about her life partner.

"We are no longer together," Karen said, "so I suppose I should have been more cautious about the adjective 'life partner,' but she remains a treasured friend, as actually does everyone I have loved or been in love with during my adult existence."

Karen recalled with amusement that New York mayor David Dinkins had appointed three women to the family court in 1990, in addition to a straight Black man: "A woman active in the lesbian community (Paula Hepner), a disabled woman (Roz Richter), and a well-known feminist (me). Poor guy, it turned out all three of us were, as my mother used to say, 'that way.'" After their swearing-in, the three women, with others, formed the first association of lesbian and gay judges in New York and marched together in the New York City Pride Parade in 1991.

At Haverford College, two miles southeast of Bryn Mawr, I met with Philip A. Bean, associate dean and dean of academic affairs, to discuss Haverford's struggle to diversify.

I graduated in 1963, when the student body of 450 was still all male and a haven of heteronormativity (so far as I knew). Arnold Zwicky, the domestic partner of Jacques H. Transue, who started at Haverford in my class of 1963 and died in 2003, called the 1960s "very bad for gay people." Zwicky said most gay men hid their sexual orientation if they understood it at all. He said you could know that you were attracted to men "but still not appreciate it as a defining fact about you, especially if you're a man who likes women as people and friends and can be sexually responsive to women."

Zwicky said Transue and he both felt "the considerable pressure to follow the life script—both of us looked forward to having children. It was easy to marry [a woman] and have the appearance of a normal married life." Zwicky, who, like Transue, married a woman, said regular sexual experiences in marriage could be "perfectly pleasant but not deeply moving." Only when their continuing attraction to men moved from fantasies to real experiences did they fully identify themselves as gay.

Bean, the associate dean, who is openly gay, said that today, in contrast, individual students may silently struggle with real or perceived hostility from their families and hometown neighbors, but the climate at Haverford for gay and lesbian students had long been "virtually a nonissue."[13] The college's alumni/ae magazine would soon feature a lengthy cover article, "Just Married," about the same-sex weddings of nine alumni/ae couples.[14]

Haverford's student Queer Discussion Group, according to its website, met once a week at a "safe, confidential place for students who are queer and/or questioning their gender/sexuality." The Gender and Sexuality Studies Program offered an interdisciplinary, six-course concentration or minor in partnership with Bryn Mawr College.

Kenzie Thorp, '15, the cohead of Haverford's Sexuality and Gender Alliance, saw Haverford as "a very liberal bubble." Students "were accepting but not aware," she said. "I'm comfortable being the crazy person with the rainbow flag."

Bean said challenges involving diversity remain at Haverford. He stressed the importance of making elite colleges like Haverford accessible to students from the first generation of their families to attend college—students who might face serious financial challenges. "There is no more powerful engine of socioeconomic mobility than higher education," Bean said.

Otherwise, Haverford appeared to be a model of multiculturalism. Bean said students of color comprised 35 percent of Haverford's entering class. Fifty-five percent of the once all-male student body was now female. In 2010, the *Journal of Blacks in Higher Education* reported Haverford "leads the way" among the highest-ranked liberal arts colleges in its percentage of African American full-time faculty members.[15]

Even a snarky review on College Prowler (now Niche.com), a website that publishes college reviews written by current students, awarded Haverford a B+ for diversity and suggested the only students who might feel like outsiders were "super religious or Republican."

Alyssa, Dan, and I headed for Washington, D.C., where the superreligious were often fans of Republican politicians and the Republicans were far from outsiders.

CHAPTER 11

Washington, D.C.

A Renegade Officiates at the Marriage of a Jew and a Christian

Dan, Alyssa, and I crossed the Mason-Dixon line—what the *Onion* jokingly calls the IHOP–Waffle House line—to Washington, D.C. Twain worked there for two months in 1867 as private secretary to Senator William M. Stewart, a Nevada Republican, for six dollars a day. Stewart fired Twain. The senator groused about the "seedy suit" and "scraggy black hair" that distinguished Twain, who also apparently got drunk on Stewart's whiskey. After Twain lost that job, he continued to contribute letters to Horace Greeley's influential *New-York Tribune* and other newspapers.[1] In a humorous letter to the *Tribune* titled "The Facts Concerning the Recent Resignation," he reported on his resignation as clerk of the Senate Committee on Conchology: "If I were to detail all the outrages that were heaped upon me during the six days that I was connected with the government in an official capacity [he said the Committee did not provide someone with whom he could play billiards], the narrative would fill a volume."

Almost a century later, during the summer of 1963, I interned as a reporter for the *Washington Post*, although a major reason for my presence in the district was to pursue Nancy Geiger, a twenty-year-old Bryn Mawr College junior whom I had started dating while a senior at Haverford. Nancy rejected me that summer in favor of Paul, whose last name I have conveniently forgotten. But by 1967, Nancy, a Jew, and I, a lapsed Protestant, were seeking a rabbi to marry us.

Nancy had grown up attending services at Temple Shalom, a Reform congregation in suburban Chevy Chase, Maryland. She had dutifully attended Sunday school and knew from her family's history what it meant to be a Jew. Her mother's family, the Moëds of Suchowola, Poland, traced their ancestors back through generations of rabbis to Rabbi Moshe Ben Nachman in thirteenth-century Spain. Nachman had left Catholic Spain—where Jews were forced to live primarily in segregated Jewish quarters and wear a yellow badge on their clothing—to settle in Palestine.[2] At the end of the nineteenth century, the Moëds went into the diamond business in Antwerp. But they "scattered in all directions" when the Nazis invaded Belgium in 1940. The Nazis caught nine Moëds and murdered them at Auschwitz.[3]

In 1967, when many U.S. Jews were marrying non-Jews (a *Look* magazine cover story warned of "The Vanishing American Jew"), Nancy and I could not find a Washington-area rabbi who would marry us. The rabbis saw inter-marriage as a threat to marital happiness and Judaism.[4]

But Edwin H. Friedman, a rabbi who had founded the Bethesda Jewish Congregation with twenty families in 1964, was willing to meet with Nancy and me. He grilled us about our values and family histories before agreeing to marry us. Looking back on that meeting, I suspect he anticipated what one intermarriage expert forecast almost a half-century later—that Jewish women would continue to marry gentile men, raise their children as Jews, and, paradoxically, "contribute to a renaissance of Jewish religious and cultural identity formation and practice from within their intermarriages."[5] I certainly approved of my children's being raised as Jews. I was in the 90 percent of fourth-generation Italian Americans of mixed origin.[6] The more mixed my children the merrier.

Nancy and I filled our wedding ceremony at the Woman's National Democratic Club in Washington with Jewish rituals. Under a chuppah, a canopy that symbolizes the home that husband and wife build together, I stomped a wine glass placed on the floor. Friedman joked this was the last time I would get to put my foot down.

Why was Friedman willing to marry us when no other area rabbi would? He told us he was writing a book on intermarriage. Nancy recalls, "If we let him interview us, he would be happy to marry us." However, I suspected he also had other reasons for marrying us. I couldn't ask him—he died in 1996—but his daughter, Shira Friedman Bogart, a San Francisco advertising executive and writer, offered two theories.

First, her father grew up in multicultural worlds with egalitarian zeitgeists. Judaism for him was "more than a religion focused on a deity or a god," Bogart said. Her father, ever the intellectual with a "progressive view on religion," found Judaism part of a way of thinking about his life, not only as a rabbi but also as a family therapist, leadership trainer, and, for five years, a community relations specialist at the White House. "He worked for Lady Bird Johnson on civil rights," Bogart said. "It was his job to kind of spread equality."

Second, Friedman adopted a "1960s mentality, challenging everything," Bogart said. With the emergence of Reconstructionist Judaism and the field of family therapy, Friedman faced "the choice of living forever in a world that is old or trying to discover one that is new," Bogart said. His liberal Jewish congregation rented space in 1967 from the Bradley Hills Presbyterian Church in Bethesda. Friedman cared only that the church was a house of prayer, his daughter said. "It just didn't matter to him what religion it was."

A friendship developed between the congregations. Thirty years later, Bradley Hills Presbyterian and Bethesda Jewish committed to spend $1 million to build a shared space, Covenant Hall. The congregations' covenant, on display in the building, reads in part: "We see this relationship as a living example of understanding and respect among people of different heritage."[7]

That statement could apply to our marriage, which reached the half-century mark in 2018. Nancy and I and our children, while they were young, celebrated Hanukkah (dreidel playing mixed with the opening of presents). And, until the children left for college, we also held a Passover Seder using a Haggadah written by Nancy's father. Nancy did not, however, join a Jewish congregation or consistently celebrate Jewish holidays after we moved from Washington to Southbridge, Massachusetts, where a more conservative Judaism prevailed. One of our daughters grew up an unaffiliated agnostic, the other sampled various religions and, toward the end of high school, chose Catholicism. She is raising her five children as Catholics.

I like to think my nuclear family has positive potential in a pluralistic society. Some experts see the growth in America of an "interfaith space" that defies the boundaries of Judaism and other religions and embraces religious difference and intermarriage.[8] Perhaps the members of my family will be less insular and more understanding—and more likely to dispel ignorance and deflate bias—than if all of us were of one faith.

———

Washington, D.C., possessed no Ghigliones, not even a Little Italy, that I could inflict on Alyssa and Dan. You could see the work of Italians, however, in the city's monumental buildings, from the Capitol to the National Cathedral. Attilio Piccirilli and his four brothers sculpted the statue in the

Lincoln Memorial. Andrew Bernasconi created the six statues along the front of Union Station. "This city has been carved in stone as a monument to some of the most sacred values of the country, such as democracy and egalitarianism," the historian Alan Kraut said. "And who built it? Who actually laid hands on? It was these sons of another land—of Italy."[9]

I did ask Dan and Alyssa to meet three friends of mine, starting with William A. Davis Jr., an African American with whom I'd gone to law school. Davis, president of Davis Property Ventures, Inc., invited the three of us to his club, the University Club of Washington, D.C., for breakfast. The dining room's maître d'hôtel told us that Dan, dressed in road trip short pants, failed to meet the club's dress code: "Creased slacks (no denims)." Davis led us out of the club to a nearby hotel. He said with a reassuring laugh that not long ago he, as an African American, would not have been allowed to enter the University Club.

I also introduced Alyssa and Dan to two Hispanic journalist friends, Evelio Contreras and Ray Hernandez, who had risen from small-town newspapers to work at the *Washington Post* and *New York Times*.

How did Evelio and Ray think about their identity?

At a Starbucks in Chevy Chase, Ray reminisced about a career that had taken him from cub reporter for my small daily in Massachusetts to Washington-based investigative reporter for the *New York Times*, the world's most powerful newspaper.

Ray had arrived at the *Times* shortly after Arthur Ochs Sulzberger Jr. became publisher in 1992. Sulzberger believed diversity was a moral issue—"the single most important issue" the *Times* faced. He transformed what had once been a virtually all-white (and mostly male) newsroom—"often only one Negro reporter, rarely more than two," Gay Talese wrote in 1969.[10] The 1990s were "a great time to be there," Ray said.

Ray and I ended by discussing the sense of identity of his two sons, one in college, the other in high school. The forty-five-year-old Ray recalled his "very rich upbringing where Spanish was the language at home, and the family, the food, the music, everything was very Hispanic." He felt fortunate to have experienced his mother's Ecuadoran and father's Puerto Rican cultures. "I see myself as a Hispanic man of color," Ray said. "It informs me in a way that it doesn't inform my children."

His sons grew up in a middle-class suburb of Washington, D.C. "We don't speak Spanish at home," Ray said. His sons "have never shown a great interest in what it means to be Hispanic. They know it intellectually, but it's not woven into the fabric of their lives the way it was for me. Part of me is sad," Ray said.

He paused, "On the other hand, there's an advantage in not feeling like the Other." His sons were moving beyond the categories of race and ethnicity that often defined and confined people.

Twenty-nine-year-old Evelio Contreras, at the time a *Washington Post* videographer, tied his journalism to his identity, which is tied to where he grew up: Eagle Pass, Texas (city slogan: "Where Yee Haw Meets Olé"), across the Rio Grande from Piedras Negras, Mexico. He said he had a divided understanding of himself. He was a first-generation Mexican American with a strong connection to the United States, but he also had deep bonds with Mexico.

His mother, who sewed clothes, and his father, who worked construction, stressed education for Evelio and his siblings: "They taught us about working hard in school."

When he was six or seven years old, he traveled with his parents to the state of Washington to pick fruit and work in canneries. When his mother took him to school there, school officials ignored her. "Because she spoke Spanish, they acted like she couldn't talk to them," he said. "She wasn't important. And I could see how they treated us migrant kids, like we weren't smart. And I knew I was smart at that age. I had a lot of self-awareness as a kid . . . just constantly questioning, 'Why am I here, why are these people acting this way?' And I would see my mom cry all the time, quietly by herself, so I was always a witness to her pain." He also witnessed migrant families risk death by attempting to cross the rushing Rio Grande from Mexico into Eagle Pass.

Such experiences shaped Evelio's journalism. As a teenager, he wrote for the bilingual *News Gram*, an Eagle Pass newspaper. In addition to reporting on crime and city hall, Evelio wrote a Sunday column, "Eye on Eagle Pass," that featured profiles of people facing hardship or trauma. "I would find the blind cross-country runner," Evelio said. "That's where it all started for me." Wherever he later worked, and whatever the form of his storytelling—article, photo, or video, he was "telling local-column stories."

Eagle Pass "felt like 99 percent Mexican," Evelio said. "There were no African Americans." He said Northwestern University's Medill School of Journalism represented his first major experience with diversity. He spent 2000–2001, his first year, exploring a different student community each

Evelio Contreras

quarter: African Americans in the fall, Asian Americans in the winter, and the student daily newspaper staff, largely white, in the spring. Used to the directness of Eagle Pass residents, he found he needed to study whites to learn "how to read what they were saying."

In his junior year, Evelio reported for ten weeks from Johannesburg and Cape Town for South African newspapers. Still the local columnist, he recalled his "most memorable experience" in South Africa as accompanying a *(Johannesburg) Star* health reporter on a visit to the home of a young orphan who had AIDS. The sister of the orphan had attached a make-believe machine—"almost like a toy," Evelio said—to her brother. Although the machine wasn't connected to anything and provided no medication, Evelio recognized its importance. In a world of suffering and death, the machine offered hope. "Every story needs hope," Evelio said, even when little or no hope exists.

He kept pursuing local-column stories. As a reporter in 2007 for the *Roanoke Times*, he spent five months hanging out with a thirty-three-year-old immigrant, a hardworking construction worker from Mexico City who reminded Evelio of his father. The resulting five-part series focused on the immigrant's effort to get license plates for his car, Evelio wrote, "even though he doesn't have a driver's license, and even though he is not in the country legally." The immigrant refused to buy a fake Social Security number and driver's license. "He wants to do it right," Evelio wrote, "or as right as he can under the circumstances."

Evelio would leave the *Washington Post* in 2012 to join *CNN Digital* as a content producer and editor based in New York. He continued to seek local-column stories. One story focused on Angelica, a Guatemalan mother, and her fourteen-year-old son, Jesus, who had illegally entered the United States from Mexico. The mother had left her two oldest children behind to undertake the arduous two-thousand-mile trip with Jesus from Guatemala to the Arizona border. Smugglers stole their possessions, leaving them with only five or six dollars. The U.S. Border Patrol arrested Angelica and Jesus. After learning they were headed to Mississippi to meet with Jesus's father, the Border Patrol set a deportation hearing for mother and son in a nearby Alabama city thirty days later and directed them to a Greyhound station in Tucson.

Evelio, who had met up with them in Tucson, rode with Angelica and Jesus on the two-day bus trip to Tupelo, Mississippi. That Angelica and Jesus had little money "was a big part of the story," Evelio said. Jesus's father encouraged Angelica to ask Evelio for money so she could buy food on the trip. Evelio felt journalism's code of ethics required him to refuse to give her money. He needed to maintain the role of the dispassionate observer and avoid the risk that someone could accuse him of buying a good story by purchasing food for Angelica and Jesus. So the mother and son ate little more than the trail mix that volunteers at the Tucson bus station had provided. The empathetic Evelio declined to purchase meals for himself on the two-day trip.

Evelio's bus-trip video, *Reuniting, a Son's Dream*, was the first part of a planned series on the effects of deportation on a family. When I contacted Evelio in 2018, he was beginning an even more ambitious personal video project—it might take a decade—about the impact of drug trafficking on a family living in the United States and Guadalajara, Mexico, home to the drug cartel New Generation Jalisco.

Many of the people Evelio chooses to feature in his videos are outsiders—loners without friends or family to help them overcome life's challenges. "I value everyday life," he said. "And the extraordinary moments in ordinary people's lives."

For an extremely different view of what it means to be a journalist of color, Alyssa, Dan, and I drove to downtown Washington, D.C., to interview Juan Williams, a Fox News political analyst. The U.S. capital was experiencing startling change. In a city once 70 percent Black and known as Chocolate City, skyrocketing housing prices were contributing to rapid white gentrification. The *Washington Post* headlined a 2011 report "Number of Black D.C. Residents Plummets as Majority Status Slips Away." Seven years later, even the homeless were being pushed out of their tent cities by developers seeking to build luxury housing. The *Post*'s report quoted Roderick Harrison, a Howard University demographer: "Clearly, D.C. is one of the most polarized cities by income and education in the country."[11]

We met Williams in the late afternoon at Johnny's Half Shell, a seafood restaurant on North Capitol, in the same building as the Fox News television studios. Dan, Alyssa, and I had just finished lunch. Williams encouraged us to order dessert while he tackled a plate of oysters.

During twenty-three years at the *Washington Post*, Williams served as a national correspondent and political columnist. He wrote a well-received biography of the first African American on the U.S. Supreme Court, *Thurgood Marshall: American Revolutionary* (1998). His book *Eyes on the Prize: America's Civil Rights Years, 1954–1965* (1987) accompanied the first season of the fourteen-hour *Eyes on the Prize* documentary TV series. His documentary writing earned him an Emmy.

But his writings and remarks also generated controversy. In 1991, when Anita Hill accused Clarence Thomas, nominated for a seat on the U.S. Supreme Court, of sexual harassment, the *Post* published a Williams column that downplayed the gravity of the charges against Thomas. Female *Post* staffers accused Williams, the defender of an accused harasser, of being a harasser himself. In an article titled "A Secret No More," Carolyn Weaver reported, "Only after a protest by 116 newsroom employees did the paper concede that the charges against Williams were founded."[12]

Williams remained a fan of Supreme Court Justice Thomas. In a tribute to him, after twenty years on the court, Williams called Thomas "a leading black conservative," who was admirably independent: "His race neutral approach is a sharp contrast to race conscious programs approved to remedy past discrimination."[13] Jack White, a former *Time* magazine columnist, denounced Williams for trying to "remake Thomas into a black nationalist icon instead of the Uncle Tom that many blacks consider him to be."[14]

Another controversy occurred in 2010 while Williams was working for both National Public Radio and Fox News. Williams contended on Fox's *The O'Reilly Factor* that fear of Muslims should not be used to restrict their rights. But, Williams said, "When I get on the plane, I got to tell you, if I see people who are in Muslim garb and I think, you know, they are identifying themselves first and foremost as Muslims, I get worried, I get nervous."[15]

NPR terminated Williams's contract two days later. Fox signed Williams to a three-year contract reportedly worth $2 million, and Williams wrote a book critical of NPR titled *Muzzled: The Assault on Honest Debate* (2011). Williams said NPR's double standard defended the expression of certain ultraliberal views but not his views. During our conversation he said of NPR, "I don't fit in their box. I'm not predictable, Black, liberal."

Later, in response to concerns about a white police officer's killing of an unarmed Black man, Williams questioned racial profiling, excessive force, and use of military equipment by police. But he also said on Fox, "We have to be honest about crime in the Black community." To Williams's way of thinking, such crime, primarily committed by young Black males, exacerbates race relations: "White people say, 'Well, I don't want to associate with people who are lawless.'" Williams criticized Jesse Jackson, Al Sharpton, and other civil rights leaders for not addressing Black crime. "They really don't exercise power to benefit the Black community," he said. "In my mind, they exercise power to the benefit of themselves."

Alyssa, Dan, and I sought Williams's opinion about a vexing challenge for Washington, D.C., and America: how to respond to a Black underclass that seems to lack the education and support network to succeed. The *Washington Post* columnist Eugene Robinson had recommended to us a domestic Marshall Plan, equivalent to the huge U.S. effort after World War II to rebuild European economies. The Harvard professor Henry Louis "Skip" Gates Jr. had called for a second civil rights movement.

But Williams took a strikingly different approach, reflected in the title of his 2007 book, *Enough: The Phony Leaders, Dead-End Movements, and Culture of Failure That Are Undermining Black America—and What We Can Do About It*. Williams judged it unrealistic to count on help from new government programs: "Now, it's politically untenable to get more money for [economic] stimulus." He stressed individual responsibility—being accountable for one's circumstances and educating oneself (in a speech he repeated an unverified Twain quote: "A man who does not read has no advantage over a man who can't read").

"What would I say to my daughter, what would I say to my sons? 'Here's what you can do to help yourself,'" Williams continued. He suggested staying in school and the job market, waiting until you have a job before getting married and having children, and being realistic. "Don't think you're going to be a rap star," he said.

The fifty-seven-year-old Williams was born in Panama and described his roots in the West Indies and his sense of Black people there not as broken but as strong and capable. He talked about the significantly higher educational level in the West Indies and the emphasis on taking advantage of academic opportunities.

He credited the civil rights movement and the Reverend Martin Luther King Jr. with opening doors for him. He recalled a time when the *Washington Post* had no Black writers. Pointing to the infrequency of Black TV anchors, Williams said race remained "a real ceiling and a real issue for me."

For his children, however, Williams thought race was less important. His daughter, Rae, was married to a white man. His two sons, Antonio and Raphael, found race "real but not defining."

The generational difference was captured in a Fox segment in which Williams took his two sons along King's route for the 1963 March on Washington for Jobs and Freedom. Then Williams escorted his sons to the new Martin Luther King Jr. Memorial and reminded them they never had to live in segregation. "I grew up in a world that was being changed by Dr. King," Williams said to his sons. "But for you, you grew up in a world that's already been changed."[16]

Williams's walk along the route of the 1963 March on Washington caused me to recall my March on Washington experience and to seek out my roommate from that summer, who had had a life-changing experience at the march.

CHAPTER 12

In the South

Underreporting Protests and Resegregating Schools

Jim MacRae, the only African American in my Haverford College class, and I had roomed together in Washington, D.C., during the summer of 1963, which was made famous by the March on Washington for Jobs and Freedom and the Reverend Martin Luther King Jr.'s "I Have a Dream" speech. From Washington, D.C., Alyssa, Dan, and I headed to Jim's hilltop farm near Schellsburg, Pennsylvania, which is about 150 miles northwest of Washington, between Harrisburg and Pittsburgh.

Jim, who was seventy and had retired at fifty-five from the White House's Office of Management and Budget, and Nancy, his wife of forty-seven years, gave Dan, Alyssa, and me a tour of their hundred-acre farm. It featured a two-story brick country house, a tree house eighteen feet up, a smokehouse, a garden house, and a swimming pool. "We do go on vacations," Nancy said. "But people say, 'Why?'"

Over lunch we talked race. Jim's father, a 1924 graduate of Pennsylvania's Lincoln University, the first degree-granting historically Black university in America, served as the school's dean of students for twenty-one years. Jim said his father and mother decided Jim would be one of three Black students to desegregate a local elementary school. "We were the guinea pigs," Jim said.

When a fifth-grade teacher, offended by Jim's impertinence while correctly answering a question, pulled Jim home and told his mother her son was suspended for two weeks, Jim's mother rose and said: "You take your hands off my son. He will never go back." The next day, Jim's parents enrolled him in Westtown, a Quaker boarding school near Philadelphia, where for most of his years there he was the only Black student in his class.

In his first week at Haverford College—"even less" diverse than Westtown, Jim said—he telephoned an attractive, much-sought-after Bryn Mawr College first-year blonde for a date. She said yes. Jim recalled that Roy David, another Haverford freshman, after learning of Jim's success, said to him, "You got a date with her? But you didn't tell her you were Black." Jim shot back, "If you had called her, would you have told her you were Jewish?"

Jim's entry in his senior yearbook was almost the only one for our year that did not have an essay about him written by a Haverford classmate. Jim attached no significance to the essay's absence, mentioning that he had lived in language houses distant from student dorms for three of his four years. As for not ever attending a college reunion, he said, "There is no animus."

Jim talked about two groups of African Americans—those who seek a completely Black experience where they live and play ("They are not comfortable in the wider world") and those "who have learned the code" and are comfortable anywhere.

Jim also reminisced about August 28, 1963, which was the day that he met Nancy Kerber, a March on Washington participant and Vassar graduate who became his wife.

Jim and Nancy, who is white, did not believe their children and grandchildren, unlike our generation, attached great significance to categories of color and race. "They'll be fine," Jim said. Caroline, his blonde-haired granddaughter, at age nine had brought an Asian American friend to meet him. "I told you my grandfather was African American," Caroline said proudly.

Jim's optimism about the generations of his children and grandchildren left me eager for us to reach the South as soon as possible. Perhaps we would feel Jim's optimism about racial understanding there too. He encouraged us, however, to take the time to stop nearby at the newly opened national memorial for Flight 93. He recalled hearing the boom from United's Boeing 757 as it plowed upside-down, at 563 miles per hour, into a field eleven miles away. The airliner, hijacked on September 11, 2001, by four terrorists, was apparently intended to strike the U.S. Capitol. But the flight's passengers and crew rushed the terrorists. No one—not the thirty-three passengers, seven crew members, or four hijackers—survived the crash.

A memorial of a different kind greeted us nine miles southeast of Pittsburgh. We stopped at Bell Avenue and Thirteenth Street in dying North Braddock. Reflecting the death of the steel industry once dominant in the area, the borough's population of 15,679 in 1940 had slid to 4,857 by 2010. A German shepherd at 1223 Bell Avenue growled menacingly at us from behind a sign that read, WARNING: CROSS THE LINE, YOUR ASS IS MINE.

We walked down Thirteenth, a street of rectangular stones and orange bricks that sloped steeply toward the Monongahela River and its steel mills. At least half of the houses—including many fine brick structures—stood abandoned. The borough's median house price in 2009 had fallen to $9,050, down 25 percent from the previous year and still dropping.

Alyssa, who grew up in Pittsburgh, responded to my disbelief about devastated North Braddock: "It could be very much the same the next town over, two towns over." We drove northwest along Braddock Avenue, the main commercial street of neighboring Braddock, to see entire blocks of abandoned buildings. "So, who's depressed yet?" Alyssa asked from the back of the van. Braddock, with 2,159 residents in the 2010 census, had lost 90 percent of its 1920s population.

I thought about Braddock again in 2016, when the Republican presidential candidate, Donald Trump, won Pennsylvania, which was traditionally Democratic. How did that reversal happen? The writer Dave Eggers, who drove from Pittsburgh to the Philadelphia suburbs a month before the election, recalled seeing "nothing but Trump/Pence signs . . . not one sign, large or small, in support of [Hillary] Clinton." He repeated the political strategist James Carville's quip about Pennsylvania's being "Pittsburgh and Philadelphia with Alabama in between."[1]

Although Braddock, which is two-thirds Black, voted 10 to 1 for Clinton, it wasn't just the white voters between Pittsburgh and Philadelphia who handed the state to Trump, according to John Fetterman, then Braddock's Harvard-educated mayor (2005–19) and more recently Pennsylvania's lieutenant governor. Fetterman told a reporter, "If Trump's support is kind of the finger that older white Americans are giving to this country for breaking its promises and leaving them behind, I can kind of understand it. We've had a Democrat in the White House for eight years. And the Democrats are in control of Allegheny County. If you look around here, you have to wonder if it's made much of a difference."[2]

We continued on to Pittsburgh, which lost nearly half its population in the last century. The Hill District, the center of Black culture depicted in nine of the ten plays in August Wilson's Pittsburgh Cycle, had fallen victim to urban renewal in the 1950s. In targeting the area's overcrowded substandard housing, in part to make way for the Civic Arena, redevelopment displaced eighty thousand residents and destroyed the Hill's social network. White residents might tout Pittsburgh today as the trendy Paris of Appalachia. But Black residents might recall that, between 1950 and 1990, 70 percent of Hill residents and four hundred businesses disappeared. Today, the Hill symbolizes segregation as well as economic decline. Urban renewal helped turn Pittsburgh, "a jumble of ethnically mixed neighborhoods," Mark Whitaker writes in *Smoketown*, "into an increasingly stark patchwork of white and Black."[3]

We stopped for the night eleven miles south of the Hill District, at the suburban Bethel Park home of Alyssa's family. I was awarded the second-floor bedroom normally occupied by Alyssa or her sister, Maria. Words by Michael Ignatieff, the Canadian author and academic, that Alyssa had taped to the mirrored door of the bedroom's closet, reminded me of my good fortune in being able to travel the United States for three months. Ignatieff had written: "One of the greatest feelings in life is the conviction that you have lived the life you wanted to live—with the rough and the smooth, the good and the bad—but yours, shaped by your own choices, and not someone else's." I had hoped to experience the full range of Americans, and I was doing just that.

The next day, racing almost three hundred miles southward, Alyssa, Dan, and I stopped briefly in Cincinnati, which critics had described throughout its history as boringly out of date. Twain, who worked there as a printer for T. Wrightson and Company in 1856–57, supposedly said (although the quote cannot be authenticated): "When the end of the world comes, I want to be in Cincinnati because it's always twenty years behind the times."

Our next stop, Lexington, Kentucky, only eighty-six miles from Cincinnati and home to horses, bourbon, and University of Kentucky basketball, was our first city in the South. Once the capital of the state's slave trade, Lexington was the birthplace in 1803 of Twain's mother, Jane Langston. She married John Marshall Clemens in 1823 and, with him, owned six slaves.

The retired newspaper editor John S. Carroll, a Haverford College classmate of mine, spoke with us about contemporary race relations in Lexington as an almost native son of the South. Although best known for his ten years as editor of the *Baltimore Sun* and five years as editor of the *Los Angeles Times* (during which the staff won thirteen Pulitzer Prizes), John had spent much of his childhood in Winston-Salem, North Carolina, where his father edited the *Journal and Sentinel*.

John, sixty-nine, recalled as a boy not knowing any African Americans, "except for people who were household servants," he said. "The Blacks were completely shut out of the world that I inhabited, and it was a world that had money and opportunities and political power." While Winston-Salem still had "a long way to go," John said, it now had its share of Black business executives, political leaders, doctors, and lawyers.

John became editor of the morning *Lexington Herald* in 1979 (two years later, the *Herald* merged with the afternoon *Lexington Leader*, and John assumed the editorship of the combined paper). He soon learned about a skeleton in the paper's closet. During the 1960s, the papers "hadn't covered the civil rights demonstrations in other cities or had reduced them to little briefs and put them so far back in the paper that nobody saw them," John said. The publisher "didn't want to give local Blacks ideas, didn't want them to be misbehaving and demonstrating and getting violent."

Even worse, the *Herald* and *Leader* downplayed the early Main Street sit-ins in Lexington that were held fifty yards from the papers' front door, John said. The demonstrations, as early as July 1959, occurred more than a half-year before the sit-ins at the Woolworth's in Greensboro, North Carolina, that had inspired young people nationwide. The Lexington newspapers swept the local sit-in campaign "under the rug and it didn't become part of history," John said.

Later, during John's time as the *Herald-Leader*'s editor, a staff member proposed as a joke that the paper make up for its enormous lapse by running a brief correction on page 2, where the *Herald-Leader* usually acknowledged minor errors of fact and spelling. The correction would read: "It has come to the editor's attention that the *Herald-Leader* neglected to cover the civil rights movement. We regret the omission."

In 2004, the *Herald-Leader* chose the fortieth anniversary of the Civil Rights Act of 1964 to publish a detailed account of Lexington's overlooked civil rights history. The exposé recounted Audrey Grevious's memory of the city's first lunch counter sit-ins—"the cold, wet shock she felt as a waitress poured a glass of Coca-Cola all over her, while the whites standing behind her hissed, 'Nigger!'"[4]

———

At John Carroll's suggestion, Dan, Alyssa, and I drove to the office of the *Herald-Leader* to interview the columnist Merlene Davis about race in present-day Lexington. Alyssa wrote:

At the beginning of the interview, Merlene Davis playfully cursed John Carroll, her former editor, for recommending we interview her. Davis, a

Merlene Davis

gregarious, warm woman who pretended to be ornery, was worried about the interview. She furiously wiped her forehead, afraid she was going to be too shiny on camera. "Lord have mercy!" she cried several times.

Davis had no need to worry. She was a natural storyteller and provided one of our most powerful interviews. At the University of Kentucky, she was studying to become an English teacher when she "somehow got wrapped up in the civil rights era." She decided, "I don't need college!"

She started a family. Then, at twenty-eight, she went back to the university. Eventually, she participated in a summer program for minority journalists and found her career.

After a stint as a Memphis Press-Scimitar *reporter, she moved to the* Herald-Leader *in 1980, writing obituaries and reporting crime on a 3:00 p.m.-to-midnight shift that was difficult for a single mother. When invited to write a thrice-weekly column in 1986, she refused at first, in part worried that if she failed it would block the road for Black journalists in the future.*

In the end, Davis agreed to write the column. She recalled, "There was no one else saying what I had to say and it needed to be said." Her column, which candidly dealt with racial issues, succeeded immediately.[5]

Davis lived the issues from an early age. She skipped the fifth grade, she said, not because she could but because she had to. She was one of a few Black students to integrate Mary Lee Cravens Elementary School in Owensboro, Kentucky. "We all ended up in the sixth grade because, as far as I could tell, Mrs. Olive Bopp was the only teacher in the school that would take us," Davis said. "So I have no idea what the fifth grade's like."

Instead, she sat through two sometimes painful years of sixth grade. Davis developed a severe stiff neck in the classroom. Her mother suggested that she was holding in a lot of tension.

Davis's mother, who had wanted her daughter to integrate the school system, then told her something that stayed with her. "She said, 'You know, you'll be okay as long as you remember you cannot be as good as your white classmates,'" Davis recalled. "'You have to be better than.'"

"Better than" is the motto that Davis adopted. She raised her three children to be "better than" as well. Her daughter took her advice, became trilingual, and spent time in Japan. She excelled. One of her sons didn't. He chose drugs and was about to enter the prison system, Davis said.

Davis was not optimistic about overcoming prejudice. "I don't see it as improving," she said. "I see it as changing. We just gotta step on somebody to make ourselves taller, and I don't know why."

Lexington marked our trip's transition from the North to the South, and Davis explained some of the differences. She described the South as less diverse and less accepting. The South's reputation for hospitality was not the reality. "All I know is, we're not hospitable, we're not welcoming," Davis said. "We will do it publicly, but behind closed doors, what are we saying?"

It wasn't strictly the dynamic between Blacks and whites, either. Jews, Native Americans, and Hispanics had all faced and continued to face prejudice. The Black community, Davis said, was not accepting of gays and lesbians. "Why would you stomp on somebody else when you've been stomped on?" Davis asked. "I don't understand."

Davis was frustrated with all groups. She said, "I keep hearing little tidbits, little slights, that make me go, 'I thought we crossed that barrier.'"

The words of Merlene Davis and John Carroll about the racial divide in Lexington, Kentucky, came back to me four years later, on June 14, 2015. That day, I returned to Lexington to attend a memorial service for John, who had died from Creutzfeldt-Jakob disease, a rare brain disorder, at seventy-three. The service was held in First Presbyterian Church, founded in 1784, long a symbol of white Lexington. "Many in the congregation," the church's history notes, "had significant investments tied up in slavery."[6]

Two African Americans participated in the service. Dean Baquet, executive editor of the *New York Times*, told how John's vision for a newsroom inspired him. The soprano Calesta Day moved me and others to tears with her a cappella "Amazing Grace."

But only one African American—the *Herald-Leader*'s editorial page editor, Vanessa Gallman—was in the audience. At the reception after the service, Gallman said, "Everybody assumed I was the singer [of 'Amazing Grace'], as if that would be the only reason I would be there."

Merlene Davis, whom John had hired in 1980 during his tenure as the *Herald-Leader*'s editor, could not attend his memorial service because that day she was expected to help with a funeral at her home church, Wesley United Methodist. "When you age, you cook at my church," she said. She estimated that the membership of her church was 95 percent Black.

Not only the membership of Lexington's churches raised the issue of race. On the day Davis retired, she could name only four African Americans who remained on the paper's news staff of fifty to sixty, and she included Rufus M. Friday, president and publisher, as one of the four. "Racial diversity is just gone," Gallman said. "It has an impact on our coverage. A lot of things happen that we don't see."

As she had when we interviewed her in 2011, Davis worried that the country, not just Lexington, refused to address the issue of race. Yes, an African American had been elected president. Yes, an African American ran the *New York Times* newsroom. But race was still an "infected boil that stinks—it's just a bunch of pus," Davis said. Rather than go to a doctor and address the boil, Americans just slap a Band-Aid over it and use Febreze to try to mask the odor. The presence of African Americans in leadership positions, Davis said, "is supposed to make it smell better." But the infected boil of race still stunk.

From our conversation with Merlene Davis about the present of race, Alyssa, Dan, and I drove south for three hours on U.S. 27 and U.S. 127 to rendezvous with the past. Mark Twain never lived in Jamestown, Tennessee, population 1,959. But the town made the most of its claim that Twain was conceived somewhere within its borders early in 1835. In front of the Mark Twain Inn, uniformed veterans from the Mark Twain American Legion Post 137 collected donations from the drivers of passing vehicles. North on Main Street, next to Mark Twain Avenue, and across from Mark Twain Apparel, sat Mark Twain City Park. It featured the Mark Twain Spring, which supposedly supplied water to Twain's parents, and a carved wooden statue of—surprise!—Mark Twain.

———

We had planned to visit, only a couple of hours away, the Tennessee State Fairgrounds—home to everything Nashville, from Rollergirls games to short-track car races to gun shows. But, as Dan detailed, we spent the day at a hospital instead:

> I woke up with the motel room light in my eyes because I had been sleeping with at least one lamp on every night since the start of the trip. Vestigial childhood anxiety about the dark had made a ruthless comeback after years of tactical repression. And being untethered to the places we visited had made me much more vulnerable to the demons of my past.
>
> But before I noticed the light, I noticed the headache. It was a searing, shrieking headache that conjured medieval images of tiny demons hammering a man's head with picks and scythes.
>
> I dialed Alyssa's number, woke her up, requested pain medication and hobbled next door, arms outstretched, eager for Advil.
>
> "Do you want two or three?" Alyssa the apothecary asked.
>
> "Three," I winced.
>
> "You don't look so good," Alyssa said.
>
> "I know." I thanked her and downed the pills with a swig of water.
>
> The pills didn't help. We were due in an hour at the Tennessee State Fairgrounds to meet Sami Safiullah, a high school friend of mine who was now a student at Vanderbilt University. Sami was going to take us to an Eid al-Adha celebration, a Muslim feast to honor Abraham's sacrifice of his young son Ishmael. I had grand plans to film the prostrations and the sermon and interview Sami afterward to learn what it was like to be a Muslim in Nashville.
>
> I grabbed the video equipment and walked out of the motel room, my head beating like so many taiko drums. Alyssa, who had learned by watching YouTube videos, had wrapped herself in a green hijab. I thought to myself,

"Well, if Alyssa has the stick-to-it-iveness to see what Eid is all about, surely I could deal with this headache."

Unfortunately, I threw up in the fairgrounds parking lot and hugged Sami (it had been more than a year since I last had seen him) over the vomit. Loren and Alyssa decided I should go to the hospital.

We had been putting in fourteen hundred miles a week and interviewing incredible people with moving stories every day. Sometimes it was easy to forget that I was indeed mortal and subject to the whims of illness and bad luck just like everyone else.

In the emergency room of the Vanderbilt University Medical Center, I dozed off for hours at a time in a hideous greenish hospital gown. Nurse Nikeisha Michaeux stuck my arms three times with needles, looking for a vein that wasn't flat.

As the IV drip seeped its saline contents into my body and as I looked over at my travel companions—Loren, ever the workaholic, busy on his laptop, and Alyssa, propped against the wall, sleeping and reading in equal measure—I felt incredibly blessed.

Here I was—living the road trip dream of every American romantic, a dream fabled in countless travelogues and backed by millions of ad dollars on the Travel Channel. This hospital visit wasn't an inconvenient setback at all. It was all part of the package. It was a fine-print clause in the job description for vagabonds. But cephalgia, the doctor's diagnosis, disappointed me. I had nothing more than a bad headache. By the next day, the debilitating pain had entirely dissipated.

Driving the 212 miles west on Interstate 40 from Nashville to Memphis, Alyssa, Dan, and I found it difficult not to sing or shout the music of the South. We were leaving behind Music City USA, home to the Grand Ole Opry and the Country Music Hall of Fame, and heading for Blues City, also known as the Birthplace of Rock 'n' Roll. Mark Twain often visited Memphis, a Mississippi River city, during his steamboat piloting years of 1857–61. His most traumatic visit occurred in June 1858, when an explosion aboard the *Pennsylvania* put his nineteen-year-old brother, Henry, a third clerk on the steamboat, in a Memphis hospital. Twain rushed to Memphis and stayed with Henry until his death about a week later. Twain called Memphis the Good Samaritan City.

But a century later, in the 1950s and 1960s, many Black Memphians failed to see segregated Memphis as a good Samaritan. Towering public park statues honored Jefferson Davis, the president of the Confederacy, and Nathan Bedford Forrest, a Confederate general and the first grand wizard of the Ku Klux Klan. In 1968, hundreds of Black sanitation workers had struck for more than two months to protest deadly working conditions and poor pay. In sympathy, the Reverend Martin Luther King Jr. took part in the strikers' protests and exhorted them to persevere: "I've been to the mountaintop. . . . We, as a people, will get to the promised land!" The next evening, James Earl Ray, a white racist, assassinated King at a downtown motel.

Memphis's *Commercial Appeal*, with an all-white news staff, published white supremacist editorials and a daily cartoon that featured a demeaning caricature of an African American named Hambone, who spoke in a parody of Black dialect. The paper also opposed the integration of Memphis's public schools. In the Withers Collection Museum and Gallery on Beale Street, Dan, Alyssa, and I met with Dwania Kyles, who made history as one of the Memphis 13, a group of first-graders who desegregated the city's all-white schools in 1961.

Kyles, a New York wellness consultant, had returned to Memphis for the first showing of a documentary about the Memphis 13 by Daniel Kiel, a University of Memphis law professor. An Ernest Withers photo of Kyles and other Memphis 13 children looked down upon us as we interviewed her. In thousands of photos, Withers captured the tinderbox of tension that engulfed segregated Memphis in Kyles's era. Withers photographed a 1950s bumper sticker: DON'T BUY GAS WHERE YOU CAN'T USE THE REST ROOM. In another Withers photo, white protesters carried a sign at city hall in 1960: SEGREGATION OR WAR.

In that environment, the local NAACP searched for Black families willing to subject their young children to the strain of desegregating Memphis's schools. Most families declined. But Dwania's parents could hardly say no. They had moved from Chicago two years earlier to be part of the civil rights movement. Dwania's father, the Reverend Samuel "Billy" Kyles, chaired the NAACP's education committee. Kyles, who was pastor of Monumental Baptist Church, would be on the Lorraine Motel balcony with the Reverend Martin Luther King Jr. when he was assassinated.

On October 3, 1961, Dwania Kyles, and two other Black children, Harry Williams and Michael Willis (now Menelik Fombi), desegregated Memphis's Bruce Elementary School. "That first morning, the police came to my house

Dwania Kyles

to escort us to school and protect us from the howling mob," Reverend Kyles said. "When we got to the school, the police had it surrounded. No howling mob—the police were the mob. As we walked up the sidewalk lined with police, the cops said the nastiest things: 'Why don't you get that black bitch out of here? Why don't you niggers stay in your place?'"[7]

"I wasn't the new kid in the class. I was the new nigger in the class," Dwania Kyles said. "And I remember I didn't have any friends. I couldn't wait for playtime so I could see Harry or Mike."[8] Kyles said they learned how to protect themselves psychologically "so we weren't destroyed by it as a five-year-old and six-year-old. That was hard, very hard. I really lived in my head a lot."

At least two Black students, Leandrew Wiggins and Clarence Williams, who attended Rozelle Elementary School, did not finish the year. Harry Williams lasted three years at Bruce. "I was constantly looking over my shoulder," Harry Williams recalled. "I was scared. . . . There was days I didn't want to go."[9] Nearly half of the Memphis 13 did not remain through sixth grade in the four schools they desegregated.

Kyles was the only one of the Memphis 13 to go straight through the city's public schools, graduating from Bellevue Middle School and then Central

High School. She decided that she, unlike her siblings, would go to a historically Black college or university. She attended Spelman College in Atlanta and graduated from Howard University in Washington, D.C. "I just wanted to have that experience with people who look like me and talk like me," Kyles said.

But Kyles discussed her Memphis school days almost with nostalgia. At a reunion of the Memphis 13, "nobody was really bitter," she said. They recognized they were part of what she called a "life-changing experience, not just for us but for the whole city as well."

The closest the generation of her twenty-six-year-old daughter, Ashli, had been able to get to that kind of experience, she said, was Barack Obama's campaign for president: "He did reignite that fire that was viciously put out in the 1960s with the assassination of so many forward-thinking leaders who were so young."

Kyles worried that her daughter's generation was being deliberately held back, because of "economic inequality practices and the widening gap between the haves and have-nots." Memphis, America's poorest large metropolitan area, was part of the problem: nearly 50 percent of Black children lived in poverty, and the median income of the county's Black residents stood at about half of the median income of local whites'. Whatever her daughter's generation faced, Kyles was proud of what she and twelve other five- and six-year-olds had accomplished. They nonviolently desegregated a city school system of 51,815 students. "I've done my part," she said.

In 2018, on the fiftieth anniversary of the assassination of the Reverend Martin Luther King Jr., Memphis activists emphasized what remained to be done. The flight of manufacturing and white residents had left Memphis with a low-wage economy and a declining population. The city's homicide rate ranked among the highest in the country. Memphis remained stuck in what King called "the dark and desolate valley of segregation."[10]

Still, Memphians pointed to signs of progress. The renovated National Civil Rights Museum helped draw 11.5 million tourists to the city annually. Mark Russell became the first African American in the 176-year history of the *Commercial Appeal* to lead the newspaper. The city announced it would award a tax-free grant of $50,000 to each of fourteen surviving Black sanitation workers from the 1968 strike, men who lacked the city pensions that had been provided to other city workers.[11] And the Confederate statues came down. Otis Sanford, a University of Memphis journalism professor, said,

"From a racial standpoint, we're at a much better place now than we've ever been."[12]

I had a personal interest in our next stop, Holly Springs, Mississippi, fifty miles to the south of Memphis. Was it, from a racial standpoint, at a much better place now than when I spent a summer there almost a half-century earlier?

CHAPTER 13

Mississippi

A Black College, Highway 61 Blues, and Racism Redux

I was uneasy about returning to Mississippi. In the summer of 1964, dubbed Freedom Summer because of the civil rights efforts in Mississippi, I and others had viewed the road south into the state as dangerous, even deadly. The comedian and civil rights activist Dick Gregory said he would have gone south but his Blue Cross coverage had expired. "Then again," Gregory added, "better it than me!"[1]

In the summer of 1964, Holly Springs, Mississippi, population fifty-seven hundred, seemed determined to remain segregated. No surprise. Billed by its Chamber of Commerce as "Where the Old South Meets the New," Holly Springs reveled in its history as a Confederate stronghold ("home of 13 generals") and center of King Cotton. The enslaved people who worked the region's cotton plantations produced more bales of cotton "than any similar division of land in the world," a historian of Holly Springs bragged. The same historian claimed the slaves "were fairly well-treated, cared for . . . if anything, rather fortunate in their servitude."[2]

In 1964, Sam Coopwood, Holly Springs mayor, city judge, clothing store owner, and former police chief, explained how fortunate the city's Black residents were in the early 1960s: "Last Saturday this colored man backed out into traffic. He couldn't pay the $7 fine so I told him to come back when he could. I don't know anywhere in the world where they turn a man out to get money."[3]

Following passage of the Civil Rights Act of 1964, which outlaws racial segregation in schools, employment, and public accommodations, hastily lettered signs sprouted in Holly Springs. At Landruth's, a combined tackle shop and restaurant, three cardboard placards read "Membership Only." The movie theater closed, and the owner announced plans to reopen it as a private membership "recreation club." The public library removed its tables and chairs and, according to Black residents, transferred all its good books to a private collection.

My unease about returning to Mississippi dated from one summer night in 1964 when I learned my identity could get me killed. Earlier, during the 1963–64 school year, I had joined other Yale Law School students in starting the Southern Teaching Program. The foundation-funded program arranged for fifty-three graduate and professional students to teach that summer at thirteen historically Black colleges in the South. James Dodson, Granger Ricks, and I were among the six white students from Yale and Columbia Medical School who volunteered to teach at Rust College in Holly Springs.

Freedom Summer's spirit of social change grabbed hold of us. I filled my Rust writing course with Ralph Ellison, Richard Wright, and other Black writers; as adviser to the college's newspaper, I encouraged students to cover the activities of Freedom Summer.

During Freedom Summer, civil rights workers in Holly Springs and across Mississippi registered Black residents to vote, established an integrated Mississippi Freedom Democratic Party, and started alternative Freedom Schools. The free schools taught young and old African Americans Black history and civil rights as well as reading, writing, art, music, and math.

White supremacists retaliated. The Mississippi State Sovereignty Commission, a segregationist espionage and propaganda agency, spied on civil rights activists and suspicious outsiders, including those of us teaching at Rust.

Sometimes the Sovereignty Commission appeared to do more than spy. Frank Cieciorka, a Holly Springs civil rights worker from California, insisted he and others were targeted for violence because whites easily recognized their license plates. Mississippi required people to register their cars within thirty days of arriving in the state.[4] State officials reserved a special sequence of license plate numbers for civil rights workers, and the Sovereignty Commission distributed the numbers across the state.[5] James Chaney, Andrew Goodman, and Michael Schwerner, who had gone to Philadelphia, Mississippi, to investigate the arson of a Black church, were arrested for speeding by sheriff's deputies. The deputies had been given the make, model, color, and license plate of their station wagon. A mob greeted their release and executed the men.[6]

Goodman and Schwerner were young white New Yorkers. I was too. I worried about setting foot off the Rust campus at night. A young woman had written in the mimeographed newspaper of the Holly Springs Freedom School that she was not shocked at the loss of Chaney, Goodman, and Schwerner: "Many of our people have come up missing and nothing was said or done about it." Bruce Johnston, a Southern Teaching Program volunteer at Rust, had been run off the road by white men in a pickup truck. And Wayne Yancey, a Black freedom worker who had been driving from Memphis to Holly Springs, had died in a head-on auto collision that many people believed "was caused by local white racists," the civil rights leader Larry Rubin said.[7]

But one evening toward the end of the summer, momentarily overcome by starvation and stupidity, Dodson, Ricks, and I piled into my fire-engine red Corvette with New York license plates (what was I thinking, driving such a car into Mississippi?) to grab a snack at a roadside restaurant.

At the restaurant, four young white male muscleheads overheard our conversation about Rust and stopped at our table on their way out. As if they were simply drawling, "Nice evenin', y'all," the four threatened to kill the three of us.[8]

Frozen by fear, I sat motionless and speechless. I realized the odds did not favor us. Ricks, a pudgy graduate student in history who wore dark glasses because he was blind, could not strike fear in the rednecks. Nor could I, a bespectacled bantam.

Dodson, twenty-nine, a lanky doctoral candidate in international relations, barked at the locals about his four years as a Marine sergeant: "You really don't want to mess with us." But Ricks, in his strong Georgia accent, invited the locals to bring it on. Dodson recalled thinking to himself, "Uh-oh, we're in for it now."

The locals, however, sauntered away. We soon found they had slashed my car's right rear tire. A police officer arrived. He blamed the slashed tire on us. Ricks remembered the officer's words: "Well, as long as you hang around with those sons of bitches [at Rust], anything can happen."

I realized my association with Rust and identity as one of the unwelcome visitors from the North—what a Sovereignty Commission investigator labeled a communist-inspired "outside bunch of civil rights agitators"—threatened my life.[9] Later, after searching the Sovereignty Commission's files, I understood that the identity of other people at Rust had marked them as much more vulnerable prey. The Sovereignty Commission targeted African American gays, Black Muslims, women and men in interracial relationships, and the college's Black president. I was a white male outsider who at

David Beckley

summer's end could return north to the safety of law school classes. Once I left Mississippi, the Sovereignty Commission wouldn't care about me.

My anxiety about reentering Mississippi in 2011 was mixed with excitement. I looked forward to seeing David Beckley, a former student of mine who was in his nineteenth year as president of Rust, and his wife, Gemma, who chaired Rust's social work department. As Alyssa, Dan, and I traveled the country, I was impressed by people like the Beckleys who transformed institutions by staying put.

David Beckley, a native of nearby Shannon, had graduated from Rust in three years (classmates recalled Beckley's saying he would someday head the college), served in Vietnam, and earned his doctorate at the University of Mississippi.

In the early 1960s, Rust had lost full accreditation. No faculty member held a doctoral degree. By the time Dan, Alyssa, and I interviewed Beckley, 62 percent of Rust's faculty had doctoral degrees, and the college was fully accredited. Rust's endowment, once virtually nonexistent, stood at $25 million (in 2020, the endowment reached $47 million).

In the early 1960s, almost 70 percent of Rust's students came from Mississippi, the poorest state and long considered the worst in the country in terms of public education. The area's schools operated on a reduced split schedule, encouraging students to work in the cotton fields in season. Senator James K. Vardaman, Democrat of Mississippi (1913–19), explained that educating the Black man "simply renders him unfit for the work which the white man has prescribed, and which he will be forced to perform. . . . The effect is to spoil a good field hand and make an insolent black cook."[10]

By the time we visited, Rust drew more than half of its nine hundred students from states other than Mississippi. Rust also attracted seventy to eighty students from outside the United States. We interviewed three students from Africa—Nigel Chimbetete from Zimbabwe, Omolola Dawodu from Nigeria, and Sandi Litia from Zambia.

Faced with few resources and isolated from much of the outside world, small historically Black colleges like Rust could have been satisfied to, in James Baldwin's words, "make peace with mediocrity."[11] But David Beckley appeared to be transforming Rust into a college relevant in a globalizing world.

Gemma Beckley, whom I had not seen in a quarter century, described another major challenge. When we had last met, she had told me about her fieldwork in the Mississippi Delta, where many girls as young as twelve became pregnant, dropped out of school, and started families. Later, for a 2014 book, she again interviewed people in the Delta who complained about a high school graduation rate of only 41 to 42 percent: "The largest single factor that keeps these kids from graduating is teen pregnancy. They have a child-care day care set up in the middle school."[12]

So had there been progress? Gemma Beckley admired how well African Americans "have done, how well women have done, even given so much of the discrimination, injustice." But she said that young African American women face challenges unknown to earlier generations in Mississippi.

Segregation had provided "more clarity in many ways in what you were fighting for," she said. In that era, African American women sought not only survival but also more control of their lives, and they attended college in greater numbers than African American men. "Some of that has been lost," Gemma Beckley said, "a loss of a certain level of determination, pride, recognition of how important it was culturally to evolve."

In rural Mississippi in the twenty-first century, she also suggested, the struggle to survive economically meant some families spent more hours working and less time teaching and supervising their children. "The children fall prey more often to many destructive things that are hurled at them more than in the past," she said. She believed drugs, crime, and school absenteeism were as great a problem in rural Mississippi as they were in cities. "Our [local] dropout rate is greater than it was twenty years ago," she said.

The Marshall County Youth Court in Holly Springs had an increasingly heavy caseload. The court "can't get through the whole [daily] docket," she said. Lynn Pullen, the regional director and a twenty-five-year veteran of Youth Services, acknowledged that the caseload and the severity of cases—including assaults and burglaries—had increased, in part because of more gang activity.

Gemma Beckley recounted the sorry history of school desegregation in Mississippi. In 1962–63, eight years after the U.S. Supreme Court's 1954 decision in *Brown v. Board of Education*, not one African American student attended a Mississippi public school with a white student.[13]

The legacy in Marshall County, Gemma Beckley said, was that the private Marshall Academy remained predominantly white, and public schools were largely segregated by race. The Black schools, often underfunded and understaffed, were failing. She cited a study that showed that by eighth grade poor Black students were three to four years behind wealthier white students in reading and four to five years behind in math.

Gemma Beckley saw a need to focus on poor families, both Black and white, not just the families' schoolage children. "It's cultural now, not just racial," she said. She also worried that students who are compelled to go to school by adolescent offender programs "are acting out . . . are just not going to conform" in school. The teachers, she said, are "half-scared of these kids."

One school reform proposal called for the establishment of a Knowledge Is Power Program—a public charter school with free tuition, open enrollment, and college prep instruction. But Gemma Beckley sounded skeptical. "When they talk about vouchers, when they talk about charter schools," she said, "these are just another way to resegregate." A half century after I spent Freedom Summer there, Mississippi appeared to be succeeding at its long-held goals of racial subjugation and segregation.

The day we drove the thirty miles south on Route 7 from Holly Springs to Oxford, the *Daily Mississippian*, the University of Mississippi's student newspaper, led page 1 with an article about "the color line" in the Student Union cafeteria.

According to the reporter, this was a not uncommon scenario: a white transfer student approaches a cafeteria table filled with African American students and asks if anyone is sitting in an open chair. "The black students look at her awkwardly for wanting to sit with them." The white student "flees to another table in the back of the Union," where she sits with other white students.

The article recalled a cafeteria incident from 1965. At the time, the university's mascot was Colonel Rebel, a stereotypical plantation master, and the school's symbols were the Confederate flag and the song "Dixie." When Verna Bailey, the first Black female student at the university, entered the cafeteria, students hissed and shouted, "Here comes the nigger, here comes the nigger." They threw food at her as she took her tray from the cafeteria line.[14]

After our trip, I telephoned Renee Ombaba, a 2014 master's graduate of the University of Mississippi's Center for the Study of Southern Culture, for an update on race relations in the cafeteria and across the university. Ombaba, twenty-four, is the Massachusetts-born daughter of a Kenyan father and a Zambian mother, professionals who were part of an ongoing wave of well-educated African immigrants.[15]

Ombaba said the university's Student Union cafeteria remained "a major issue." A white student's tweeted complaint—that the front of the cafeteria looked like the student body at historically Black Jackson State—went viral.

The dispute about space in the cafeteria, Ombaba said, "represented how people feel about the entire university. There are covert acts of violence or microaggressions [discriminatory insults and actions] to keep minorities from entering spaces that whites don't feel African American or other non-white students should occupy."

While Ombaba felt comfortable with her professors, she believed institutional racism at the University of Mississippi allowed for cultural exclusion as well as physical exclusion of many African American students. Faculty and administrators nudged African Americans toward the social work department and education school, she said. The message to an African American student intent on studying chemistry might be, "You shouldn't be a chemistry major, you're not smart enough."

Fraternities, sororities, and other student organizations also reflected, Ombaba said, "an environment where it is okay to display your xenophobia." On the night of President Obama's reelection in 2012, white students burned an Obama campaign sign and chanted anti-Obama racial slurs. A scuffle between thirty to forty Black and white students caused someone to tweet, "It's a riot on campus," Ombaba said. Soon four hundred to five hundred students had gathered to see what was happening.

The next day, at the office of the William Winter Institute for Racial Reconciliation, Ombaba discussed the incident with professors. "A lot of African American students were afraid to come to school," she said. "How do we deal with this?" Ombaba said she and her professors felt that "we had to react quickly so that the students could feel safe again." She helped organize a candlelight vigil. Nearly seven hundred people held copies of the University Creed (its first principle: "I believe in respect for the dignity of each person") as they marched in the dark from the Student Union to the Lyceum, a university center.

The university undertook other initiatives. The handbook for entering students, which originally focused on effective study skills, addressed issues of race and inclusion as well. An action plan ranged from creating a vice chancellor for diversity and inclusion to changing the name of Confederate Drive to Chapel Lane.

But Ombaba spoke of a fear that the university could still go backward. A September 2013 production at the university of *The Laramie Project*, a play about the brutal 1998 murder of Matthew Shepard, a gay college student in Wyoming, made national headlines after homophobic heckling by audience members. In February 2014, three first-year students were expelled for placing a noose around the neck of the statue of James Meredith, the first Black student to enroll at the university, and draping over his face an early Georgia state flag that featured the Confederate battle emblem.

Mississippians needed to address the racism that remained a part of their lives, Ombaba said. Rather than merely reacting to individual racist and homophobic incidents, she said, Mississippians had to tackle the larger societal system of massive resistance to racial justice that condoned, and even invited, discrimination.

While Ombaba knew institutional racism was a problem not just at the University of Mississippi or in Mississippi, she committed to addressing it in Mississippi. Many African Americans left the state after graduating from the university, but she planned to stay. "I love the South, I love the state, and I love this place we call home," she said. "If you love this place, you should be willing to learn about it and want to change it."

An hour and a half south of Oxford, we reached Money, Mississippi, home to the crumbling remains of Bryant's Grocery & Meat Market. The store was the site of an incident that led to fourteen-year-old Emmett Till's horrific murder, which in turn helped kick-start the civil rights revolution.

On August 14, 1955, Till and his cousin, Wheeler Parker, who were on vacation from Chicago and visiting Till's great-uncle, purchased candy at Bryant's. Parker and Simeon Wright, another of Till's cousins, said they saw Till wolf-whistle at Carolyn Bryant, who owned the store with her husband, Roy.

Two weeks later, Roy Bryant and his half-brother, J. W. Milam, kidnapped Till. After beating, torturing, and shooting the boy in the head, they used barbed wire to tie a seventy-five-pound cotton-gin fan to his neck. Then they tossed his body in the Tallahatchie River.

That morning, Leflore County sheriff George Smith arrested Milam and Bryant on suspicion of kidnapping. The charge was changed to murder when Till's body turned up three days later. Mamie Till Bradley demanded that the battered and bloated body of her son be returned home and displayed in an open-casket funeral for, she said, "the whole world to see." The September 15, 1955, issue of *Jet* magazine featured a photo of the corpse—swollen, hacked head; one eye bulging out of its socket, the other gouged out; mouth and tongue torn and twisted; teeth smashed.

The photo stirred African Americans. Shortly after Till's murder, Rosa Parks, seamstress and NAACP activist, refused to give up her seat to a white passenger and move to the back of a bus in Montgomery, Alabama. Police arrested her for violating the state's bus segregation laws. Later she said, "I thought about Emmett Till and I just couldn't go back."[16]

A jury of twelve white men acquitted Bryant and Milam after deliberating only sixty-seven minutes. A juror said the men would have taken less time if they had not stopped to drink sodas. Later, Bryant and Milam confessed to Till's murder.

Seventy-year-old Charlie Brunson recalled for Alyssa, Dan, and me the 1950s, when a less moldy Money had several hundred residents, a cotton mill, and five or six stores to the east of Bryant's Grocery. But the stores were torn down after the post office closed in 2010. As for the railroad station across the road from Bryant's, now relocated behind it, "all the old folks used to gamble in there." One man lost his five-thousand-acre farm.

We learned more about Money from Sylvester Hoover, owner of Delta Blues Legends tours in Greenwood, Mississippi. He described the life of his father, who picked cotton on the twenty-two-hundred-acre Whittington plantation on Money Road (County Road 518), which runs between Money and Greenwood. As a day laborer, he was paid a dollar a day. To get ahead, he also made moonshine whiskey, which he sold for five dollars a gallon.

When Hoover's mother paid for supplies at the plantation commissary with a five-dollar bill, the commissary operator questioned her. Hoover explained, "You didn't have no right to have no five-dollar bill. They wanted to dictate the way your family lived."

In a good year, Hoover's family picked five hundred bales of cotton. But at the year-end accounting, the plantation owner always claimed Hoover's father still owed him money, Hoover said. A study by the Yale anthropologist Hortense Powdermaker estimated that only a quarter to a third of plantation owners accounted honestly.[17] "It was just a conspiracy. You never got ahead, never," said Hoover. "If I owe you a nickel, I can't move."

Physical as well as financial intimidation—the threat of rape and murder—shadowed the plantation's workers. Hoover's parents insisted his sisters leave Mississippi by age thirteen—"My mother didn't want the boss man to fool with them"—and his brothers by fifteen. Hoover's siblings left for Chicago and other northern cities. "They won't come back," Hoover said.

In front of Bryant's Grocery stood a sign—"Marker No. 1 on the Mississippi Freedom Trail, dedicated May 18, 2011," the fiftieth anniversary of the Freedom Rides. I took that sign to be a mark of progress in a state that still celebrates Confederate Memorial Day and Confederate Heritage Month. (But vandals stole an Emmett Till memorial sign erected in 2008 at the Tallahatchie River and threw it in the river; replacement signs were defaced with bullet holes, forcing the erection in 2019 of a five-hundred-pound bulletproof sign with a surveillance system.)[18]

Brunson said Harry Ray Tribble, a local businessman, had bought the ghostly remains of the Bryant's Grocery and the service station next door. Nobody knew what he would do with the store and service station. Open a tourist business? A civil rights museum?

Two local sites already honored Emmett Till. At the Emmett Till Historic Intrepid Center in Glendora, Mississippi, eighteen miles from Money, Johnny B. Thomas, the fifty-eight-year-old mayor of Glendora and executive director of the center, said rumor had it that Tribble had rejected an offer from Leflore County of $50,000 for Bryant's Grocery and the abandoned service station next door. Wielding a light green fly swatter, Thomas added, between slaps at flies, "Some others said he wanted three million dollars for the entire property—two, three, maybe four acres."

A Mississippi Civil Rights Historical Sites grant program, I later learned, had awarded Tribble and Annette T. Morgan, his sister, $152,004.80 to restore the service station next to Bryant's, which they did. Tribble, sixty-two, insisted the county never offered $50,000 for the service station and Bryant's Grocery. He talked about getting another grant to restore Bryant's Grocery to create a small Emmett Till museum. "We're not going to bulldoze it down," he said. "I've got all the stuff that went in the original store."

But he was also offering to sell "the whole town" of Money, fifteen to seventeen acres, for $3.2 million. If he made a financial killing, local citizens could be excused for recalling his father's role in another kind of killing—the murder of Emmett Till. His father had served on the jury that acquitted Till's killers.

Streaking south ten miles from moribund Money on Money Road, past miles of cotton and soybean fields, we crossed the Tallahatchie River and suddenly entered the world of cotton-plantation prosperity on Greenwood's appropriately named Grand Avenue.

During the avenue's construction in 1910, the *Greenwood Enterprise* had proudly predicted Grand—with its one thousand stately oak trees, distinctive tree-lined grass median strip, and elegant mansions—would become "the prettiest and swellest piece of property anywhere in the South."[19]

Soon we arrived at another symbol of white Greenwood—a forty-foot-high marble monument to Confederate soldiers next to the Leflore County Courthouse. At the monument's 1913 dedication, the president of the Varina Jefferson Davis chapter of the United Daughters of the Confederacy declared there was "no cause more just or more righteous than the cause for which the Confederate soldiers contended."[20]

We found no monument to Fannie Lou Hamer and the other local African Americans who were soldiers in the civil rights war of the 1960s that was fought, in part, at that same county courthouse. Hamer, a forty-one-year-old sharecropper's wife and plantation timekeeper, was thrown off the plantation when she tried to register to vote in 1962. One of twenty children born to a family of Delta sharecroppers, Hamer proved an eloquent spokesperson for the Mississippi Freedom Democratic Party, which challenged the all-white, segregationist Mississippi delegation to the Democratic National Convention in 1964. She also ran for Congress that year against a white incumbent who had been elected twelve times. "I'm showing the people that a Negro can run for office. All my life I've been sick and tired. Now I'm sick and tired of being sick and tired,"[21] she famously said.

Greenwood served as a headquarters of the White Citizens' Council and a battleground for the Ku Klux Klan. In 1963, Greenwood's Byron De La Beckwith, a member of the council and the Klan, drove to Jackson and assassinated Medgar Evers, field secretary of the National Association for the Advancement of Colored People, by shooting him in the back with a high-powered hunting rifle.

Black Mississippians made Greenwood the starting point for a voter registration campaign that eventually became the national focus of such organizations as the Student Nonviolent Coordinating Committee (SNCC). Greenwood was an obvious target for a voter registration drive. Two-thirds of its twenty thousand residents were Black, but only 250 were registered to vote. Before the end of the 1960s, however, three-quarters of the town's eligible Black residents would be registered to vote.

The registration drive inspired Greenwood residents, including June E. Johnson and her parents, to help SNCC. While returning from a voter registration training workshop in South Carolina, the fifteen-year-old Johnson and other activists sought to eat at a bus station's whites-only restaurant in Winona, Mississippi. They were arrested, locked in the local jail, and savagely beaten. "Blood was streaming down the back of my head, and my dress was all bloody," she said.[22] An all-white jury cleared the sheriff and other participants in the beating.

Johnson refused to stop her voter registration work. In the 1970s she served as plaintiff and paralegal investigator for lawsuits to end racial discrimination by Greenwood and Leflore County. In 1978, she became the first African American woman candidate for the Leflore County Board of Supervisors. Johnson died in 2007 at age fifty-nine of kidney failure, having spent her life stubbornly fighting injustice. A SNCC worker once said she "would argue with a stop sign."[23]

I interviewed Johnson's youngest brother, Benton, at Century Funeral Home, a symbol of the South's racial divide. White-owned funeral homes employed white embalmers for white customers. Black-owned funeral homes employed Black embalmers for Black customers. Century, Greenwood's preeminent Black funeral home, had handled the body of Emmett Till before it was returned to Chicago and later the cancer-riddled body of Fannie Lou Hamer.

Benton Johnson, fifty-seven, worried that present-day Greenwood, with high unemployment and little opportunity, was in worse shape than when his sister and Hamer fought the Jim Crow system in the 1960s and 1970s. "We can't put everything on the white folk," he said. "I would say the struggle done turned into a financial thing. It ain't just Blacks and whites divided. It's Blacks and Blacks divided." Some Blacks still struggled for justice, Johnson said, whereas others cared only about "something to put in their pocket."

Johnson did not sugarcoat the reality of the civil rights era: "Most of the [Black] people around the town did what white people said. If you were the type who couldn't go along with what they said to do, you had to leave."

After his mother's early death, Johnson was raised by his maternal grandmother, Emily Johnson Holt. She warned him never to go beyond the railroad tracks and Johnson Street, where Black residents shopped and socialized.

Greenwood's racial boundaries continued to go deeper than geography. School resegregation left Greenwood High School 98 percent Black (the state department of education gave the school a grade of F for 2013–14); whites flocked to largely white private schools.

Greenwood businesses paid heed to racial boundaries. The restaurateur Mack "Booker" Wright, who had once employed Johnson, had worked as a bow-and-scrape waiter at Lusco's, a famous family-owned restaurant that, when I visited in 2012, had the look of the Depression-era speakeasy it once was. Wright had appeared in a nationally televised documentary, Frank De Felitta's *Mississippi: A Self-Portrait*, in 1966. Wearing his black bow tie and white waiter's coat, a smiling Wright told the television audience what he would tell his white customers at Lusco's: "Glad to see y'all. We don't have a written menu, I'd be glad to tell ya what we're gonna serve tonight."

After reciting the lengthy menu, Wright continued to smile as he explained to viewers how his customers responded: "Some people nice, some is not. Some call me Booker, some call me Jim, some call me John, some call me nigger. All that hurts, but you have to smile. . . . The meaner the man be, the more you smile, although you're crying on the inside or you're wondering, 'What else can I do?'

"I'm trying to make a living. Why? I got three children. I want to give them an education. . . . I just don't want my children [to] have to go through what I go through with 'Hey, tell that nigger to hurry up with that coffee!'"[24]

I met Karen Pinkston, a fourth-generation owner of Lusco's, who recalled what happened after Wright appeared on television: "Well—the phone started ringing off the wall. *All* of the customers were calling out here and telling Marie [Lusco], 'We *never* want Booker to wait on us again. Never.' When Booker came in, he heard the phone and he heard the calls. And he just turned around, and he told them he was sorry, and he just walked out the door and left."[25]

I talked by telephone with Yvette Johnson, Wright's granddaughter. In a 2017 book titled *The Song and the Silence*, Johnson describes Wright's later life.[26] He suffered a beating after his appearance on television. But the restaurant he opened after leaving Lusco's, Booker's Place, became "the most successful, most popular eatery for Blacks in the Delta," she said.

Benton Johnson, who washed dishes and cleared tables there, said the restaurant attracted white customers. In 1973, Lloyd Louis Cork, an African American who used the nickname "Blackie," started taunting two white customers. Wright demanded that Cork leave. Cork walked to the table of the whites and pushed their plates off the table. Wright tossed Cork from the restaurant. Cork returned with a sawed-off shotgun and shot Wright, who died three days later.

Both Yvette Johnson and Karen Pinkston, the fourth-generation owner of Lusco's, were quite happy to let that ugly history be history. Johnson decried historians' focus on Greenwood's "extreme racists" and not other white residents, "people that we would've had dinner with and let our children visit with."

Perhaps Greenwood was beginning to write a different kind of history. In 2009, despite its two-thirds Black majority, Greenwood replaced Sheriel F. Perkins, who is Black, with the politically independent Carolyn McAdams, who is white, as its mayor. "Trust, it turns out, trumps race," writes the historian Gene Datell.[27] McAdams balanced the city's budget, spearheaded revitalization efforts, and started the Mississippi Delta's first municipal recycling program.

"I'm going to be here until I die, so I want Greenwood to sustain itself as a city," she said. "It can't do that with just one race."[28] For three years in a row, readers of the local daily selected McAdams as Greenwood's favorite elected official. She won reelection to a four-year term in 2013 and 2017.

We drove fifty-three miles west from Greenwood on Route 82, through Leland to Greenville, a Mississippi River town, population three thousand in the 1870s, that Twain found "full of life and activity." Before returning to Leland, we ate dinner at seventy-year-old Doe's Eat Place, a dilapidated dive entered through the kitchen. Doe's, winner of a James Beard America's Classics Award in 2007, began in 1941 as a honky-tonk that served buffalofish and chili to the neighborhood's Black residents. When a white doctor began coming for a meal between calls, white locals soon learned about the quality of the food. Doe's accommodated the racial policy of the day by practicing the reverse: Blacks came to the front door, whites to the back. "Shug" (short for Sugar) Signa, who is married to the grandson of the original owner, explained the Doe's experience: "People come together, never meet a stranger—it's the American way."[29]

After Doe's, we headed east to Leland. With van windows open, we blared a mix of music that spanned our generations. Alyssa and Dan chose indie pop rock—groups like The Drums and Future Islands. I blasted jazz and blues from the LP record era. The blues moved me, though I remembered what the playwright August Wilson has blues singer Ma Rainey say: "White folks don't understand the blues. They hear it come out but they don't know how it got there. They don't understand that's life's way of talking. You don't sing [the blues] to feel better. You sing because that's a way of understanding life."[30]

Leland, home of the Highway 61 Blues Museum, oozed the blues. It was played at such juke joints as Boss Hall's Lounge and captured on seven downtown wall murals devoted to B. B. King and other blues greats. The 61 Blues Museum displayed a 1908 magazine article that said as many as ten thousand people flocked to town from surrounding plantations for craps games, kept women, blind-tiger booze, and the blues, played on corners and in clubs and cafes until daylight.

When we started south on Route 61 from Leland, the Delta blues seemed the most appropriate music to boom. Sylvester Hoover, the owner of Delta Blues Legends tours in Greenwood, had stressed the marriage of the blues and the flat alluvial floodplain of northwest Mississippi's delta. He had handed me a nine-foot canvas sack that a plantation worker would drag behind him, picking daily at least seven thousand bolls of cotton, enduring the pricks of the barbed cockleburs, and filling the sack with 100 to 160 pounds of cotton. "If you drag one of these, you'd sing the blues," Hoover said. "The land made the music, the music made the land. They couldn't have happened without each other."

In Twain's time, the Mississippi River dealt deliverance and death. The Mississippi buried the town of Napoleon, Arkansas, under water. The Mississippi also transported African American sharecroppers escaping north from plantations.

Sylvester Hoover shows a canvas bag used to pick cotton. Photo by Claudia Stack from the film *Sharecrop* (2017 Stack Stories LLC).

Highway 61, known as the Great River Road, followed the course of the Mississippi and ran by Alligator, Panther Burn, Rolling Fork, Onward, and other towns with tantalizing toponyms. The Delta blues juke joints, plantations, shotgun houses, and deadly history made Highway 61 a symbol of the state of Mississippi.

Natchez, our final stop in Mississippi on Highway 61, was "the last of the beautiful hill cities," Twain said, as he steamed south on the river to New Orleans. But the civil rights struggle of the 1960s in Natchez was hardly beautiful. Hardscrabble white men from neighboring rural towns, the journalist and Natchez native Vern E. Smith wrote shortly before our arrival in Natchez, "joined with white supremacists and dominated the work force of the city's main employers, . . . and soon, local law enforcement." Ernest Avants, a Klansman from Bogue Chitto, Mississippi (population 887 in 2010) who was later convicted of murder, described Natchez derisively: "The Jews own [Natchez], and the Catholics run it, and the niggers enjoyed it." Against such murderous whites, the Black community, Smith writes, "organized demonstrations, an economic boycott, and countered the Klan violence and the lack of police protection by arming themselves."[31]

On the day of our visit, the *Natchez Democrat* carried a front-page Veterans' Day story—"A Wrong Righted: New WWI Plaque Includes Omitted Names"—that reported the four brass World War I memorial plaques affixed in 1924 to Memorial Hall (now the Natchez federal courthouse) carried the names of only white veterans, 552 in all.[32] Shane Peterson, a graduate student at California State University, Northridge, researched the Black veterans of World War I while working as an intern on the Natchez Court House Project, a catalogue and preservation project of Reconstruction-era court records. Peterson concluded that the absence from the monument of the names of 581 Black Army troops "was no clerical error; this was 'Jim Crow.'"[33]

Alyssa, Dan, and I left behind the Delta, home of the blues, and headed 175 miles south to New Orleans, where Jim Crow was "practiced in a more polite manner," according to the rocker Chuck Berry.[34] I still hoped New Orleans, despite its reputation for traditional jazz, would finally provide an opportunity for me to hear Delta blues live.

CHAPTER 14

New Orleans

A Polyglot Port City with a Multicultural Menu

Only after leaving Mississippi, home of the Delta blues, did I finally hear the blues live. At the southern end of the original Highway 61 in New Orleans, the eighty-two-year-old St. Roch Tavern (nicknamed St. Roach in honor of its resident pests) hired a blues band to play aside its smoke-clouded cheap-booze bar (pitcher of beer: $6). In the rear, five twentysomething gutter punks (T-shirt: "Rude, Crude and Socially Unacceptable") shot pool at a worn table so ancient that it rivaled a table described by Twain as from "the Old Silurian Period, and the cues and ball of the Post-Pliocene."

J.D. & the Jammers, a four-man blues band, unpacked for their 8:30 p.m. start. Fiddling with a lime-green, battery-operated rotary hand fan as he downed a preshow whiskey, the band's leader, J. D. Hill, outlined his half-century career. One of eight children, the son of a choir-singing mother and a harmonica-playing father, Hill, fifty-six, had worked for three decades in New Orleans and environs with Buddy Guy, Junior Wells, and other blues greats.

He showed me a surgical scar on the back of his neck, then self-consciously touched his wired jaw. Three young robbers on bikes had beaten him, break-ing his jaw in two places, all for $13. He was happy to still be able to play blues harmonica gigs, if often for only $20 to $30 a night. His favorite refrain during the evening, as he passed a plastic tip jug, was, "For the needy, not the greedy."

As the lights dimmed, Hill donned a black hat and dark glasses. "We don't want to look like people on the street," he said. He put a tambourine he had stomped into an oblong under his right black-canvas shoe and began to play. He tapped, tapped, tapped the beat on the tambourine to keep time for the band. His first song, especially its verse about getting away from here and being too young to die, conjured up images of deadly Highway 61.

But as the night wore on, the blues seemed more celebratory. I began to feel happier and, perched on a bar stool, moved more freely to the rhythm. It wasn't the booze. I was nursing a Coke. Chris Joplin, the drummer, explained the music to me at intermission: "Even the sad parts of the blues are catharsis."

Toward the end of my time at St. Roch, a Black woman and a white woman, both smiling broadly, rose to dance. They moved together happily and freely. I thought of a line from a James Baldwin short story about a blues musician: "Freedom lurked around us and I understood, at last, that he could help us to be free if we would listen."[1]

Later on, Alyssa, Dan, and I caught a different kind of New Orleans music at Preservation Hall on St. Peter Street in the French Quarter. But first we listened to forty-year-old Ben Jaffe, his brow furrowed, describe the vision of his parents, Allan and Sandy Jaffe. Ben said they had founded Preservation Hall "to create a dignified environment where these aging African American musicians could carry on a tradition that was slowly disappearing without anybody's notice."

I had visited New Orleans in the summer of 1965, several years after Allan and Sandy's arrival, to spend my days as a law student researching the case of Edgar Labat and Alton Poret, two New Orleans African Americans who had spent fourteen years on death row at Louisiana State Penitentiary for allegedly raping a white woman. I had devoted my nights to listening to the Preservation Hall band. Sandy Jaffe, seated at the hall's front gate with a basket in her lap, charged me only 50 cents, half the regular admission.

The weathered hall from the early 1800s framed the music being played inside, encouraging me to feel that for my "student rate" I was listening to authentic traditional jazz of historic value. I heard Allan Jaffe play tuba with such talented African Americans in their eighties and nineties as the trombonist Jim Robinson and the clarinetist George Lewis. I also experienced the Jaffes' French Quarter world of, in Ben Jaffe's words, "thinkers and outsiders and poets and musicians and artists and wheeler dealers." Bill Russell, a sixty-year-old ragtime violinist, modernist composer, and leading historian of New Orleans music, fixed friends' violins for free. Potbellied and

Ben Jaffe

porkpie-hatted Larry Borenstein, forty-six, one-time illusionist, rare-book dealer, and currency speculator, sold two-thousand-year-old pre-Columbian art (that landed him in Mexican jails three times) and contemporary Noel Rockmore paintings of Preservation Hall musicians.

How did Ben Jaffe explain the soul-invigorating New Orleans that Preservation Hall represented? He saw New Orleans as northern Caribbean—a city of French, Spanish, African, and Native American culture, food, music, and architecture that just happened to be in the Deep South.

Visitors to early nineteenth-century New Orleans encountered, two historians explained, "the prevailing French language of the city, its dominant Catholicism, its bawdy sensual delights [and] its proud free Black population—in short, its deeply rooted creole traditions."[2] Sold by Napoleon to the United States with the rest of the Louisiana Purchase in 1803, the city Americanized, becoming both a magnet for Irish, German, Italian, and other European immigrants and the South's main cotton and slave market. Crowded interracial neighborhoods fell prey to Jim Crow. Twentieth-century metropolitan New Orleans began to look more like other segregated U.S. cities—a Black core surrounded by a ring of white suburbs.

But New Orleanians fought in the 1960s to defeat proposals for both an uptown river bridge and a riverfront expressway that would have decimated the French Quarter, the mythologized symbol of the city's devotion to fine food, art, jazz, and other pleasures of the senses. "Our pleasure bar is much higher here than in any other city that I know," Ben Jaffe said. "We're very serious about enjoyment."

Jaffe grew up in the French Quarter, lived two blocks from Preservation Hall, and spent his early life listening to—and learning—traditional New Orleans jazz. He became a part of a largely African American world. Following his father's death from cancer at fifty-one in 1987, Ben took over his father's role of playing tuba in the Preservation Hall Jazz Band.

He also sought to preserve a community and way of life. "Every time I see another Walmart going up, it breaks my heart that it's chipping away at the soul of America," he said. He saw Walmart "as a metaphor for everything that's becoming too big and too much."

The New Orleans world of traditional jazz, he said, "gives us hope. It allows us to mourn. It's a way for us to celebrate and to honor people. And that's what's important to me, those traditions." People from other countries, he said, came to New Orleans to find the meaning of life in the city and its music. Those who stayed, he said, realized "it's not one thing."

He pointed to the experience of the pianist Mari Watanabe from Japan. The first time she encountered New Orleans musicians playing in a funeral procession, it was as a tourist, the second time as a performer, the third time as a mourner for a musician she knew well. She had become a part of the community.

The way of life of his New Orleans, Jaffe suggested, should spread across the world. "If everybody would dance a little bit more, and sing a little more, and celebrate life—not Bourbon Street celebration, Preservation Hall celebration—if they would celebrate the way we celebrate, the way we honor people with our music, the way we celebrate at funerals, the way we're able to mourn people, it just would be a better place for everyone."

New Orleans—60 percent Black, 31 percent white—also celebrated white supremacy, slavery, and segregation. The city's Confederate statues honored President Jefferson Davis and Generals Robert E. Lee and P. G. T. Beauregard; an obelisk saluted white militia that had rioted against integrated police forces in 1874. In 2017, when New Orleans removed the Confederate statues, Mayor Mitch Landrieu said they celebrated "a fictional, sanitized Confederacy, ignoring the death, ignoring the enslavement, ignoring the terror that it actually stood for."[3] He recalled New Orleans was once home to America's largest slave market in a state where 540 people were lynched.[4] Observing the present-day city, New Orleanian Sarah M. Broom writes that outsiders' romanticized image of the Big Easy—sophisticated, progressive, diverse, and distinctive—"comes at the expense of its native black people, who are, more often than not, underemployed, underpaid, sometimes suffocated by the mythology that hides the city's dysfunction and hopelessness." Broom decries, "for the average local, the life-and-death nature of life lived in the city."[5]

A dramatic example of that life-and-death existence caused us to visit two neighborhoods. Hurricane Katrina's devastating winds and rain walloped the Gulf Coast on August 29, 2005, and took more than eighteen hundred lives (fourteen hundred of them in New Orleans), displaced two million people, and produced $130 billion in damage. The storm surge that breached the levees of New Orleans and put much of the below-sea-level city under water for almost two months hit the predominantly Black working-class Lower Ninth Ward the hardest. Even before the storm the area suffered from high poverty. But when the storm ripped homes from their foundations and federal rebuilding money failed to cover the cost of reconstruction, hundreds of families took buyouts. They turned over their properties to the state instead of rebuilding. At least one-third of the Lower Ninth stood empty. In 2015, a decade after the hurricane, only 38 percent of the Lower Ninth's pre-Katrina population of fourteen thousand had returned.[6]

Sustainable, solar-powered, pastel-colored "Brad Pitt houses," built through the actor's foundation, beautified a portion of Tennessee Street. But elsewhere, unoccupied water-stained houses with smashed windows and aging Federal Emergency Management Agency trailers, meant to provide temporary housing, suggested the Lower Ninth might never fully recover. Daniel Aldrich's 2012 study of the recovery compared the Lower Ninth to "a ghost town that could double as a movie set for post-apocalyptic wastelands."[7]

The Village de l'Est Vietnamese neighborhood in the city's northeast corner, however, showed few signs of Hurricane Katrina. Aldrich raved about the neighborhood's "amazing recovery," but Alyssa, Dan, and I realized Village de l'Est had significantly less to recover from than did the Lower Ninth. Two years after Katrina, 90 percent of the Vietnamese businesses had reopened and 90 percent of the residents had returned. "Even as they were evacuating, they organized. They built a website and had a Vietnamese broadcast," Aldrich said. "They raised their own money. They built an urban farm, their own medical facility, and schools. They weren't waiting for FEMA or the city."

Aldrich credited cohesiveness and collective action for Village de l'Est's success: "When New Orleans allowed residents to return in October 2005, Village de l'Est residents did so en masse, with the parish church organizing to supply necessities. . . . When five hundred signatures were needed to prompt Entergy—the local utility—to restore electrical power to the neighborhood, more than a thousand residents signed by the end of the day."[8]

Dan Tham captured the neighborhood's spirit in his interview of resident Giuseppe Anthony Tran:

> On the fortieth anniversary of Saigon's fall, Vietnamese immigrants and their children gathered alongside Vietnam War veterans to reflect on the dramatic events that forever changed all their destinies—the siege of South Vietnam's capital; the evacuation of American soldiers, who would return home from defeat; and the Southeast Asian boat people fleeing the communist takeover.
>
> In the Vietnamese diaspora, it's referred to as Ngày Mất Nước, the Day We Lost Our Country. But in New Orleans, the Vietnamese community commemorated the four decades since April 30, 1975, a little differently. "Everywhere else, they were mourning," Giuseppe Anthony Tran said. "Here, we celebrated forty years of success. . . . Evaluating ourselves and seeing what we've done." He described experiences during those forty years that demonstrated breathtaking resilience, moxie, and a shining sense of humor, wholly unexpected given the circumstances.
>
> That combination worked out quite nicely for the Vietnamese man with an Italian name. It kept him alive. It took him from one delta to another, from fields of jasmine rice to fields of Jazzmen rice, a local variety of the aromatic grain that's advertised as music for your mouth. "It tastes better than jasmine," Tran said with a laugh.
>
> He was born in the Year of the Dragon, 1964, to a family of rice farmers in Hà Tiên, a beach town at the southernmost tip of Vietnam. During his childhood, an unexploded shell jutted out from the ground right in front of his house. Every day the little boy, then known as Toan (Vietnamese for "safe, secure"), would touch the shell with wonder.
>
> Tran didn't know it would explode one day. "The war became something that was familiar to the people," he said. "To the point that we weren't scared

as much." The soundtrack of "the bombing and the guns and everything" accompanied Tran's entire childhood. Until April 30, 1975, when a tenuous peace was reached.

Like a Vietnamese Huckleberry Finn, Tran, then sixteen, decided to flee the country on a raft with eleven other young Vietnamese—total strangers, most of them teenagers. "My mom saved a lot to put me on board," Tran said. "I would say equivalent to $400. That's a lot in Vietnam in the eighties! We were poor as any other citizen."

He was the youngest of seven siblings, just two years shy of military age. He would either leave the country then or never have the chance. "Living under the communists, you get the feeling that you don't have another day to live," he said. "Everything is controlled. That's why I told my parents, 'I don't see any future here.'"

He left on the night of April 30, 1981, while the communists were celebrating six years since the end of the war.

"Officials and police and everyone in office were getting drunk and having a party. I used that moment to escape on a raft," Tran said. The plan was for the twenty-five-foot raft to transport more than a hundred people to a boat. They docked at the mouth of the Mekong River, a vital channel the color of caramel, and waited for the boat to come and take them away from Vietnam. But no boat showed up. As night gathered, so did a crowd of eager would-be escapees. Finally, the twelve pulled anchor and left on the raft.

Tran saw many people pull up in smaller vessels to get onto theirs. "If we waited another second, we would have been overloaded with people," Tran said. "The minute we started the engine, it made so much damn noise. Like a lawn mower. Officials heard it and started firing at us. On that night, the thirtieth, we left with eight big holes in the raft. We had to plug the holes with our shirts."

Tran prayed that the raft would float in one direction: away.

It was everyone's first time at sea. No one knew how to properly maneuver the raft. They had no compass, no map. By night they faced heavy storms. By day the sun fried their skin into "rice paper," Tran recalled. Once in a while they would see a boat in the distance, but the engine wasn't strong enough to take them there in time.

Four times, Tran said, Thai pirates showed up, seeking women and valuables. A little girl, eleven or twelve years old, as Tran remembers, was aboard the raft. When the pirates came the first time, Tran knew they would be after her.

"To protect her, I took a big can of engine oil and dumped it on her," Tran said. "She looked really filthy and so when the pirates looked at her, they said, 'Just forget it.'"

He started fantasizing about land. "After a day or two on the vast ocean, you don't see anything but the blue sky and the water. And the waves were so huge, you didn't think you were going to survive," he said. A devout Roman Catholic, Tran began reciting the last rites each night before sleeping.

Finally, early on the morning of their fifth day at sea, Tran saw a seagull in the open sky. He knew from his childhood spent by the sea that when you see birds, land is near. "It was so wonderful."

Eventually, they landed at the border between Malaysia and Thailand. Although it was a poor village in the province of Narathiwat, it was not Vietnam.

Once word spread that a group of Vietnamese refugees had arrived in the village, the government of Thailand took them in, placing the group in the Songkhla Refugee Camp. At this point, Tran had no shirt, no shoes, and no money.

UNICEF sheltered the tens of thousands of refugees at Songkhla and supplied them with barely enough food and water. Tran started craving meat and certain comfort foods.

"When you're hungry, you come up with all sorts of crazy ideas. I dreamed I would fry an egg as big as a blanket," Tran said. "I would cover myself up and eat at the same time."

Tran volunteered to work for the UNICEF office. One day he found a magazine while he was cleaning up. "I was so happy," Tran said. "So I grabbed it. Actually, I stole it." In his hands Tran held an old edition of a Vietnamese magazine from New Orleans.

Tran took the magazine back to his tent to show his friends. As he flipped through the pages, he happened upon the name of his older brother, Tuong, an ordained priest who had fled Vietnam for the United States in 1975. Tran hadn't heard from him in more than six years. Tran learned from the magazine that his brother was the editor of Dân Chúa, which he had started in the late 1970s to connect Vietnamese Catholics living in the United States.

Tran wanted to send his brother a letter, but he had no money for paper or stamps. "So I asked a priest for a small sheet of paper. I wrote, 'Please help me' and an address and that's it." The priest mailed the letter for him.

In two months, Tran received a letter from his brother with a twenty-dollar bill enclosed. He learned that Tuong had helped settle the very first

Giuseppe Anthony Tran

Vietnamese refugees to arrive in Louisiana. Tuong also assured Tran that he would contact their mother to let her know that her youngest son had made it to safety.

"It was so huge," Tran said. "My life started from there." Wielding the American money with pride, Tran bought "a whole lot" of eggs. That night, for dinner, Tran fried all the eggs but could eat only a quarter of them. "I couldn't take it anymore, you know?" Tran laughed. "I choked on the eggs."

After two years of statelessness, Tran started making plans with his older brother to come to the United States. Tuong, however, was a priest and wasn't allowed to take in another person. He asked an Italian American couple he knew through Catholic Charities to cosponsor Tran.

Francisco Giovanni and his wife, Evelyn, who lived in Chicago, took Tran in, named him Giuseppe Anthony, and put him through high school and college. "That's why I'm in love with Italy," Tran said. "I'm an Italian Vietnamese living in America!

"Coming to America was like a leap into heaven," Tran said. Every day in his new country, Tran took the bus to the library and borrowed an armload of books to read. "Education is something that my parents and godparents wanted for me," Tran said.

At first, learning English was the "most troublesome" for Tran. One day during his first winter, Tran took a walk around downtown Chicago. As he approached a pedestrian crossing, he couldn't understand the DON'T WALK sign on the crosswalk signal. So he hopped on a bus and immediately asked to be dropped off as soon as the bus crossed the road. Looking back on that episode, Tran guessed that the bus driver probably "cursed me for such a stupid action."

But he was determined. Unable to adapt to the freezing Chicago winters, he moved to New Orleans and became the first Vietnamese student at Brother Martin High School. After graduation from there in 1984, he entered St. Joseph Seminary College in Covington, Louisiana, and earned degrees in philosophy and psychology. He moved on to Notre Dame Seminary in New Orleans and trained for the priesthood, which he would leave in order to focus on bringing his family to the United States from Vietnam.

Tran eventually settled in Village de l'Est, a neighborhood known for its Vietnamese community. The river there is crowded with lily pads. The soupy air circulates languidly around the signs in Vietnamese for restaurants and grocery stores, attorneys and dentists, Catholic churches and Buddhist temples. Many of the men living there are fishers or shrimpers by trade. In Village de l'Est, there's the distinct feeling of quê hương. Homeland.

The immigrant population liked the area because it so resembled the country they had left: the tight-knit community and the subtropical climate, the landscapes and the faces, the familiar food and the language spoken.

"The unity is there," Tran said. "It's lovely." He had been to other Vietnamese communities in Texas and California, but nothing compared to Village de l'Est.

In 1997, Tony Tran went back to Vietnam for the first time in almost twenty years. His mission was to bring his mother to Louisiana.

On the flight into Tan Son Nhat International Airport, Tran noticed the rusty-looking rooftops of Saigon. Overgrown weeds choked the airport's runway. He found he had no attachment to the country of his birth. He also found that every step he took to get to his mother required a financial transaction—bribe an official here, placate an officer there with cold, hard cash. Tran paid a couple of authorities $200 each to accompany him. "They followed me like the FBI," he said.

He had learned that his family now lived in Biên Hòa, just outside Saigon. He walked into his mother's house and surprised her. "I'm glad that she didn't faint!" Tran said.

At the end of his one-week visit, Tran told his mother that he would do everything in his power to bring her to the United States. And later that year he did. In 2000, Tran returned to Vietnam to fulfill his mother's wish that he bring the remains of his father, who had died in 1972, to the United States. They fit into his carry-on luggage in a tiny basket. When we talked, his mother was ninety-four years old and lived in the West Bank of New Orleans, where his father was buried. Tran's mother died in 2018 at the age of ninety-seven and was buried with his father.

For the Vietnamese community, which had so often experienced exodus and relocation—from North to South Vietnam, from Vietnam to refugee camps, from those camps to America—the devastation wrought by Katrina in 2005 was yet another experience of moving from one place to another. It took Tran twenty-eight hours to reach Dallas from New Orleans, usually an eight-hour trip.

As Tran told it, two weeks after the storm the displaced Vietnamese "came right back and fixed their homes. We shoveled out the mud and picked up. Cleaned up. Came back strong."

Tran served as the parish coordinator of the Mary Queen of Vietnam Church. He was a community leader and the assistant to the Reverend Dominic Nghiem. Tran's wife, whom he met at the library in 1994, was a nurse. They had two boys—Mark, a student at Loyola University, and Tri On (Vietnamese for "grateful"), a sophomore in high school.

Over a meal of Vietnamese food at Ba Mien Restaurant, Tran said, "With my life, I feel I had more than I wished for. Looking back on the journey, everything was a blessing all along."

On Thanksgiving Day of 2011, not long after our visit, Tran learned he had cancer of the spleen.

"Kind of ridiculous, huh?" he said.

For the first eight months, he underwent "all sorts of treatment, testing, radiation, chemo, medical examinations," he said. "Now I'm on pills."

Tran said the cancer caused a terrible growth on his skin. "It felt like leprosy. I was so worried," he said. His doctor told him she had never seen anything like it.

Despite, or maybe because of, his experiences, from war to escape, cancer to Katrina, Tran insisted there was nothing to be afraid of, that he had all sorts of reasons to be happy.

"I try not to take everything seriously," he said. "It's a life-changing experience. I'm taking it easy with everything, while I still have another day to *live. So, what the heck, this is just a little cancer, huh?"* In 2020, Tran was still *working at the church, and his cancer was in remission.*

Moved by New Orleanians like Giuseppe Anthony Tran and by the cele-bratory, over-the-top spirit of the city, we left New Orleans feeling the way Twain felt about the city's special place in American life. He wrote that Americans have not seen the United States until they have experienced New Orleans and its Mardi Gras: "New Orleans seldom does things by halves."

CHAPTER 15

Outliers

From Prison Inmates to American Indians

When the Civil War broke out in 1861, Mark Twain knew his regular visits to New Orleans as a steamboat pilot were numbered. He headed upriver from New Orleans to St. Louis as a passenger on the *Nebraska*. Governor Claiborne Jackson of Missouri, a slave state, rallied fifty thousand Missourians to join the militia to fight for the South. A conflicted Twain returned to his hometown of Hannibal and became a member of an inept Confederate militia, the Marion (County) Rangers, for two weeks: "I knew more about retreating than the man who invented retreating."

When Lincoln appointed Orion Clemens, Twain's brother, secretary of the Territory of Nevada, Twain saw an opportunity to distance himself from the Civil War. He accepted the unpaid position of assistant secretary of the Nevada Territory and headed west with his brother, achieving freedom from the war.

In 2005, Wilbert Rideau achieved a different kind of freedom. He walked free after spending forty-four years behind bars in Louisiana—one-quarter of those years on death row. The Supreme Court had thrown out his first conviction because of prejudicial pretrial publicity, and appeals courts rejected two other convictions by all-white juries. He was convicted of manslaughter by a mixed jury in 2005 and was released, having served many more years than the term for manslaughter. Until he walked free, the media told Rideau's story two ways.

First, they portrayed him as a man wronged by the legal system, given the rejection of those three convictions by appellate courts. The U.S. Supreme Court had overturned Rideau's first conviction for murdering a bank teller, Julia Ferguson, in the aftermath of a botched bank robbery because, with a sheriff's help, a local television station had broadcast a "covertly filmed interview" of Rideau, subjecting him to what Justice Potter Stewart called "kangaroo court proceedings."[1]

Second, the media portrayed Rideau as "the most rehabilitated prisoner in America."[2] A ninth-grade dropout, Rideau achieved what no prison journalist and few professional journalists have accomplished. His editorship of the *Angolite*, the newsmagazine of Louisiana State Penitentiary (known as Angola), earned it seven nominations for a National Magazine Award. Rideau himself won a George Polk Award and a Robert F. Kennedy Journalism Award. As an inmate, he worked as a correspondent for NPR's *Fresh Air* and coproduced and narrated *Tossing Away the Keys*, a documentary for NPR's *All Things Considered*. He codirected the Academy Award–nominated film *The Farm: Angola, USA*.

But when Rideau walked free, some media chose a third way to tell his story: by focusing on the victims of the 1961 crime that had sent him to prison and the anger that led to threats on his life after his release. A 2005 *Los Angeles Times* article, written from Lake Charles, Louisiana, Rideau's hometown, used in a headline a quote from Kenneth Rue, an electrical contractor, about Rideau: "If he came back [to town], he'd be pushing up daisies." A separate *Times* article quoted an email writer who planned to hire a contract killer to "bump off" Rideau.[3]

Six years after Rideau's release, we visited him to learn what life was like for him in the non–New Orleans portion of Louisiana, what the novelist John Kennedy Toole called "the heart of darkness, the true wasteland."[4] Rideau asked that we not name the Louisiana community where he lived. Life in prison had made Rideau wary of people on the outside.

"Life is good out here," Rideau said. He loved and felt loved by his wife, Linda LaBranche, once a Shakespeare scholar at Northwestern University, who played a key role in gaining his freedom. He makes a living as a consultant to lawyers in capital cases, which gives him a sense of accomplishment.

His consulting work permits him time, after decades of closely regulated prison life, to be on his own. "I'm free," Rideau laughed. "I want to say, 'Free, partly white, and twenty-one.' You know, in the South, color is everything, race is everything."

Rideau should know. After his three convictions by all-white juries were thrown out, he had to stand trial for a fourth time. That jury of two Black women, one mixed-race woman, one Black man, seven white women, and one white man found him not guilty of murder. A murder verdict would

Wilbert Rideau and
Linda LaBranche

have meant a life sentence. Instead, the jury convicted him of manslaughter, which carried a maximum sentence of twenty-one years. Hence his immediate release for time served.

Rideau saw signs of racial progress on the outside—for example, three-quarters of the cashiers at a local Walmart were African American. "There's change," he said.

He quickly added, "But there's not change. The entire criminal justice system—cops, courts, prisons—is run by whites." For instance, "white juries or functionally white juries—one or two Blacks on it"—decide the fate of defendants who are often nonwhite. An 1898 state constitutional convention dominated by white supremacists virtually ensures that the few African Americans selected for a Louisiana jury, however skeptical they may be of an accused's guilt, have little or no say in the jury's conclusion; the state became one of only two (Oregon is the other) that does not require a unanimous jury for conviction in felony cases. A 10–2 vote is sufficient to convict. (In a 2020 case involving a Louisiana man convicted 10–2 of murder, the U.S. Supreme Court outlawed split verdicts, ruling that juries nationwide must be unanimous to acquit or convict a criminal defendant.)

His comment about the criminal justice system recalled my introduction to that system. In 1965, to interview inmates on death row in Angola (where Rideau had served much of his sentence), I had to obtain the approval in nearby St. Francisville of Judge John R. Rarick, a segregationist firebrand who called the civil rights movement a communist conspiracy. He flew the Confederate flag in his courtroom. The day the 1964 Civil Rights Act passed

Congress, he flew the American flag upside down and began stamping his mail "Resist."

Rarick personified the white-supremacy South that favored use of the n-word or "colored" when identifying Rideau. Ironically, Rideau questioned whether "Black" or "African American" was the best way to identify him in an increasingly multiracial America where an interracial marriage, like his, was no longer uncommon. He recalled being labeled colored as a boy and thought the term more appropriate today, because people labeled Black or African American were more often than not shades of brown. "'Colored' fits better," Rideau said, "because that's where the [skin color of the] country is going anyway."

Rideau thought people who talked about America as postracial deluded themselves. He pointed to the white vote in Louisiana for the white supremacist David Duke when he was a candidate for governor. Duke, a founder of the National Association for the Advancement of White People, opposed former governor Edwin W. Edwards in a runoff in 1991. Duke received 671,009 votes to Edwards's 1,057,031. But Duke claimed victory: "I won my constituency. I won 55 percent of the white vote." Exit polls indicated he was right.[5]

Exit polls in the 2008 presidential election showed President Barack Obama lost the nationwide white vote to John McCain, 55 to 43 percent, and in 2012 to Mitt Romney, 59 to 39 percent. Indeed, in every presidential election for the past half century a majority of whites voted against the Democratic candidate.[6] Many whites, especially those with what pollsters call "high racial resentment scores," wanted to "take back America," Rideau said.

Alyssa, Dan, and I planned to stop in Angola to interview Warden Burl Cain, whose emphasis on religion was ballyhooed in a *New York Times* article.[7] Rideau was less than enthusiastic about Cain and prison religion. In his 2010 memoir he had criticized Cain as being "about power, control, and money," but he told us that, after visiting other U.S. prisons, he thought Cain was a better prison warden than many others. The two had some history. When Cain first became the warden at Angola, he had sought to turn Rideau into a snitch, then to convert him to the warden's brand of evangelical Christianity. When that failed, Rideau said, Cain targeted Rideau's *Angolite* for censorship. Cain could be "a bully—harsh, unfair, vindictive," Rideau said.[8]

As for organized religion in prison, Rideau said, "I just saw too much." Priests, chaplains, and ministers visited Angola to save souls but seemed unconcerned about the mortal lives of the people whose souls they were busy saving: "Coming there made them feel good about themselves, and a little self-righteous."[9]

Rideau ended by talking about his difficult search for work. He carved out a career that proves the T. S. Eliot epigram—success "is what we can make of the mess we have made of things."[10] Rideau repeatedly expressed remorse for his victims: "I realize words are pretty inadequate. But that's all I've got right now." He also reinvented himself yet again, teaching in continuing legal education programs and working as a consultant for defense attorneys in more than fifty problem capital cases.

In a problem case, the defendant might refuse to cooperate in his own defense, become a disciplinary problem, or volunteer to be executed. Typically, the defendant, an African American or Latinx who feels alone and does not understand the criminal justice system, is represented by "a white guy, middle-aged, maybe even country club," Rideau said.

Rideau helps the lawyer understand the uncooperative defendant and counsels the defendant, who often was misinformed by fellow prisoners. "The problem is not often what the prisoner tells you it is," Rideau said.

In a criminal justice system that "just locks people up," Rideau believes his participation regularly makes the system more just. "Quite often it ends up saving someone's life," he said.

Despite the justice system's injustice and the continuing power of racism, he hailed the millennial generation, which accepts integration and intermarriage. Speaking as one septuagenarian to another, Rideau said, "Once we older people die off, the world will be better."[11]

On our way to Angola, we stopped off at the Baton Rouge home of Chung Kim Do to pick up pomegranates and gourds she wanted us to deliver to Dan's mother, Kim Hoa Nguyen, in Salt Lake City; they had been childhood friends back in Vietnam. Dan interviewed Chung Kim Do, who insisted we call her Miss Kim:

Miss Kim, a fifty-eight-year-old single mother, raised six children in Baton Rouge.

Despite her love for her new homeland, she was skeptical of Western medicine. She refused to administer Tylenol when she could call upon the healing properties of ginger and other herbs.

When doctors were unable to completely remove a large and painful cyst on her son Kent's lower back, Miss Kim took matters into her own hands. Every night she tiptoed into Kent's room, rolled him over, and lifted his pajama top. She spat on the cyst and gently rubbed her saliva into the lesion as her son slept. Five nights later the cyst was gone. Kent looked embarrassed as his mother told us what she had done.

Miss Kim was a beauty school graduate and clearly had taken to heart the lessons she had learned there. She was wearing a pin-striped business suit and jeweled earrings. Her hair was tastefully bouffant.

Her laugh was a barely audible, joyous eruption, and her eyes moistened with sadness or pride in accord with the story she was telling. A particularly wet-eyed story was the one about how she got to America.

"I don't understand," Miss Kim said, looking upward. "God blessed me."

She was born in 1953 in a small hamlet called Pleiku, where my mother was also raised. I visited Pleiku once. I remember, as I sputtered along on a motorcycle behind my father, seeing a severed dog's head for sale in the market. When we drove back through, the head was gone.

Miss Kim's family was poor and only got poorer with the end of the Vietnam War because of the family's affiliation with the losing South Vietnamese government. In their childhood days, my mother had bought afterschool treats for both of them—pâté chaud, a meat-filled flaky pastry, sweet mung bean soup, pouches of sour frozen yogurt.

My mother finished high school, but Miss Kim dropped out after the ninth grade to help sell trinkets and candy at her family's store. She reluctantly married a Chinese man for the sake of financial stability. They had six children.

After her husband died in a motorcycle accident, Miss Kim decided to leave Vietnam. "Bring me anywhere but here," she said. "I wanted my children to have a good future. I had dreams. I dreamed my children would have a good education."

Someone from a Catholic ministry helped Miss Kim and her children— aged three to eighteen—get to the United States by going through the Philippines.

In 1994, she arrived in Baton Rouge unable to speak English. She started working in a factory, skinning fresh-caught fish and shelling crabs. After five months, Miss Kim knew she had no future there. She went to beauty school and subsequently opened her own nail salon. "The customers so love me," Miss Kim said with a laugh.

In 2003, with the help of her son Ben, who had just graduated from pharmacy school, Miss Kim bought a spacious house with room for all her children and in-laws.

Miss Kim plans to convert her nail salon into a beauty school, so she can teach others the trade. "If I was still in Vietnam, I'd be poor," Miss Kim said. "I appreciate America very, very, very much."

———

Burl Cain, sixty-nine, warden of Angola for seventeen years, had arranged for us to view the eighteen-thousand-acre prison, the largest maximum-security penitentiary in America (20 percent larger than the island of Manhattan), from the Mississippi River.

That's the way Mark Twain saw the same land: from the river. Angola was once a slave-breeding plantation, then a cotton and indigo plantation, and, after the Civil War, a prison. The slightly inclined beach, unlike the tall bluffs elsewhere on the Mississippi, allowed steamboat roustabouts during Twain's time to harvest wood to serve as steamboat fuel. But we motored up and down the Mississippi aboard a gas-fueled, twenty-eight-foot prison pontoon boat while Captain Randy Robinson explained why few inmates tried to escape on the fourteen-mile river side of the prison: the water's frigid temperature, its treacherous turbulence, and the "spooky, spooky" current. During heavy storms, the river floods; twice in recent years the penitentiary has had to temporarily evacuate two thousand inmates to other prisons.

Later, we drove past a line of 150 inmates marching into a prison field to harvest vegetables under the watchful eye of a rifle-toting guard on horseback. Nicknamed "the Farm," the penitentiary produced enough vegetables to feed more than eleven thousand inmates housed in five state prisons. The state spent only $1.50 to feed each inmate three meals daily, said Gary Young, the prison official who accompanied us.

In a prison that officially categorized everyone as white or Black, we asked to interview inmates who were racial or ethnic outliers. Nudged by lawyers from the Louisiana chapter of the American Civil Liberties Union, Cain made available an African American Muslim, a Vietnamese American, a Hispanic, and two Indigenous people, from Canada and Oklahoma. Whatever their differences, they responded similarly to a question about what they missed most: family and freedom.

Only Scott Meyers, an Indigenous person from Canada, responded differently. He said, "Knowing my philosophy, I was probably more in prison when I was on the street—with drugs, alcohol, gangs, and the unknown." As for his current prison stay—a sentence of 149 years at hard labor without benefit of parole, probation, or suspension of sentence—he said, "I learned a lot more about myself in here."

In seeking his return to Canada to serve out the remainder of his prison term, Meyers and his advocates raised two questions, one extraordinary, one ordinary for Louisiana. The extraordinary: Meyers had been subjected to the "Sixties Scoop," a Canadian practice that began in the 1960s and took twenty thousand Indigenous children from their families, placed them in usually middle-class, non-Indigenous foster homes, or put them up for adoption in Canada or elsewhere.[12] Meyers was adopted by a New Orleans family.

Second, Meyers and his advocates questioned the length of his sentence for armed robbery and attempted second-degree murder, noting the dramatic contrast with the sentence given to Nathaniel Williams, who also was implicated in the armed robbery. After Williams testified against Meyers, officials reduced the charges against Williams to attempted manslaughter and simple robbery. He was given a suspended sentence of five years at hard labor on each of the two counts and placed on active probation for six months.[13]

Louisiana courts hand out lengthy sentences, even death sentences, with extraordinary ease. Louisiana's Caddo Parish, for instance, recorded more death sentences per capita between 2010 and 2014 than any other U.S. county with four or more death sentences. Dale Cox, Caddo's acting district attorney, believed Louisiana needed to "kill more people."[14]

We broke from our interview of Meyers for a five-course prisoner-produced lunch at a dining center for Angola guests called the Ranch House. There, Dan spoke in Vietnamese with Hao "Hop Sing" Nguyen, who helped prepare the lunch, the first time Nguyen had had a chance to speak Vietnamese in years. The meeting shook Dan. Nguyen, who bore a resemblance to some of Dan's uncles and spoke in their same broken English, had spent most of his life behind bars and was likely to die there. "What if, like Hao, I had immigrated to the U.S. from Vietnam, fell in with the wrong crowd, and ruined someone's life and my own?" Dan said. "As an Asian American growing up with this notion of the 'model minority' (I didn't know any Asians who had been to jail or had substance abuse problems, etc.), to meet Hao was to almost see a looking glass reflection of myself. An inverse world."

Hao "Hop Sing" Nguyen

Dan, Alyssa, and I were gorging on chocolate chip cookies and lemon meringue pie when we were summoned to the office of Warden Cain, an affable, Santa Claus–shaped true believer in religion's ability to rehabilitate.

Cain displayed for us his several sides—preacher-propagandist, nontraditional penologist, teacher on parenting, and, in the words of the journalist James Ridgeway, "genius PR man."[15] Flattering us, Cain said he had been a Twainiac since childhood. His mother, a fourth-grade teacher, had encouraged him to read Twain. Cain said he played Go Fish with a deck of cards that featured Twain and other U.S. authors: "I always wanted to get Mark Twain."

Cain outlined his philosophy for running a prison: "Good food, good medicine, good play, and good praying. . . . We do all those four components, and we just rock 'n' roll." In a prison containing few Muslims and Buddhists and a lot of what Cain called Bapticostals, he promoted studying the Bible, praying, avoiding profanity, and achieving what he termed "moral rehabilitation."

A prison extension school operated by the New Orleans Baptist Theological Seminary trained inmates to become preachers who could spread the gospel at other Louisiana prisons, as well as at Angola. The penitentiary's six thousand inmates—including eighty-three death row occupants and four thousand lifers—were encouraged "to find meaning to their existence in prison" by "believing in Jesus Christ as Savior."[16]

Prison experts failed to credit Cain's evangelical ministry for order at Angola.[17] Ben Cohen, a lawyer who represented Angola prisoners, said, "I'm not an expert on Christianity. But the prison is run on fear, not the prospects of redemption. Inmates, guards, even lawyers are afraid of Cain."[18]

Cain's Angola helped explain Louisiana's reputation as having one of the harshest criminal justice systems in the world. An eight-part *(New Orleans) Times Picayune* series in 2012 began, "Louisiana is the world's prison capital. . . . Louisiana's incarceration rate is nearly triple Iran's, seven times China's, and 10 times Germany's."[19]

With some of the stiffest sentencing guidelines in the United States, Louisiana filled Angola with prisoners who were serving life without parole. Cain subjected Angola inmates to record-setting stints in solitary confinement, some prisoners for more than forty years, even though the United Nations special rapporteur on torture determined that solitary confinement for longer than fifteen days should be banned. The special rapporteur cited scientific studies that establish "some lasting mental damage is caused after a few days of social isolation." (Despite his treatment of inmates, Cain looked out for Cain, using prison employees to renovate his Baton Rouge home and conducting private real estate dealings that led to investigations, lawsuits, and his resignation in 2016.)[20]

Prisoners and a former staffer had complained to us about being required to classify themselves on penitentiary forms as either Black or white, even though they identified as something else. Indigenous peoples, for example, were identified as white. I asked Cain about the prison's Black-or-white classification system. In a Louisiana accent so thick Alyssa later joked that she needed subtitles, Cain said the prison did not care about race or ethnicity in melting-pot America: "We just all Americans . . . and we don't refer to anyone as African Americans or English Americans or Vietnamese. You can tell he is Vietnamese, you know, because of the way he looks. We really don't get into all that. We just don't care. We just Americans." But just Black or white Americans.

After our day at Angola, we rumbled north toward Arkansas through Louisiana towns with memorable monikers like Tallulah, Transylvania, and Waterproof.

A widow who owned a plantation had lured a contractor into running the railroad through her plantation, then dumped him. So he named the water stop for an old girlfriend, Tallulah, not for the plantation owner.

Dr. W. L. Richards, a major landowner and alumnus of Transylvania University in Kentucky, named a town after his school. But the town chose to identify with a different Transylvania. A black bat adorned its water tower. Its general store, with a painting of Count Dracula on a window, advertised: "We're always glad to have new blood in town."

In the 1830s, when many spots for wagons crossing the Mississippi were regularly under water, a strip of land that was not submerged took the name Waterproof, although the village had to move three times to escape floodwaters.

In Little Rock, an interview helped us understand race in a city made famous in 1957 by nine Black students who, escorted by armed troops, integrated Central High School. Adjoa A. Aiyetoro, director of the new Institute on Race and Ethnicity at the University of Arkansas at Little Rock, laid out the institute's plans, including an ambitious research project on institutional racism in the Arkansas legal system.

Aiyetoro showed us what she called the "graffiti board." More than two hundred students had stuck favorite quotes about addressing racism and other identity challenges on the board, which was titled "Face It to Fix It." Many quotes encouraged action. Muhammad Ali: "Don't count the days, make the days count." But Margaret Atwood was the most quoted: "I hope people will finally come to realize that there is only one 'race'—the human race—and that we are all members of it."

We headed northeast on Route 67 toward Keokuk, Iowa, where a young Sam Clemens, writing as Thomas Jefferson Snodgrass (he would not use the pseudonym Mark Twain until almost a decade later), worked as a printer in the mid-1850s. Keokuk was a tired Mississippi River town. The historian Kristin L. Hoganson's description of the mythical heartland town captured Keokuk: "White, rural, and rooted, full of aging churchgoers, conservative voters, corn, and pigs."[21]

A 2016 study of Keokuk, which had lost almost 40 percent of its population of sixteen thousand since the 1960s, used such phrases as "neighborhood blight" and "living in poverty." Keokuk was suffering more than other Iowa communities of its size.[22] Many of its residents felt threatened. They worried about losing their way of life and their jobs to undocumented immigrants at home and manufacturers abroad.

The town worked to stem further losses. It sought to keep Lee County's office from moving elsewhere, to reopen the local office of Iowa Workforce Development, and to find a buyer for Keokuk Steel Castings, which was almost a century old, when its owner announced its two hundred workers (down from five hundred) would be laid off and the plant's work moved to Mexico.[23]

Keokuk's economic plight symbolized a decline that extended beyond Iowa's borders. As of 2013, rural towns across America were facing a crumbling demand for labor, shrinking wages and benefits, the exodus of educated young people, and more people dying than being born—"the first time that's happened since the dawn of universal birth registration in the 1930s." A study proclaimed rural America "the new 'inner city.'"[24] Key measures of socioeconomic well-being—such as income, college graduation, and male labor-force participation—ranked communities like Keokuk among the nation's most troubled.

Keokuk could be seen as a Donald Trump town as much as a Sam Clemens–Mark Twain town. It was not only whiter (92 percent white) and poorer than much of Iowa, it was less educated.[25] While Obama had carried Iowa by 5.8 percentage points in 2012, Trump won the state by about 9 percentage points in 2016. Trump's margin of victory in Lee County was 16 points, almost 80 percent bigger than his margin across Iowa. No wonder Trump said while campaigning: "I love the poorly educated." White noncollege voters, heavily Republican, will be 44 percent of the eligible voters nationally in 2020 and could well allow Republican presidential candidates to continue winning the Electoral College through 2036, despite their loss of the popular vote.[26]

An expert in partisanship characterized as brilliant Trump's pitch to those who felt they were America's educational, economic, racial, religious, and geographical losers.[27] Multiple identities—white, conservative, rural, evangelical Christian, poor in terms of income and education—multiplied many times created a sense that Trump's antiestablishment, antielitist, antientitlement Republican Party best represented Lee County.

When Trump visited nearby Iowa communities to campaign, he chose to offer no policy proposals but to provide, as one reporter wrote, "a relentless bragging exercise about his own wealth-generating powers." Trump said: "I will be the greatest jobs president that God ever created, believe me. Believe me! Believe me!" An Iowan added: "The only one talking about jobs was Trump."[28]

Our time in Keokuk left me feeling that the town had a special significance for America's future as well as its past. Anticipating presidential elections in 2020 and beyond, prognosticators warned that the Democrats stood little chance of winning back blue-collar white voters in communities like Keokuk without addressing their key issues, such as jobs, wages, and schools.[29]

Next we headed to Muscatine, Iowa, where Sam Clemens had helped his brother Orion put out the *Journal* newspaper in summer 1854, before they worked together in Keokuk. Muscatine's manufacturing base appeared to be stronger than Keokuk's. In 2017, Monsanto announced a $50 million plant expansion that would increase its workforce to four hundred.

But what we found more interesting than Muscatine's manufacturing present (chemicals and office furniture) and past (mother-of-pearl buttons and lumber) was how the city chose to celebrate Twain and the Mascoutin (sometimes called Muscatine) Indians, who lived in the area during the 1700s and 1800s.

A bronze statue of a handsome, half-clad Native American looks toward the Mississippi from the city's Riverside Park. The statue was erected in 1926 by the Improved Order of Red Men, a white male fraternal organization founded in the early nineteenth century, that claims its roots are in the Sons of Liberty of the 1770s. The statue celebrates legendary Native Americans as "exemplars of liberty who helped white Americans develop democracy." But the Improved Order of Red Men has not celebrated living Native Americans, barring them from membership until the 1970s. In 2019, the organization's staff declined to say whether the order had any Native American members.[30]

Dozens of volunteers had made a two-story Twain puppet that dominated the lobby of a downtown shopping center. The giant Twain was constructed from chicken wire, cotton batting, sheep's wool, plastic tubing, and paper recycled from the *Muscatine Journal*, where Twain published his early travel writings—eight letters from Philadelphia, Washington, D.C., and St. Louis—in 1853–55.

Twain's *Muscatine Journal* letters represent his ignorant, racist youth; he disparaged Jews, Native Americans, Catholics, and abolitionist U.S. senators.

Loren Ghiglione admires a Mark Twain papier-mâché figure in a Muscatine, Iowa, shopping center.

The letters celebrated three senators—Henry Clay, John C. Calhoun, and Daniel Webster—who helped pass the Fugitive Slave Act.

But Twain changed. He proclaimed toward the end of his life, "I have no race prejudices, and I think I have no color prejudices or caste prejudices nor creed prejudices. Indeed I know it. All that I care to know is that a man is a human being—that is enough for me; he can't be any worse."

A sociological study suggested Black and Brown immigrants working in new meatpacking plants and similar factories were key to the survival of heavily white Iowa small towns like Muscatine: "Strangers represent the best chance for the future and, simultaneously, the end of an old way of life."[31]

Rusty Schrader, the news editor of the *Muscatine Journal*, agreed. He said the Muscatine area saw diversity "more as an opportunity than a challenge." Muscatine (17 percent Hispanic/Latinx, according to the 2010 census), and the neighboring small towns of Columbus Junction (48 percent Hispanic/Latinx) and West Liberty (52 percent Hispanic/Latinx), had embraced diversity the way Keokuk had not. Significantly, the Diversity Service Center of Iowa, which helps newcomers and employers with their immigration issues, chose to locate in Muscatine.

Muscatine supported the newcomers. In 2016, when Donald Trump attended a service at Muscatine's First Presbyterian Church as a presidential candidate, he heard the Reverend Dr. Pam Saturnia tell the congregation that Syrian refugees and Mexican migrants should be welcomed, not shunned: "Share Jesus with the ones who need him."[32] In 2017, dozens marched outside Muscatine City Hall to stand in solidarity with immigrants and refugees: "We're not gonna let xenophobia, racism, bigotry into our community," said the rally organizer Nick Salazar. A lecturer that year at the Muscatine Library titled her presentation of the history of Hispanics in Muscatine "Migration Is Beautiful."[33]

We decided to head west across the Great Plains from where Twain headed west, St. Joseph, Missouri. Twain and his brother Orion began their odyssey from St. Joseph in 1861. They paid $200 each for overland stagecoach tickets to Carson City, Nevada Territory. Stagecoach passengers stretched their necks and strained their eyes to catch sight of Pony Express riders racing almost two thousand miles at up to 25 mph to deliver the mail in about ten days from St. Joseph to Sacramento. The Pony Express Museum in St. Joseph taught us about the daring riders—some as young as eleven, all about 125 pounds or less—armed with rifle, revolver, horn, and Bible. Dan and Alyssa loved the riders and made small crayon drawings of them—"so free, so American," Alyssa said.

We left Route 36, the Pony Express Highway, in northeastern Kansas to learn about the area's American Indians and my mother's farm-family parents, Hettie Fletcher Haskin and Loren Haskin, my namesake. Indigenous people had lived in the area of Kansas (named for the Kanza Indians, "People of the South Wind") since the Ice Age, eleven thousand years ago. The Haskins (the name comes from a diminutive for the Old Norse name Asketin), immigrants from England, were among the white settlers who illegally squatted on American Indian land or obtained it legally in the nineteenth century.

We had been on the road for more than two months. I had promised a four-day Thanksgiving break so that each of us could fly home from Kansas City, Missouri, to reunite with family, sleep in comfortable beds, and eat a traditional Thanksgiving turkey.

Dan, however, looked forward to an untraditional turkey. When he was a boy, Dan and his family had Vietnamese food for Thanksgiving—fried rice, pho, egg rolls, and a dozen other dishes. When he was nine or ten, his family visited Bac Thanh Dong, a friend who served what Dan called a "white Thanksgiving": turkey, mashed potatoes, corn, and cranberry sauce. Dan and his brother, Trung, loved it and insisted their parents serve "American Thanksgivings" in the future. "Fast-forward ten years or so," Dan said. "I'm in college, my brother has green hair, and my family is strictly vegan/vegetarian." Dan, home from our trip, was served "two or three brands of tofu turkey . . . or, as my mom, calls it 'Foturkey.' My mom should have stayed in her lane and made her amazing Vietnamese food, because the mashed potatoes were bland and watery (vegan mothers hate butter), and, naturally, the tofu turkey was as gross as it sounds."

As much as we enjoyed being home, we also loved being in motion, even if we questioned our motivation. "The three of us are curious people who have a powerful, irresistible urge to understand *why*," Dan said. "We are seekers to a fault. But I think underlying that, for myself at least, is a darker motivation—the fear of death and not seeing everything I want to see before I die. It's an existential, perhaps selfish, drive to know this world we live in. To feel everything." Alyssa questioned her history of eagerly throwing herself into weeklong and monthlong excursions, not just our trip: "Everything had to be new, everything demanded to be tasted, touched, toppled."

After our Thanksgiving home visits, Alyssa, Dan, and I headed back to Hiawatha, in northeastern Kansas, where my grandparents, Hettie and Loren Haskin, had married in 1897. In nearby Morrill, where my great-grandparents and grandparents had lived, we interviewed seventy-five-year-old Robert Herbster. Three generations of his family had worked the 160 acres that had made up my great-grandfather John Fletcher's farm. I showed Herbster a photo I had taken of three generations of his family in 1980, when I first visited the farm to interview him. The photo, in a way, told the story of American farming. In the generation of Robert's parents, independent local farmers could make a decent living on crops from hundreds, not thousands, of acres.

When I visited in 1980, Robert and Mary, his wife, struggled to keep working his small farm. Agribusiness giants were beginning to dominate farming. Eventually, as a few farms got gargantuan, Robert and other local farmers got out. Absent the farmers, Morrill's bank and many other businesses closed. Robert moved into Morrill and took a job with Wenger Manufacturing in Sabetha, Kansas, before retiring in 2009. Mary worked at the grain elevator in Morrill.

Their two sons, Marty and Mike, born in 1969 and 1971, also did not farm, instead choosing engineering work at manufacturing plants that made air filtrators and seed treaters in Sabetha and Wetmore, Kansas.

The story of Kansas's disappearing farmers became the story of the disappearing state: Kansas ranked among the ten states with the greatest population loss between 2010 and July 2013. Rural Kansas's population had been declining since the Great Depression.[34]

Perhaps anticipating the fate of farmers in Morrill and throughout Kansas, my Haskin grandparents took the railroad west in 1901 and settled in Pomona, California. There, my grandfather sold furniture for Wright Bros. & Rice. Later he would become an owner of the store. But farm life in Morrill survived in the family's souls and stories. Grandpa Loren loved recounting how he raised sheep. Great-grandmother Fletcher told tales of being frightened when American Indians rode through the farm on raids. Once, as a child, she was kidnapped. The Indians returned her the next day unharmed.

We drove south on U.S. 75 from Morrill toward Topeka. The area was home to many American Indians—the Ioway, Sac-Fox, and Kickapoo—and sensitive to Indian attitudes. In 2000, the mascots for Hiawatha's high school, middle school, and elementary school changed from Redskins, Warriors, and Braves to Red Hawks, Hawks, and Junior Hawks.

When I saw a road sign for the Kickapoo reservation, I made an impromptu left turn for a visit. I confess, the tribe's euphonious name caught my eye. Perhaps the Kickapoo name helps explain why a New Haven company used traveling medicine shows in the late nineteenth century to pitch Kickapoo Indian Sagwa, Kickapoo Buffalo Salve, Kickapoo Indian Cough Cure, and Kickapoo Indian Worm Killer (though I doubt any Kickapoo had ever experienced, much less endorsed, those quack medicines).[35]

We drove in search of the real Kickapoo—a proud tribe with, as the historian A. M. Gibson writes, "a remarkably independent spirit and a studied hostility toward acculturation."[36]

Although Twain never wrote about the Kickapoo nation, he did claim to report from "personal observation" about American Indians in Nevada. Twain called the warrior who headed the Washoes a demeaning name that sounded a bit like Kickapoo, "Hoop-de-doodle-doo." Twain said Hoop-de-doodle-doo shed giant vermin, smelled like a stinkpot, and resembled "a very long and very bob-tailed bird in a cage that isn't big enough for him," thereby perpetuating the stereotype of the subhuman Indian.[37]

Signs directed us to the Kickapoo Tribe's fifteen-year-old Golden Eagle Casino, Brown County's largest employer with a staff of four hundred. Dan, Alyssa, and I each gambled two dollars. Dan and I lost our money almost immediately. Dan later reflected on the experience: "The only interaction most of the outside world has with this tribe and many others is exactly this: a dusty, garish, depressing casino. There's so much more culture and richness and nuance to the Kickapoo than that. It's like how Americans only see and understand Vietnam through Vietnam War films, and they don't really see anything else of us besides the Charlies and gooks in the jungle."

Alyssa won $2.75, with which she purchased a bottle of water from a vending machine that also dispensed a free bottle of Mountain Dew (Alyssa: "Mountain Dew has the color and flavor of battery acid, but the point is, it was free").

From the casino, we found our way to the Kickapoo Tribal Council's headquarters, a joined pair of double-wide trailers. The stern face, Mohawk hairstyle, and muscular body of fifty-year-old Curtis Simon Sr., a member (soon vice chair) of the Kickapoo Tribal Council, belied his easygoing and friendly manner.

Simon emphasized the tribe's intention to remain an independent sovereign tribe. The sixteen hundred enrolled Kickapoo had their own fire department (Simon headed it for four years), police department, court system, senior citizen center, water treatment plant, land department, health clinic, farm, and roads department.

A separate department sought the return of human remains and funerary objects under the 1990 Native American Graves Protection and Repatriation Act. Simon had served on a nine-member Kansas board that fought the disturbance of Indian burial mounds and unmarked graves and the possession of Indian skeletal remains by museums and universities.

Despite the Kickapoo's concern about federal domination and tribal dependency, the tribe continued to seek federal funding—what wags called "hunting the federal buffalo." Even with federal assistance, 40 to 50 percent of reservation workers remained unemployed.

To increase employment, maintain the reservation's independence, and overcome water shortages, the tribal council had begun planning in the

Curtis Simon Sr.

1970s to build a twelve-hundred-acre reservoir. In 1998, Congress approved an agreement between the Kickapoo and the neighboring counties' watershed board to build the reservoir dam. Some landowners, however, would not sell their land.

The watershed board refused to use its power of eminent domain to take the land. "They are reluctant to condemn white man's land for the benefit of Kickapoo Indian people," Steve Cadue, then chair of the Kickapoo, told the Associated Press. In 2013, a U.S. District Court ruled the Kickapoo could not compel the watershed board to use its power of eminent domain to take private property for the reservoir. The reservoir remains unbuilt.[38]

Simon drove us to the Kickapoo's casino for lunch, then to the Kickapoo Nation School, a K–12 school with ninety-one students in Powhattan, a sleepy village of thirty households. The only tribally controlled school in Kansas, the Kickapoo school, like other Indian schools, was inadequately funded.[39]

A sign proclaimed the school HOME OF THE WARRIORS. Wall murals in the school's gym captured the warrior spirit. One, created by Simon, shows a young, bare-chested Kickapoo with flowing black hair astride a prancing gray horse. The Kickapoo's raised right hand holds a bow, his left hand a round blue shield with a thunderbird in red at its center.

Simon introduced us to Howard Allen, fifty-three, who taught the Kickapoo language to all of the school's students in kindergarten through sixth grade. After the sixth grade, Allen said, the Kickapoo language was an elective. Considered endangered, Kickapoo, like Mandarin Chinese, is a tonal language. The pitch of a vowel, high or low, can change a word's meaning. Allen held his hands as far apart as possible to make the point that Kickapoo and English were "not similar at all."

Of the hundreds of Native American languages that once existed in North America, more than half had disappeared. Allen underscored the importance to young Kansas Kickapoo of mastering their language. "That's the only way they would understand the tribe," its culture and ceremonies, he said.

In the past, government boarding schools had removed Kickapoo children from their homes to "get rid of our culture and language," Allen said. The boarding schools forced assimilation. In addition to suppressing tribal languages, they cut off children's braids, assigned them non-Native names, and rejected Native religious beliefs. One historian called the schools' efforts to eradicate all Native identity and culture "education for extinction."[40] And literal extinction too. A report found malnourished, mistreated, overworked Native boarding school students were six times more likely to die in childhood than the rest of American children.[41] Allen saw the Kickapoo Nation School as an antidote to education for extinction.

Allen, like Simon, said the Kickapoo needed to fight to retain their right to self-govern. "Native Americans on a reservation have to follow more laws than anyone else in the United States," he said. The American Indian Religious Freedom Act of 1978 was intended to eliminate interference with the free exercise of Native American religions. "It was still unenforced," Allen said.

He also cited article 7 of the Treaty of Greenville, which in 1795 gave the Kickapoo and other tribes "liberty to hunt . . . without hindrance or molestation" on tribal lands ceded to the United States. "If we tried to exercise [that right] we would be arrested," Allen said. "We have a need for deer. I don't know why we couldn't work something out."

But Allen had a theory about why the Kickapoo and the government had failed to reach agreement. He spoke of the cultural differences between the more spiritual Native Americans and the more materialistic, goal-oriented dominant culture. Asked to explain the cultural differences, Allen said,

"There is no ten-page pamphlet on our culture. It's just everywhere. The humor is different. No knock-knock jokes, but stories about real life, where something funny happens to somebody." Allen also noted the number of treaties negotiated by lying representatives of the dominant culture. "Our people tell the truth," he said.

If we had any doubt about whether Allen saw us as representatives of that dominant culture, the doubt seemed to disappear when he said he wanted to teach us a word before we left. He pointed to a skunk woven into the carpet. "Chi-ca-ga," he said. He pointed to a baby skunk woven into the carpet. "Chi-ca-goa," he said. He sounded the word for the city next to where our trip had begun, Chicago.

Although we had not asked to shoot Allen's photo, he said, stone-faced, that he did not want us to take his picture for religious reasons. "If you understand quantum physics," he added, "you might understand my reasoning." I did not understand quantum physics. But I thought I understood how Allen viewed our taking his photo. Photo taking could be seen as a symbol of the untrustworthy white culture's taking of Native lands and identity and the destruction of American Indians' way of life.

James C. Faris begins his critical history of photographs of Native Americans by describing the viewpoint of the photo-shooting "dominant, aggressive, and exploitative majority foreign culture." The dominant culture sought a permanent record that might have commercial value. It did not care that the photographs, which it perceived as reality, failed to capture Native Americans' lived experiences. "What is outside the frame?" Faris asked. "What is not focused? What are the silences to be listened (watched) for?"[42] What truths do photographs, usually posed, fail to tell or even hide?

Alyssa wrote in her diary, "I think in Allen's mind the differences between our two cultures are insurmountable. He spoke very softly, and sometimes he would break off into Kickapoo, leaving us clueless and also powerless. He was extremely wary of us, as journalists and 'suits and ties.'

"Decades of mistrust and misunderstanding have pushed their tribe to double-, triple-, quadruple-check every line of every document in efforts to prevent what happened in the past when they were robbed of their land," Alyssa continued. "We went there with our goal-oriented questions and academia-informed perspectives and asked them to conform to it. Allen didn't want to. It's sovereignty they want."

I left the Kickapoo reservation with a sense that the melting-pot model of mixing and merging, which had worked well for many immigrants to the

United States, needs to leave room for American Indians, many of whom have been targets of land seizures and forced removal and therefore reject assimilation into the mainstream culture. They live by their own distinctive vision and values.

Dan, Alyssa, and I resumed our drive south on U.S. 75 with a question in mind from our visit to Muscatine. The prevailing view among many Anglos there was that Mexicans were newcomers to the region, "with no permanent Hispanic residents until the middle of the 1960s."[43] But an exhibit in Topeka would tell a quite different story about the region.

CHAPTER 16

Coming to America

Mexicans Immigrate to Kansas, Chinese and Italians to California

In Topeka, we met Andy Valdivia, a goateed sixty-three-year-old whose vividly colored murals were part of the exhibit *From Mexico to America: Through the Eyes of Kansas Artists* at the Brown v. Board of Education National Historic Site.

One Valdivia mural captures the story of Mexican immigrants arriving in Topeka by railroad to escape poverty and the violence of the Mexican Revolution of 1910–20. They worked for the Atchison, Topeka and Santa Fe Railway and lived in cramped boxcars and bunkhouses, often without indoor bathrooms, electricity, or running water. They were not permitted in the public pool or movie theaters—except the "Mexican Heaven" balconies, next to the "Crow's Nest" sections for Black moviegoers. Mexicans were allowed only takeout at restaurants. A typical sign read COLOREDS, MEXICANS AND INDIANS SERVED IN SACKS ONLY.

Valdivia's murals also told the story of later generations of Mexican Americans—of distinguished military service overseas, graduation from college as well as high school, and employment in skilled and professional positions.

The setting for Valdivia's murals—the historically Black Monroe Street School, before it became the Brown v. Board of Education National Historic Site—illustrated the nation's history of school segregation and recent school resegregation. In 1879, the *Topeka Colored Citizen* charged Monroe Elementary was so mismanaged "that many children in it are just where they were 2–3 years ago."[1]

The newspaper claimed Black children were intentionally held back to prevent them from entering the city's integrated junior high schools. To gain

Andy Valdivia

space for students, teachers at Monroe Elementary converted a bathroom and an office into classrooms by adding tablet-arm chairs and blackboards.[2]

Monroe, one of four segregated elementary schools for African Americans in Topeka, was a target of the Supreme Court's 1954 decision ending racial segregation in public schools. A 2009 study found U.S. public schools more segregated than they were a half-century earlier. Most nonwhite schools were segregated from white schools by income as well as race, the study concluded.[3] Some critics blame Supreme Court rulings, including a 2007 decision about the voluntary desegregation plan of Seattle Public Schools. The decision invalidated use of race as a criterion in school zoning decisions.

But in Kansas, at least, it was hard not to think that institutions other than the Supreme Court were also responsible for school resegregation. I had grown up thinking of Kansas as all-American, moderate Republican, and middle of the road as well as middle of the country, the placid Plains state that was home to Dwight Eisenhower's Abilene and Clark Kent/Superman's Smallville. But Kansas had become a bastion of the rabid right.

The Topeka preacher Fred Phelps and his disciples picketed the funerals of gay people, carrying signs that read GOD HATES FAGS. The Kansas school board tried to expunge references to evolution from state science teaching guidelines. Kansas paid law firms $1 million to defend a raft of antiabortion laws enacted after Sam Brownback became governor in January 2011. The legislature passed anti-Muslim legislation that prohibited local courts from relying on Shariah and other foreign laws, despite no evidence of Kansas courts' doing so. The legislature also passed a provision that required proof of citizenship when residents registered to vote, a provision challenged in 2016 as a violation of federal law.[4]

Brownback pursued a "march to zero income taxes," killed state agencies, and slashed the state budget, targeting public schools and infrastructure (a 2013 civil engineering report awarded Kansas's bridges a D+).[5] The conservative legislature pushed private-school vouchers and "parental choice" formulas that drove funding toward whiter rural and suburban districts and capped the growth of urban districts, which had increasingly large numbers of low-income students of color. In 2017, the Kansas Supreme Court unanimously ruled that the state's funding of public education was unconstitutionally low and inequitable.[6] At the same time, the achievement levels and graduation rates of Kansas's African American and Latinx students slid. White students were also hurt. In *Dying of Whiteness*, Jonathan M. Metzl notes: "Kansas students plunged to dead last in the United States in student scores on some sections of national proficiency exams. . . . The state also fell into the bottom ten states in the percentage of high school graduates who pursued college education." In the words of Booker T. Washington: "You can't hold a man down without staying down with him."[7]

The austerity tax cuts intended to jump-start the Kansas economy actually helped jump-stall it. After losing jobs in 2015, Kansas ranked forty-sixth among all states in private-sector job growth in 2016. Kansans' support for the economic and educational self-destruction promoted by the far-right legislature and governor mirrored the behavior of the characters in William H. Gass's novella *In the Heart of the Heart of the Country*. Gass's small-town midwesterners "for years have voted squarely against their interests."[8]

Brownback's backlash austerity ravaged the financial structure put in place to make sure that poorer, inner-city schools did not fall behind wealthy suburban ones. The austerity also, sadly, shredded school desegregation efforts. A 2011 study noted that African Americans who spent five years in desegregated schools were healthier and wealthier than their counterparts in segregated schools. They earned about 25 percent more in annual family income than those who never had the opportunity to attend desegregated schools.[9]

David L. Kirp, a professor of public policy at the University of California, Berkeley, said of the study results, "By itself, racial mixing didn't do the trick [of raising Black achievement levels], but it did mean that the fate of black and white students became intertwined. School systems that had spent a pittance on all-black schools were now obligated to invest considerably more on African-American students' education after the schools became integrated."

In general, smaller and better-equipped classes, the inclusion of better-off families, and teachers' higher expectations improved the lives of students, Kirp said.[10] Court-ordered school desegregation worked. It did not deserve to die.

We zig-zagged north on country roads to get to Interstate 80 in Nebraska. As we entered Nebraska, a road sign announced a state motto: "The Good Life." That motto prompted me to check the Internet for alternative mottos: "The White Life," "The 'N' Is for Knowledge," and "Safe Sex: We Mark the Sheep That Kick."

Alyssa was ready with another motto once we reached Lexington, Nebraska: "The Smelliest Place on Earth." Lexington residents blamed the STABL Inc. rendering plant, which converted dead animals from farms and feedlots into such products as Happy Hound dog food.

Great Plains towns like Lexington faced life-or-death decisions, said the Reverend Paul J. Colling, the fifty-four-year-old pastor of St. Ann's Catholic Church in Lexington. He served as vicar on Hispanic issues for the Grand Island diocese, which encompasses fifty thousand square miles of Nebraska.

Colling said the towns could have remained virtually 100 percent white, a choice many residents favored. But they would have lost their few factories to towns that welcomed large numbers of low-paid, nonunion workers, a majority of them immigrants.

In 1990, city leaders of Lexington, population sixty-six hundred at the time, said, "'This is what we gotta do if we're going to survive,'" Colling recalled.

So Mexican, Guatemalan Indian, Cuban, Colombian, El Salvadoran, and African immigrants flocked to Lexington to work at the IBP (Tyson Fresh Meats since 2001) plant. Soon Tyson employed 2,100 workers to process 4,000 head of cattle daily in a 600,000-square-foot plant.[11]

Lexington, only 4.9 percent Hispanic in 1990, became 63 percent Hispanic by 2010. The town's population of 10,230 also included an estimated 1,300 Somali refugees, who were not fully counted in the 2010 census.

Prejudice against immigrants still existed in Lexington, Reverend Colling said. But he believed the community was becoming "really, really open." He said the town had begun attracting whites because of its diversity.

Critics of the packing plant claimed it created in Lexington a class of vulnerable immigrant working poor. Many workers were undocumented and therefore in no position to demand better pay or regular hours. We talked with Ana Maria Hermosillo, forty-five, whose husband worked at Tyson. She worried about immigrants who were "applying but not being called" for work. She also pointed to the cut in workers' hours, from forty-eight to thirty-seven a week. In addition, the threat of automation loomed; in 2015, when Tyson announced a $47 million plant expansion involving partly automated delivery systems, company officials said the expansion would add no new jobs.[12]

Christopher Leonard, author of *The Racket: The Secret Takeover of America's Food Business*, sees the Tyson plant in Lexington as part of a national crisis. He charges that a handful of companies, led by Tyson, control the nation's meat supply; consumers pay more for food, and Tyson towns like Lexington struggle. He said Tyson "has expanded in economically marginal areas, and it has kept those areas economically marginal." But a study by agricultural economists of the trade-offs faced by meatpacking communities concluded that "while case studies have focused on the costs of adding large processing facilities, the worst cases must surely be the towns where those jobs have been lost."[13]

At St. Ann's, which offered two masses in English and two in Spanish, Colling said he tried "to help the community blend as much as I can." He encouraged whites to experience the Our Lady of Guadalupe Fiesta, which included Mexican dancers wearing traditional handmade costumes. He applauded Tyson's effort to accommodate Mexican and Latin American workers who attached great significance to family funerals: "They'll just leave [for their hometowns in Mexico or Latin America] and can be gone for a week."

But tough challenges remained, Colling said. He bemoaned the closing of Haven House, a shelter for people who arrived in town virtually penniless. Haven House had provided 4,714 bed-nights and 24,381 meals in 1991–92, its first year.[14] Colling's church was beginning a study to see if establishing an immigration office for the parish would be feasible.

As we were leaving Lexington, Colling encouraged us to talk with other residents downtown. We visited Washington Street, the main thoroughfare, which had the usual downtown stores but also two importers of Mexican and Latin American goods, the African International Food Market, and Freddy's, a Somali bakery and restaurant.

Although Colling had never visited Freddy's, he had told us it did not admit women. He warned Alyssa, "You can't go in!" So, of course, we visited Freddy's. Alyssa was welcomed. But perhaps Freddy's helped prove Lexington's business diversity did not necessarily mean that people mixed. At lunchtime, Freddy's had four customers, all Black men; two doors away, Madeline's Cafe & Bakery had seventeen customers, all white women.

Alyssa, Dan, and I thought a lot about whiteness. Alyssa, who grew up in a virtually all-white world, said the humiliating personal experiences related by the people of color we interviewed made her realize how her whiteness sheltered her from feeling humiliated: "I had to ask myself, did I ever do anything, as a white person, to make someone feel [humiliated] this way?" On our trip, she came to understand that being white in America meant "not having to think about your race or your ethnicity."

Dan recalled times growing up when he was made to feel self-conscious about his race and ethnicity: "I wish whiteness weren't the default and everything else an aberration or deviation." He felt our trip had helped him resist believing all white people harbored racist ideas. Except for being the only person offered chopsticks at the Japanese restaurant in Marion, Indiana, he was "pleasantly surprised by the open-mindedness of folks, especially white folks."

To stay on schedule, we needed to reach Wyoming by that night. So we drove two hours west from Lexington on Interstate 80 before stopping in Julesburg, Colorado. We stayed there for only one hour, the same amount of time Mark Twain spent there on his seventeen-hundred-mile stagecoach ride west in 1861.

Twain reveled in the story of J. A. Slade, the overland stagecoach agent in Julesburg. Slade, a sharpshooting vigilante, was said to have killed twenty-six men for stealing from the stagecoach company. Slade cut off the thieves' ears and sent them as keepsakes to their relatives. The result, said Twain: "Slade's coaches went through, every time!"

We returned to Interstate 80 and, with Red Bull Alyssa at the wheel, drove west in the evening darkness to Laramie, Wyoming. The next morning, we located where Matthew Shepard, beaten, bloodied, and unconscious, was found tied to a log fence on October 7, 1998. The site sat at the intersection of Pilot Peak and Snowy View Roads. Despite the houses in the distance, we felt the desolation of the snow-covered ground, steely-gray sky, and funereal silence.

Alyssa spoke of the site's isolation: "What a way to die. Alone."

The "lack of acknowledgment" disturbed Dan: "How do we memorialize something we are so ashamed of? Do we need to? What happens to our collective memories of these horrific murders when the overwhelming response to them is forgetfulness, ignorance—or, worse, indifference?"

Shepard's shoes and the bloody gun used to pistol-whip him were found in the truck of Aaron McKinney, twenty-two. McKinney received two consecutive life terms without the possibility of parole; Russell Henderson, his twenty-one-year-old accomplice, received two consecutive life terms.

Under Wyoming and federal law, crimes committed because of the victim's sexual orientation could not be prosecuted as hate crimes. On October 28, 2009, after a congressional battle of more than ten years, President Barack Obama signed into law the Matthew Shepard and James Byrd, Jr. Hate Crimes Prevention Act (Byrd, an African American who lived in Jasper, Texas, was chained to the back of a pickup by three white men and dragged one and a half miles to his death on June 7, 1998). The law made it easier to investigate and prosecute hate crimes.

We were unable to interview Judy Shepard, Matthew's mother and the head of the Matthew Shepard Foundation, while we were in Laramie. Finally, in 2013, following her standing-room-only lecture, "The Meaning of Matthew," at Indiana University, I discussed with her the portrayal of her son and the Laramie location where her son had been left to die.

Judy Shepard saw no reason to visit the location or put a memorial to Matthew there. "Matt's not there," she said. "I don't need that visual in my head." She finally agreed to let the University of Wyoming place a bench on its campus in his memory. "They promised it would be under lights and constantly patrolled. It's in a beautiful location, and I'm glad we did it because it's the only thing in Laramie that is a memorial [to Matthew]," Shepard said. A bench plaque says of Matthew: "He continues to make a difference. Peace be with him and all who sit here."

Judy Shepard was less pleased with the State of Wyoming. Faced with "the opportunity to really change things and set a good example," she said, the Wyoming House of Representatives, on a 30–30 vote, failed to pass a hate crimes bill.

She saw the nation's less populated areas, not only Wyoming, as "diversity challenged." Colleges and universities in the Deep South rarely invited her to speak. "Even in California, which you think is very open, you go inland and it's just as bad as anyplace else," she said.

But there was progress nationally, which she attributed to the "open, vocal support" of Obama and Vice President Joe Biden. "It's like he [Obama] gave his permission [for the public] to support LGBT rights."

She ended her lecture with a Cherokee parable that could be interpreted as a tale about the public's attitude, pro and con, toward her son and other members of the LGBT community.

"A tribal elder told his grandson about a battle that goes on inside people," Shepard began. "He said, 'My son, the battle is between two wolves. One wolf is evil. It is anger, envy, regret, greed, arrogance, self-pity, guilt, resentment, inferiority, lies, false pride, superiority, and ego. The other wolf is good. It is joy, peace, love, hope, harmony, serenity, humility, kindness, benevolence, empathy, generosity, truth, compassion, and faith.' The grandson thought about it for a minute and asked his grandfather, 'Which wolf wins?' And the tribal elder simply replied, 'The wolf you feed.'"

Driving west from Laramie on Interstate 80, Alyssa, Dan, and I slalomed through a snowstorm before reaching Salt Lake City, the community along our route that I suspected would be most unlikely to honor Mark Twain. Twain took aim at the powerful Church of Jesus Christ of Latter-day Saints, or Mormons. He criticized the Book of Mormon ("chloroform in print, . . . half modern glibness, and half ancient simplicity and gravity") and Valley Tan, a potent whiskey developed by Mormons, who were supposed to refrain from drinking.

Twain joked about planning to lead a great reform to end polygamy. Joseph Smith, founder of the Latter-day Saints, took thirty to forty wives, some already married and at least one only fourteen years old.[15] But Twain said he ended his reform effort once he saw Mormon women. "The man who marries sixty of them," he wrote, "has done a deed of open-handed generosity so sublime that the nation should stand uncovered in his presence and worship in silence."

Twain observed that Utah locals, not just Mormons, despised "low and inferior" outsiders like him. I, too, felt like an outsider amid all the business-dressed, fresh-faced Latter-day Saints. Perhaps there was an explanation for the wrinkle-free faces. In 2007, *Forbes* ranked Salt Lake the most vain U.S. city, based in part on the number of plastic surgeons per 100,000.[16]

Although Utah was 62 percent Mormon as of 2012, Mormons were a minority in Salt Lake City. Hispanics, Asians, Pacific Islanders, Native Americans, and African Americans had a significant presence, as I was reminded by our brief stopover with Dan's parents, Kim Hoa Nguyen and Hoa Tram. Kim and Hoa had fled Vietnam by boat shortly after the Vietnam War and, like many refugees and immigrants who moved to Salt Lake City before them, settled on the west side, where they had lived for three decades.

The heart of Kim and Hoa's home was the kitchen and adjacent dining area with a cylindrical table and a misleading eight chairs. Misleading, because when Kim cooked her five-course vegan feasts, the house filled almost instantly with forty or so hungry family members and friends. Dan recalled that, after his high school graduation, "we had four family reunions in just three weeks. My mom would spend two to three days preparing for each of them." So it was no surprise when, three years after our visit, Kim and her brother Binh Nguyen opened All Chay (*chay* means "vegan" in Vietnamese), a strip mall restaurant among Hispanic businesses that quickly earned rave reviews on Yelp and Urbanspoon.

Salt Lake City was not only racially and ethnically diverse. It ranked first nationally among midsize cities—"less-expected locales"—for gay and lesbian couples.[17] That might surprise anyone familiar with Mormon history. Spencer Kimball, the twelfth Latter-day Saints president, spoke in 1980 of homosexuality as a heinous and diabolical perversion. He demanded homosexuals resist and repent. The same year, Edmund White published *States of Desire: Travels in Gay America*. After visiting Salt Lake City's gay scene, White wrote, "Mormons do not live in their own century and country."[18]

He described the failed program of aversion therapy instituted by Mormons: shocks applied to gay men as they looked at homoerotica to condition them to dislike the pictures. In a later session, photos of nude women were shown to them without the shocks. White quoted a therapist specializing in same-sex relationships who noted the high rate of suicide among gay Mormons: "Oh! Those Mormons! What are they doing to their children? They seem to produce more homosexuals and yet they treat them so cruelly!"[19]

Interviewed in 2012, three decades after he wrote *States of Desire*, White, seventy-two, saw a glimmer of hope in the Mormon religion's habit of "revising itself": for example, of shedding polygamy and accepting Black bishops.

Mormons, White said, "personally are wonderful people, kind, thoughtful, and public-spirited," and Salt Lake City, no longer majority Mormon, has "one of the biggest gay pride parades in the world." But, he continued, "Mormons, I think like all Christian religions, their effect on homosexuality is disastrous."

White survived the repression of homosexuality in the 1950s and 1960s ("When I worked for Time-Life from 1962 to 1970, I had to refer to my boyfriends as women; otherwise I would have been fired").[20] He called himself a pleasure-loving throwback to the 1970s, what he labeled the golden age of promiscuity ("I like sex a lot and I tend to have it a couple times a day and with different people"). White told me a gay person may find comfort in a "private religion where it's just a question of him and God and what he believes." But a gay man will not find comfort in the dogma of the Mormon religion—or, indeed, in the doctrines of the three monotheistic religions, White said. "There is a deep fundamental hatred of pleasure itself and sexuality and homosexuality in particular," he added.

In 2015, as if to prove the point, the Mormon church toughened its doctrinal standards for members. To become church members, children of same-sex couples had to leave their parents' homes and wait until they were eighteen, then disavow same-sex relationships. Only then could they obtain the approval of church leadership and be baptized. At a time when more Mormons were openly identifying as gay and supporting same-sex marriage, the church labeled Mormons in same-sex marriages apostates and required them to endure church disciplinary hearings that could lead to excommunication.[21]

The church's edict resulted in Mormons "leaving the church in droves," according to the *New York Times* (perhaps as a result, the church in 2019 reversed one part of its edict, permitting children of same-sex couples to be baptized without having to abide by the 2015 requirements).[22]

Troy Williams, dubbed Salt Lake City's "gay mayor" because of his championing of the LGBT community, beat the crowd in leaving the church, as Dan reported:

> *In July 2009, Mormon security officials detained a gay couple after one man kissed the other on the cheek near the Mormon temple in Salt Lake City.*
> *Matt Aune and Derek Jones were walking home through a popular pedestrian thoroughfare that the city had sold to the Mormon church in the 1990s. When Aune kissed Jones on the cheek, the church security guards handcuffed the couple because of their public display of affection.*

Troy Williams, forty-two, was outraged. Inspired by the sit-ins of the civil rights era, he and local activists organized three "kiss-ins" at the plaza where the security guards had handcuffed Aune and Jones. "We took back that space," Williams said.

Williams was the producer of RadioActive, a progressive, often political, talk show, on KRCL 90.9 FM. The aim of KRCL, a nonprofit community radio station, was to "represent diverse cultural perspectives—there's not a big market for what we do," Williams said with a laugh.

He was raised Mormon in Eugene, Oregon. "Growing up Mormon wasn't a horrible thing. It's very family oriented. You feel this sense of belonging," Williams said. "So, when you're pushed out because of your [sexual] orientation, there's this deep sense of loss."

Williams went through all the motions of a good Mormon boy. He did his mission, a rite of passage for male Latter-day Saints, in England; he attended Brigham Young University; and, in what he called a sublimation of his sexuality, he became a right-wing conservative and volunteered at the Utah Eagle Forum, part of an antiabortion, antigay national organization.

"I thought I could just run from who I was by hiding in an organization that was the exact opposite of what I feared I would become," Williams said. "And that kind of sublimation causes all kinds of emotional, psychological pain."

"I prayed to Heavenly Father: 'Please, please make me straight,'" Williams said. "'Please help me have these desires for women.' And, thankfully, God ignored every single one of my prayers." Williams said he hoped he had made up for his prayers by leaving the faith and "being a good left-leaning activist here in Utah."

Williams's activism caused a Salt Lake Tribune reporter to name him the "gay mayor of Salt Lake City."[23] For Williams, Salt Lake City was the ideal place to be a queer activist.

"Salt Lake City is actually a very progressive town," Williams said. "We have not elected a Mormon or Republican mayor for over thirty years." In 2009, the Salt Lake City Council unanimously passed ordinances that protect LGBT residents from housing and employment discrimination.

Every month, Williams met with other members of the LGBT community to talk about activism and projects. He said activism on issues of sexual orientation and gender expression in Utah could be a model for other marginalized groups in the United States. "If you go into large, urban centers of queer people, you see lots of divisions," Williams said. "Here in Utah we don't have that kind of luxury to have those divisions. We just don't."

For all the disagreements the Mormons had had with gays and lesbians, and vice versa, Williams said the two groups had a lot more in common than people would believe. "Mormons and queer people know what it's like to be hated for being different," Williams said. "So they ought to have empathy."

Mormons were radical communitarians who practiced a different marital form, polygamy. They fled the United States in the mid-1800s and settled in the Salt Lake Valley, ensconced in the Rocky Mountains and flanked by desert. When the Utah Territory was incorporated into the United States in 1896, Mormons felt they needed to assimilate and prove that they were just regular Americans.

Marginalized and persecuted groups tend to show they have assimilated as "good, worthy Americans" by ostracizing another group, Williams said. "They forget their own history of oppression and start to contribute to the oppression of others. That's what the Latter-day Saints have done."

Natalie Palmer-Sheppard, a fifty-four-year-old Black Mormon, made clear that race, not just sexual orientation, was an issue for the Church of Jesus Christ of Latter-day Saints. Long before Palmer-Sheppard, a family therapist and mother of six, became a Mormon, the church discriminated against its Black members.

Her troubles, however, involved more than racial discrimination by the church. Not long after moving from Cincinnati to Salt Lake City, she drove with her son Ronnie, then seven, to a gas station. A car filled with young white men in tuxedos arrived. One of the men, Palmer-Sheppard recalled, "tried to take the pump out of my hand and I said, 'Really? Seriously?' He said, 'You dumb little Black nigger, give me the pump.' And so, I took the pump and I squirted him. I squirted the gasoline all over him. And his friend started getting out of his car—and I squirted him too. And they just kept using the n-word."

She returned the nozzle and hose to the pump stand, got back into her car, and, as she was about to drive away, shouted, "You just better be glad I don't have a match."

Other tales of trouble involved her children. A seminary teacher told Ronnie that, as a Black Mormon, he would "never be anything in this church." His mother consulted leaders of Genesis, an organization of Black Latter-day Saints, who helped her confront the seminary's leadership. The teacher was fired. But Palmer-Sheppard's son abandoned the church.

Natalie Palmer-Sheppard

She, however, remained a committed Mormon. She originally came to the church, she said, as an angry Black woman: "I was ghetto. I recognized that there were changes that needed to occur in my life." She earned a university degree and became a licensed clinical social worker.

She adopted less confrontational ways of dealing with racism. As a therapist for the Utah Division of Child and Family Services, she called on a dysfunctional white family for a court-ordered family therapy session. The husband told her, as she stood without an umbrella in heavy rain at his front door, "I don't let your kind in my house." Palmer-Sheppard quietly talked herself inside and, over time, helped the husband and his wife regain their children from foster care.

Palmer-Sheppard developed techniques for dealing with racism. Destinae, Palmer-Sheppard's then-four-year-old daughter, was playing with a girlfriend when a girl new to the neighborhood joined them and said to Destinae's friend, "If you're going to play with her, I can't play with you because she's just a little Black nigger." A neighbor suggested that Palmer-Sheppard visit the new girl's parents to confront them.

Palmer-Sheppard refused to do that. The next Sunday she spoke at the local Mormon temple's testimony meeting about what had happened to her daughter. She concluded by saying, "If you're all who you say you are, and you're walking in the footsteps of Jesus Christ, none of my children should ever have to experience that again."

After the meeting, a man came up to Palmer-Sheppard with his daughter. Palmer-Sheppard recalled: "He said, 'This is my daughter, Izzie, and she is the one who offended your daughter, and she really doesn't know what that means. And we really wanted to come to your house to talk to you and Destinae and straighten it out.'" The father and daughter did visit, Palmer-Sheppard said. "She and Destinae are friends off and on now."

Racism thrived everywhere, though more subtly among Utahns, Palmer-Sheppard said. "They will smile and grin at you, and you may learn later that they called you some kind of name. But you have to be a better person. In order for that mind-set to change, in order for things to be better for your children, you have to learn how to act in a situation instead of reacting to it. And that's the reality."

———

Behind schedule, we sped west across Nevada and California, planning to stop only at places where Twain worked. The best part of the six-hour drive west on Interstate 80 from Salt Lake City to Unionville, Nevada, where Mark Twain played at prospecting for silver and gold, was the last half hour. We exited the interstate and drove south at sunset on Nevada Route 400. OPEN RANGE signs dotted the rural road. Each sign featured a black bull on a yellow background, topped by two fluttering red flags. At three miles, lying on the roadside, a dead coyote nestled on the stomach of a dead black cow.

At seventeen miles, we left the desert-like brushland and climbed a gravel canyon road to the ghost town of Unionville, where animals far outnumbered its fifteen humans. Mitzi Jones, eighty-seven, and her son, David, sixty-two, owners of the Old Pioneer Garden bed-and-breakfast, had three dogs, four cats, twenty-five chickens, and a gaggle of goats and lambs. The Joneses put us in a restored circa-1861 guesthouse. The front two rooms (Twain reportedly ate dinner in the rear one) had adobe walls two feet thick.

Twain's Unionville consisted of eleven cabins and a liberty pole.[24] A state historical sign marks "the remains of Mark Twain's cabin." But the Joneses said Twain actually lived in a nearby dugout. He built it, as he wrote in *Roughing It*, "in the side of the crevice and roofed it with canvas, leaving a corner open to serve as a chimney, through which the cattle used to tumble occasionally, at night, and mash our furniture and interrupt our sleep." Twain tried prospecting for gold, scratching with a pick and sinking a shaft, but soon quit.

We ate dinner at a long wooden table off the kitchen with the Joneses, two out-of-towners, and a neighbor, Frank McCuskey, a sixty-nine-year-old transplanted Texan who retired in his fifties from teaching shop in the nearby Winnemucca, Nevada, school system.

Dinner felt festive, four days after Twain's birthday, a day before David Jones's, and on Dan's twenty-first. David Jones offered glass after glass after glass of red wine. We adopted Twain's advice to "never refuse to take a drink—under any circumstances." Sometime after the lasagna main course (vegetarian in Dan's honor) and more rounds of wine, Dan barely blew out the eight candles on his birthday carrot cake.

The conversation turned to the danger of driving at night in the valley below, where people tested the road's 70 mph speed limit and killed or maimed cattle, bears, antelope, and deer. The Joneses, with a rifle standing near their front door, recalled when a cougar killed a half-dozen of their lambs and goats. He was treed and shot to death.

The killings reminded me of another time and another desert I would have preferred to forget. Following my parents' divorce in 1946, when I was five, I lived with my mother, Rita, and my aunt and uncle, Josephine and Loren Haskin, in the Coachella Valley desert of California for three years. The 160 acres of crater-pocked sand and scrub—grandly called Haskin's Haystack Mountain Ranch—had served as a training ground for General George Patton's Third Army tank battalions.

I associated that desert with death. A coyote had killed Suzy, my wirehaired dachshund. Uncle Loren used a shovel to guillotine a rattlesnake coiled in the shade next to our back door.

My uncle, without children of his own, acted as a father to me. He was "Loren," I was "Little Loren." He let me ride Buster, his fifteen-year-old swaybacked horse, taught me to shoot, and offered advice.[25]

So I was devastated to read a clipping from the *Pomona Progress-Bulletin*, his hometown paper, four years after I left California. Mailed to me in New York City, where I had moved following my mother's death, the clipping reported my uncle "was the victim of an 'unloaded' gun that discharged into his abdomen" when one of his dogs "apparently playfully jumped at the gun as his master was preparing to shoot ground squirrels."

But I later learned that my aunt, after quarreling with my uncle about his plan to end their ten-year marriage, her third marriage, shot-gunned him to death. Judged insane, she spent the rest of her life in San Bernardino's Patton State Hospital. She died there in 1967 at age sixty-two.

Despite those melancholy memories, I found it hard not to be mesmerized the next morning by the golden light of the rising sun, the elegance of a row of swaying poplars, and the glisten of icicles hanging from trees and buildings in Unionville.

After offering us a gargantuan breakfast of scrambled eggs, baked apples, French toast, and oatmeal with walnuts and raisins, the Joneses showed us reminders of Twain's era in Unionville: a rusted pistol; a hard block of opium embossed with a Chinese character; and an 1870 census that listed dozens of Chinese toiling as cooks, laborers, and house servants, and a twenty-six-year-old Irish woman, Elisabeth Lee, who was working as a prostitute.

The Joneses' collection of Unionville-area ammonites provoked the most thought. The rock-hard fossils of invertebrate spiral sea creatures from two hundred million years ago reminded us that, in the age of the universe, our lives were less than a breath. A century after Twain's death, we toasted the longevity of his popularity. But Twain himself chose to emphasize the brevity of human existence: "The fleeting of a luminous mote through the thin ray of sunlight—and it is visible but a fraction of a second."

From Unionville, we hurried southwest to Virginia City, near the California border. Sam Clemens first used the Mark Twain byline as a reporter at the *Territorial Enterprise* there. Tales about his time in Virginia City focus not only on his journalistic escapades but also on his life as a heavy-drinking, sexually active young single. Scholars suggest he slept with prostitutes and chambermaids and maybe even a saloon-hopping male roommate or two.[26] So Alyssa, Dan, and I visited a photo studio to have our picture taken against a Twain-era saloon backdrop, dressed as carousing barmaid and bank robbers.

One of the greatest thrills of a road trip is to find what you are not searching for—and to find it more fascinating than what you were seeking. We planned to visit the Angels Camp Museum in Angels Camp, California, to view its exhibit about Mark Twain and the local "Jumping Frog" story that made him famous. But the tales of Susan Rudolph, the museum's archivist, about local residents proved even more engrossing. Rudolph, forty-nine, a Pasqua Yaqui Indian on her mother's side, told how the Miwok Indians,

In Virginia City, Nevada, a mining town where Twain prospected and wrote for the *Territorial Enterprise* newspaper, Dan Tham (left), Alyssa Karas, and Loren Ghiglione play bank robbers and barmaid at Priscilla Pennyworth's Old Time Photos.

residents of the area for thousands of years, were forced to live on a reservation near Eight Mile Road. The area's Mexicans were also required to live on the town's outskirts and excluded from working in the mines. Whites felt Native Americans and Mexicans "worked too cheap," Rudolph said.

Chinese, however, were allowed to settle in town and mine. They were said to mine scientifically, "after Euro-Americans had removed the more readily available gold."[27]

Given the history of my great-grandfather Angelo Ghiglione, who arrived in New York from near Genoa, Italy, in 1872, I was surprised to learn immigrants from the Genoa area came to this remote mountain mining town at roughly the same time. In the museum's archive, Rudolph showed us the remains of an exhibit about local Genovese who, after trying mining, went into law, government, and business. Olivia Rolleri, a widow with ten children to raise, ran the Calaveras Hotel so successfully that she was able to buy other businesses, including ranches to raise beef and a butcher shop that supplied her hotel.[28] The Genovese, Rudolph said, "made a lot of money off those miners."

When we left Angels Camp, Alyssa, Dan, and I headed toward a rendezvous near San Francisco with a nonrelative, Frank Ghiglione, another financially successful Italian American entrepreneur (who had a curious tie to the jumping frog contest of Calaveras County that Twain's story chronicled).

CHAPTER 17

San Francisco

A Porn Star Comes to Our Rescue

We left Calaveras County, home to the frog-jumping contest that Twain made famous, and headed toward San Francisco. We stopped off at the island of Alameda, California, to interview Frank Ghiglione, who had his own frog-jumping story. Five years earlier, Ghiglione (no relation) and friends had bought several Alameda frogs to enter in the contest. What were their names, I asked, thinking theirs might rival that of the record holder (21 feet, 5¾ inches), Rosie the Ribeter.

"Losers is what I call them," Ghiglione quipped. The Alameda frogs, he said, had no chance against behemoths from Africa. "My frog almost had a heart attack," he said.

———

As a Twainiac with a Genovese/Ligurian last name, I started my visit to San Francisco on Telegraph Hill. Twain once lived there, and at the top of the hill, in front of Coit Tower, stood a statue of Christopher Columbus, given to San Francisco in 1997 by the mayor of Genoa and the president of Liguria. The statue proclaimed Columbus "discoverer of America," although, of course, America really had been discovered by Indigenous peoples thousands of years before Columbus's visit to the Western Hemisphere.

Americans, not only Italian Americans, cast Columbus as a discoverer—"forward-looking / inventive daring not afraid of fools and bigots," the poet Robert Viscusi writes. But Columbus Day, which San Francisco's Italian Americans claimed to have first organized in 1869, Viscusi says, "will go the way of the dinosaur."[1] Cities and states will continue replacing Columbus Day with Indigenous People's Day. And the heroic Columbus of myth and children's verse, he who sailed the ocean blue, likely will fall to the historians' Columbus, an adventurer and slaver who "used torture and mutilation" to control Indigenous peoples.[2]

Walking around Coit Tower, I felt on the top of the world. I could see as far as the Napa hills, fifty miles away, and looked down upon the financial district. There, off Sansome Street, a runty Mark Twain alley ends in a tiny park that celebrates Twain, the writer of stories that appeal to children as much as adults. Statues of six stomping children and nine large frogs leaping on lily pads recalled Twain's famous tale, "The Celebrated Jumping Frog of Calaveras County."

Twain's trip west to San Francisco represented an early stage in the lifetime evolution of a young, ignorant racist who ultimately would don the mantle of a nonracist. In *Roughing It* (1871), Twain demeaned the Native Americans of the West—specifically the Goshoot Shoshone and "the despised Digger Indians of California." American Indians were "treacherous, filthy and repulsive," he wrote. "They deserve pity, poor creatures; and they can have mine— at this distance. Nearer by, they never get anybody's."

San Francisco stood for the segregation and subjugation of not only American Indians. Many African Americans arrived in San Francisco during World War II to work in the shipyards. The Fillmore District, a jazz-jumping neighborhood, earned a reputation as the Harlem of the West. But an urban renewal plan proposed "a clean sweep and a new start . . . a green city" that few Black residents could afford. The developer Justin Herman, who was responsible for carrying out the urban renewal plan in the 1960s, acknowledged that "without adequate housing for the poor, critics will rightly condemn urban renewal as a land-grab for the rich and a heartless push-out for the poor and nonwhites."[3] (Herman's racist policies led the city's Recreation and Park Commission and its Board of Supervisors to strip his name from the Justin Herman Plaza and rename it Embarcadero Plaza in 2017.) Local African Americans predicted the city, which had a Black-white residential ratio of 1:7 in 1970, would wind up with a citizenry in which only one resident in one hundred is Black.[4]

I wanted to learn more about the people of San Francisco who were often disparaged: the Chinese immigrants who entered the United States through San Francisco Bay's Angel Island and the Native Americans who were called Diggers because they supposedly searched for wild roots. Descriptions of the swarthy Digger drew attention to the similarity between the word *digger* and the country's most potent racial epithet, *nigger*.[5]

Indigenous peoples had been in the San Francisco area for more than ten thousand years. I visited Misión San Francisco de Asís (popularly known as Mission Dolores), founded by Spanish priests in 1776. I asked Andrew A. Galvan, the mission's fifty-eight-year-old curator and a former Franciscan seminarian, about the mission's treatment of American Indians. Galvan, a descendant of the Ohlone, Bay Miwok, and Patwin Indians whose lands once occupied the greater San Francisco Bay region, downplayed the mission's impact on Native Americans: "The Spanish [priests] were the least of the evils." The greatest devastation came later, following the discovery of gold in 1848, from mistreatment and murder by miners, Galvan said. A California Indian population of 275,000 in the late 1700s had dwindled to 30,000 after the gold rush.[6]

The Mission Dolores cemetery, jeweled today by rose bushes and cypress trees, made clear, however, that in an earlier era the Spanish missions not only forced conversion to obliterate the local Indians' names, languages, and culture but also helped decimate the area's Native Americans. Vincent Medina, a twenty-seven-year-old assistant curator at the mission and a member of the Chochenyo Ohlone community, said almost six thousand Native Americans constituted the largest group buried there.

Spanish priests such as Junipero Serra, founder of the California missions who was given sainthood by Pope Francis in 2015, saw the missions as utopian Christian communities to help the Indians and save their souls. The Indians were to be civilized and made into good Catholics who would lead "lives of great peacefulness and holiness."[7] In reality, the missions were, Medina said, "horrible places—similar to concentration camps."

Once baptized, Indians were held against their will. They were treated as slaves, their land taken, their labor exploited. A detachment of soldiers shackled and whipped those who tried to flee. Unmarried Indian women were forced to live in *monjerias* (nunneries) and work as spinners and weavers when they were not being driven into the mission for mass or lessons in church doctrine. By 1843, the mission's total Indian population of at least one thousand had been reduced to "eight aged starvelings."[8]

The California State Board of Education mandated a unit on the early missions. Medina recalled his required fourth-grade class field trip to Mission San José in Fremont in 1996 "to visit the place my ancestors built and were enslaved in." The woman who served as the tour guide proudly told Medina and his classmates: "'The friendly, faithful, and peaceful Indians were happy to accept the Spanish culture and the Catholic faith!'"

Vincent Medina

Medina writes: "I felt embarrassed and annoyed to hear that while surrounded by my classmates."[9]

That experience drove him to work at Mission Dolores, where he offered an Ohlone perspective on the history of the missions. When Gabriel, his younger brother, faced his fourth-grade Mission San José assignment, Medina told him about an 1829 rebellion there. Indians attacked the Spanish at the mission because of their abuses.

Gabriel and Vincent Medina bought the usual mission-assignment supplies from an arts and crafts store, including plastic figurines of Spanish priests and horses. But they also purchased flame-colored cellophane, toothpicks to paint and insert into the mission model to look like arrows, and G.I. Joe figurines that they transformed into Ohlone militia. Gabriel's mission project told the story of Mission San José under siege, as Ohlone fighters set fires and occupied the bell tower. Gabriel proudly titled his project, "You Gotta Do What You Gotta Do."

Vincent Medina also committed to a larger challenge, to change the way the story of the missions was told and taught throughout California. Some mission curators resisted. But he helped the California Indian Culture and Sovereignty Center develop a website about Indian opposition to the missions. He also learned the language of his tribe to assist in reviving Chochenyo as a spoken language. He worked at Heyday, the publisher of books about California Indians, as an outreach coordinator. His blog, *Being Ohlone in the 21st Century*, documents his community's revitalization.[10] He is determined, he said, "to make concrete change happen."

Our visit to Angel Island, which is north of Alcatraz in San Francisco Bay, forced me to rethink the version of American history I had learned in school. If the Angel Island Immigration Station was mentioned at all, it was portrayed as the Ellis Island of the West, welcoming hundreds of thousands of Chinese and other immigrants.

But the real story of Angel Island contradicted the feel-good version. Between 1910 and 1940, the Angel Island Immigration Station's years of operation, more people left the United States from there (665,430) than arrived (550,469). Immigrant processing that took a few hours at Ellis Island took days, sometimes years, at Angel Island. Angel Island accepted people from eighty countries. But the discriminatory way they were greeted—many, especially Chinese, expelled from the United States on the basis of race, class, gender, and nationality—told a sadder version of the nation's immigration story.

Mark Twain, who visited Angel Island in 1864 as a reporter for the *San Francisco Daily Morning Call*, learned firsthand as the *Call*'s police reporter about the mistreatment of the Chinese. He covered the kidnapping of Chinese girls to staff Chinatown's brothels, the exploitation of Chinese railroad workers, and the California statute that allowed whites to testify against everyone but permitted Chinese to testify against only other Chinese.

During his daily thirteen hours as the *Call*'s police reporter, Twain saw the Chinese, Edgar M. Branch writes, "as victims of an 'enlightened' and 'Christian' and 'civilized' way of life."[11] Twain claimed he was fired by the *Call* in part because of his indignant piece about street bullies abusing peaceful Chinese.

We took the San Francisco–to–Angel Island ferry to view what was once a detention facility for Chinese immigrants. The December cold and the emptiness of the immigration station's two-story wooden barracks gave the buildings the feel of a prison. That was fitting. The barracks were last used to house Japanese prisoners during World War II.

The Chinese immigrants who came to Angel Island between 1910 and 1940 were treated little better than the Japanese prisoners. Two hundred Chinese were stuffed into a one-thousand-square-foot room. Three-high bunk beds were stripped of the mattresses provided to other immigrants. Only bare bulbs offered light. Laundry hung from the walls and ceiling. Suitcases covered the floor.

With the Chinese Exclusion Act of 1882 in force, many immigrants lied about their identity, pretending to be the children—"paper sons" or "paper daughters"—of Chinese merchants or U.S. citizens. If they succeeded in entering the United States, they lived in constant fear of detection and deportation.

Eddie Wong, the fifty-year-old executive director of the Angel Island Immigration Station Foundation, told us about his father, who arrived at Angel Island as a fifteen-year-old on forged papers. He started attending school in San Francisco. "Someone did not get paid off," Wong said. "Someone informed on his whole false family. He was arrested in Francisco Junior High School and taken here [to Angel Island] for a month, then sent back to China."

Wong's father waited a year, bought more forged papers, returned to Angel Island with a false brother, and survived three weeks of interrogation. Immigration officials grilled Wong's father and the false brother to make sure their version of their lives matched those provided by their supposed parent.

Maxine Hong Kingston captured the treachery of the interrogators' trick questions:

> Those who came back after being examined told what questions they had been asked. "I had to describe all the streets in my village." "They'll ask, 'Do you have any money?' and 'Do you have a job?'" "They've been asking those questions all this week," the cooks and janitors confirmed. "What's the right answer?" asked the legal fathers. "Well, last week they liked 'No job' because it proves you were an aristocrat. And they liked 'No money' because you showed a willingness to work. But this week, they like 'Yes job' and 'Yes money' because you wouldn't be taking jobs away from white workers." The men groaned. "Some help."[12]

Wong's father decided he would not settle in the Bay Area again because people "talked too much, so he moved to Chicago," Wong said. His father worked as a driver for the Hong Kong Noodle Factory in Chicago's Chinatown, next to Little Italy. "He remembers mobster Al Capone loved Chinese food and [that] the Chinese and Italians did not get along because the Italians would beat up and rob the Chinese," Wong said. "And the Chinese would not report it" out of fear they would be deported.

Wong's father was forced to confess a second time to being a false citizen because another brother had confessed. "And he had to wait five years to become a citizen," Wong said. His father's message was always to behave or risk deportation. "I kind of roughly knew that, because whenever friends came over [to the house], they'd call him by a different name. So it was very curious to me why he had at least three names: an American name, Frank Wong; his false Chinese name, Wong Fook Goey; and his real Chinese name, Wong Moon Tung."

That life of fear was captured in the Chinese calligraphy on the Angel Island Immigration Station's walls: "Sadness kills the person in the wooden building," one poem said. Immigration station officials repainted the walls to cover up what they deemed graffiti. But the poets then carved into the walls expressions of their longing to escape confinement. Maintenance crews filled the carvings with putty and repainted the walls. Still, more than two hundred poems and other works remained visible.

The Angel Island experience haunted its survivors. Tet Ming Yee, whose papers were real, entered the United States after being held for six months on Angel Island. Exclusion laws kept his wife and daughter out of the country for fourteen years. Only after repeal of the exclusion laws and his honorable discharge from the U.S. Army following service in World War II was Yee able to become a U.S. citizen and bring his wife and daughter to the United States.

Before he died in 1996 at eighty-five, he wrote a poem about his time at Angel Island. The poem ends:

> The memories are etched in my bones and in my heart.
> Today we can stand proud as Chinese Americans.
> But I will never forget what happened here on Angel Island,
> Where our pain was carved in silence.[13]

Alyssa, Dan, and I returned to downtown San Francisco to visit Charles Reich, once a controversial law professor of mine. Pundits have a habit of anointing a few writers as so gifted that they capture the spirit of a decade. Sam Tanenhaus, editor of the *New York Times Book Review* from 2004 to 2013, chose Francis Fukuyama for the 1990s, Allan Bloom for the 1980s, and Christopher Lasch for the 1970s.[14]

But my choice for the 1970s is Reich. On September 26, 1970, the *New Yorker* published Reich's "Reflections: The Greening of America." His article applauded a student-generation counterculture that sought "a more human community." The article generated more letters to the *New Yorker* than any other article to that date in the magazine's history. When my fifty-seven-hundred-circulation, factory-town *Southbridge (Massachusetts) Evening News* reprinted the article along with local pro-and-con reactions, it provoked a record-setting barrage of brickbats and bravos. Random House soon published *The Greening of America* as a book that topped best-seller lists and eventually sold more than two million copies.

Reich, the scholarly law professor with the perfect pedigree (editor-in-chief of the *Yale Law Journal* and clerk for U.S. Supreme Court Justice Hugo L. Black), became a rock-star celebrity. The media, he worried, were "trying to turn me into a fifth Beatle."[15]

Despite the popularity of *The Greening of America*, or perhaps because of it, many academic and media critics savaged the book.[16] "*The Greening of America* did me in as far as academe was concerned," Reich, eighty-four, told Alyssa, Dan, and me. "I would never be the same after that." He resigned

Charles Reich

from the Yale Law faculty and in 1974 moved to San Francisco. "It was with the goal of being as far away as I possibly could be still in the United States— as far away from New York, where I grew up, New Haven, Washington, D.C.—to get some distance from my former life."

Seen in the 1970s as a counterculture advocate, Reich critiqued the counterculture movement that was hogging the headlines during our trip, Occupy Wall Street. "They'll never get anywhere with what they're doing now because they're appealing to someone else to do something," Reich said, whether the someone else was Congress, the president, or business. "My message is: 'You're going to have to do it yourself.'"

Reich saw a staggering agenda to tackle. He worried about the two million inmates in U.S. prisons, the spread of nuclear weapons ("I'm not sure we won't blow ourselves up completely in the next few years"), the unnecessary role of the U.S. military abroad, and the "scandal and disgrace" of the U.S. economy, with millions of jobs sent overseas, sometimes with tax support.

During the 1960s, he believed in reform and felt he was doing some good. A half-century later, he no longer talked reform. He saw himself as a dissenter in his own country: "I don't like what is going on. I don't think this is a good future."

But Reich saw greater tolerance among Americans than in the past. The progressive private schools he attended in New York—Lincoln School and City and Country School—had no Black students. He began his law career in 1952, at a time of discrimination against Jews, people of color, and women. At Cravath, Swaine & Moore in New York, where all the lawyers and stenographers were male, Reich said his boss, Donald C. Swatland, told him, "Women are frivolous, women belong at home, women are not designed for business."

Reich noted the greater acceptance today of same-sex marriage. But he downplayed his identity as a gay man. "I represent a different group—an unknown minority, probably forty million or more—people who live alone." He described himself as a loner who could not live with another person. "That trumps sexual orientation completely," he said. At his age, Reich said, his sexual orientation "has almost no relevance to my life."

As a seventy-year-old, I hated being reminded that my body and brain weren't what they once were when it came to sex. Not surprisingly, for me our trip lacked the sexual hijinks of Kerouac's *On the Road*. Alyssa, a half-century my junior, fantasized in San Francisco about cute Cosmo, who was sleeping on the couch (Alyssa and Dan were crashing at a cooperative house where a high school friend of Dan's lived; I was staying with Northwestern alums). Dan remained loyal to his boyfriend, Brian Cacioppo, although Dan joked: "I could have had a lover in every port." But his dating experience raised serious questions for him. Was he being fetishized by his white partners? Were the stereotypes of small, weak Asian men and large, strong white men producing a paradigm of sex and sexual hierarchy? Is being on top, to quote Dan, "not just sexual but social, economic, cultural, imperial, and white"?

As we left Reich's apartment, he reiterated he was a dissenter but a dissenter with hope for humanity. He walked with a cane, and when he climbed on a bus, people rushed to give him a seat. "You get the best of human nature. . . . I get the feeling that people are very nice."

The United States, however, had become a corporate tyranny "taken over by a small minority of powerful interests." On his website in 2019, he contrasted the United States under FDR—"we felt that the country was in good hands and on the right track"—with that of America under Trump. Reich showed a photo of a bizarre make-believe bird, titled "the Goofus bird—just the creature for today's crazy world."

When Reich died in 2019 at ninety-one, his obituary in the *New York Times* said his career goal "had been 'to make people think.' By that measure, he succeeded."[17]

An experience in San Francisco reminded us of Alyssa's motto that everything in life is either a good time or a good story. One evening, our van, which we had parked at the high-traffic intersection of Ninth and Folsom, fell victim to smash-and-grabbers.

They shattered a passenger-side window and escaped with our video camera, two laptop computers, and Alyssa's two suitcases. They left behind eight heavy cartons of research files. Maybe the thieves had been reading Twain. In "Advice for Good Little Boys," he said: "You ought never to take anything that don't belong to you—if you cannot carry it off."

The loss of irreplaceable video interviews and photos hit us hard, in part because we were exhausted after almost three months on the road. Alyssa wrote in her diary the next day: "We're ready to be done and go to bed for days and days and be left alone."

Standing on the street corner, looking at the black shards of the van's window glass covering the sidewalk, the three of us responded emotionally, if somewhat differently.

Alyssa telephoned her mother. "I felt calm, but my legs were shaking," she recalled. "And then I started to sob without realizing it. I tried to hold it in, leading to silence when I couldn't choke out the words. And then I burst into real, hard, gasping sobs. That lasted for a few minutes, and then I was done, and I accepted it, and moved on: 'It's just stuff. No one was hurt.'"

Dan returned from a Chinatown dinner with his uncle Binh, shocked by the loss of not only our tripod and expensive camera but also hours of interviews. He hugged Alyssa and cried. At first, I played the calm, collected adult. I called the San Francisco police, expecting a squad car would arrive momentarily. No police came. I called the police again and again, growing angrier and angrier. No one came. Finally, hours after my first call, I gave up. We drove to a nearby police station to report our loss.

The story got better the next morning. Someone named Kimberly Kills tweeted Alyssa and asked where she was. Alyssa replied, "San Francisco," and learned that Kills had found one of her suitcases after midnight, half open, clothes strewn on the sidewalk, in Oakland, about ten miles from San

Francisco. In arranging for us to meet Kills at a Starbucks in Oakland to pick up her bag, Alyssa said, "I think she's a porn star."

Alyssa appeared to be right. KimKills.com called Kills "one of the hottest, natural transsexual porn stars on this planet." Kills described herself as a twenty-eight-year-old transgender male-to-female model who performed in adult films. She listed her specialty as "experienced rope bottom and fetishist/kink lifestyle."

When we arrived at the Oakland Starbucks, Kills was drinking a cup of coffee and typing on her laptop. She could have been a university student attracted to Oakland by its punk scene. She displayed a heart tattoo on her neck and an angel tattoo on her shoulder. Her black T-shirt carried a catchphrase from *No Way Back*, a 1976 blaxploitation film: "Never trust a woman with her clothes off."

Kills posed for a photo with Alyssa. They looked like sisters. For us, Kills was a sister of kindness, going out of her way to make sure Alyssa's suitcase was returned to her.

Later, during a telephone conversation, she said she had been out of work and was in need of clothes when she came across Alyssa's suitcase on the street. She saw a stylish new dress hanging out of Alyssa's bag. But Kills found Alyssa's business card in the suitcase and tweeted her. "I just thought it was the right thing to do," Kills said.

Kills had something personal to say about the identity issues that were the focus of our trip, especially sexual orientation. She labeled her own sexual orientation as polyamorous bisexual. The child of parents who divorced when she was about two, Kills grew up a military brat who moved every two or so years from town to town across America. At seventeen, she joined the U.S. Army and served two years. "I wanted to fight who I was," she said.

Her nomadic life continued. After stays in eight U.S. cities, she "lost a solid place to live" and spent two years on the road. Finally, she said, "I landed in Oakland burnt out and found a nice, torn-down, shithole, punk venue to live at."

When Alyssa checked the contents of her suitcase, almost everything was present, including a voodoo doll she had bought for protection at Marie Laveau's House of Voodoo in New Orleans. The only missing item of note was Ron Powers's biography of Mark Twain.

No doubt our erudite smash-and-grabbers wanted to read about Twain's time in San Francisco, which he called "the most cordial and sociable city," perhaps to learn how they could be even more hospitable to out-of-towners.

Alyssa Karas (left) and Kimberly Kills

Alyssa, Dan, and I left San Francisco without conducting one interview that seemed especially timely. We had arrived in San Francisco on December 7, the seventieth anniversary of the bombing of Pearl Harbor by the Japanese. Hysteria had gripped the West Coast as residents worried about Japanese and Japanese American intelligence agents and saboteurs. Under Executive Order 9066, the government banished more than 117,000 U.S. citizens and resident aliens of Japanese descent from the West Coast to distant internment camps (critics called them concentration camps). Our visit to Seattle provided an opportunity to make up for our failure to interview a Japanese American who was exiled to one of those camps.

CHAPTER 18

Seattle

*Uprooted Native Americans and Root-Planting
Asian and Italian Immigrants*

Our failure in San Francisco to interview a Japanese American survivor of Executive Order 9066 led me to search Seattle for someone who had lived through what the historian Roger Sale considers the darkest moment in Seattle history: "Japanese Americans . . . were captured like criminals, hauled away to concentration camps, and made to bear collectively a guilt that in fact was not even the responsibility of a single one, since no one in Seattle was ever charged with collaboration with the government of Japan."[1]

William Toshio "Tosh" Yasutake, a Japanese American born in Seattle in 1922, lived at the Hearthstone retirement community with his Japanese American wife, Fumi, who was born in New York in 1926. Sitting in their book-lined living room, they were surrounded by Japanese art: origami, landscape paintings, and a cloth curtain in the doorway to their bedroom that reproduced Katsushika Hokusai's famous woodblock print, *The Great Wave off Kanagawa.*

Tosh heard about the Pearl Harbor bombing while attending services at Blaine Memorial United Methodist Church.[2] He returned home with his brother, Joe, and sister, Mitsuye. They huddled around a radio in the living room of their parents' four-bedroom house on Beacon Hill, a racially diverse neighborhood in southeast Seattle.

Their mother, Hide, remained at the family's church to attend a women's group meeting. Their father, Jack, was leading a senryu poetry club meeting at the Maneki Restaurant downtown. Around noon, the doorbell rang. Four FBI agents demanded to speak to Jack, who had served as a U.S. Immigration and Naturalization Service interpreter for twenty-three years.

The children provided the name and address of the downtown restaurant. One agent left for the restaurant and arrested Jack. Without charging him with a crime, the agent took Jack to a holding cell at the Immigration and Naturalization Service office and never informed his family where he had been jailed.

The other agents entered the Yasutake home. While one agent watched the Yasutake children in the living room, his gun resting on his knee, the two other agents tore up the house. They emptied kitchen cabinets plate by plate. They rolled up rugs and ripped up floorboards.

Hide Yasutake flung open the front door and cried out in Japanese, "What's going on? Who are these people?" The agent guarding her children stood and yelled, "Speak English! Don't speak Japanese!" He ordered her to join her children in the living room. She and her children sat together silently, afraid to speak.

Hours later, the agents left with Jack Yasutake's journal notes and manuscripts of his community club speeches written in Japanese; all his film, including family photos; letters from relatives in Japan; clippings from Japanese newspapers and magazines; and books in Japanese.

Fortunately for the Yasutakes, the FBI agents had failed to spot a safe hidden in the back of a closet, behind hanging clothes, in Mitsuye's bedroom. When the government froze Jack Yasutake's bank accounts, the $1,000 in the safe helped pay for food and other essentials. The only source of family income until April 1942, when the family was expelled from their home under Executive Order 9066, was the $15 a week Mitsuye, a high school senior, earned as a housekeeper and babysitter. Tosh, a premed major in his first year, had dropped out of the University of Washington after the Pearl Harbor attack to seek work. He responded to daily want ads, but nobody would hire him.

After stops at internment camps in Missoula, Montana, and Santa Fe and Lordsburg, New Mexico, Tosh's father landed in the high-security camp at Crystal City, Texas. A migrant labor camp before the war, Crystal City housed as many as 3,374 Japanese Americans and German Americans—so-called enemy aliens. Today, an engraved granite stone there reads, "World War II concentration camp, 1943–1946."

Army troops escorted Tosh, his mother, his siblings, and more than seventy-three hundred other Japanese Americans to temporary barracks built on the Western Washington Fairgrounds in Puyallup, thirty-five miles south of Seattle. Public relations officials called the barracks surrounded by barbed wire Camp Harmony. Mitsuye later wrote a poem called "Evacuation" that helped capture the irony of Camp Harmony's name: "As we boarded the bus / . . . the *Seattle Times* / photographer said / Smile! / so obediently I smiled / and the caption the next day / read: / Note smiling faces / a lesson to Tokyo."[3]

Three months later, the Yasutakes endured a thirty-hour ride by train and bus to the arid, rattlesnake-and-sagebrush desert of the Minidoka, Idaho, internment camp. Barbed-wire fence and watchtowers enclosed tar-papered barracks. Tosh refused to call Minidoka a concentration camp, a term he reserved for Buchenwald and other Holocaust camps. "That's what the Jews went through," he said.

But Minidoka was no desert resort. Storms of fine dust "would come in like smoke" through cracks in the windowsills, Tosh said. "My mother spent a lot of time packing those cracks with sheets and old clothes." He ate Vienna sausages gritty from dust storms for almost every meal for several weeks: "To this day I don't like Vienna sausages."

Tosh insisted, however, that his autobiography could be titled *One Lucky Guy*. He worked as an attendant and later a medical technician in the hospitals at Puyallup and Minidoka and therefore benefited from better food and facilities. While at Minidoka, which had the highest ratio of volunteers for the U.S. Army of the ten internment camps, he enlisted.

He was reluctant at first because he would have to serve in a segregated unit—all Japanese American soldiers, headed by two white officers. "That's why I was the very last one of about five hundred from Minidoka to volunteer," he said. "But I finally decided to volunteer because I thought it would help my dad get released a bit earlier."

Tosh's luck held while serving as a combat medic in the 442nd Infantry Regiment. Sniper fire was killing medics at such a rapid rate that they removed the red cross from their armbands and helmets. "It's such a good target," Tosh said. While he was fighting in the Vosges forests in northern France, shrapnel hit his right leg below the knee. Tosh called the embedded shrapnel a life-saving "million-dollar wound"—although it took months to heal.

"I'm still carrying the shrapnel," Tosh said. "I have always felt very lucky that I survived. The fellow who replaced me was killed in action within days of replacing me, and the fellow who replaced him was seriously wounded. I was wounded just before the Lost Battalion battle [that decimated the 442nd]. That's the reason I'm alive. Survival is a matter of luck."[4]

William Toshio "Tosh"
Yasutake

I asked Tosh to show me his war medals. From his living room closet, he brought out the Purple Heart, the Bronze Star with Oak Leaf Cluster, the French Knight in the Order of the Legion of Honor, and the Congressional Gold Medal. As I held each of Tosh's medals, reminders of the bravery of the 442nd, I thought about the soldiers' imprisonment in Minidoka and other internment camps. Perhaps their record of both perseverance in the camps and triumph on the battlefield helped accelerate acceptance of Japanese Americans.

Perhaps Japanese Americans' postwar record of accomplishment helped too. All three Yasutake sons—Tosh, Joe, and Mike—earned doctoral degrees and served society as professionals: Tosh as a salmon-disease researcher, his brothers as psychologist and Episcopal minister.

Tosh called their sister, Mitsuye Yamada, who did not obtain a doctoral degree, "the smart one in the family." A poet and retired professor of English, Yamada and the Chinese American feminist activist Nellie Wong were the subject of a 1981 documentary, *Mitsuye and Nellie: Asian American Poets*, by the Academy Award winners Allie Light and Irving Saraf.

But racism and other forms of discrimination persisted generation after generation. Japanese Americans were not the only targets during World War II. In 1941, when Mussolini's Italy declared war on the United States and signs posted in Italian neighborhoods warned, DON'T SPEAK THE ENEMY'S LANGUAGE! SPEAK AMERICAN!, Dr. August J. Ghiglione, my great-grandfather's third son, had to obtain a copy of his New York City birth certificate to prove he was a U.S. citizen or risk being thrown in an internment camp for those suspected of loyalty to Mussolini's Italy.

Lucius Horiuchi, a former U.S. Foreign Service officer, saw an echo in the deliberations of a presidential policy team established to address the Iranian hostage crisis of 1979–81: "Some members of the team wanted 'camps' to be reopened to be ready to hold all Iranians and Americans of Iranian parentage. In times of national stress, of pending war or of war, many may again turn against those who can be labeled and categorized—be it hyphenated Americans or whomever some in the majority wish to be rid of."[5]

In this generation, President Trump's anti-immigrant, antirefugee initiative has taken many forms. He has slashed to eighteen thousand a year the number of refugees that the United States will admit (down from 110,000 in Obama's last year), with Muslim refugee admissions cut the most. The criminalization of immigration also has had an impact. The legal scholar Michelle Alexander writes, "Minor legal infractions, ranging from shoplifting to marijuana possession to traffic violations, now routinely prompt one of the nation's most devastating sanctions—deportation."[6]

One form of Trump's attack on immigrants resembles the internment camps of World War II. Immigrant families and children, including asylum seekers, requesting entry to the United States, have been told, "Our country is *full.*" They have been caged in detention centers, with prolonged delays in processing and deaths among the detained. Thousands of children have been forcibly separated from their parents, all in the name of national security. "History is repeating itself," writes Michiko Kakutani. "This time without even the pretext of war, and with added heartbreaking cruelty."[7]

———

Many Americans view Vietnamese Americans as outliers, dark and different, even dangerous. Only 36 percent of Americans wanted to accept Vietnamese refugees in 1975, when the Vietnam War ended. In recalling his mother, who came to America that year as a Vietnamese refugee, the Pulitzer Prize–winning novelist Viet Thanh Nguyen wrote, "She did not speak fluent English, but she did well enough to contribute more in taxes than many Americans. She was and is heroic, but many Americans would see her only as an outsider, including the one who put a sign in a shop window near my parents' grocery store: 'Another American driven out of business by the Vietnamese.'"[8] Dan,

Julie Pham

Alyssa, and I visited Julie Pham, who, like Viet Thanh Nguyen's mother, was a successful Vietnamese American businesswoman, at the office of the region's Vietnamese-language newspaper. Dan wrote about that visit:

One day, an elderly Vietnamese man walked into the Seattle office of Người Việt Tây Bắc, *the largest and oldest newspaper for Vietnamese immigrants in Washington State. He wanted to place a classified ad in the twenty-eight-year-old biweekly.*

The man ran the ad only once. It called for the person who had left his luggage in the man's house for months to take it away. Once the paper got into the hands of the Vietnamese community, those who knew the leaver of the luggage reminded him to remove it.

Julie Pham, thirty-three-year-old managing editor, told us about the man and his ad. "People are really hungry to feel connected," Pham said. "I look around and I see that the need for news is growing. There are constant streams of immigration. And they [immigrants] turn to the newspaper to help them understand and acclimate to the world here.

"The Vietnamese community is the most linguistically isolated, with the highest percentage of limited English proficiency," Pham said. "The newspaper links people with news of their homeland, of Vietnam, and also with local news, so they can understand their new homeland as well." Pham saw her family's newspaper as stoking a sense of community for the third-largest Asian

population in the state. Người Việt Tây Bắc *provided everything, from news of business openings to recommendations of dentists to classified ads subtly asking for the removal of luggage.*

In 1979, when she was just two months old, her family decided to flee Vietnam. Subjected to pirates, overcrowded makeshift boats, and storms on the open waters, many of the estimated 1.5 million Vietnamese who tried to escape failed to survive their attempts. Pham's parents rarely talked about the family's escape, but they had told her she cried a lot and that they were hungry, thirsty, and unsure of what was going to happen next.

Pham's father and mother were two of the 823,000 Vietnamese refugees the United States had accepted.[9] Pham's father delivered pizzas and her mother worked as a dental assistant during their first few years in Seattle. Her father eventually realized that he didn't like working for other people. Inspired by the influx of Vietnamese boat people in the Pacific Northwest, he started Người Việt Tây Bắc, *an offshoot of the national* Người Việt *newspaper headquartered in Orange County, California.*

Pham's work at the paper sharpened her business acumen. "I always say I got my real-life MBA *by working at the newspaper," she said.*

But her formal educational pedigree also was impressive. After graduating from UC Berkeley in 2001, Pham received a doctoral degree in history from the University of Cambridge in 2008, as a Gates Scholar. She then spent time living in France, Germany, and the country she left as an infant. "I learned how American I was by being abroad," Pham said.

Pham was sympathetic to second-generation Vietnamese Americans. She did not really engage with Vietnamese culture and understand her parents on a deeper level until she learned Vietnamese after college. Hers was an American experience more than it was an immigrant one.

But she prized the role played by her immigrant father. "At the end of the day, ethnic media, they're all businesspeople," Pham said. "They're all immigrant, refugee, minority entrepreneurs."

The achievements of Julie Pham, like the achievements of Giuseppe Anthony Tran of New Orleans, Chung Kim Do of Baton Rouge, and other Vietnamese Americans Dan interviewed, demonstrate the value to America of immigrants. Despite the claim that immigrants rely heavily on costly public services, Zoltan L. Hajnal, an immigration expert, writes, "The data show that immigrants are generally not a burden on America. They work hard. They use relatively few government services. They contribute to the economy."[10]

Indeed, Vietnamese immigrants exemplify what the author Anand Giridharadas calls the "immigrant advantage." Because they came from a family-centered, collectivist society where the government did little for them, they behave in the United States as if they cannot count on government. "In America," Giridharadas writes, "they reap the advantages of being self-starters."[11]

Julie Pham is among the most recent in a long line of entrepreneurs who spent time in Seattle. Mark Twain and my great-grandfather, Angelo Francesco Ghiglione, traveled to Seattle at about the same point in their lives as Pham's parents to recover from the same problem: financial ruin.

In July 1895, the fifty-nine-year-old Twain began a yearlong round-the-world lecture tour—122 performances in 71 cities—to pay off creditors. Before heading abroad, he lectured on August 13 in Seattle, then a city of forty-five thousand, to a standing-room-only audience of twelve hundred. "To tell the story of such a lecture is like trying to narrate a laugh," a *Seattle Post-Intelligencer* reviewer wrote somewhat apologetically. "Those who heard the lecture enjoyed it, and those who did not, cannot conceive of it."[12] Twain's lecture tour allowed him to pay off his creditors by 1898.

A. F. Ghiglione was fifty-eight when he arrived in Seattle from New York four years later. He had liquidated his underfunded Lower East Side pasta company and, following the discovery of gold in the Yukon in 1896, decided to move far west. All he knew was the manufacture of pasta. He was fourteen when he started making pasta in Italy in 1858. While an indentured pasta maker in New York, he saved money by working as the factory's night watchman and sleeping part of the day in the building. "Why pay for rent?" his granddaughter Hazel Rispoli recalled he had said. "He learned the business. He took it over." It became A. F. Ghiglione & Sons.

He reinvented his pasta company in Seattle. The firm twice moved to larger quarters within the city, finally to brick buildings on Sixth Avenue in South Seattle. Each day, the firm's two dozen workers, all Italian American, turned seven tons of semolina flour, made from North and South Dakota hard durum wheat, into forty kinds of pasta.

The company prospered. Angelo had a reputation for innovation. He hired a flying salesperson (to cover Hawaii, Australia, the Philippines, New

Zealand, and Asia), started cooking classes, published a pasta cookbook, and promoted his egg noodles and macaroni in newspaper and trolley car ads as "better for you than Sirloin Steak."

Perhaps he was a bit too innovative. In 1907, he advertised his macaroni as "freshly made in Seattle, in a clean, new factory—better than the imported article, which is old and stale long before it reaches your door." By 1916, however, his company was charged with violating the Food and Drugs Act by selling domestic macaroni as "Gragnano Macaroni Brand Italian Macaroni, Quality Insuperable, Prepared for Exportation," in packages decorated with an Italian scene. Convicted of mislabeling—selling domestic macaroni as imported pasta—the company paid a $100 fine.

Angelo died at eighty-three of a stroke in 1927. Sons Charles and Frank took over the company. Depression-era disasters struck. The sons invested in Dease Creek Mining and other get-rich-quick mining stocks. Marie Wilham, granddaughter of A. F. Ghiglione, told me that in the '29 crash "all the Ghigliones lost their shirts—they had enough worthless stock to paper all their homes."

A. F. Ghiglione & Sons also suffered from a dishonest bookkeeper who loved numbers so much that he kept two sets of books. And Charles and Frank, penny-pinching managers, failed to modernize, Hazel Rispoli said. Guido Merlino of the competing Mission Macaroni Company "started to buy all up-to-date machinery," said Paskey DeDomenico, chairman of the Golden Grain Macaroni Company, another competitor. "The Ghigliones had all the junk machinery."

Robert Bruce Driscoll struck the death blow. A monomaniacal firebug who said he was "sore at the world," Driscoll torched 140 Seattle buildings between 1931 and 1935, including two buildings of A. F. Ghiglione & Sons in December 1932.[13] The damage to the two buildings amounted to $100,000 (about $1.7 million today).

The insurance company, beset by dozens of fire claims, took two years to pay. Charles and Frank lacked the business sense to deal with such a calamity. Following the fire, "they had the opportunity to put their labels on competitors' product and keep their customers," said Maybelle Lucas, another A. F. granddaughter. "But there was too much pride. They just closed. And they couldn't get back on the shelves." By the time Charles and Frank resumed production, the competitors of A. F. Ghiglione & Sons "had grabbed all its customers," DeDomenico said.

A. F. Ghiglione was tough for his sons to follow, personally as well as professionally. He was the quiet, gentle patriarch—six feet tall, 220 pounds, with mustache and muttonchops—who liked the good life and made it possible for his family to experience it. He kept a garden and purchased freight cars of California grapes to make his own wine. Into the 1920s, A. F. and his wife, Maria, traveled to mountain resorts in Alaska, California, and Washington, where, according to Wilham, "they took their own chef so that Grandpa could have his good Italian cooking."

A. F. Ghiglione's children and grandchildren remembered him proudly as, in Maybelle Lucas's words, "brave, courageous, and ambitious." He "dared come to a strange country with no money and no ability to speak the language—yet he achieved so much. When he died, he left a flourishing business that gave employment to many."

He also gave them a version of the American dream. Helen C. De Lorenzo was sixteen when she came to Seattle from Genoa in 1920 and went to work for A. F. Ghiglione & Sons. She earned eight dollars—later fifteen—a week, weighing and packing pasta. A. F., then seventy-six and white-haired with a Santa Claus beard, would sit and talk with her in their Ligurian dialect. "He was really very good to me," she said. "He told me he came to America with only a dollar in his pocket. He said, 'I was just like you. If you work hard and be honest, you will succeed.'"

I admired the entrepreneurial drive of my great grandfather and succeeding generations of Ghigliones. Indeed, it seemed especially appropriate to celebrate immigrants' entrepreneurial drive in Seattle, "one of the world's preeminent innovation hubs" of high-tech start-ups. Immigrants began one quarter of the U.S. high-tech firms started between 1965 and 2005. Immigrants or their children founded about 40 percent of all Fortune 500 companies in 2010. Immigrants and their descendants were more than drivers of the economy. They were, writes Paul Taylor, author of *The Next America*, "our face to the world."[14] Their life stories embodied prized American values: tolerance, dynamism, optimism, and pluralism.

But I found even greater inspiration in the life of my great-grandfather's third son, Dr. August J. Ghiglione, who cared for Seattle's Italian Americans from 1905 until his death in 1949 and had served them as Italian consul for the Pacific Northwest from 1907 to 1914.

Alyssa, Dan, and I stayed in Seattle with John Ghiglione, the doctor's son and my second cousin once removed, and John's wife, Joann. On a fifteen-minute trip that recalled 170 years of the region's racial history, John drove Dan, Alyssa, and me to Dr. Ghiglione's Seattle home in the Leschi neighborhood. From John's predominantly white Capitol Hill neighborhood, we drove south on Martin Luther King Way through the Central District, which was more than 70 percent Black in the 1960s. Restrictive racial covenants and bank redlining had kept Blacks out of other Seattle neighborhoods. Rising housing prices and an influx of whites that began in the Central District in the 1980s had encouraged Black residents to leave the neighborhood. By 2014, African Americans made up only 20 percent of the Central District's population.

We continued south from the Central District to the Leschi neighborhood, named for the chief of the Nisqually tribe who fought the Treaty of Medicine Creek of 1854, engineered by Isaac I. Stevens, Washington's first territorial governor. Leschi was executed by hanging, and the treaty's "final settlement"—a phrase similar to the phrase used by the Nazis for their extermination of European Jewry—took four thousand square miles of Native nations' richest arable land and forests and restricted the Nisqually and other tribes to three isolated reservations on six square miles of the least hospitable land.[15]

The front door to Dr. Ghiglione's century-old house at 333 Thirtieth Avenue South was locked, but luckily one of the second-floor tenants, Carly Reiter, a thirty-seven-year-old teacher at the Seattle Girls' School, was out walking her ten-year-old cat, Coyote George the River Pig. A decade earlier, Reiter, a fan of Mark Twain's Huck Finn, had taken a twenty-five-hundred-mile, 121-day solo canoe trip down the Mississippi, from Bemidji, Minnesota, to Baton Rouge, Louisiana. Along the way she stopped at a bar. A five-week-old kitten climbed out of a farmer's milk crate and into her lap. Reiter took the cat aboard her canoe. The kitten promptly walked into the water. But Reiter and Coyote George the River Pig survived the Mississippi. And Alyssa, Dan, and I took their presence in Seattle, at the last stop in the West on our trip, to be a good omen: Twain was with us from our odyssey's beginning to its end.

Dan, Alyssa, and I were disappointed that the rebuilt garage to Dr. Ghiglione's house no longer stood. The garage had made headlines in 1910. When the Black Hand, a criminal syndicate formed by Italian immigrants, tried to extort money from other Italian immigrants, Dr. Ghiglione had

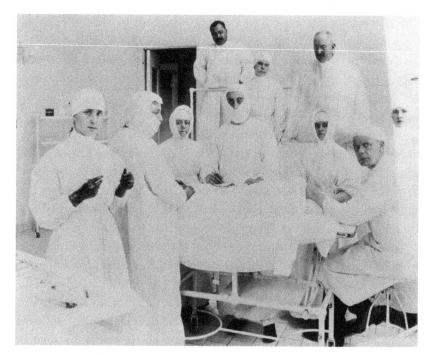

Dr. August J. Ghiglione (center, in mask, facing the camera) is about to operate at Seattle's Providence Hospital, circa 1914–20.

aided police in breaking up the plot. For a time, he traveled with a bodyguard and carried a gun in his car. On a December night, he put his Pope-Hartford in his garage. He, his wife, and their two children retired for the evening. Shortly after midnight the garage exploded.

The blast blew open the kitchen door. The house's crockery and windows—and reportedly the windows of houses several blocks away—shattered. The *Seattle Daily Times* carried front-page photos; the headline shouted, "Dynamite Outrage Perpetrated Against Italian Consular Agent Ghiglione."[16] Dr. Ghiglione appealed for police protection for his family and home.

The police ignored him. Under the headline of "The Shame of Seattle," the *Post-Intelligencer* editorialized about the corrupt police, the partnership between Police Chief Charles W. Wappenstein and criminal classes, and the chief's unwillingness to protect Dr. Ghiglione and his family.[17]

When Dr. Ghiglione wasn't dealing with corrupt police, he helped meet the medical needs of impoverished Italian Americans. His patients were primarily truck gardeners and laborers from southern and central Italy who lived in neighborhoods with nicknames like Garlic Gulch. Orly Alia, a retired construction worker, recalled an uncle who stacked ninety-five-pound bags of cement from a rapidly moving line, ten hours a day, seven days a week. Alia said, "They wore themselves out, and they were gone by the time they were sixty."[18]

Dr. Ghiglione spoke his patients' Italian dialects, wrote out prescriptions in English or Italian, depending on the patient's first language, and conveniently forgot to charge patients who lacked the money to pay. Hazel Rispoli, his daughter-in-law, said: "He came to your house and never got half the money owed him. The Italians were all poor. You didn't ask for payment [from them]. It always was, 'Pay when you can.'"

Dr. Ghiglione more than compensated for what his father perceived as his own failings. Despite his success in business, A. F. Ghiglione had never obtained an education. He saw the clubs that other Seattle businesspeople joined as beyond his reach. But Dr. Ghiglione assumed leadership positions in Italian American and civic organizations. He was elected staff president of Columbus Hospital and Providence Hospital, the largest private hospital in the state. Having developed a reputation as a top surgeon (a *Post-Intelligencer* headline: "Rare Operation Saves Baby Girl"), he was also elected president of the Seattle Academy of Surgeons.[19]

As Italian consul during World War I, he served a region that eventually included Oregon, Washington, Idaho, and Montana. He helped send three thousand subjects of the Kingdom of Italy—who were required to enlist at age twenty for three years of service—to join Italian forces against the Austro-Hungarian Empire before the United States entered the war in 1917. He was knighted Cavaliere, and later Cavaliere Ufficiale della Corona d'Italia, by Italy's king, Victor Emmanuel III.

When a *Seattle Times* reader disparaged Italian, Chinese, and Japanese immigrants in 1910, Dr. Ghiglione attacked the reader's ignorance and misinformation. He defended immigrants' patriotism and dismissed the reader's call for immigration restrictions as amounting to "air bubbles."

In response to the reader's claim that Italians were violent criminals, Dr. Ghiglione cited a study of Italians in America that concluded: "Generally speaking, they are gentle drudges—honest, faithful, and inoffensive."[20] He foresaw an America enriched and enlivened for generations to come by its immigrants, by people of different races, ethnicities, religions, and visions of what life in the United States could be.

CHAPTER 19

What We Learned about America

As Dan, Alyssa, and I left Seattle to begin our return home, I did not experience what the travel writer John R. Humphreys called "the grand finale" after reaching the Pacific.[1] No answer to the question I asked in the introduction—Is America's identity at a turning point?—immediately came to mind. No profound truths about the trip's meaning bubbled from my brain. I was overcome by weariness and an indecisiveness—indeed, a humbling humility—about what conclusions we could draw from our interviews.

First, I doubted whether our interviews, given the contradictory views expressed, allowed us to reach a simple, straightforward conclusion about such controversial identity issues as race and racism in the United States. Two African Americans—the retired federal official James B. MacRae and the journalist Ellis Cose—had talked with optimism about the next generations in their families. Cose, for example, said that when his then-nine-year-old daughter, Elisa, judged people, "race really doesn't enter into the equation with her."

But two other African Americans—the Chicago actor Karen Aldridge and Merlene Davis, a Lexington, Kentucky, newspaper columnist—were pessimistic that America's racial divide would disappear anytime soon. "I don't see it as improving," Davis said.

Certainly, the misconduct by heavily white police departments offered nothing postracial. Nor did the employment disparity and the gap in wealth between races. Segregation continued to befoul America's housing and schools. And crime statistics showed that young African American men were nine times more likely to die in a homicide than their white counterparts.[2]

Second, I doubted the brief time we had to interview people during the trip allowed us to capture their complete stories in all their complexity. For example, at the retirement in 2015 of Merlene Davis, the *Lexington*

Herald-Leader columnist, she revealed a shocking story that the three of us had missed.

Over the years, numerous writers of obscene anonymous letters had promised to kill her. But one anonymous letter writer went further. He threatened to rape her daughter: "I know where your daughter goes to school. It's time she becomes a woman." Davis's editor insisted Davis call the police about that letter. A white officer came to her home. Davis recalled, "He read the letter and he said, 'You know I've been mad at you enough times to say something similar.' I knew not to go to the police from then on about my letters."

Third, our hit-and-run interviewing was an unscientific, inexact tool to capture the true feelings of people about identity.

Despite continuing doubts about our interviews and trip, I took solace in Dayton Duncan's road rules in *Out West*, his odyssey retracing Lewis and Clark's three 1804–6 journeys from St. Louis to the Pacific. Duncan's last road rule: "The final value of any expedition is not what you failed to discover but what you found in its place."[3] Here are six things Alyssa, Dan, and I found:

- Hollowed-out cities and towns, especially small towns, their residents hurt by deprivation and despair. "The poverty and destituteness of certain places haunted me," Alyssa said, "and some of our interview subjects carried around such hurt." Dan said his rose-colored lenses were now tinted with "speckles of dark doubt and disappointment." I recalled the words of the novelist Richard Russo, who said small towns had become places "where people are hanging on to home and hanging on to pride, and hanging on by a thread."[4]
- Our extraordinary ignorance about the American Indian. We learned during our visit to the Kickapoo reservation in Kansas, for example, that a majority of Native Americans live in cities, not on reservations, and that American Indians are not dying off. Although Native Americans are increasingly active in the life of the nation (Minnesotans elected an Ojibwe lieutenant governor of the state and Native members of Congress doubled from two to four in the 2018 election), we observed a widespread ignorance of Native Americans and an assumption that their time had passed, which made them virtually invisible to most Americans. We began to understand that civil rights for Native Americans are not the same as civil rights for African Americans and other marginalized U.S. citizens. The

Kickapoo and other sovereign Native nations deserve the preservation of their autonomy and trust relationships with the U.S. government, as outlined in the Constitution, laws, and treaties. And American Indians' collective, communal values deserve the appreciation of those non-Natives who believe in the mythic American dream of rugged individualism.

- The exceptional contribution of refugees and immigrants to communities across America. This suggests the elusive goals of rational, fair refugee resettlement and immigration reform deserve Americans' immediate attention. The United States needs to control its borders. But the policies and politics of anti-immigration—of border troops and armed citizen vigilantes, criminal prosecution of unauthorized immigrants, forcible separation of migrant children from their parents, campaigns to "Buy American, Hire American"—downplay an important truth: refugees and immigrants greatly benefit the United States. Population growth, to which refugees and immigrants contribute, "accounted for roughly half of the potential economic growth rate" of the United States between 2007 and 2017. Refugees "brought in $63 billion more in government revenues [in 2007–17] than they cost."[5] Refugees and legal and undocumented immigrants, on the whole, are good citizens. They serve with distinction in the military (an estimated eight thousand noncitizens join every year). Once in the country, both legal and undocumented immigrants are less likely to break the law than native-born citizens. They work at jobs on farms and in meatpacking plants and health care facilities that many native-borns refuse. Immigrants outperform native-borns in starting businesses, earning patents, and winning "genius grants" and other prizes for intellectual performance.[6] In short, they do not repudiate but instead reinforce American values.

- Evidence of growing income inequality. Charles Reich's description of the United States as a corporate state "taken over by a small minority of powerful interests" stuck with us. So did the speed with which the Occupy Wall Street movement flamed and fizzled. Capitalism, driven to maximize profits and ignore how it affects the environment and future generations, appears to be failing America. Those in power seem to have grown increasingly indifferent to addressing the plight of the poor. Politicians seek to slash funding for safety net programs. Taxes on the rich do not rise when income inequality and economic hardship increase. The future offers little hope of changing laws written to benefit the rich.[7]

- Americans' increasing ease in being themselves—whether their identities are tied to their gender, sexual orientation, race, religion, or ethnicity. New forms of assimilation have softened the borders between Black, white, and Brown, between those assigned at birth to be male and those assigned to be female, and between other categories of Americans that traditionally have seen themselves as different and distinctive. But Islamophobia, homophobia, misogyny, and other forms of dehumanizing discrimination refuse to die. Reported anti-Semitic incidents increased 57 percent in 2017, the largest annual increase in almost four decades.[8] Dr. Larry Mass, when he spoke with us in 2011, said he was worried about a demagogic leader's fomenting the public targeting of African Americans, Muslim Americans, or gays: "History can turn on a dime."

- No end to racism despite greater inclusiveness. Indeed, an Associated Press poll around the time of our trip reported that racial prejudice had not become less pervasive since the United States elected its first Black president in 2008. Racial prejudice had increased, with 51 percent of Americans expressing prejudice against African Americans.[9] As a student in the early 1960s, I had naively believed—following passage of the Civil Rights Act of 1964 and the Voting Rights Act of 1965—that my generation would end racial discrimination. But residential and school segregation and resegregation (with failing schools a staple of low-income Black communities that no longer benefited from court-mandated school desegregation), gerrymandering, voter ID laws, sentencing disparities, and other forms of systemic racism were proving tough foes. As they defend their privilege, white Americans have adapted these barriers to keep discrimination alive and thriving. Even white progressives, the sociologist Michael Eric Dyson argues, all but forget the needs of the Black and Brown working classes: "The real unifying force in our national cultural and political life, beyond skirmishes over ideology, is white identity masked as universal, neutral and, therefore, quintessentially American."[10] Whiteness is the unexamined social norm that blinds many white people to the systemic racial inequities that shackle the most disadvantaged.

But Alyssa, Dan, and I also found positive, if slightly different, messages in our trip about the United States. Alyssa said she concluded the trip with "a deep, deep love for America, and I still feel that Americans have a collective drive and respect for innovation, for boldness, for freedom, for the outsized."

From all our road trip adventures, dinner conversations, and unending interviews, Dan saw America at its best as "a grand story about determination and forgiveness and community."

I found myself reading more and revising the version of U.S. history I had first absorbed from school textbooks. That version largely erased the network of Native American nations and their systems of roadways, trade, and agriculture. It focused from the start on white guys of European heritage—explorers, claimed territories (New France, New Netherlands, and New Spain, as well as the British colonies), and Pilgrims, Puritans, and pioneers ("Euro-Americans in motion").[11] Native Americans and African Americans were virtually invisible.

I also found myself returning to questions asked by Ellis Cose when we interviewed him in New York: "How are we going to be an American family? What does it mean to be this America that is evolving?" I decided that today's Genus Americanus, recalling the term coined by the novelist John Steinbeck, is, increasingly, in Steinbeck's words, "rooted in all races, stained and tinted with all colors."[12] However ideologically segregated America appears to be becoming, it is a diversifying pluralistic nation. I like to think it recognizes the potential of outgrowing racial and other identity boundaries and aspiring to the universal.

Writers like Constance Rourke and Albert Murray make clear that Native Americans and other Americans of color have helped make American identity distinctive.

Rourke notes, for example, that frontier whites adopted Indian dress and used Indian weapons. Of the Boston Tea Party, Rourke writes, "it may well be a question whether the participants enjoyed more dumping the tea in the harbor or masquerading in war paint and feathers with brandished tomahawks."[13]

Even Twain, who often mocked American Indians, described himself in the early 1860s as an "ignorant half-breed" and representative of "red men." He saw Indians as incarnations of "his truest, natural Self."[14]

Murray argues Americans are a three-dimensional composite that he labels Omni-Americans—part Yankee ingenuity, part American Indian, and part African American. Whether a Pilgrim or a twentieth-century immigrant, the "very act of arrival" in America exposes the newcomer to American culture and traditions. Even swarthy Sicilians and other darker-than-white immigrants, "as they struggle and finagle to become all-white (by playing up their color similarities and playing down their cultural differences), inevitably acquire basic American characteristics—which is to say Omni-American" characteristics—part African American and part Native American.[15]

While guarding against romanticizing the American Indian, I also found myself embracing a set of values that seemed to be part of the lives of the Native Americans we interviewed: sustaining the environment; broadening the notion of family so that society has few outcasts; diminishing the power and wealth gap between those with the most and least; loving place, its beauty, natural resources, and personal meaning; working with joy and a minimum of rancor and resentment; living with humility, realizing your insignificance in the universe.[16]

Those values suggest questions for a modern society that worships at such shrines as technology, economic growth, innovation, and city life. And they caused me to change my priorities at Northwestern University. To diminish my ignorance about American Indians, I volunteered for the university's Native American Outreach and Inclusion Task Force and later chaired the steering committee for One Book One Northwestern, a program that encouraged all entering students that school year to read Thomas King's *The Inconvenient Indian: A Curious Account of Native People in North America* (2012) and attend some of the seventy-five lectures, exhibits, and other events about Native Americans throughout that year.

I started teaching an oral history course, Native Americans Tell Their Stories. My students and I interviewed dozens of American Indians who provided moving accounts of adjusting to a diasporic life in Chicago after leaving their homelands. They grew to be more "of America," writes the historian David Treuer, not merely "in America."[17]

I was profoundly affected by the stories Native Americans told us. For instance, the eighty-eight-year-old Susan Kelly Power, said to be the oldest Native American in Chicago, compared herself to the sixty-seven-million-year-old Dakota dinosaur, a fossil found in 1999 in North Dakota on land that, she said, once belonged to her family. Her great-grandfather was Chief Mahto Nunhpa (Two Bears) of the Upper Yanktonais Dakota. Her mother, Josephine Gates Kelly, was the first female leader of the Standing Rock Sioux Reservation's tribal council in North Dakota. Power called her mother "an activist against any injustice, a superstrong mother, who raised her eight children alone, without welfare, without handouts, without anything."[18]

Susan Kelly Power

Power pointed to a plastic basket that contained approximately two hundred short stories about her reservation childhood that she had written over more than seven decades: "It was hard when I was growing up. We survived the Dust Bowl. We survived the Indian Reorganization Act that destroyed the old way of government." She planned to leave her stories to her daughter, Susan Power, who graduated from Harvard and Harvard Law School and became a writer.

Susan Kelly Power remembered the reservation fondly, as a place blessed with families and few distractions. At seventeen, she left the reservation for a housekeeping job in Chicago. Later, she worked as a secretary, then book buyer, for A. C. McClurg, a publishing firm. A federal urban relocation program brought tens of thousands of Native Americans to Chicago beginning in 1952. Power helped lead the Indian Council Fire and other local social clubs for Native Americans, who lacked telephones, cars, and other means to connect. She reunited seventeen Native American children with their birth families and initiated education programs that allowed Indians to ward off what she called cultural genocide. She advocated, her daughter recalls, "for the downtrodden, for those who didn't understand their legal rights and so would get taken right and left."[19]

In 1960, Susan Kelly married Carleton Gilmore Power, whose Pilgrim ancestors had arrived in North America three centuries earlier and helped establish the original colony in Massachusetts.[20] When she told her husband she got along with his female eastern white Anglo-Saxon Protestant relatives, he joked in response, "You know why? They think they're the elite of the land. You Sioux know you are."

The couple moved to a South Side Chicago bungalow so their daughter could attend an integrated Catholic school, St. Philip Neri, and the family could live in an integrated community. Power's husband died in 1973.

Susan Kelly Power became a fiery spokesperson for Native Americans. Her daughter remembered traveling east at thirteen with her mother to learn her father's family history. On a side trip to Plymouth Rock, her mother "just, well, lost it," Susan Power said. Surrounded by tourists, Susan Kelly Power whispered loudly to her daughter, "Look at them, look at them worshipping this rock that was the beginning of so much loss and grief and theft and geno-cide." She charged the fence surrounding the rock and spat over its edge.

"She launched into a passionate speech about the plague this early group turned out to be for Native peoples, invoking the eloquent words of Malcolm X, speaking of the African American experience: 'We didn't land on Plymouth Rock. The rock was landed on us.' No one dared to shout back," her daughter said. "Mother can be fierce. She continued to present our perspective on the colonizing of America until we were suddenly joined by young people who worked at the nearby Plimouth Plantation—tribal members who staffed the Wampanoag homesite and heard from tourists that an 'Indian woman is going off by the rock!' They urged Mom on, delighted— no, relieved—by the balm of her anger, how she forced a space for our story, our version, where there was no space."[21]

When Susan Kelly Power felt Native Americans in Chicago were not treated with respect, she acted with the same ferocity that she had exhibited at Plymouth Rock. She spent a night in jail for a sit-in at the Chicago office of the Bureau of Indian Affairs. She integrated the Marshall Field Garden Apartments, one of the city's first subsidized housing developments, in 1959.

She helped lead the removal of the 1893 Fort Dearborn Massacre Monument from the lobby of the Chicago Historical Society. The nine-foot bronze statue by Carl Rohl-Smith depicted one Indian warrior driving a spear into the chest of a drowned white man and another Indian warrior about to deliver a blow to a white woman with her baby at her feet. While the statue also featured the rescue by the Potawatomi chief Black Partridge of the white woman and her baby, Power complained to the historical society about the statue's stereotypical depiction of Indians as savage murderers.

Power's daughter remembered what her mother said as she berated historical society officials: "This is the only monument to the history of Indians in this area that you have on exhibit. It's a shame because it is completely one sided. Children who see this will think this is what Indians are all about." The statue disappeared and, despite a campaign to relocate it to a Chicago park, appears likely to never come out of storage.[22]

Susan Kelly Power said Native Americans should not regurgitate the opinions they thought whites and other members of the dominant culture want to hear from Indians. She compared herself to the Contraries of certain Great Plains tribes who danced in the opposite direction of other tribal members.

As my interview with Susan Kelly Power came to a close, she grew quietly philosophical. "I think we all have something to teach each other. The early teachers [of Native Americans] assumed we were dumb and we had to be changed—instead of . . . saying, 'Let's learn about these people, and we'll combine what's good in us with what's good in them because we're all going to be part of this great country.'"

She said she avoided asking people where they worked and lived: "That's what the dominant society does all the time." Whites and other members of the dominant society try to judge people, she said. "'Are you worth knowing? Are you rich enough for me to pay attention to you? Are you important enough for me to pay attention to you?' We [Indians] don't do that. If you're nice enough, if you're kind enough, that's what matters." Power applauded the role of the Sioux grass dancer—"a person who opens doors to make life easier for other people."

She stressed the importance of Native Americans' survival to the survival of all Americans. Any continent that has Indigenous people, Power said, should try to help them survive as a people. "If we don't survive," she said, "the rest of you won't."

The Native Americans like Susan Kelly Power whom I met in Chicago, the American Indians at Northwestern and at the Sand Creek Massacre National Historic Site in Colorado, and the Menominee and Northern Cheyenne I visited in Wisconsin and Montana, respectively, all greatly enriched my life. They encouraged a revision of my priorities: advocate for nature, aspire to greater humility, not more awards and other ephemera; become in spirit a Sioux grass dancer (even if I can't dance) to make life easier for my family, friends, and others; and pursue the values that parents and teachers everywhere encourage children to adopt.

Recently, I visited the class of Joy MacMillan, eight, my joyful third-grade granddaughter. A large, colorful classroom poster proclaimed in bold letters: "In this classroom . . . we will put our BEST SELF forward by: helping others, . . . being active listeners, . . . and by being generous with our words and actions." Nearby the children listed the attributes they planned to pursue in 2020 to be their best selves. Joy wrote: "Curious, helpful, and thoughtful (I will start thinking more about other people than about me)."

Dayton Duncan's last road rule emphasizes enjoying a road trip for itself, whatever the trip's purpose. Before Alyssa, Dan, and I left Seattle, we attended the rollicking, cake-all-over-your-face first birthday party of Tinley Ann Tyson, the great-great-great-granddaughter of A. F. Ghiglione. That party made clear how much I loved the opportunities our trip had provided: the time with Ghigliones, whether we were related or not; the companionship of Dan and Alyssa; the conversations with friends and strangers who took us in for a night or the better part of a week; the admittedly rare roadside stops for a sunset or solitude; the willingness of the 150 people we interviewed to answer questions about everything from religious beliefs to sex-change operations; the moments of discovery, about myself as well as America.

That first birthday party amid generations of Ghigliones reminded me that I was privileged and not just as a straight white male with upper-middle-class means who lived in the United States, a land of freedom, the rule of law, and enormous resources. I had the good fortune to be son, grandson, and great-grandson in an immigrant clan that prized education, family, independence, and the pursuit of whatever dream I chose to pursue.

Epilogue

Hope for America's Future

Mark Twain argued it is perfectly acceptable for someone my age not to wax optimistic about life. "The man who is a pessimist before forty-eight knows too much; if he is an optimist after it, he knows too little," Twain wrote.

Certainly, I had reason to be a pessimist. The federal government, in the time of Trump, pursued policies that benefited the wealthy and undermined the rights of many Americans, be they Muslim, African American, Native American, transgender, female, gay, immigrant, or refugee. And even my university, which saw itself as progressive, practiced admissions policies that favored recruited athletes, legacies, and the affluent. Some of those policies—which critics labeled affirmative action for whites—were part of what Richard V. Reeves calls "hoarding mechanisms" practiced by the upper middle class, the top fifth of the population. The affluent live in good neighborhoods and send their children to good schools that increase the likelihood they will attend universities like Northwestern. "American meritocracy," Daniel Markovits contends, "has thus become precisely what it was invented to combat: a mechanism for the dynastic transmission of wealth and privilege across generations."[1]

In June 2020, as this book was about to go to press, Americans had even more reason to be pessimistic. Two pandemics were devastating the United States. COVID-19 infected Americans in the millions, cost jobs in the tens of millions, and caused more than one hundred thousand deaths. A centuries-old history of violence against African Americans and Native Americans—a racial injustice pandemic—culminated in the horrific killing of George Floyd, an African American, caught on video. While a white Minneapolis police officer's left knee kept Floyd's neck pinned to the ground for more than eight minutes, he pleaded, "You're going to kill me, man. I can't breathe." Sign-carrying protesters in more than two thousand communities in all fifty states, as well as around the world, called for an end to police brutality and racial discrimination. The protests, the public health crisis, and the economic recession left Americans across the political spectrum reeling. Americans in recent decades have consistently labeled themselves optimists about the nation's future. But a survey of voters in June 2020 by NBC News/ *Wall Street Journal* concluded that "eighty percent of voters now believe the country is spiraling out of control."[2] Among the voters, pessimism reigned.

Nevertheless, I choose to be optimistic. If we are optimistic about our ability to change the pessimism-causing policies and practices of our universities, governments, and other institutions, we are more likely to produce the energy needed to achieve progress. Pessimism means lowering our heads and trudging toward despair and death. Optimism represents opportunities for change we will never see if, with lowered heads, we study only the ground.

But optimism also demands realism. Americans need to be more committed to sustained action to combat institutionalized discrimination, whether laws and policies or other means are responsible for the discrimination. To fight structural discrimination requires hard work, especially for white Americans, who must overcome what Robin DiAngelo, a trainer on racial justice issues, calls "the apathy of whiteness."[3] Oblivious and unreachable, they need to permit themselves to be reached. They need to recognize and address their internalized superiority, unconscious bias, and racial privilege. They also need a dogged determination to take action against discrimination, a determination that borders on a permanent state of righteous anger. Heather Heyer, the millennial killed protesting the "Unite the Right" rally in Charlottesville, Virginia, in 2017, offered a relevant catchphrase: "If you're not outraged, you're not paying attention."[4]

Many enraged whites participated in the protests that followed the killing of George Floyd. They carried Black Lives Matter posters and shouted antiracism slogans. Prognosticators talked about a seismic shift among white people in favor of real change. But the *New York Times* columnist Charles M. Blow rightly asked whether the protests represented true change "or an activist-chic summer street festival for people who have been cooped up for months. . . . This has to be a forever commitment, even after protest eventually subsides." There is perhaps a disturbing lesson from 2014. The tumultuous protests after the killing in Ferguson, Missouri, of a black eighteen-year-old, Michael Brown, at the hands of a white police officer failed to remake American policing.[5] And Americans still needed to address systemic racism and white privilege, not only in law enforcement but also in housing, employment, education, medical care, and every other aspect of their lives.

Those who seek change cannot expect to meet success with techniques and tactics that merely mimic those of earlier civil rights movements. Contemporary efforts may need to be more radical and revolutionary. They may need to be global, taking full advantage of social media and previously unimagined coalitions of people seeking change. Experts in activism suggest success depends on strategic leaders' building coalitions that strengthen relationships among members.[6] I believe millennials, usually defined as those born between the early 1980s and the early 2000s, have the capacity to build and lead the required coalitions, equipping individual participants to act collectively.

The media often dismiss millennials as the me generation, driven by narcissism and a sense of entitlement; the boomerang generation, content to live in their parents' homes well into adulthood; the Peter Pan generation, pampered and determined not to grow up; and the conventional generation, "more comfortable with their parents' values than any other generation in living memory."[7]

But millennials (and even younger Americans) of all races played key roles in the protests following the killing of George Floyd. The attitudes and habits of these millennials offer hope. An innovative 1991 study of eighteen generations in America, 1854 to 2069, predicted "can-do" millennials would "achieve and excel," exhibiting "new civic energy and devotion to community."[8] Millennials choose to be appropriately skeptical of institutions—from organized religion to marriage to government to corporations. They question capitalism—and its meritocracy myth, that people succeed in proportion to their hard work and abilities—as much as they question socialism. Half call themselves political independents. They are America's most racially diverse generation. And, despite higher levels of student loan debt and poverty, they are more upbeat than earlier generations about America's future. They are "eager to make a difference," a Deloitte survey found.[9]

I ground my optimism about millennials in the behavior of the students I taught until recently at Northwestern. Admittedly, my students are not representative of their generation, despite Northwestern's dramatic efforts to overcome socioeconomic privilege in admissions. Nevertheless, these millennials appear to evince greater tolerance, empathy, and global understanding than previous generations of students.[10] They remind me of the title of a 2010 Pew Research Center report on millennials: "Confident. Connected. Open to Change." In sit-ins and rallies that echo protests from my student days in the 1960s, these students proclaim "Black lives matter!" and target such issues as discrimination on the basis of sexual orientation or gender expression, the university's investment in the fossil fuel industry, the erasure of Native Americans, debilitating student debt, sexual harassment (#MeToo), and the lack of inclusive faculty, staff, and student communities.

I view millennials as budding change makers. They embrace activism, albeit "often organic and largely leaderless" activism ("a social network approach to social justice"). And they embrace empathy. Ending this book with a couple of stories about empathetic millennials struck me as all important. Pete Seeger, the late folk singer, civil rights marcher, and antiwar protester, said, "The key to the future of the world is finding the optimistic stories and letting them be known."[11]

The first story involves the initial meeting of MIXED, the Mixed Race Student Coalition, at the beginning of Northwestern's 2013–14 school year. MIXED hoped to create a space for discussion among multiracial students and others interested in mixed-race topics.

Their generation represents a revolution in thinking. I had been reading Twain on multiracial relationships—what his contemporaries called intermixture or miscegenation. He saw no future for such relationships. When a reporter in Calcutta, India, asked him about the likelihood of intermixture in society, Twain said, "Not the slightest."

Laws against multiracial relationships carried well into the twentieth century. Not until 1967 did the U.S. Supreme Court rule in *Loving v. Virginia* that antimiscegenation laws are unconstitutional. Hostility toward multiracial relationships lasted well into the twenty-first century. But many millennials see their multiracial upbringing as a point of pride.

I first met Kalina Chen Silverman, who describes herself as "half Chinese and half white, with a culturally Jewish emphasis," in September 2012. She was a first-year journalism student at Northwestern. As her academic adviser, I watched as she sought to find her place at the university.

She seemed to find herself when a classmate, Tori Marquez, and she started MIXED at the end of their first year. "I went to a couple events hosted by the Chinese Students Association and Hillel, and I didn't feel like I fully fit in," Silverman said. At the first meeting of MIXED, she definitely fit in. The slogan of the forty-five students who attended: We're 100 percent mixed.

The officers of MIXED began the meeting by describing their own racial and ethnic mixtures. They sounded like the United Nations: Kemi Areke,

The founding members of MIXED include, left to right, Kathy Del Beccaro, Kalina Chen Silverman, Tori Marquez, Catherine Sham, and Maria Voelk.

Indian and Nigerian; Kathy Del Beccaro, Italian, Japanese, Irish, Apache, and Cherokee; Marquez, Peruvian, Scottish, German, and Polish; Roman Tamas, Hungarian and Jamaican; Catherine Sham, Chinese, Irish, and French.

Del Beccaro said, "For me, being mixed race has always been cool. Growing up, I got a lot of questions about my ethnicity but only positive responses that made me feel unique in a good way." She felt especially connected to her Italian and Japanese heritages: "I am proud of my ancestors and proud of myself—every part of it."

Professor Nitasha Sharma, who taught a mixed-race experience course at Northwestern and was married to "a nice Jewish Black guy," served as MIXED's faculty adviser. In creating MIXED, Marquez and Silverman had to make a variety of decisions, Sharma said. Should MIXED as a multiracial organization work in alliance with For Members Only, Northwestern's Black student group, and similar student organizations? Should MIXED represent and welcome all students, including those who are not multiracial? Should MIXED challenge the assumption of monoracial categories of people that perpetuates a hierarchy of color, with white at the top, mixed-race in the middle, and Black at the bottom?

Marquez and Silverman opted for inclusivity and equality. "They're so sharp. And they're so *professional*," Sharma said. "They really made a great group." (Following graduation from Northwestern in 2016, Silverman worked in Singapore as a Fulbright research scholar studying cross-cultural empathy and continued to develop *Big Talk*—makebigtalk.com—a social impact project and documentary video series about skipping the small talk to have more momentous conversations with people around the world.)

MIXED's meeting reminded me that the fastest-growing group of children in America's ethnic and racial goulash is not a single ethnic or racial group. It is multiracial. A 2017 Pew Research Center study reported that 17 percent of all new marriages in the United States in 2015 were interracial or interethnic, more than five times the 3 percent rate in 1967, the year the Supreme Court decided *Loving*. The rapidly growing birthrate of multiracial children was expected to increase between 2018 and 2060 by 176 percent, while whites were dying faster than they were being born in a majority of states.[12]

In the 2000 census, for the first time, Americans could identify as belonging to more than one race. In 2010, more than nine million Americans so identified, up 32 percent from the 2000 census, more than three times the 9.2 percent increase reported by single-race individuals. Many Americans were feeling free to think anew about how they viewed themselves. Some were even going so far as to adopt a view that the Roman playwright Publius Terentius Afer had expressed more than two millennia ago: "I am human, I think nothing human alien to me."[13]

And many Northwestern students were becoming less provincial and more globally aware, as I learned from journalism students working in 2013 and 2014 as reporting interns in Cape Town and Johannesburg, South Africa. Those students provided a second optimistic story about their generation.

I asked my two dozen Northwestern advisees how their time in South Africa had affected their sense of their own identities. Their answers made clear how different they were from the students I first took to South Africa in 1999. The 2013 and 2014 students were much more global in their perspective and experience. They had lived, studied, and worked in locations around the world—in Brazil, Canada, China, Colombia, El Salvador, England, France, Germany, Italy, Malaysia, Morocco, Senegal, South Korea, Spain, and Turkey. Many students, regardless of their economic status or background, spoke foreign languages and viewed their South African internship as just one more opportunity to absorb the world beyond U.S. borders.

Those global experiences were providing the students with opportunities to address race, ethnicity, and other identity issues that were sometimes an uncomfortable part of their lives in the United States. Christina

Christina Cala (left) mentors Brieana Sealy.

Cala, who reported for the Cape Town bureau of the South African *Sunday Times* newspaper, was typical. Of Colombian ancestry, Cala grew up in Los Angeles and recalled being identified there as Mexican. "That bothered me a lot," she said, noting differences in Mexican and Colombian slang, food, and class signs and symbols. "As I grew older, saying I was from Colombia meant having people immediately ask about cocaine, drug cartels, and violence." A Northwestern friend even liked to call her Cocaine Cala.

Cala, who majored in Spanish as well as journalism, had managed four reporting experiences abroad, not only in South Africa but in Peru (to report on sacred monuments), Germany (to report on nanomedicine treatments), and Spain (to report on arts and culture). In Peru and Spain Cala easily blended in with locals. In advance of her Cape Town reporting internship, she worried that South Africans would be less accepting. "But Capetonians were quick to take me in," she said.

She thought her experiences abroad are part of key differences that mark her generation: "We see more diversity in our schools, we see more diversity on our TVs and computers, and we have voices and fields of study exploring narratives other than the dominant white American narrative. I think that makes us more empathetic." (Following graduation in 2014, Cala went to work for National Public Radio, eventually becoming a producer at *TED*

Radio Hour; in 2018, she and three other women of color at NPR started a mentoring program across all NPR departments that, by the third stage, had reached more than one hundred women of color.)

The millennials' travel offered them the opportunity to overcome the biases and blind spots that afflict all of us, including myths of white supremacy, and systems of oppression based on class, race, religion, gender, and sexual orientation. The T-shirt that Alyssa, Dan, and I gave out to people who hosted us during our drive around America carried a shortened version of Twain's words from *Innocents Abroad*. Millennials seemed to have taken those words to heart: "Travel is fatal to prejudice, bigotry, and narrow-mindedness. . . . Broad, wholesome, charitable views of men and things cannot be acquired by vegetating in one little corner of the earth all one's lifetime."

The question remains whether millennials will not only pursue their own personal and career goals but will also work tenaciously to overcome bias and achieve a better America, an America of democratic, shared ideals, an America that unites. At minimum, millennials need to vote (barely half of eligible millennials voted in the 2016 presidential election versus 70 percent of baby boomers); millennials are estimated to be 40 percent of the electorate in 2020. But to achieve a better America, millennials also must commit to re-creating the nation—to not being satisfied with the United States as it is.

Progress will continue so long as the millennials and each succeeding generation aggressively strive to achieve change. Mark Twain's life and literature suggest Americans can change, as individuals and collectively as a nation. He invited Americans to be more self-aware, more understanding, and more compassionate: "What is the most rigorous law of our being? *Growth*. . . . *We change* and must change, constantly, and keep on changing as long as we live."

I see millennials as more empathetic, more globally aware, and better equipped than any previous generation to achieve positive change in the United States and the world. That change must come.

Acknowledgments

Five exceedingly generous alumni/ae of Northwestern's Medill School of Journalism contributed $30,000 to make possible the trip that resulted in this book: Nanette DeMuesy, North Canton, Ohio; Bruce E. and Carol Hallenbeck, Santa Ana, California; Mary Lou Song, Los Altos, California; and Howard Dubin, Evanston, Illinois.

Throughout the trip, dozens of friends, family members, alumni/ae, and parents of alumni/ae of Northwestern University and Haverford College took us into their homes and provided extraordinary hospitality.

We also benefited from the contributions and support of Northwestern faculty: Kevin Boyle, Abigail Foerstner, Ava Greenwell, Nitasha Sharma, David Standish, and Claire E. Sufrin. At Medill, deans John Lavine and Brad Hamm, associate deans Mary Nesbitt and Craig LaMay, and program directors Beth Bennett, Michelle Bitoun, Janice Castro, and Jon Marshall provided time during the academic year for me to research and write. Technologies specialists at Medill—beginning with Rachel Venegas, who created the model for the book's map of our route—and Rachel Rooney, IT/reference librarian at the West Tisbury, Massachusetts, Free Public Library, helped me overcome my computer illiteracy.

Mick Gusinde-Duffy, executive editor for scholarly and digital publishing at the University of Georgia Press, believed in this book's publication when many other acquisitions editors did not. A special thanks to him and the superb team at the University of Georgia Press, including Jason Bennett, Melissa Buchanan, Jon Davies, Melissa Gamble, Erin Kirk, Rebecca Norton, Beth Snead, and Steven Wallace.

A highlight of the research for this book—and of my life—was a 2009 fellowship to the Bogliasco Foundation's villa outside Genoa that permitted me to research my Ghiglione family roots in northern Italy. Anna O'Connor, my marvelous Genovese guide and interpreter, filled each day with humor as well as history. My wife, Nancy, not only joined me during the research trip but also patiently endured the eight years of absences and late nights it took me to research, write, and rewrite this book. To her and to my daughters, Jessica and Laura, I am forever grateful.

I wanted the text to be as free of end notes and other scholarly trappings as possible. For that reason, I have not cited the sources of Mark Twain quotes—virtually all are easily accessible—or the interviews conducted by Alyssa Karas, Dan Tham, and me. R. Kent Rasmussen, the author of numerous books about Twain, kindly reviewed an early draft of this book for the accuracy of its references to Twain. But any errors of fact and infelicities of language belong to me. That said, readers beware: page-number references to *New York Times* articles are to articles in Midwest and New England editions of the *Times* that serve communities where I lived while writing this book.

There would be more errors in the book if drafts had not been critiqued by Alyssa and Dan, my traveling companions and coauthors; Polly Kummel, an extraordinary copy editor; the talented Medill work-study students Princess-India T. Rayne Alexander, Elise Echeverria, Kahlil Ellis, Olivia Exstrum, Jacob Meschke, Hayat Norimine, Rita Oceguera, Ali Pelczar, Sharon Song, and Brooke Workneh; and my friends Mike Rodell, Doug Foster, and George Geers.

When George returned his edited manuscript, he wrote that my students' writing strengthened the book: "Such a generational work. I would suggest that one or both take the trip in 40 years in tribute to Twain and you." I love ending with the idea that four decades from now Alyssa and Dan might follow up on our trip with their own odyssey across America.

Notes

Introduction

1. Walter F. White, *A Man Called White* (1948; repr., Athens: University of Georgia Press, 1995), 3; Fukuyama, *Identity*, 25.

2. Derek M. Norman and Aaron Randle, "'Gay,' 'Femme,' 'Nonbinary': How Identity Shaped These 10 New Yorkers," *New York Times*, July 5, 2019, A15.

3. Kwame Anthony Appiah, "'Speaking as a . . . ,'" *New York Times*, August 12, 2018, SR4.

4. John Sides, Michael Tesler, and Lynn Vavreck, *Identity Crisis: The 2016 Presidential Campaign and the Battle for the Meaning of America* (Princeton, N.J.: Princeton University Press, 2018), 42.

5. Appiah, *Lies That Bind*, 167; James Poniewozik, "Problem Was the Event, Not the Jokes," *New York Times*, May 1, 2018, C1.

6. Nell Irvin Painter, "What Is Whiteness," *New York Times*, June 20, 2015, https://www.nytimes.com/2015/06/21/opinion/sunday/what-is-whiteness.html ?module=inline; Charles Murray, *Coming Apart: The State of White America, 1960–2010* (New York: Crown Forum, 2012), 84.

7. bell hooks and Amalia Mesa-Bains, *Homegrown: Engaged Cultural Criticism* (Cambridge, Mass.: South End, 2006), 73.

8. Of course, in making the trip, I could be accused of joining, in the words of Claudia Rankine, "all the 'woke' white men who set their privilege outside themselves—as in, I know better than to be ignorant or defensive about my own privilege. Never mind that that capacity to set himself outside the pattern of white male dominance *is* the privilege." Claudia Rankine, "Brief Encounters with White Men," *New York Times Magazine*, July 21, 2019, 43.

9. "Toni Morrison, the Art of Fiction No. 134," *Paris Review*, no. 128 (fall 1993), https://www.theparisreview.org/interviews/1888/toni-morrison-the-art-of-fiction -no-134-toni-morrison; Dick Gregory, with Shelia P. Moses, *Callus on My Soul: A Memoir* (New York: Longstreet, 2000), 256.

10. Richard Russo, *The Destiny Stuff: Essays on Writing, Writers and Life* (New York: Alfred A. Knopf, 2018), 181.

11. Levy, *Huck Finn's America*, xviii.

12. Alexander, *New Jim Crow*.

13. Samuel Langhorne Clemens did not begin using his pen name of Mark Twain until February 1863, when he was twenty-seven, but for simplicity's sake, I usually refer to Clemens, whatever his age, as Twain.

14. Powers, *Dangerous Water*, 18.

15. Daniel Okrent, *The Guarded Gate: Bigotry, Eugenics, and the Law That Kept Two Generations of Jews, Italians and Other European Immigrants Out of America* (New York: Scribner, 2019), 99.

16. Ibid., 344.

17. Christopher Ingraham, "Three Quarters of Whites Don't Have Any Non-White Friends," *Wonkblog, Washington Post*, August 25, 2014, http://www. washingtonpost.com/news/wonk/wp/2014/08/25/three-quarters-of-whites-dont-have-any-non-white-friends/; Michael I. Norton and Samuel R. Sommers, "Whites See Racism as a Zero-Sum Game That They Are Now Losing," *Perspectives on Psychological Science* 6 (May 18, 2011): 215–18, http://pps.sagepub.com/content /6/3/215.

18. Matt Sedensky, "AP-NORC Poll: Political Divide over American Identity," *APNews.com*, March 6, 2017; Stephen Hawkins, Daniel Yudkin, Míriam Juan-Torres, and Tim Dixon, *Hidden Tribes: A Study of America's Polarized Landscape* (New York: More in Common, 2018), 8, http://hiddentribes.us/pdf/hidden _tribes_report.pdf.

19. Ortiz, *Sand Creek*, 86. See also "The Future of the United States" in Dunbar-Ortiz, *An Indigenous Peoples' History*, 218–36.

20. Hunter Thompson, *Fear and Loathing in Las Vegas: A Savage Journey to the Heart of the American Dream* (New York: Vintage, 1971), 18.

CHAPTER 1. Hannibal, Missouri

1. Robinson Meyer, "The Cyclical Nature of Campus Media," *North by Northwestern*, March 8, 2013, alpha.northbynorthwestern.com/story/the-cyclical -nature-of-campus-media/.

2. Lori Belknap, email to author, June 10, 2016.

3. Fishkin, *Lighting Out for the Territory*, 61.

4. Judith Yaross Lee, *Garrison Keillor: A Voice of America* (Jackson: University Press of Mississippi, 1991), 32.

5. Vogel, *Mark Twain's Jews*, 1, 3; Andrews, *City of Dust*, 91.

6. From the gravestone for Injun Joe Douglass, who died on September 29, 1923, and is buried in Mount Olivet Cemetery, Hannibal, Missouri.

7. Gayle Rubin, "Thinking Sex: Notes for a Radical Theory of the Politics of Sexuality," in *Culture, Society and Sexuality: A Reader*, ed. Richard Parker and Peter Aggleton, 2nd ed. (1999; New York: Routledge, 2007), 161, 162.

8. Rikki-Lee Burley, "Hannibal-LaGrange Denies Openly Gay Student's Re-Admittance," March 25, 2014, *KBIA.org*, https://www.kbia.org/post/hannibal-lagrange-denies-openly-gay-students-re-admittance#stream/.

9. Malcolm X, "Malcolm X on Afro-American History," in *Malcolm X on Afro-American History*, ed. Steve Clark (New York: Pathfinder, 1970), 24.

10. Brent Staples, "How Italians Became 'White,'" *New York Times*, October 13, 2019, SR4. See also Louise DeSalvo, "Color: White/Complexion: Dark," in Guglielmo and Salerno, *Are Italians White?*, 28.

11. Christine Kenneally, *The Invisible History of the Human Race: How DNA and History Shape Our Identities and Our Futures* (New York: Viking, 2014), 191.

12. Andrews, *City of Dust*, 36.

13. Dennis Wepman, *Immigration: From the Founding of Virginia to the Closing of Ellis Island* (New York: Facts on File, 2002), 163.

14. Cosco, *Imagining Italians*, 10.

15. Mark Stolarik, "Immigration, Education, and the Social Mobility of Slovaks, 1870–1930," in *Immigrants and Religion in Urban America*, ed. Randall M. Miller and Thomas D. Marzik (Philadelphia: Temple University Press, 1977), 112.

16. Andrews, *City of Dust*, 246.

17. City of Hannibal, "Community P.R.I.D.E. Project," 2019, www.hannibal-mo.gov/community-pride/about/; Ashley Szatala, "Company Redevelops Houses, Wants to Help Hannibal Community," *Herald-Whig*, March 4, 2017, https://www.whig.com/20170304/company-redevelops-houses-wants-to-help-hannibal-community.

18. Enrico Moretti, *The New Geography of Jobs* (Boston: Houghton Mifflin Harcourt, 2012), 4.

19. James Risen and Tom Risen, "Donald Trump Does His Best Joe McCarthy," *New York Times*, June 25, 2017, SR2.

20. Theoharis, *A More Beautiful and Terrible History*, 24; Daniel Marans and Mariah Stewart, "Why Missouri Has Become the Heart of Racial Tension in America," *Huffington Post*, November 16, 2015, www.huffingtonpost.com/entry/ferguson-mizzou-missouri-racial-tension_us_564736e2e4b08cda3488f34d.

21. "Hannibal's Black Schools," Jim's Journey: The Huck Finn Freedom Center, 2019, http://www.jimsjourney.org/education/.

22. Fishkin, *Writing America*, 8.

23. Anderson, *White Rage*, 3.

24. Greil Marcus, *Mystery Train: Images of America in Rock 'n' Roll Music* (New York: Plume, 2015), 155.

25. T. S. Eliot, "The Dry Salvages," *The Complete Poems and Plays, 1909–1950* (New York: Harcourt, Brace, 1952), 130.

CHAPTER 2. St. Louis

1. Vanessa Varin, "'Pure Americanism': Building a Modern St. Louis and the Reign of Know Nothingism," master of arts thesis, May 2012, Louisiana State University, 5.

2. Dred Scott v. John F. A. Sandford, 60 U.S. 393, 407 (1857).

3. F. Kaplan, *Singular Mark Twain*, 236.

4. Christa Case Bryant, "Bridging Black and White: How St. Louis Residents Are Trying to Surmount Racial Inequities Post-Ferguson," *Christian Science Monitor Weekly*, January 1 and 8, 2018, 28; Gerald Early, "St. Louis: The Midwestern Long Good-Bye," in Sandweiss, *Seeking St. Louis*, 977.

5. Tim Elfrink, "'It's Still a Blast Beating People': St. Louis Police Indicted in Assault of Undercover Officer Posing as Protester," *Washington Post*, November 30, 2018, https://www.washingtonpost.com/nation/2018/11/30/its-still-blast -beating-people-st-louis-police-indicted-assault-undercover-officer-posing -protester/; Associated Press, "Federal Prosecutors to Charge Two More St. Louis Officers," *AP News*, November 13, 2019, https://apnews.com/e360ef7f0c6c42 abaf9cbb2d4780fe93.

6. Early, *Daughters*, 165.

7. Early, *"Ain't But a Place,"* 253.

8. Ibid., 255.

9. Pulitzer's company sold the paper in 2005 after 127 years of ownership.

10. Brawley, *Gay and Lesbian St. Louis*, 81.

11. Sheila T. Murphy and Leroy Aarons, "Perception vs. Reality: Comparing Actual Newspaper Coverage of Lesbian and Gay Issues with Readers' Impressions," 1999 preliminary draft, in the personal files of Loren Ghiglione.

12. "Mazy Gilleylen, 11, Is a Transgender Child," *St. Louis Post-Dispatch*, September 25, 2016, https://www.stltoday.com/news/multimedia/mazy-gilleylen -is-a-transgender-child/collection_452f8baf-7e92-5756-b6af-05bc89dafcd4.html.

13. In 2019, after nineteen years at the *St. Louis Post-Dispatch*, Moore accepted a voluntary separation package in a round of cost-cutting at the newspaper. He became the communications director for St. Louis County executive Sam Page, and he works on LGBTQ issues, among other things. As for advocating coverage of the LGBTQ community, Moore said, "No one at the *Post-Dispatch* has stepped into my former role, which is sad."

14. Francis X. Clines, "Shepherding a China Report Past the Partisan Routines," *New York Times*, May 24, 1999, https://www.nytimes.com/1999/05/24/us /public-lives-shepherding-a-china-report-past-the-partisan-routines.html.

15. Mormino, *Immigrants on the Hill*, 97.

16. Joseph Wheless, *Forgery in Christianity: A Documented Record of the Foundation of the Christian Religion* (New York: Alfred A. Knopf, 1930), 406.

17. Edward O. Wilson, *The Meaning of Human Existence* (New York: Liveright, 2014), 154.

18. Elizabeth Dias, "A Silent Crisis for Gay Priests," *New York Times*, February 18, 2019, A1; Frédéric Martel, *In the Closet of the Vatican: Power, Homosexuality, Hypocrisy* (London: Bloomsbury Continuum, 2019), xi; Wills, *Future of the Catholic Church with Pope Francis*, 211; Karen Armstrong, "A God for Both Sexes," *Economist*, December 21, 1996, 65.

CHAPTER 3. Chicago

1. Austin, *High-Risers*, 31.

2. Amanda Seligman, "North Lawndale," *Encyclopedia of Chicago*, 2004–2005, http://www.encyclopedia.chicagohistory.org/pages/901.html; Frank James, "Martin Luther King Jr. in Chicago," *Chicago Tribune*, January 3, 2008, http://www.chicagotribune.com/news/nationworld/politics/chi-chicagodays-martinlutherking-story-story.html.

3. Milliken v. Bradley, 418 U.S. 717, 815 (1974) (Marshall, J., dissenting).

4. Frank Rich, "Post-Racial Farce," *New York Magazine*, May 20, 2012, http://nymag.com/news/frank-rich/racism-2012-5/.

5. See R. Barry Ruback and Daniel Juieng, "Territorial Defense in Parking Lots: Retaliation Against Waiting Drivers," *Journal of Applied Social Psychology* 27, no. 9 (May 1997): 821–34.

6. David Masci and Gregory A. Smith, "7 Facts About American Catholics," Pew Research Center, October 10, 2018, https://www.pewresearch.org/fact-tank/2018/10/10/7-facts-about-american-catholics/.

7. See Robert T. Teranishi, Carola Suárez-Orozco, and Marcelo Suárez-Orozco, "Immigrants in Community Colleges," *Future of Children* 21, no. 1 (spring 2011): 153–69.

8. Jan Hoffman, "Estimate of U.S. Transgender Population Doubles to 1.4 Million Adults," *New York Times*, June 30, 2016, https://www.nytimes.com/2016/07/01/health/transgender-population.html.

9. Jaime M. Grant, Lisa A. Mottet, Justin Tanis, Jack Harrison, Jody L. Herman, and Mara Keisling, *Injustice at Every Turn: A Report of the National Transgender Discrimination Survey* (Washington, D.C.: National Center for Transgender Equality and National Gay and Lesbian Task Force, 2011), 3, https://www.hivlawandpolicy.org/sites/default/files/Injustice%20at%20Every%20Turn.pdf.

CHAPTER 4. The Rust Belt

1. Fishkin, *Writing America*, 9.

2. Carr, *Our Town*, 19.

3. David Margolick, *Strange Fruit: Billie Holiday, Café Society, and an Early Cry for Civil Rights* (Philadelphia: Running Press, 2000), 15.

4. Ibid., 17.

5. Dorian Lynskey, *33 Revolutions Per Minute: A History of Protest Songs, from Billie Holiday to Green Day* (New York: Ecco, 2011), 8.

6. Cameron, *A Time of Terror*, 91. On state-sanctioned terrorism against African Americans, see Stewart E. Tolnay and E. M. Beck, *A Festival of Violence: An Analysis of Southern Lynchings, 1882–1930* (Urbana: University of Illinois Press, 1995), 48–50.

7. James Allen, Hilton Als, John Lewis, and Leon Litwack, *Without Sanctuary: Lynching Photography in America* (Santa Fe, N.Mex.: Twin Palms, 2000), 176.

8. Kerouac, *On the Road*, 309.

9. "History Cleveland's Columbus Day Parade," *La Gazzetta Italiana*, October 2010, https://www.lagazzettaitaliana.com/local-news/7621-history-cleveland -s-columbus-day-parade.

10. Longworth, *Caught in the Middle*, 124.

11. Robert W. Fairlie, *Immigrant Entrepreneurs and Small Business Owners, and Their Access to Financial Capital* (Washington, D.C.: Small Business Association Office of Advocacy, 2012), https://www.sba.gov/sites/default/files/rs396tot.pdf; Marie Jastrow, *Looking Back: The American Dream Through Immigrant Eyes* (New York: W. W. Norton, 1986), 19.

12. Kathleen Grimm and Jessica Bauer Walker, *Challenges and Opportunities of Community Health Workers in Buffalo, N.Y.* (Buffalo: Community Health Foundation of Western & Central New York, January 2011), 3–5.

13. Jesse McKinley, "A Surprising Salve for New York's Beleaguered Cities: Refugees," *New York Times*, February 21, 2017, A19.

14. Reigstad, *Scribblin' for a Livin'*, 44.

15. Brian Meyer, Lou Michel, and Jay Ray, "Site Meant for Celebration Turns Nightmarish; As Patrons Leave Downtown Restaurant a Barrage of Gunfire Creates a Bloody Mess," *Buffalo News*, August 15, 2010.

16. Margaret Sullivan, "Despite Pain, Community Should Know the Truth," *Buffalo News*, August 29, 2010.

17. Ibid.

18. Harold McNeil, "Black Community Voices Outrage over Story on City Grill Victims; Editor of News Hears Demands for Apology," *Buffalo News*, September 2, 2010.

19. Margaret Sullivan, "News Is Reaching Out to East Side Community Perhaps, in the Long Run, This Painful Episode Will Prove to Be Something Positive," *Buffalo News*, October 31, 2010.

20. Driscoll, *Mark Twain Among the Indians*, 129.

21. Ibid., 8, 350, 351.

22. Breyer and Kamalakar, *300 Miles to Freedom*, 2011.

23. Barbara S. Ramsdell, "The John W. Jones Story," John W. Jones Museum, 2002, https://www.johnwjonesmuseum.org/the-john-w-jones-story.

24. "Elmira Union Civil War Prison," Civil War Journeys, January 16, 2019, https://www.civil-war-journeys.org/elmira_prison.htm.

25. Josh Pais, dir., *7th Street*, 2002, 7thstreetmovie.com.

CHAPTER 5. New York City

1. Sherwood Anderson, *Winesburg, Ohio: A Group of Tales of Ohio Small-Town Life* (New York: Modern Library, 1947), 303.

2. Hope Edelman, "No Quick Fix for Childhood Grief," *New York Times*, August 26, 2019, A19.

3. Maxine Harris, *The Loss That Is Forever: The Lifelong Impact of the Early Death of a Mother or Father* (New York: E. P. Dutton, 1995), 122.

4. Frank Spadola, *For Whom I Live* (New York: Las Americas, 1956).

5. James Barron, "Private School, After Closing, Sells All It Has," *New York Times*, August 4, 1988, B3.

6. Samuelsson, *Yes, Chef*, 126, 72.

7. Ibid., 213.

8. Ibid., 303.

9. Ibid., 312.

10. Byfield, *Savage Portrayals*, 2.

11. Benjamin Weiser, "Settlement Approved in '89 Jogger Case; City Deflects Blame," *New York Times*, September 6, 2014, A17.

12. Michael Wilson, "Trump Draws Criticism for Ad He Ran After Jogger Attack," *New York Times*, October 23, 2002, https://www.nytimes.com/2002/10/23/nyregion/trump-draws-criticism-for-ad-he-ran-after-jogger-attack.html; Peter Baker, "A President Who Fans, Rather Than Douses, the Nation's Racial Fires," *New York Times*, January 12, 2018, https://www.nytimes.com/2018/01/12/us/politics/trump-racism.html.

13. Ellis Cose, "Trump's Monumental Challenge on Race," *USA Today*, November 10, 2016, https://www.usatoday.com/story/opinion/2016/11/10/donald-trump-white-men-jim-crow-ellis-cose/93558380/.

14. "We are the 99 percent," a slogan used by the Occupy movement, draws attention to the income and wealth gap between the richest one percent of society,

which has a disproportionate share of income, influence, and capital, and the bottom 99 percent represented by Occupy.

15. Ruth Milkman, Stephanie Luce, and Penny Lewis, *Changing the Subject: A Bottom-Up Account of Wall Street in New York City* (New York: Murphy Institute, City University of New York, 2013), 47, docs.wixstatic.com/ugd/90d188 _f7367c3e04de4e94a6f86f9e6b1023ed.pdf.

16. John-Manuel Andriote, *Victory Deferred: How AIDS Changed Gay Life in America* (Chicago: University of Chicago Press, 1999), 49–51.

17. Mass, *Confessions of a Jewish Wagnerite*, 267.

18. James Kinsella, *Covering the Plague: AIDS and the American Media* (New Brunswick, N.J.: Rutgers University Press, 1989), 32.

19. Mass, *Confessions of a Jewish Wagnerite*, 137, 177, and 187.

CHAPTER 6. Five Points

1. Charles Dickens, *American Notes and Pictures from Italy* (London: Oxford University Press, 1957), 89 and 90.

2. Ann M. Ryan, "Mark Twain and the Mean (and Magical) Streets," in Ryan and McCullough, *Cosmopolitan Twain*, 43.

3. His lecture tours and writing took him across America and around the globe. He wrote about people everywhere—from western U.S. mining camps to Jerusalem in the Near East, from Missouri villages to African capitals. The narrator in "Extract from Captain Stormfield's Visit to Heaven," the last book Twain published in his lifetime, finds heaven occupied by people of all backgrounds, faiths, tastes, and races. In the American section, Indigenous peoples are the vast majority, with whites a tiny minority: "You can't expect us to amount to anything in heaven, and we *don't*," the white narrator explains.

4. "Queer Foreign Quarter: Mulberry Bend Park and Its Curious Inhabitants," *New York Times*, July 12, 1896, 32.

5. Lee died while in office in 2017; Quan left office in 2015.

6. Nadia Y. Kim, "Critical Thoughts on Asian American Assimilation in the Whitening Literature," *Social Forces* 86, no. 2 (December 2007): 562, 571.

7. See C. N. Le, "Multiracial/Hapa Asian Americans," Asian Nation: Asian American History, Demographics, and Issues, 2019, http://www.asian-nation.org /multiracial.shtml.

8. Roger Ebert, *The Great Movies II* (New York: Broadway Books, 2005), 277.

9. Robin Pogrebin, "In Little Italy, Saving the Past by Rebuilding It," *New York Times*, April 15, 2013, C1.

10. Sam Roberts, "Little Italy, Littler by the Year," *New York Times*, February 22, 2011, A20.

11. Joel Perlmann, *Demographic Outcomes of Ethnic Intermarriage in American History: Italian-Americans Through Four Generations*, working paper no. 312

(Anandale-on-Hudson, N.Y.: Levy Institute, Bard College, August 2000), http://www.levyinstitute.org/pubs/wp312.pdf.

12. Richard N. Juliani, *Building Little Italy: Philadelphia's Italians Before Mass Migration* (University Park: Pennsylvania State University Press), 102.

13. Alexander Betts, "Survival Migration: A New Protection Framework," *Global Governance: A Review of Multilateralism and International Organizations* 16, no. 3 (July–September 2010), 361–82.

14. Harry Hearder, *Italy in the Age of the Risorgimento 1790–1870* (London: Longman, 1983), 152; "The Poor Italians," *New York Times*, December 15, 1872, 8.

15. William W. Morris to the editor, *New York Times*, December 19, 1872, 2.

16. Francis Lam, "The Mysteries of Manhattan's Curry Row," *New York Times Magazine*, May 3, 2015, https://www.nytimes.com/2015/05/03/magazine/the-mysteries-of-manhattans-curry-row.html.

17. Francis X. Clines, "An Artist, an Arsonist and an Island of Trump Fans in New York," *New York Times*, April 10, 2017, A20.

18. The office of MIT's registrar confirmed that Ghiglione '32 graduated in just one year but could not confirm that he earned "the highest grades ever earned to that date."

19. Sharon Cooper, ed., *Dotty Bowe and Her Legacy* (Cambridge, Mass.: MIT, 2011), 4. Ann Ghiglione fulfilled her requirements for a bachelor's degree in mathematics, with minors in French and education, in three and a half years and attended the University of Strasbourg for her last semester.

20. Bix, *Girls Coming to Tech!*, 225.

21. Audrey Buyrn, interview by Catherine Poon, July 25, 2011, for the Margaret MacVicar Memorial AMITA Oral History Project, Institute Archives and Special Collections, MIT Libraries, 9.

22. Hopkins, "Changing Status and Number of Women in Science," 7.

23. Ibid., 8.

24. Julia Belluz, "DNA Scientist James Watson Has a Remarkably Long History of Sexist, Racist Public Comments," *Vox*, January 15, 2019, https://www.vox.com/2019/1/15/18182530/james-watson-racist.

25. Hopkins, "Changing Status and Number of Women in Science," 10, 9.

26. Ibid., 10.

27. "Enrollments 2018–2019," MIT Facts, https://web.mit.edu/facts/enrollment.html, and "Faculty and Staff," MIT Facts (as of October 2017), http://web.mit.edu/facts/faculty.html.

CHAPTER 7. New Haven

1. Virginia Willis to author, October 12, 1990.

2. Frances Sumner to author, September 2, 1990.

3. Isabel F. Smith to Mabel R. Hastings, May 26, 1932; Henry P. Eames to Hastings, June 1, 1932. Hastings was the secretary for the drama department at Yale. In 1980, long before privacy regulations governing colleges and universities were made as stringent as they are today, Yale made my mother's records available to me when I asked to see them.

4. Eames to Hastings; Smith to Hastings.

5. Rita Haskin to Allardyce Nicool, March 19, 1934. Nicool was the chair of Yale's drama department.

6. Yale University School of the Fine Arts catalog for 1933–34, 64.

7. Virginia G. Drachman, *Sisters in Law: Women Lawyers in Modern American History* (Cambridge, Mass.: Harvard University Press, 1998), 48.

8. "American University Development," *Self Culture* 2, no. 3 (December 1895): 571.

9. "Helen Hadley Hall," Yale University Visitor Center, https://visitorcenter. yale.edu/book/helen-hadley-hall.

10. Hope, *Pinstripes and Pearls*, 105.

11. Ibid., 17.

12. Claire Cain Miller, "Pay Gap Is Because of Gender, Not Jobs," *New York Times*, April 24, 2014, http:///www.nytimes.com/2014/04/24/upshot/the-pay-gap-is-because-of-gender-not-jobs.html.

13. Claudia Goldin, "A Grand Gender Convergence: Its Last Chapter," *American Economic Review* 104, no. 4 (2014): 23.

14. Elizabeth Olson, "'A Bleak Picture' for Women Trying to Rise at Law Firms," *New York Times*, July 24, 2017, https://www.nytimes.com/2017/07/24/business /dealbook/women-law-firm-partners.html.

CHAPTER 8. North toward Boston

1. Alwood, *Straight News*, 287.

2. Ibid.

3. Ibid., 50.

4. J. Kaplan, *Mr. Clemens and Mark Twain*, 181.

5. A poll conducted in April 2011, about six months before our trip, found that 61 percent of Americans had an unfavorable view of Islam and only 33 expressed favorable views. Shibley Tehhammi, "What Americans Really Think About Muslims and Islam," *Markaz* (blog), Brookings, December 9, 2015, https://www .brookings.edu/blog/markaz/2015/12/09/what-americans-really-think-about -muslims-and-islam/.

6. Brian Knowlton, "Muslim Women Gain Higher Profile in U.S.," *New York Times*, December 27, 2010, https://www.nytimes.com/2010/12/28/world /middleeast/28iht-muslim28.html.

7. Ingrid Mattson, "How Muslims Use Islamic Paradigms to Define America," in *Religion and Immigration: Christian, Jewish, and Muslim Experiences in the United States*, ed. Yvonne Yazbeck Haddad, Jane I. Smith, and John L. Esposito (Walnut Creek, Calif.: AltaMira, 2003), 203.

8. Samuel P. Huntington, *The Clash of Civilizations and the Remaking of World Order* (New York: Simon and Schuster, 1996), 29.

9. Gallup Center for Muslim Studies, "In U.S., Religious Prejudice Stronger Against Muslims," January 21, 2010, http://www.gallup.com/poll/125312/religious -prejudice-stronger-against-muslims.aspx?version=print.

10. "Foreign Fighters Expand Terrorist Groups, Panel Says," *New York Times*, November 1, 2014, A7.

11. The circulation of the *Emporia Gazette* was 3,904 at the end of World War I. Sally Foreman Griffith, *Home Town News: William Allen White and the Emporia Gazette* (Oxford: Oxford University Press, 1989), 214.

12. Mellinger, *Chasing Newsroom Diversity*, 102, 106, 177–78.

13. American Society of Newspaper Editors, "Newsroom Diversity Survey: 2015 Census," press release, July 25, 2015, https://members.newsleaders.org/content .asp?contentid=415.

14. Dolores Courtemanche, "Men Not Likely to Monopolize the League of Women Voters," *Worcester Telegram*, May 11, 1975, D1.

15. Mellinger, *Chasing Newsroom Diversity*, 68; Steve Chawkins, "Jean Sharley Taylor Dies at 91; Groundbreaking L.A. Times Journalist," *Los Angeles Times*, October 13, 2015, http://www.latimes.com/local/obituaries/la-me-jean-sharley -taylor-20151014-story.html.

16. Mellinger, *Chasing Newsroom Diversity*, 44, 69.

CHAPTER 9. Boston

1. Treuer, *Heartbeat of Wounded Knee*, 410–11.

2. Akilah Johnson, Nicole Dungca, Liz Kowalczyk, Andrew Ryan, Todd Wallack, Adrian Walker, and Patricia Wen, "Boston. Racism. Image. Reality: The Spotlight Team Takes on Our Hardest Question," *Boston Globe*, December 10, 2017, https://apps.bostonglobe.com/spotlight/boston-racism-image-reality/series /image/.

3. Andrew Ryan et al. (Spotlight Team), "A Better Boston? The Choice Is Ours," *Boston Globe*, December 16, 2017, 1.

4. Ana Patricia Muñoz, Marlene Kim, Mariko Chang, Regine O. Jackson, Darrick Hamilton, and William A. Darity Jr., *The Color of Wealth in Boston* (Boston: Federal Reserve of Boston, Duke University, and the New School, March 25, 2015), https://www.bostonfed.org/publications/one-time-pubs/color-of-wealth .aspx.

5. Nicholas Kristoff, "When Whites Just Don't Get It, Revisited," *New York Times*, April 3, 2016, SR9.

6. Primeau, *Romance of the Road*, 115; Beauvoir, *America Day by Day*, 382.

7. Linda Villarosa, "The Hidden Toll," *New York Times Magazine*, April 15, 2018, 31.

8. See Nancy R. Nangeroni, "Rita Hester's Murder and the Language of Respect," *Sojourner, the Women's Journal*, February 1999, http://www.gendertalk.com/language-of-respect/.

9. Daniel Vasquez, "Stabbing Victim a Mystery to Many, Police Seeking Clues in Allston Slaying," *Boston Globe*, November 30, 1998, B1.

10. Jessica Van Sack, "Undercover 'John' Takes on Trannies, Pimps," *Boston Herald*, July 7, 2008, https://www.bostonherald.com/2008/07/07/undercover-john-takes-on-trannies-pimps/.

11. Dan Piepenbring, "How Mark Twain Tried to Get Rich Quick—Again and Again," *New Yorker*, October 25, 2017, https//www.newyorker.com/books/page-turner/how-mark-twain-tried-to-get-rich-quick-again-and-again.

12. McDonald, *Golden Passport*, 1.

13. Harvard Business School African American Alumni Association, "Lillian Lincoln Lambert," 2019, http://hbsaaa.net/lillian-lincoln-lambert.php. I am indebted to Liam Sullivan of the Baker Library of Harvard Business School for information from its History Archives about the school in the 1930s.

14. David Carr, "The Devil Wears Teflon," *New York Times*, July 10, 2006, https://www.nytimes.com/2006/07/10/business/media/10carr.html.

15. Harvard Business School, "Training Course in Personnel Administration, 1937–1944," *Building the Foundation: Business Education for Women at Harvard University*, n.d., http://www.library.hbs.edu/hc/wbe/exhibit_training.html.

16. Jodi Kantor, "Harvard Business School Case Study: Gender Equity," *New York Times*, September 7, 2013.

17. McDonald, *Golden Passport*, 578.

18. David Gelles and Claire Cain Miller, "Schools Teach M.B.A.s Perils of 'Bro' Ethos," *New York Times*, December 26, 2017, A15.

CHAPTER 10. Philadelphia

1. D. H. Lawrence, *Studies in Classic American Literature* (New York: Doubleday Anchor, 1953), 72.

2. Wilkerson, *Warmth of Other Suns*, 418.

3. Chicago Commission on Race Relations, *Negro in Chicago*, xxiv.

4. Jennifer Szalai, "The Original Siamese Twins, Examined Yet Again," *New York Times*, April 5, 2018, C6.

5. Richard N. Juliani, *Building Little Italy: Philadelphia's Italians Before Mass Migration* (University Park: Pennsylvania State University Press, 1998), 315.

6. Pew Research Center, "Political Polarization in the American Public."

7. Ibid.; David A. Moss, "Fixing What's Wrong with U.S. Politics," *Harvard Business Review*, March 2012, https://hbr.org/2012/03/fixing-whats-wrong-with-us-politics.

8. Jason Baumann, introduction to *The Stonewall Reader*, ed. Baumann (New York: Penguin, 2019), xxii.

9. Zacks, *Chasing the Last Laugh*, 47.

10. Morris, *Gender Play in Mark Twain*, 16.

11. Dr. Richard von Krafft-Ebing, *Psychopathia Sexualis with Especial Reference to the Antipathic Sexual Instinct* (New York: Physicians and Surgeons, 1924), 438.

12. Alyssa Banotai, "A Summer of Activism: From Bryn Mawr to Shanghai, Four Students Landed Summer Internships with an LGBTQ Focus," *Alumnae Bulletin*, November 2014, 22.

13. After seventeen years in the dean's office, Philip Bean left Haverford on March 27, 2019, to become the executive director of the Central New York Conservancy in his hometown of Utica.

14. "Just Married," *Haverford*, fall 2014, 54–62.

15. "Black Faculty at the Nation's Highest-Ranked Liberal Arts Colleges," *Journal of Blacks in Higher Education*, 2010, http://www.jbhe.com/news _views/65_blackfaculty.html.

CHAPTER 11. Washington, D.C.

1. Muller, *Mark Twain in Washington, D.C.*, 82–83; J. Kaplan, *Mr. Clemens and Mark Twain*, 58.

2. Jules Moëd, "Genealogy of the Moëd Family," 1990, 1, typescript in the files of Loren Ghiglione.

3. Henny Moëd Roth, *Just a Jewish Girl: A Pictorial Family Album of Pre-World War II, Antwerp, Belgium* (Los Angeles: Jans Custom Photobooks, 2011), 30, 8.

4. McGinity, *Still Jewish*, 203. According to a 2010 survey of 2,450 Americans, same-faith couples report higher rates of "marital satisfaction" than do their interfaith counterparts. See Riley, *'Til Faith Do Us Part*, 125.

5. Riley, *'Til Faith Do Us Part*, 216. See also Susan Katz Miller, "Being 'Partly Jewish,'" *New York Times*, November 1, 2013, A31.

6. Joel Perlmann, *Demographic Outcomes of Ethnic Intermarriage in American History: Italian-Americans Through Four Generations*, working paper no. 312 (Anandale-on-Hudson, N.Y.: Levy Institute, Bard College, August 2000), http://www.levyinstitute.org/pubs/wp312.pdf.

7. Simon Hyoun, "Crossing the Threshold: How a Presbyterian Church and an Independent Synagogue Share Space," *PBS.org*, 2004, http://www.pbs.org /thecongregation/indepth/crossing.html.

8. Seamon, *Interfaith Marriage in America*, 170–71.

9. Barbara Matusow, "Washington, Italian Style," *Washingtonian*, June 1999, 48.

10. Alex S. Jones and Susan E. Tifft, *The Trust: The Private and Powerful Family Behind the New York Times* (Boston: Little, Brown, 1999), 651; Gay Talese, *The Kingdom and the Power* (New York: World, 1969), 326.

11. Eugene L. Meyer, "Conflict in Washington: Growth vs. Housing Its Poorest Can Afford," *New York Times*, June 6, 2018, B7; Carol Morello and Dan Keating, "Number of Black D.C. Residents Plummets as Majority Status Slips Away," *Washington Post*, March 24, 2011, https://www.washingtonpost.com/local/black -dc-residents-plummet-barely-a-majority/2011/03/24/ABtIgJQB_stort.html.

12. Carolyn Weaver, "A Secret No More," *American Journalism Review*, September 1992, http://ajrarchive.org/Article.asp?id=1688.

13. Juan Williams, "After 20 Years Justice Clarence Thomas Has Made His Imprint on the Supreme Court, Conservatism and the Black Experience in America," *Fox News*, October 22, 2011 (last updated May 7, 2015), http://www. foxnews.com/opinion/2011/10/22/after-20-justice-clarence-thomas-has-made-his -imprint-on-supreme-court.html.

14. Jack White, "What Happened to Juan Williams?" *Root*, October 22, 2011, https://www.theroot.com/what-happened-to-juan-williams-1790866494.

15. Williams appeared on the show on October 18, 2010, www.youtube.com /watch?v=_Tp2vod3klA.

16. "Juan Williams and His Sons Retrace the Steps of MLK!" *Fox News*, October 24, 2011, https://www.youtube.com/watch?v=DxBGSZTuy4k.

CHAPTER 12. In the South

1. Dave Eggers, "None of the Old Rules Apply: Travels Through Post-Election America," in *What We Do Now: Standing Up for Your Values in Trump's America*, ed. Dennis Johnson and Valerie Merians (New York: Melville House, 2017), 194.

2. D. D. Guttenplan, "Seeking an Upset, Sanders Campaign Searches for Votes in Pennsylvania's Lost Communities," *Nation*, April 7, 2016, https://www .thenation.com/article/seeking-an-upset-sanders-campaign-searches-for-votes -in-pennsylvanias-lost-communities.

3. Whitaker, *Smoketown*, 323.

4. Linda Blackford and Linda Minch, "Front-Page News, Back-Page Coverage," *Lexington Herald-Leader*, July 4, 2004, https://www.kentucky.com/news/special -reports/article210138324.html.

5. Some information about Merlene Davis's early journalism career comes from Davis, interview by Betty Baye, April 30, 2015, Kentucky Civil Rights Hall of Fame Oral History Project, https://kentuckyoralhistory.org/ark:/16417/xt7xks6j438m.

6. First Presbyterian Church, "History of First Church," n.d., https://fpclex.org /about-us/history/.

7. Juan Williams, *My Soul Looks Back in Wonder: Voices of the Civil Rights Experience* (New York: AARP/Sterling, 2005), 154–55.

8. Linda A. Moore, "The First Steps—Satchels, Big Hopes Weighed Heavy on 13 First-Graders as They Made History 50 Years Ago Integrating Memphis Schools," *Commercial Appeal*, October 2, 2011, A1.

9. *The Memphis 13*, directed by Daniel Kiel, 2011, http://thememphis13.com/.

10. Alan Blinder and Jerry Gray, "A Dampened Dream: Fifty Years After the King Assassination, Memphis Is Dogged by Poverty, Segregation and Violence," *New York Times*, April 4, 2018, A12; Holland Cotter, "Where the Dream Is Still Alive," *New York Times*, April 1, 2018, AR 14.

11. Alan Blinder, "Decades Later, Memphis to Compensate Black Sanitation Strikers of 1968," *New York Times*, July 25, 2017, https://www.nytimes.com/2017/07/25/us/memphis-sanitation-workers-strike-grants.html.

12. Emily Yellin and Richard Fausset, "How Memphis Hopes to Move On, Now That Statues Are Down," *New York Times*, December 21, 2017, https://www.nytimes.com/2017/12/21/us/memphis-confederate-statues-parks.html.

CHAPTER 13. Mississippi

1. Dick Gregory, *From the Back of the Bus* (New York: E. P. Dutton, 1962), 23.

2. William B. Hamilton, *Holly Springs, Mississippi, to the Year 1878* (Holly Springs, Miss.: Marshall County Historical Society, 1984), 30, 23.

3. Loren Ghiglione, "A Summer in Mississippi," *Yale Law Report*, 11, no. 2 (winter 1965): 28.

4. Bruce Anderson, "In Memoriam: Frank Cieciorka," December 3, 2008, http://theragblog.blogspot.com/2009/01/frank-cieciorkas-self-inscribed-eulogy.html; Council of Federated Organizations, "Memo to Accepted Applicants (#2)," [1964?], Michael J. Miller Civil Rights Collection, University of Southern Mississippi, https://digitalcollections.usm.edu/uncategorized/collection_7ab8c6d0-eb82-4e44-b8c5-975804d31ab2/. The memo tells volunteers that Mississippi required outsiders to obtain Mississippi license plates within sixty, not thirty, days.

5. The Mississippi State Sovereignty Commission files contain a "List of Freedom School Teachers That Have Bought Tags in Marshall County," signed by J. M. Ash, Holly Springs, Mississippi, sheriff and tax collector. Frank Cieciorka, his 1960 Studebaker, and his new license plate number (47–8–473) are on the list, along with the names, cars, and license plates for seven other civil rights workers in Holly Springs. All eight license plates begin with the number 47. This is document SCR ID # 99–132–0–2–1–1–1; to access the Sovereignty Commission files online, go to http://www.mdah.ms.gov/arrec/digital_archives/sovcom/#basicname.

6. Anderson, "In Memoriam"; Laura Parker, "Civil Rights Museum in Mississippi Arouses Hope—and Distrust," *National Geographic*, June 24, 2014,

http://news.nationalgeographic.com/news/2014/06/140623-mississippi-civil
-rights-museum-history-freedom-summer.html.

7. Calvin Trillin, *Jackson, 1964: And Other Dispatches from Fifty Years of
Reporting on Race in America* (New York: Random House, 2016), 28; Larry Rubin,
"A Walk in Holly Springs: 1964" Civil Rights Movement Archive, winter 1964,
http://www.crmvet.org/nars/rubin.htm.

8. The four rednecks fit the Mississippi author Willie Morris's description of
the brawny white "'redneck' boys" who stayed one rung above the bottom of the
social pecking order by beating down Blacks. Willie Morris, *North Toward Home*
(Boston: Houghton Mifflin, 1967), 21–22.

9. One method of accessing this quote from a May 19, 1964, report by Tom
Scarbrough, Sovereignty Commission investigator between 1960 and 1968, is to
use the "basic folder search" access system for Sovereignty Commission Online
at http://www.mdah.ms.gov/arrec/digital_archives/sovcom/. Type in "Marshall
County" for the folder title (that county is the location of Rust College, Holly
Springs, Mississippi) and click. Then click on "Marshall County [2–20–1]." Finally,
click on file SCR ID #2–20–1–75–6–1–1, which is page 6 of Scarbrough's report,
and scroll within the "Zoom Level" box to "Printer Friendly." Click on it.

10. Steve Fraser, *Class Matters: The Strange Career of an American Delusion* (New
Haven, Conn.: Yale University Press, 2018), 204.

11. James Baldwin, "A Letter to My Nephew," in *The Fire Next Time* (New York:
Vintage, 1993), 7.

12. Duncan and Beckley, "Dahlia Twenty Years Later," 14.

13. Erwin Chemerinsky, "The Segregation and Resegregation of American Public
Education: The Courts' Role," *North Carolina Law Review* 81 (2003): 1603.

14. Cohodas, *Band Played Dixie*, 124.

15. Eugene Robinson, *Disintegration: The Splintering of Black America* (New
York: Anchor, 2011), 165–66.

16. Stanley Nelson, dir., *American Experience: The Murder of Emmett Till*, PBS,
February 3, 2004.

17. Hortense Powdermaker, *After Freedom: A Cultural Study in the Deep South*
(New York: Viking, 1939), 86.

18. Aimee Ortiz, "Till Memorial Replaces Sign a Fourth Time. It's Bulletproof,"
New York Times, October 22, 2019, A13.

19. "The Boulevard," *Greenwood Enterprise*, April 21, 1910, http://www.
aboutgreenwoodms.com/grand-boulevard.html.

20. "The Greenwood (Miss.) Monument," *Confederate Magazine*, December
1913, aboutgreenwoodmississippi.com/confederate-monument.html.

21. Fannie Lou Hamer, "Testimony Before the Credentials Committee,
Democratic National Convention, Atlantic City, New Jersey, August 22, 1964,"

American Radio Works, http://americanradioworks.public radio.org/features
/sayitplain/flhamer.html.

22. Dittmer, *Local People*, 171.

23. Patricia Sullivan, "Civil Rights Activist June Johnson," *Washington Post*, April
18, 2007, http://www.washingtonpost.com/wp-dyn/content/article/2007/04/17
/AR2007041701988.html.

24. *Mississippi: A Self Portrait: Booker Wright*, documentary by Frank De Felitta,
NBC News, May 1, 1966.

25. "Karen Pinkston, Fourth Generation Owner and Cook," interview by Amy
Evans, June 12 and 19, 2003, Lusco's Restaurant, Greenwood, Mississippi, http://
www.southernfoodways.org/interview/karen-pinkston/.

26. Yvette Johnson, *The Song and the Silence: A Story about Family, Race, and
What Was Revealed in a Small Town in the Mississippi Delta While Searching for
Booker Wright* (New York: Atria Books, 2017).

27. Gene Datell, "Beyond Black and White in the Mississippi Delta," *New York
Times*, December 2, 2012, SR 4.

28. Karson Brandenburg, "White Mayors Win on Black Votes," School of
Journalism and New Media, University of Mississippi, December 3, 2014, http://
meek.olemiss.edu/2014/12/03/white-mayors-win-on-black-votes/.

29. Julia Reed, "Never Meet a Stranger," *Time*, August 6–13, 2018, 73.

30. Whitaker, *Smoketown*, 331.

31. Vern E. Smith, "Ghosts of Mississippi," *Defenders Online*, March 4, 2011,
http://www.thedefendersonline.com/2011/03/04/ghosts-of mississippi/ (last
accessed October 1, 2011).

32. Lindsey Shelton, "A Wrong Righted: New WWI Plaque Includes Omitted
Names," *Natchez Democrat*, November 11, 2011, 1A.

33. Shane Peterson, "The World War I Memorial Project: Natchez, Adams
County, Mississippi," October 18, 2011, http://shanepeterson.com/oldweb
/natchez-memorial-hall-project.html.

34. Michael Tisserand, "A Racism Harder Than Stone," *New York Times*, May 9,
2017, A23.

CHAPTER 14. New Orleans

1. James Baldwin, "Sonny's Blues," *Partisan Review* 24, no. 4 (summer 1957): 358.

2. Hirsch and Logsdon, *Creole New Orleans*, xi.

3. John Williams, "Rethinking the Old South," *New York Times*, March 20, 2018, C5.

4. Mitch Landrieu, "Speech on the Removal of Confederate Monuments in New
Orleans," *New York Times*, May 23, 2017, https://www.nytimes.com/2017/05/23
/opinion/mitch-landrieus-speech-transcript.html?src=me&_r=0.

5. Broom, *Yellow House*, 301, 328.

6. Roberto E. Barrios, "Hurricane Katrina's Forgotten Survivors," *Sapiens*, May 22, 2016, https://www.sapiens.org/culture/hurricane-katrina-lower-9th-ward/.

7. Aldrich, *Building Resilience*, 130.

8. Ibid., 131.

CHAPTER 15. Outliers

1. Rideau, *In the Place of Justice*, 48.

2. George H. Colt, "The Most Rehabilitated Prisoner in America," *Life*, March 1993, 70.

3. Lianne Hart, "Prisoner's Release After 44 Years Reopens a Town's Old Wounds," *Los Angeles Times*, January 23, 2005, http://articles.latimes.com/2005 /jan/23/nation/na-lakecharles23; Scott Gold and Lianne Hart, "Released Louisiana Man Is in Seclusion After Threats," *Los Angeles Times*, January 18, 2005, https:// www.latimes.com/archives/la-xpm-2005-jan-18-na-rideau18-story.html.

4. John Kennedy Toole, *A Confederacy of Dunces* (New York: Grove, 1980), 22.

5. Tyler Bridges, *The Rise of David Duke* (Jackson: University Press of Mississippi, 1994), 236–37.

6. Steve Phillips, "Make Trump's Racism an Issue," *New York Times*, July 31, 2019, A29.

7. Erik Eckholm, "Bible College Helps Some at Louisiana Prison Find Peace," *New York Times*, October 5, 2013, http://www.nytimes.com/2013/10/06/us/bible -college-helps-some-at-louisiana-prison-find-peace.html?pagewanted=all.

8. Rideau, *In the Place of Justice*, 242; James Ridgeway, "God's Own Warden," *Mother Jones*, July–August 2011, http://motherjones.com/politics/2011/07/ burl-cain-angola-prison/.

9. Rideau, *In the Place of Justice*, 343.

10. T. S. Eliot, *The Family Reunion* (New York: Harcourt, Brace, 1939), 114.

11. Wilbert Rideau, telephone interview by author, August 4, 2014.

12. See Crey and Fournier, *Stolen from Our Embrace*, 30.

13. The facts of the case are outlined in *State of Louisiana v. Scott Meyers*, 97–KA-2584 (La. App. 4 Cir. 11/24/99), http://caselaw.findlaw.com/la-court-of -appeal/1071554.html.

14. Campbell Robertson, "The Man Who Says Louisiana Should 'Kill More,'" *New York Times*, July 8, 2015, A1.

15. Andrew Cohen, "At Louisiana's Most Notorious Prison, a Clash of Testament," *Atlantic*, October 11, 2013, http://www.theatlantic.com/national /archive/2013/10/at-Louisianas-most-notorious-prison-a-clash-of- testament/280414/.

16. Dennis Shere, *Cain's Redemption: A Story of Hope and Transformation in America's Bloodiest Prison* (Chicago: Northfield Publishing, 2005), 27.

17. See, for example, Tanya Erzen, *God in Captivity: The Rise of Faith-Based Prison Ministries in the Age of Mass Incarceration* (Boston: Beacon, 2017), and Maya Lau, "Burl Cain Claims Angola Transformation, but Prison's Violence Era Preceded Him by Decades," *(Louisiana) Advocate*, January 3, 2016, https://www. theadvocate.com/baton_rouge/news/crime_police/article_c2c84230-f700-5c00 -936c-85933b4b73be.html.

18. Cohen, "At Louisiana's Most Notorious Prison." The lawyer quoted is no relation to the author of this article.

19. Cindy Chang, "Louisiana Is the World's Prison Capital," *(New Orleans) Times-Picayune*, May 13, 2012 (updated October 14, 2017), https://www.nola.com /crime/index.ssf/2012/05/louisiana_is_the_worlds_prison.html. See also Charles M. Blow, "Plantations, Prisons and Profits," *New York Times*, May 20, 2012, A17.

20. "Solitary Confinement Should Be Banned in Most Cases, UN Expert Says," *UN News*, October 18, 2011, https://news.un.org/en/story/2011/10/392012- solitary-confinement-should-be-banned-most-cases-un-expert-says; Maya Lau and Gordon Russell, "Angola Warden Burl Cain to Resign amid Twin Probes into His Side Business Dealings," *(Baton Rouge) Advocate*, December 9, 2015, https://www .theadvocate.com/baton_rouge/news/politics/article_d6826c2e-136d-5a19-a62d -fcf3383887e6.html.

21. Kristin L. Hoganson, *The Heartland: An American History* (New York: Penguin, 2019), xiv.

22. Dave Swenson and Liesl Etherington, *Revisiting the Demographic and Economic Baselines for Keokuk, Iowa*, November 2016, www2.econ.iastate.edu /prosci/Swenson/Publications/Keokuk%202016_Send.pdf.

23. Kevin Hardy, "This Iowa Town Lost Its Steel Factory; Now It's Coming Back," *Des Moines Register*, December 15, 2016, https://www.desmoinesregister. com/story/money/business/2016/12/15/shuttered-iowa-factory-gets-second -chance-keokuk/95330124/.

24. Janet Adamy and Paul Overberg, "Rural America Is the New 'Inner City,'" *Wall Street Journal*, May 26, 2017, https://www.wsj.com/articles/rural-america-is -the-new-inner-city-1495817008.

25. Swenson and Etherington, *Revisiting*.

26. Rob Griffin, Roy Teixeira, and William H. Frey, "America's Electoral Future: Demographic Shifts and the Future of the Trump Coalition," Brookings, April 19, 2018, https://www.brookings.edu/research/americas-electoral-future_2018/.

27. Amanda Taub, "Partisanship as a Tribal Identity: Voting Against One's Economic Interests," *New York Times*, April 13, 2017, A10.

28. Richard Wolffe, "Donald Trump's Economic Pitch to Iowa Is Simple: The Blessing of His Midas Touch," *Guardian*, January 25, 2016, https//www .theguardian.com/us-news/2016/jan/25/donald-trump-economic-pitch-to-iowa

-is-simple-the-blessing-of-his-midas-touch; Trip Gabriel, "In Iowa, Trump Voters Are Unfazed by Controversies," *New York Times*, January 12, 2017, https://www.nytimes.com/2017/01/12/us/donald-trump-iowa-conservatives.html?_r=0.

29. Thomas Frank, *Rendezvous with Oblivion: Reports from a Sinking Society* (New York: Metropolitan Books, 2018), 220.

30. James W. Loewen, *Lies Across America: What Our Historic Sites Get Wrong* (New York: New Press, 2019), 157-160.

31. Patrick J. Carr and Maria J. Kefalas, *Hollowing Out the Middle: The Rural Brain Drain and What It Means for America* (Boston: Beacon, 2009), 14–15.

32. Robert Costa, "Trump Goes to Church in Iowa and Hears a Sermon About Welcoming Immigrants," *Washington Post*, January 24, 2016, https://www.washingtonpost.com/news/post-politics/wp/2016/01/24/reaching-out-to-iowa-evangelical-voters-trump-attends-presbyterian-service/.

33. Yessenia Chavez, "Dozens Rally and March for Immigrant Neighbors in Muscatine," *WQAD.com*, February 18, 2017, https://wqad.com/2017/02/18/dozens-rally-and-march-for-immigrant-neighbors-in-muscatine/; Zachary Oren Smith, "Migration Is Beautiful: A Look at Latino History in Muscatine," *Muscatine Journal*, September 30, 2017, https://muscatinejournal.com/muscatine/migration-is-beautiful-a-look-at-latino-history-in-muscatine/article_ca00ec4c-35ed-56ab-9e6d-1ea03f14c413.html.

34. "Kansas Sees Net Loss in Population," *Kansas City Business Journal*, March 28, 2014, https://www.bizjournals.com/kansascity/blog/morning_call/2014/03/kansas-sees-net-loss-in-population.html; Trevor Davis, "Behind the Numbers: Sociologist Says Kansas' Population Growth Not All Positive," press release, Kansas State University, March 9, 2011, http://www.k-state.edu/media/newsreleases/mar11/census30911.html.

35. Brooks McNamara, "The Indian Medicine Show," *Educational Theatre Journal* 23, no. 4 (December 1971): 431.

36. Gibson, *Kickapoos*, 5.

37. Twain to his mother, March 20, 1862. The letter was reprinted in the *Keokuk Gate City* on June 25, 1862, and appears in Branch, *Literary Apprenticeship of Mark Twain*, 233–37.

38. Andy Marso, "Kickapoo Leadership Vows to Continue Fight for Reservoir," *Topeka Capital-Journal*, December 27, 2013, https:www.cjonline.com/news/2013–12–27/Kickapoo-leadership-vows-continue-fight-reservoir; Associated Press, "Kickapoo of Kan. Still Seeking Reservoir," *Native Times*, November 3, 2012, http://www.nativetimes.com/index.php/news/tribal/8024-kickapoo-of-kan-still-seeking-reservoir; "Kickapoo Tribe in Kansas Files Lawsuit in Federal Court to End 30-Year Era of Systematic Deprivation of the Tribe's Water Rights," *NARF Legal Review* 31, no. 2 (summer–fall 2006), http:www.narf.org/nill/documents/nlr/nlr31-2.pdf; Andy Marso, "Kickapoo Ask Brownback to Intervene in Water

Spat," *Topeka Capital-Journal*, October 26, 2012, https://www.cjonline.com /article/20121026/NEWS/310269872.

39. Steve Cadue, "Legacy of *Brown*: Kickapoo Chair Says Separate and Unequal Remains a Reality," *Topeka Capital-Journal*, May 12, 2014, http://cjonline.com /news/2014-05-12/legacy-brown-kickapoo-chair-says-separate-and-unequal -remains-reality.

40. Adams, *Education for Extinction*.

41. Treuer, *Heartbeat of Wounded Knee*, 140.

42. Faris, *Navajo and Photography*, xi, 13.

43. Micheal Hutchison, "River of Steel, River of Sweat: Early Mexican American Community in Muscatine, Iowa," Iowa Women's Archives, 2016, https://migration .lib.uiowa.edu/exhibits/show/barrio-settlements/muscatine.

CHAPTER 16. Coming to America

1. Thom Rosenblum, "The Segregation of Topeka's Public School System, 1879–1951," National Park Service, April 10, 2015, https://www.nps.gov/brvb/learn /historyculture/topekasegregation.htm.

2. Ibid.

3. Gary Orfield, *Reviving the Goal of an Integrated Society: A 21st Century Challenge* (Los Angeles: The Civil Rights Project/Proyecto Derechos Civiles at UCLA, January 2009), https://civilrightsproject.ucla.edu/research/k-12-education /integration-and-diversity/reviving-the-goal-of-an-integrated-society-a-21st -century-challenge.

4. Michael Paulson, "Fred Phelps, Anti-Gay Preacher Who Targeted Military Funerals, Dies at 84," *New York Times*, March 20, 2014, A26; Suzanne Goldberg, "Creationists Defeated in Kansas School Vote on Science Teaching," *Guardian*, February 15, 2007, https://www.theguardian.com/science/2007/feb/15 /schoolsworldwide.religion; "Kansas Pays Nearly 1.2 M to Outside Law Firms to Defend Anti-abortion Laws," *Wichita Eagle*, February 10, 2015, https://www .kansas.com/news/politics-government/article9668558.html; "Kansas Law-makers Pass Anti-Islamic Law Measure," *CBS News*, May 11, 2012, https://www .cbsnews.com/news/kansas-lawmakers-pass-anti-islamic-law-measure/; John Eligon, "A.C.L.U. Challenges Kansas Voter Law Requiring Proof of Citizenship," *New York Times*, February 18, 2016, https://www.nytimes.com/2016/02/19 /us/aclu-challenges-kansas-voter-law-requiring-proof-of-citizenship .html.

5. Jonathan M. Metzl, *Dying of Whiteness: How the Politics of Racial Resentment Is Killing America's Heartland* (New York: Beacon, 2019), 202.

6. Mitch Smith and Julie Bosman, "Ruling on School Spending Adds to Kansas' Fiscal Troubles," *New York Times*, March 3, 2017, A22.

7. Metzl, *Dying of Whiteness*, 226, 254.

8. Ibid., 204; William H. Gass, *In the Heart of the Heart of the Country and Other Stories* (New York: New York Review of Books, 2015), 197.

9. Rucker C. Johnson, *Long-Run Impacts of School Desegregation and School Quality on Adult Attainments*, Working Paper 16664 (Cambridge, Mass.: National Bureau of Economic Research, January 2011), 21.

10. David Kirp, "Making Schools Work," *New York Times*, May 20, 2012, SR1.

11. Gouveia and Stull, "Dances with Cows," 86.

12. Associated Press, "Tyson Plans $47 Million Expansion of Lexington Beef Plant," *Lincoln Journal Star*, March 18, 2015, http://journalstar.com/business/local /tyson-plans-million-expansion-of-lexington-beef-plant/article_0afc88a0-11ff -5ed9-b9b3-dc962ab3dd1c.html.

13. Gouveia and Stull, "Dances with Cows," 98–104; Christopher Leonard, *The Meat Racket: The Secret Takeover of America's Food Business* (New York: Simon and Schuster, 2014), 46, 315; Georgeanne Artz, Rebecca Jackson, and Peter F. Orazem, "Is It a Jungle Out There? Meat Packing, Immigrants, and Rural Communities," *Journal of Agricultural and Resource Economics* 35, no. 2 (2010): 313. See also Georgeanne M. Artz, "Immigration and Meatpacking in the Midwest," *Choices*, 2nd quarter, 2012, http://www.choicesmagazine.org/choices-magazine/theme-articles /immigration-and-agriculture/immigration-and-meatpacking-in-the-midwest-.

14. Gouveia and Stull, "Dances with Cows," 95.

15. Laurie Goodstein, "It's Official: Mormon Founder Had Many Wives," *New York Times*, November 11, 2014, A1, A20.

16. Rebecca Ruiz, "In Pictures: America's Vainest Cities," *Forbes*, November 29, 2007, https://www.forbes.com/2007/11/29/plastic-health-surgery-forbeslife- cx_rr_1129health_slide.html#ffa94776b1be.

17. Matthew Breen, "Gayest Cities in America, 2012," *Advocate*, January 9, 2012, https://www.advocate.com/travel/2012/01/09/gayest-cities-america-2012?pg=full.

18. White, *States of Desire*, 113.

19. Ibid., 106.

20. Edmund White, foreword to *The Stonewall Reader*, ed. Jason Baumann (New York: Penguin, 2019), xi–xii.

21. Laurie Goodstein, "Mormons Sharpen Stand Against Same-Sex Marriage," *New York Times*, November 7, 2015, A11.

22. "Stung by Gay Edict, Mormons Leave Church," editorial, *New York Times*, November 19, 2015, A30; Elizabeth Dias, "Mormon Church Rescinds Policy That Stung Same-Sex Families," *New York Times*, April 5, 2019, A1.

23. Glen Warchol, "Troy Williams: The 'Gay Mayor' of Salt Lake City," *Salt Lake Tribune*, October 4, 2010; https://archive.sltrib.com/article.php?id =50379215&itype=CMSID.

24. A liberty pole, which actually dates to pre-Roman history, was a tall pole capped by a red flag and raised to call people to meetings to protest the Stamp

Act in colonial America. "The Liberty Pole," Providence Forum, n.d., https://providenceforum.org/story/liberty-pole/.

25. Dorothy Martone to author, May 15, 1980.

26. Sanborn, *Mark Twain*, 200–201, and Andrew J. Hoffman, "Mark Twain and Homosexuality," *American Literature* 67, no. 1 (March 1995): 23–49.

27. Judith Marvin, "Chinese Immigrants," *Angels Camp Museum Foundation Newsletter*, no. 4 (fall 2011): 1.

28. Ronald H. Limbaugh and William P. Fuller Jr., *Calaveras Gold: The Impact of Mining on a Mother Lode County* (Reno: University of Nevada Press, 2004), 104.

CHAPTER 17. San Francisco

1. Robert Viscusi, "Oration upon the Most Recent Death of Christopher Columbus," in *The Italian American Reader*, ed. Bill Tonelli (New York: William Morrow, 2003), 485, 486.

2. Treuer, *Heartbeat of Wounded Knee*, 24.

3. Gary Kamiya, *Cool Gray City of Love: 49 Views of San Francisco* (New York: Bloomsbury, 2013), 299, 306–8.

4. "SF Board of Supervisors Votes to Rename Justin Herman Plaza," *KGO ABC 7*, September 20, 2017, https://abc7news.com/2433951/; Thomas Fuller, "The Loneliness of Being Black in San Francisco," *New York Times*, July 20, 2016, http://www.nytimes.com/2016/07/21/us/black-exodus-from-san-francisco.html.

5. Ned Blackhawk, *Violence over the Land: Indians and Empires in the Early American West* (Cambridge, Mass.: Harvard University Press, 2006), 275.

6. Margolin, *Ohlone Way*, 58; Alyssa Landry, "Native History: California Gold Rush Begins, Devastates Native Population," *Indian Country Today*, January 24, 2014, http://indiancountrytodaymedianetwork.com/2014/01/24/native-history-california-gold-rush-begins-devastates-native-population-153230; Madley, *An American Genocide*, 3.

7. Margolin, *Ohlone Way*, 159.

8. Ibid., 166.

9. Vincent Medina, "Plastic Siege: A New Twist on the Fourth Grade Mission Project," *News from Native California* 27, no. 1 (fall 2013): 4.

10. Mariko Conner, "Q&A with Vincent Medina," Heyday Books, September 16, 2014, https://heydaybooks.com/qa-with-vincent-medina/.

11. Branch, *Clemens of the Call*, 70.

12. Maxine Hong Kingston, *China Men* (New York: Alfred A. Knopf, 1980), 55.

13. Lee and Yung, *Angel Island*, 108.

14. Sam Tanenhaus, "Hey, Big Thinker," *New York Times*, April 27, 2014, ST1, 8.

15. Rodger D. Citron, "Charles Reich's Journey from the *Yale Law Journal* to the *New York Times* Best-Seller List: The Personal History of *The Greening of America*," *New York Law School Law Review* 52 (August 2007): 406.

16. Ibid., 410–12.

17. Sam Roberts, "Charles Reich, 91; Embraced Values of Flower Children," *New York Times*, June 18, 2019, B12.

CHAPTER 18. Seattle

1. Roger Sale, *Seattle: Past to Present* (Seattle: University of Washington Press, 1976), 174.

2. This account is based not only on my interview of Tosh Yasutake but also on undated recorded video interviews by Densho: The Japanese American Legacy Project, especially those that appear in "Sites of Shame: One Family's Journey," 2005, https://densho.org/sitesofshame/, and interviews of Tosh Yasutake and his sister, Mitsuye Yamada, in Teresa Tamura, *Minidoka: An American Concentration Camp* (Caldwell, Idaho: Caxton Press, 2013), 37–52.

3. Yamada, *Camp Notes and Other Writings*, 13.

4. William Toshio Yasutake died on December 12, 2016, and his wife, Fumi, on April 15, 2018.

5. Tamura, *Minidoka*, 32.

6. Miriam Jordan, "Judge Halts Trump Policy Allowing States and Cities to Reject Refugees," *New York Times*, January 10, 2020, A11; Katie Rogers, "President Plans to Expand Number of Countries Under 2017 Travel Ban," *New York Times*, January 22, 2020, A18; Michelle Alexander, "Injustice on Repeat," *New York Times*, January 19, 2020, SR6.

7. Michiko Kakutani, "When History Repeats," *New York Times*, July 15, 2018, SR1.

8. Viet Thanh Nguyen, "Good Refugees, Bad Refugees," *New York Times*, May 20, 2018, SR7.

9. C. N. Trueman, "Vietnamese Boat People," History Learning Site, July 19, 2019, http://www.historylearningsite.co.uk/vietnam_boat_people.htm.

10. Zolton L. Hajnal, "The Democrats' Immigration Problem," *New York Times*, November 21, 2014, A27.

11. Anand Giridhardas, "The Immigrant Advantage," *New York Times*, May 25, 2014, SR5.

12. Zacks, *Chasing the Last Laugh*, 4; Ruth A. Burnet, "Mark Twain in the Northwest, 1895," *Pacific Northwest Quarterly* 42, no. 3 (July 1951): 201.

13. Statement of Robert Bruce Driscoll, taken at Seattle Fire Department headquarters, May 5, 1935, https://www.flickr.com/photos/seattlemunicipal archives/4081147984/.

14. Enrico Moretti, *The New Geography of Jobs* (Boston: Houghton Mifflin Harcourt, 2012), 74; Madeline Zavodny, *Immigration and American Jobs* (Washington, D.C.: American Enterprise Institute for Public Policy Research and

the Partnership for a New American Economy, December 2011), 7, http://www
.aei.org/wp-content/uploads/2011/12/-immigration-and-american-jobs
_144002688962.pdf; Taylor, *Next America*, 87.

15. Richard Kluger, *The Bitter Waters of Medicine Creek: A Tragic Clash Between White and Native America* (New York: Alfred A. Knopf, 2011), 73, 84-85.

16. "Scene of Dynamite Outrage Perpetrated Against Italian Consular Agent Ghiglione," *Seattle Daily Times*, December 7, 1910, 1.

17. "The Shame of Seattle," *Seattle Post-Intelligencer*, January 29, 1911.

18. Dennis Caldirola, "The Seattle Italian Story: Seattle's First Italian-Americans," Festa Italiana Seattle, n.d., https://festaseattle.com/about/local -history/.

19. Undated clipping of *Seattle Post-Intelligencer* article and photo from the scrapbook of John R. Ghiglione.

20. Dr. August J. Ghiglione to the editor in reply to George E. Ralston, *Seattle Daily Times*, February 2, 1910; Herbert N. Casson, "The Italians in America," *Munsey's Magazine*, October 1906, 123.

CHAPTER 19. What We Learned about America

1. John R. Humphreys, *The Lost Towns and Roads of America* (New York: Doubleday, 1961), 189.

2. Peter Baker and Julie Hirschfeld Davis, "Urging Persistence on Racial Gains, Obama Recalls Sacrifice in Selma," *New York Times*, March 7, 2015, A12.

3. Duncan, *Out West*, 415.

4. Patrick J. Carr and Maria J. Kefalas, *Hollowing Out the Middle: The Rural Brain Drain and What It Means for America* (Boston: Beacon, 2009), 26.

5. Ruchir Sharma, "To Be Great Again, America Needs Immigrants," *New York Times*, May 7, 2017, SR7; Julie Hirschfeld Davis and Somini Sengupta, "Administration Rebuffs Findings of Refugees' Benefit to Economy," *New York Times*, September 19, 2017, A1.

6. Frank Bruni, "Want Geniuses? Welcome Immigrants," *New York Times*, September 24, 2017, SR3.

7. Kenneth Scheve and David Stasavage, *Taxing the Rich: A History of Fiscal Fairness in the United States and Europe* (Princeton, N.J.: Princeton University Press, 2016). Brink Lindsey and Steven M. Teles contend that regressive regulations—laws that benefit the rich—are a primary cause of the extraordinary income gains among U.S. elite professionals and financial managers. Lindsey and Teles, *The Captured Economy: How the Powerful Enrich Themselves, Slow Down Growth, and Increase Inequality* (New York: Oxford University Press, 2017).

8. Maggie Astor, "Incidents of Anti-Semitism Were Up 57 Percent in 2017," *New York Times*, February 28, 2018, A17.

9. "AP Poll: U.S. Majority Have Prejudice Against Blacks," *USA Today*, October 27, 2012, A17, https://www.usatoday.com/story/news/politics/2012/10/27/poll-black-prejudice-america/1662067/.

10. Michael Eric Dyson, "Donald Trump's Racial Ignorance," *New York Times*, December 18, 2016, SR1.

11. Dunbar-Ortiz, *An Indigenous Peoples' History*, 15–31. The term "Euro-Americans in motion" comes from Juliana Barr, "Borders and Borderlands," in Sleeper-Smith et al., *Why You Can't Teach*, 15.

12. John Steinbeck, *America and Americans* (New York: Viking, 1966), 13.

13. Rourke, *Roots of American Culture*, 70.

14. Driscoll, *Mark Twain Among the Indians*, 370.

15. Murray, *Collected Essays and Memoirs*, 23.

16. This list relies heavily on Margolin's criteria in *Ohlone Way*, x.

17. Treuer, *Heartbeat of Wounded Knee*, 288.

18. This interview of Susan Kelly Power relies primarily on an oral history interview conducted by me and secondarily on an oral history interview by Susie Coleman Neilson, a Northwestern graduate who was then a student in my Native Americans Tell Their Stories course. These interviews are part of a collection of thirty oral history interviews that I donated to the Newberry Library, Chicago, in 2017. The Newberry has titled the interviews, which the library was still processing in 2020, "The American Indians of Chicago Oral History Project."

19. Susan Power, email to author, June 25, 2014.

20. Susan Power, "Attic," 161.

21. Susan Power, email to author, February 5, 2014, of her "Vignettes from Facebook."

22. Susan Power, *Roofwalker* (Minneapolis: Milkweed, 2002), 162. On the statue, see Deanna Isaacs, "Blood on the Ground/Investing in the Future," *Chicago Reader*, March 22, 2007, http://www.chicagoreader.com/chicago/blood-on-the-groundinvesting-in-the-future/Content?oid=924564.

Epilogue

1. Richard V. Reeves, *Dream Hoarders: How the American Upper Middle Class Is Leaving Everyone Else in the Dust, Why That Is a Problem, and What to Do About It* (Washington, D.C.: Brookings Institution Press, 2017), 6, 12; Appiah, *Lies That Bind*, 173.

2. Lisa Lerer and Dave Umhoefer, "Left, Right or Center, Voters See a Bleak Future," *New York Times*, June 13, 2020, A1, A23.

3. Robin DiAngelo, *White Fragility: Why It's So Hard for White People to Talk About Racism* (Boston: Beacon, 2018), 144.

4. Hawes Spencer and Richard Pérez-Peña, "Charge Is Murder in Death at

Charlottesville Protest," *New York Times*, December 15, 2017, A12. See also Ibram X. Kendi, *How to Be an Antiracist* (New York: World Books, 2019), 237–38.

5. Charles M. Blow, "White Allies, Don't Fail Us Again," *New York Times*, June 8, 2020, A25; Shaila Dewan and Mike Baker, "6 Years after Ferguson, Reform but Little Change," *New York Times*, June 14, 2020, A1, A22.

6. Hahrie Han, "The Secrets of Successful Activism," *New York Times*, December 17, 2019, A27.

7. Twenge, *Generation Me*; Sharon Bartlett and Maria LeRose, dirs., *Generation Boomerang* (Detroit: Dreamfilm Productions and Canadian Broadcasting Corporation, 2011); Tony Khuon, "Peter Pan Syndrome: What Makes the Millennials Different?" *Agile Lifestyle*, September 18, 2014, http://agilelifestyle.net/peter-pan-syndrome-complex; Willy Staley, "Golden Age," *New York Times Magazine*, October 14, 2018, 12–13.

8. Strauss and Howe, *Generations*, 342, 417, and 426.

9. Michelle Goldberg, "Why Young People Hate Capitalism," *New York Times*, December 5, 2017, A25; Pew Research Center, "Millennials in Adulthood," Social and Demographic Trends, March 7, 2014, http://www.pewsocialtrends.org/2014/03/07/millennials-in-adulthood/; Deloitte, "The Millennial Survey 2014: Big Demands and High Expectations," January 2014, https://www2.deloitte.com/ba/en/pages/about-deloitte/articles/2014-millennial-survey-positive-impact.html.

10. However, one survey found millennials "express the least prejudice . . . but only by a matter of 1 to 3 percentage points, not a meaningful difference." Scott Clement, "Millennials Are Just as Racist as Their Parents," *Washington Post*, June 23, 2015, https://www.washingtonpost.com/news/wonk/wp/2015/06/23/millennial-are-just-as-racist-as-their-parents/. Some writers doubt millennials' desire to achieve change. The data scientist Sean McElwee concludes from data: "Millennials aren't racially tolerant, they're racially apathetic: They simply ignore structural racism rather than try to fix it." Sean McElwee, "Millennials Are Less Racially Tolerant Than You Think," *Cut*, January 8, 2015, https://www.thecut.com/2015/01/millennials-are-less-tolerant-than-you-think.html.

11. Charles M. Blow, "A New Age of Activism," *New York Times*, December 8, 2014, A25; Sam Tanenhaus, "Generation Nice," *New York Times*, August 17, 2014, ST1; Jon Pareles, "Pete Seeger, Champion of Folk Music and Social Change, Dies at 94," *New York Times*, January 29, 2014, https://www.nytimes.com/2014/01/29/arts/music/pete-seeger-songwriter-and-champion-of-folk-music-dies-at-94.html.

12. Suketo Mehta, *This Land Is Our Land: An Immigrant's Manifesto* (New York: Farrar, Straus and Giroux, 2019), 192; Susan Saulny, "Census Data Presents Rise in Multiracial Population of Youths," *New York Times*, March 24, 2011, http://www/nytimes.com/2011/03/25/us/25race.html; Gretchen Livingston and Anna Brown,

"Intermarriage in the U.S. 50 Years After *Loving* v. *Virginia*," Pew Research Center, May 18, 2017, https://www.pewsocialtrends.org/2017/05/18/intermarriage-in -the-u-s-50-years-after-loving-v-virginia/; William H. Frey, "The US Will Become 'Minority White' in 2045, Census Projects: Youthful Minorities Are the Engine of Future Growth," Brookings, March 14, 2018, updated September 10, 2018, https:// www.brookings.edu/blog/the-avenue/2018/03/14/the-us-will-become-minority -white-in-2045-census-projects/; Sabrina Tavernise, "Whites a Minority in the U.S.? The Transition Is Accelerating," *New York Times*, June 21, 2018, A1.

13. U.S. Census Bureau, "2010 Census Shows Multiple-Race Population Grew Faster Than Single-Race Population," press release, September 27, 2012, https:// www.census.gov/newsroom/releases/archives/race/cb12-182.html; Appiah, *Lies That Bind*, 219.

Selected Bibliography

Works included here relate directly to the topic of identity among Americans or to one of the main inspirations for our book and travels, Mark Twain, whose works, in many ways, commented on the American identity being forged in the wake of the Civil War. Other works referenced in the book are cited in full in the notes.

Adams, David Wallace. *Education for Extinction: American Indians and the Boarding School Experience, 1875–1928*. Lawrence: University Press of Kansas, 1995.

Aldrich, Daniel P. *Building Resilience: Social Capital in Post-Disaster Recovery*. Chicago: University of Chicago Press, 2012.

Alexander, Michelle. *The New Jim Crow: Mass Incarceration in the Age of Colorblindness*. New York: New Press, 2010.

Alwood, Edward. *Straight News: Gays, Lesbians and the News Media*. New York: Columbia University Press, 1996.

Anderson, Carol. *White Rage: The Unspoken Truth of Our Racial Divide*. New York: Bloomsbury, 2016.

Andrews, Gregg. *City of Dust: A Cement Company Town in the Land of Tom Sawyer*. Columbia: University of Missouri Press, 2002.

Appiah, Kwame Anthony. *The Lies That Bind: Rethinking Identity: Creed, Country, Color, Class, Culture*. New York: Liveright, 2018.

Asch, Chris Myers, and George Derek Musgrove. *Chocolate City: A History of Race and Democracy in the Nation's Capital*. Chapel Hill: University of North Carolina Press, 2017.

Austin, Ben. *High-Risers: Cabrini-Green and the Fate of American Public Housing*. New York: HarperCollins, 2018.

Bakht, Nancy. "Mocking Mohammad: Mark Twain's Depiction of Arabs and Muslims in *The Innocents Abroad*." Master of arts thesis, English Department, College of Arts and Sciences, University of South Florida, Tampa, 2006.

Beauvoir, Simone de. *America Day by Day*. Berkeley: University of California Press, 1999.

Bix, Amy Sue. *Girls Coming to Tech! A History of American Engineering Education for Women*. Cambridge, Mass.: MIT Press, 2013.

Branch, Edgar M., ed. *Clemens of the Call: Mark Twain in San Francisco*. Berkeley: University of California Press, 1969.

———. *The Literary Apprenticeship of Mark Twain: With Selections from His Apprentice Writing*. Urbana: University of Illinois Press, 1950.

Brawley, Steven Louis. *Gay and Lesbian St. Louis*. Charleston, S.C.: Arcadia, 2016.

Breyer, Richard, and Anand Kamalakar, dirs. and eds. *300 Miles to Freedom: The Story of John W. Jones and the Underground Railroad*. New York: W&B Productions and Trilok Fusion Media, 2011.

Broom, Sarah M. *The Yellow House*. New York: Grove Press, 2019.

Byfield, Natalie P. *Savage Portrayals: Race, Media, and the Central Park Jogger Story*. Philadelphia: Temple University Press, 2014.

Cameron, James. *A Time of Terror: A Survivor's Story*. Baltimore: Black Classic Press, 1994.

Carr, Cynthia. *Our Town: A Heartland Lynching, a Haunted Town, and the Hidden History of White America*. New York: Three Rivers, 2006.

Chicago Commission on Race Relations. *The Negro in Chicago: A Study of Race Relations and a Race Riot*. Chicago: University of Chicago Press, 1922.

Cobbs, Charles E. Jr. *On the Road to Freedom: A Guided Tour of the Civil Rights Trail*. Chapel Hill, N.C.: Algonquin, 2008.

Cohodas, Nadine. *The Band Played Dixie: Race and the Liberal Conscience at Ole Miss*. New York: Free Press, 1997.

Cosco, Joseph P. *Imagining Italians: The Clash of Romance and Race in American Perceptions, 1880–1910*. Albany: State University of New York Press, 2003.

Cose, Ellis. *Color-Blind: Seeing Beyond Race in a Race-Obsessed World*. New York: HarperCollins, 1997.

———. *The End of Anger: A New Generation's Take on Race and Rage*. New York: HarperCollins, 2011.

Crey, Ernie, and Suzanne Fournier. *Stolen from Our Embrace: The Abduction of First Nation Children and the Restoration of Aboriginal Communities*. Vancouver: Douglas & McIntyre, 1998.

Davis, Townsend. *Weary Feet, Rested Souls: A Guided History of the Civil Rights Movement*. New York: W. W. Norton, 1998.

Dittmer, John. *Local People: The Struggle for Civil Rights in Mississippi*. Chicago: University of Chicago Press, 1994.

Driscoll, Kerry. *Mark Twain Among the Indians and Other Indigenous Peoples*. Berkeley: University of California Press, 2018.

Dunbar-Ortiz, Roxanne. *An Indigenous Peoples' History of the United States.* Boston: Beacon, 2014.

Duncan, Cynthia M., and Gemma Beckley. "Dahlia Twenty Years Later: New Jobs and New Politics." In Cynthia M. Duncan, *Worlds Apart: Poverty and Politics in Rural America.* 2nd ed. New Haven, Conn.: Yale University Press, 2014.

Duncan, Dayton. *Out West: A Journey Through Lewis and Clark's America.* 1987. Lincoln: University of Nebraska Press, 2000.

Early, Gerald, ed. *"Ain't But a Place": An Anthology of African American Writings About St. Louis.* St. Louis: Missouri Historical Society Press, 1998.

———. *Daughters: On Family and Fatherhood.* Reading, Mass.: Addison-Wesley, 1994.

Faris, James C. *Navajo and Photography: A Critical History of the Representation of an American People.* Albuquerque: University of New Mexico Press, 1996.

Fatout, Paul. *Mark Twain in Virginia City.* Bloomington: Indiana University Press, 1964.

———, ed. *Mark Twain Speaking.* Iowa City: University of Iowa Press, 1976.

Fede, Frank Joseph. *Italians in the Deep South: Their Impact on Birmingham and the American Heritage.* Montgomery, Ala.: Black Belt, 1994.

Fishkin, Shelley Fisher. *Lighting Out for the Territory: Reflections on Mark Twain and American Culture.* New York: Oxford University Press, 1997.

———. *Writing America: Literary Landmarks from Walden Pond to Wounded Knee.* New Brunswick, N.J.: Rutgers University Press, 2015.

Fosberg, Michael Sidney. *Incognito: An American Odyssey of Race and Self-Discovery.* Chicago: Incognito, Inc., 2010.

Friedman, Edwin H. *What Are You Going to Do with Your Life? Unpublished Writings and Diaries.* New York: Seabury Books, 2009.

Fukuyama, Francis. *Identity: The Demand for Dignity and the Politics of Resentment.* New York: Farrar, Straus and Giroux, 2018.

Fulton, Joe B. *The Reconstruction of Mark Twain: How a Confederate Bushwhacker Became the Lincoln of Our Literature.* Baton Rouge: Louisiana State University Press, 2010.

Ghiglione, Loren. "A Summer in Mississippi." *Yale Law Report* 11, no. 2 (winter 1965): 28–29.

Gibson, A. M. *The Kickapoos: Lords of the Middle Border.* Norman: University of Oklahoma Press, 1963.

Gilman, Susan. *Dark Twins: Imposture and Identity in Mark Twain's America.* Chicago: University of Chicago Press, 1989.

Gouveia, Lourdes, and Donald D. Stull. "Dances with Cows: Beefpacking's Impact on Garden City, Kansas, and Lexington, Nebraska." In *Any Way You Cut It: Meat Processing and Small-Town America.* Edited by Donald D. Stull, Michael J. Broadway, and David Griffith. Lawrence: University Press of Kansas, 1995.

Guglielmo, Jennifer, and Salvatore Salerno, eds. *Are Italians White? How Race Is Made in America*. New York: Routledge, 2003.

Harris, Helen L. "Mark Twain's Response to the Native American." *American Literature* 46, no. 4 (January 1975): 495–505.

Hirsch, Arnold R., and Joseph Logsdon, eds. *Creole New Orleans: Race and Americanization*. Baton Rouge: Louisiana State University Press, 1992.

Hope, Judith Richards. *Pinstripes and Pearls: The Women of the Harvard Law Class of '64 Who Forged an Old Girl Network and Paved the Way for Future Generations*. New York: Scribner, 2008.

Hopkins, Nancy H. "The Changing Status and Number of Women in Science and Engineering at MIT: A Celebration! (with Caveats . . .)." Keynote address, MIT 150 Symposium, Leaders in Science and Engineering: The Women of MIT, March 28, 2011, Cambridge, Mass.

Jerome, Robert D., and Herbert A. Wisbey Jr., with revisions and additions by Barbara E. Snedecor. *Mark Twain in Elmira*. 2nd ed. Elmira, N.Y.: Elmira College, 2013.

Kaplan, Fred. *The Singular Mark Twain: A Biography*. New York: Doubleday, 2003.

Kaplan, Justin. *Mr. Clemens and Mark Twain: A Biography*. New York: Simon and Schuster, 1966.

Kerouac, Jack. *On the Road: The Original Scroll*. New York: Penguin, 2007.

Krass, Peter. *Ignorance, Confidence and Filthy Rich Friends: The Business Adventures of Mark Twain, Chronic Speculator and Entrepreneur*. Hoboken, N.J.: John Wiley, 2007.

Lee, Erika, and Judy Yung. *Angel Island: Immigrant Gateway to America*. Oxford: Oxford University Press, 2010.

Levy, Andrew. *Huck Finn's America: Mark Twain and the Era That Shaped His Masterpiece*. New York: Simon and Schuster, 2015.

Longworth, Richard C. *Caught in the Middle: America's Heartland in the Age of Globalism*. New York: Bloomsbury, 2008.

Madley, Benjamin. *An American Genocide: The United States and the California Indian Catastrophe, 1846–1873*. New Haven, Conn.: Yale University Press, 2016.

Margolin, Malcolm. *The Ohlone Way: Indian Life in the San Francisco Monterey Bay Area*. Berkeley, Calif.: Heyday, 2014.

Mass, Lawrence D. *Confessions of a Jewish Wagnerite: Being Gay and Jewish in America*. New York: Cassel, 1994.

Mattson, Ingrid. *Being Muslim in America: A Conversation with Ingrid Mattson*. Video. Pittsburgh: Pennsylvania State University, February 9, 2008. http://ingridmattson.org/video/being-muslim-in-america-a-conversation-with-ingrid-mattson/.

McAdam, Doug. *Freedom Summer*. New York: Oxford University Press, 1988.

McCullough, Joseph B., and Janice McIntire-Strasburg, eds. *Mark Twain at the Buffalo Express: Articles and Sketches by America's Favorite Humorist*. DeKalb: Northern Illinois University Press, 1999.

McDonald, Duff. *The Golden Passport: Harvard Business School, the Limits of Capitalism, and the Moral Failure of the MBA Elite*. New York: Harper Business, 2017.

McGinity, Keren R. *Still Jewish: A History of Women and Intermarriage in America*. New York: New York University Press, 2009.

McIntosh, Peggy. *White Privilege and Male Privilege: A Personal Account of Coming to See Correspondences Through Work in Women's Studies*. Working Paper 189. Wellesley, Mass.: Wellesley College Center for Research on Women, 1988.

Mellinger, Gwyneth. *Chasing Newsroom Diversity: From Jim Crow to Affirmative Action*. Urbana: University of Illinois Press, 2013.

Mormino, Gary Ross. *Immigrants on the Hill: Italian-Americans in St. Louis, 1882–1982*. Columbia: University of Missouri Press, 2002.

Morris, Linda A. *Gender Play in Mark Twain: Cross-Dressing and Transgression*. Columbia: University of Missouri Press, 2007.

Muller, John. *Mark Twain in Washington, D.C.: The Adventures of a Capital Correspondent*. Charleston, S.C.: History Press, 2013.

Murray, Albert. *Collected Essays and Memoirs*. Edited by Henry Louis Gates Jr. and Paul Devlin. New York: Library Classics, 2016.

Ortiz, Simon J. *From Sand Creek: Rising in This Heart Which Is Our America*. Tucson: University of Arizona Press, 1981.

Painter, Nell Irvin. *The History of White People*. New York: W. W. Norton, 2010.

Pew Research Center. "Across Racial Lines, More Say Nation Needs to Make Changes to Achieve Racial Equality," August 5, 2015. http://www.people-press.org/2015/08/05/across-racial-lines-more-say-nation-needs-to-make-changes-to-achieve-racial-equality/.

———. "Modern Immigration Wave Brings 59 Million to U.S., Driving Population Growth & Change Through 2065," September 28, 2015. https://www.pewresearch.org/hispanic/2015/09/28/modern-immigration-wave-brings-59-million-to-u-s-driving-population-growth-and-change-through-2065/.

———. "Political Polarization in the American Public," June 12, 2014. http//www.people-press.org/2014/06/12/political-polarization-in-the-american-public/.

Power, Susan. "The Attic: A Family Museum." In *Home: American Writers Remember Rooms of Their Own*, 158–71. Edited by Sharon Sloan Fiffer and Steve Fiffer. New York: Pantheon, 1995.

Powers, Ron. *Dangerous Water: A Biography of the Boy Who Became Mark Twain*. New York: Basic Books, 1999.

———. *Mark Twain: A Life*. New York: Free Press, 2005.

Primeau, Ronald. *Romance of the Road: The Literature of the American Highway*. Bowling Green, Ohio: Bowling Green State University Popular Press, 1996.

Rasmussen, R. Kent. *Mark Twain A to Z: The Essential Reference to His Life and Writings*. New York: Oxford University Press, 1995.

Reich, Charles A. *The Greening of America*. New York: Random House, 1970.

——. *The Sorcerer of Bolinas Reef*. New York: Random House, 1976.

Reigstad, Thomas J. *Scribblin' for a Livin': Mark Twain's Pivotal Period in Buffalo*. Amherst, N.Y.: Prometheus, 2013.

Rideau, Wilbert. *In the Place of Justice: A Story of Punishment and Deliverance*. New York: Alfred A. Knopf, 2010.

Riley, Naomi Schaefer. *'Til Faith Do Us Part: How Interfaith Marriage Is Transforming Marriage*. New York: Oxford University Press, 2013.

Robinson, Greg. *After Camp: Portraits in Midcentury Japanese American Life and Politics*. Berkeley: University of California Press, 2012.

Rourke, Constance. *The Roots of American Culture*. New York: Harcourt, Brace, 1942.

Ryan, Ann M., and Joseph B. McCullough, eds. *Cosmopolitan Twain*. Columbia: University of Missouri Press, 2008.

Samuelsson, Marcus. *Yes, Chef: A Memoir*. New York: Random House, 2012.

Sanborn, Margaret. *Mark Twain: The Bachelor Years*. New York: Doubleday, 1990.

Sandweiss, Lee Ann, ed. *Seeking St. Louis: Voices from a River City, 1670–2000*. St. Louis: Missouri Historical Society Press, 2000.

Seamon, Erika B. *Interfaith Marriage in America: The Transformation of Religion and Christianity*. New York: Palgrave Macmillan, 2012.

Shepard, Judy. *The Meaning of Matthew: My Son's Murder in Laramie, and a World Transformed*. New York: Hudson Street, 2009.

Sleeper-Smith, Susan, Juliana Barr, Jean M. O'Brien, Nancy Shoemaker, and Scott Manning Stevens. *Why You Can't Teach United States History Without American Indians*. Chapel Hill: University of North Carolina Press, 2015.

Stahl, J. D. *Mark Twain, Culture and Gender: Envisioning America Through Europe*. Athens: University of Georgia Press, 1994.

Steinbeck, John. *America and Americans*. New York: Viking, 1966.

——. *America and Americans and Selected Nonfiction*. Edited by Susan Shillinglaw and Jackson J. Benson. New York: Penguin, 2003.

Strauss, William, and Neil Howe. *Generations: The History of America's Future, 1584 to 2069*. New York: William Morrow, 1991.

Taylor, Paul. *The Next America: Boomers, Millennials, and the Looming Generational Showdown*. New York: Public Affairs, 2014.

Theoharis, Jeanne. *A More Beautiful and Terrible History: The Uses and Misuses of Civil Rights History*. Boston: Beacon, 2018.

Touré. *Who's Afraid of Post-Blackness?: What It Means to Be Black Now*. New York: Free Press, 2011.

Treuer, David. *The Heartbeat of Wounded Knee: Native America from 1890 to the Present*. New York: Riverhead Books, 2019.

Tuckey, John S., ed. *The Devil's Race-Track: Mark Twain's "Great Dark" Writings*. Berkeley: University of California Press, 1980.

Twain, Mark. *The Five Jumps of the Calaveras Frog*. Angels Camp, Calif.: Angels Camp Museum, 2010.

———. *How Nancy Jackson Married Kate Wilson*. Edited by John Cooley. Lincoln: University of Nebraska Press, 2001.

———. *Pudd'nhead Wilson* and *Those Extraordinary Twins*. Edited by Sidney E. Berger. New York: W. W. Norton, 2005.

———. *Roughing It*. Berkeley: University of California Press, 1993.

———. *Tales of Wonder*. Edited by David Ketterer. Lincoln: University of Nebraska Press, 1984.

Twenge, Jean M. *Generation Me: Why Today's Young Americans Are More Confident, Assertive, Entitled—And More Miserable Than Ever Before*. New York: Free Press, 2006.

———. *iGen: Why Today's Super-Connected Kids Are Growing Up Less Rebellious, More Tolerant, Less Happy—and Completely Unprepared for Adulthood*. New York: Atria, 2017.

Vogel, Dan. *Mark Twain's Jews*. Jersey City, N.J.: KTAV, 2006.

Watson, Bruce. *Freedom Summer: The Savage Season That Made Mississippi Burn and Made America a Democracy*. New York: Viking Penguin, 2010.

Whitaker, Mark. *Smoketown: The Untold Story of the Other Great Black Renaissance*. New York: Simon and Schuster, 2018.

White, Edmund. *States of Desire: Travels in Gay America*. New York: Dutton Obelisk, 1983.

Wilkerson, Isabel. *The Warmth of Other Suns: The Epic Story of America's Great Migration*. New York: Random House, 2010.

Wills, Garry. *The Future of the Catholic Church with Pope Francis*. New York: Viking, 2015.

Yamada, Mitsuye. *Camp Notes and Other Writings*. New Brunswick, N.J.: Rutgers University Press, 1998.

Zacks, Richard. *Chasing the Last Laugh: Mark Twain's Raucous and Redemptive Round-the-World Comedy Tour*. New York: Doubleday, 2016.

Index

America, 278; Buffalo, 78; Chinese fleeing, 102; Cleveland, 71, 73; economic divide, 89, 180; Hannibal, 21; of Italians, 111; Keokuk, 222; Memphis, 180; of Mexican immigrants, 233; New Orleans, Ninth Ward, 203; student, 289; Twain on, of Italians, 111–12; Twain on, in NYC, 100
Powdermaker, Hortense, 191
Power, Carleton Gilmore, 283
Power, Josephine Kelly, 282
Power, Susan, 283, 284, 285
Power, Susan Kelly, 282–85, *283*
Powers, Ron, 262
Preservation Hall (New Orleans), 200–202
Presti, Charlie, 72
Presti, Michael, 72
Presti, Rose and Charles, Sr., 72
Presti's Bakery (Cleveland), 72
Privilege: activism and jail as, 96; author Ghiglione's other, 286; author Ghiglione's white male, 3, 125–26, 286; circles of, 95; in college admissions, 289; meritocracy as mechanism to transmit, 287; need to address racial, 288; Twain's, 3; white, 288; white male, in law, 126–27; *White Privilege and Male Privilege*, 125; whites defend, 280
Prynne, Hester, 11
Psychopathia Sexualis (Krafft-Ebing), 154
Pulitzer, Joseph, 32
Pullen, Lynn, 187

Quan, Jean, 103
Quarry Farm, 80
Quinnipiac University, 128
Qur'an, 131, 132

Racism, 13, 21, 30, 32, 69, 89, 91, 92, 206, 288; attacked in "Strange Fruit," 69; in Boston, 134; *Buffalo News* accused of, 77–78; Bunkers subjected to anti-Asian, 145; in criminal justice system, 203; in Lexington, Ky., and beyond, 169; millennials' response to, 289–92; among Mormons, 231–33; in

New Orleans, 194; no end to, 263; in Seattle, 256; segregation, 47; in St. Louis, 33; at University of Mississippi, 180–82
Racket, The (Leonard), 237
Radcliffe College, 147
Radcliffe Publishing Procedures Course, 85
Rainbow Ranch (Morse Mill, Mo.), 33
Raisin in the Sun, A (Hansberry), 45
Rarick, Judge John R., 213–14
Ray, James Earl, 178
"Real Americans," 2
Red Rooster Harlem, 86–88
Reeves, Richard V., 287
refugees, 2, 268, 279, 287; Afghan, 131; in Buffalo, N.Y., 74–75, 76; Somali, 75, 236; Syrian, 215; Trump's attitude toward, 2, 76, 268; Vietnamese, 2, 55, 206–7, 209, 241, 268, 270
Reich, Charles, 258–61, *259*; *The Greening of America*, 258; on income inequality, 279; *New York Times* obituary, 261
Reigstad, Thomas J., 77
Reiter, Carly, 274
Republicans: anti-gay, 97, 154; versus Democrats, 5; 1880 National Convention, 23; Electoral College strength of, 222; gay-friendly, 17; at Haverford College, 157; in Kansas, 234–36; McCarthyism, 91; Nevada senator and, 158; in Pennsylvania, 170; roll right, 153; Salt Lake City mayor and, 243; Staten Island and, 113; Trump in 2012, 2
"Reverse racism," 5
Rich, Frank, 46
Richard, Ronn, 74
Richards, Dr. W. L., 221
Richter, Roz, 156
Ricks, Granger, 183, 184
Rideau, Wilbert, 211–15, *213*
Rispoli, Hazel, 39, 271, 272
Ritter, Connie, *12*, 12–13
Roanoke Times, 163–64
Roberts, Edward, 76
Robinson, Eugene, 166

84; path traveled by, when young, 4; on pool table, 199; racist attitude toward Lower East Side poor, 100; as *San Francisco Daily Morning Call* police reporter, 59, 251, 256; Seattle lectures of, 271; as steamboat pilot, 149; on St. Louis, 28; as St. Louis typesetter, 28; story about parade of people, white to black, 89; on vigilante Slade, 238; Virginia City prospects and reports in, 248, 249; on virtue and money, 94; white male of privilege of, 3; writes from Washington, D.C., for newspapers, 158; Yale visit, 117, 121, 127

works: *The Adventures of Huckleberry Finn*, 12–13, 24, 79; *The Adventures of Tom Sawyer*, 15, 23, 79; "Advice for Good Little Boys," 261; "The Celebrated Jumping Frog of Calaveras County," 248, 251, 252; "A Day at Niagara," 79; *Following the Equator*, 43; *The Gilded Age* (with Warner), 3; *The Innocents Abroad*, 76–77, 110, 130, 294; *Life on the Mississippi*, 3; "1002nd Arabian Nights," 60; *Roughing It*, 3, 246–47, 252; *Those Extraordinary Twins*, 151, 152; *The Tragedy of Pudd'nhead Wilson*, 151, 152; "United States of Lyncherdom," 65

Tyson, Tinley Ann, 286

Underground Railroad, 80, 81
Unionville, Nev., 246–48
University Club of Washington, D.C., 161
University of Mississippi, 185, 187–89; action plan, 189
University of Wyoming, 239
U.S. Border Patrol, 164
U.S. Department of Homeland Security, 57
U.S. Department of State, 91
U.S. Immigration and Naturalization Service, 264, 265
U.S. Immigration Commission, 20
U.S. Supreme Court: Hugo Black, 258; *Brown v. Board of Education*, 187, 234; decision outlawing split criminal verdicts, 213; *Dred Scott* decision, 28; *Loving v. Virginia*, 290,

292; Thurgood Marshall, 44, 165; *Rideau* decision, 211; Clarence Thomas, 165

Valdivia, Andy, 233, *234*
Vardaman, Sen. James K., 186
Vatican, 42, 51, 105
Vietnam, 56, 57, 69, 70, 204–10, 215–17, 218, 269–70
Vietnamese Americans, viewed as outliers, 268
Vietnamese Association of Illinois, 55, 56, 57
Vietnam War, 56, 69, 70, 185, 204
Virginia City, Nev., 248, 249
Virginia City Territorial Enterprise, 89, 248, 249
Viscusi, Robert, 251–52
Voelk, Maria, *291*
Vogel, Dan, 15
Voting Rights Act of 1965, 280

Walsh, Andrew, 130
Wappenstein, Charles W., 275
Warmth of Other Suns, The (Wilkerson), 149
Washington, Booker T., 235
Washington, D.C., 59, 129, 149, 157, 158–67, 168, 180, 223, 259
Washington Post, 5, 59, 85, 129, 158, 161, 162, 164, 165, 166, 167
Watanabe, Mari, 202
Wayland, Francis III, 121
Weaver, Carolyn, 165
Webster, Daniel, 224
Wells, Junior, 199
Wesley United Methodist Church (Lexington, Ky.), 175
Westbrook, Jay, 71–72
Whitaker, Mark, 171
White, Edmund, 241–42; *States of Desire*, 241
White, Jack, 165
White, Walter F., 1
White, William Allen, 134–35
White Citizens' Council, 193
Whiteness: apathy of, 288; of Asian Americans, 152; *Dying of Whiteness*, 235; Karas and Tham address, 238; as unexamined social norm, 280

Printed in the USA
CPSIA information can be obtained
at www.ICGtesting.com
CBHW021436130624
10031CB00002B/26